STUDIES IN EARLY MODERN CULTURAL, POLITICAL AND SOCIAL HISTORY

Volume 16

THE FINAL CRISIS OF THE STUART MONARCHY

Studies in Early Modern Cultural, Political and Social History

ISSN: 1476–9107

Previously published titles in the series
are listed at the back of this volume

THE FINAL CRISIS OF THE STUART MONARCHY

The Revolutions of 1688–91 in their British, Atlantic and European Contexts

Edited by

Tim Harris and Stephen Taylor

THE BOYDELL PRESS

First published 2013
The Boydell Press, Woodbridge
paperback edition 2015

ISBN 978 1 84383 816 6 hardback
ISBN 978 1 78327 044 6 paperback

The Boydell Press is an imprint of Boydell & Brewer Ltd
PO Box 9, Woodbridge, Suffolk IP12 3DF, UK
and of Boydell & Brewer Inc.
668 Mt Hope Avenue, Rochester, NY 14620–2731, USA
website: www.boydellandbrewer.com

A catalogue record for this book is available
from the British Library

Contents

Contributors

TOBY BARNARD, FBA, MRIA (hon) was fellow and tutor in history, Hertford College, Oxford from 1976 to 2012 and is now an emeritus fellow. His publications include *Cromwellian Ireland: English Government and Reform in Ireland, 1649–1660* (1975; paperback, 2000), *A New Anatomy of Ireland: The Irish Protestants, 1641–1770* (2003; paperback, 2004), *Making the Grand Figure: Lives and Possessions in Ireland, 1641–1770* (2004) and *Improving Ireland? Projectors, Prophets and Profiteers, 1641–1786* (2008). He is completing a study of the cultures of print in Ireland, 1680–1784.

TONY CLAYDON gained his PhD from University College London before serving as a junior research fellow at Fitzwilliam College, Cambridge and then moving to Bangor University, where he is now Professor of Early Modern History. He is author of a number of works on late Stuart history, including *William III and the Godly Revolution* (1996); *William III: Profiles in Power* (2003); and *Europe and the Making of England, 1660–1760* (2007).

JOHN GIBNEY is a graduate of Trinity College Dublin. He was formerly a research fellow at the University of Notre Dame and the National University of Ireland, Galway. He is the author of *Ireland and the Popish Plot* (2008) and *The Shadow of a Year: The 1641 Rebellion in Irish History and Memory* (2013).

LIONEL K. J. GLASSEY is an Honorary Research Fellow in Modern History at the University of Glasgow. He studied at Lincoln College, Oxford. He has published *Politics and the Appointment of Justices of the Peace, 1675–1720* (1979) and several articles; and he edited *The Reigns of Charles II and James VII & II* in Palgrave Macmillan's 'Problems in Focus' series (1997). He is currently engaged on a new edition of Gilbert Burnet's *History of His Own Time* commissioned by Oxford University Press.

GABRIEL GLICKMAN received his BA, MPhil and PhD from Cambridge University. He was lecturer and British Academy Postdoctoral Fellow at Hertford College, Oxford between 2006 and 2012 and is now Assistant Professor of Early Modern British History at the University of Warwick. His first book, *The English Catholic Community 1688–1745: Politics, Culture and Ideology*, was published by Boydell and Brewer in 2009. Recent articles have been published in the *Journal of Modern History*, the *Historical Journal* and the *English Historical Review*.

MARK GOLDIE graduated from the University of Sussex before moving to Cambridge, where he is now Professor of Intellectual History and a Fellow of Churchill College. He has published extensively on politics, religion and ideas in seventeenth- and eighteenth-century Britain. He was general editor of *The Entring Book of Roger Morrice* (7 vols, 2006) and has edited two volumes of *The Cambridge History of Political Thought.*

TIM HARRIS received his BA, MA and PhD from Cambridge University and was a Fellow of Emmanuel College from 1983 before moving to Brown University in 1986, where he is the Munro-Goodwin-Wilkinson Professor in European History. His books include *London Crowds in the Reign of Charles II* (1987); *Politics under the Later Stuarts* (1993); *Restoration: Charles II and his Kingdoms* (2005); *Revolution: The Great Crisis of the British Monarchy, 1685–1720* (2006); and *Rebellion: Britain's First Stuart Kings* (2014).

JOHN MARSHALL is Professor and Chair of the Department of History at the Johns Hopkins University. He received his BA from Cambridge University and his PhD from Johns Hopkins. He is the author of *John Locke: Resistance, Religion and Responsibility* (1994; paperback, 1994) and *John Locke, Toleration and Early Enlightenment Culture* (2006; paperback, 2009) and co-editor of *Heresy, Literature and Politics in Early Modern English Culture* (2006).

ALASDAIR RAFFE received his BA from the University of Oxford and then studied at the University of Edinburgh, where he was awarded his PhD in 2008. He has held positions at Durham and Northumbria Universities and is now a Chancellor's Fellow in History at the University of Edinburgh. He is the author of *The Culture of Controversy: Religious Arguments in Scotland, 1660–1714* (2012) and of articles and chapters concerning Scottish religion, politics and intellectual life in the seventeenth and eighteenth centuries.

OWEN STANWOOD received his PhD from Northwestern University and taught at the Catholic University of America before taking up a position at Boston College, where he is currently Associate Professor of History. A specialist in colonial American and Atlantic history, he is the author of *The Empire Reformed: English America in the Age of the Glorious Revolution* (2011), as well as numerous articles and book chapters.

STEPHEN TAYLOR is Head of Department and Professor in the History of Early Modern England at Durham University. He has published widely on the political and religious history of England in the seventeenth and eighteenth centuries, including *The Entring Book of Roger Morrice. Vol. IV: The Reign of James II 1687–1689* (2007).

Abbreviations

B.L.	British Library
Bodl.	Bodleian Library
C.J.	*Commons Journals*
E.H.R.	*English Historical Review*
H.J.	*Historical Journal*
H.M.C.	Historical Manuscripts Commission
L.J.	*Lords Journals*
P.R.O.	Public Record Office
P.R.O.N.I.	Public Record Office of Northern Ireland
R.C.B.	Representative Church Body Library
R.O.	Records Office
T.N.A.	The National Archives
U.L.	University Library

Unless otherwise stated, all works cited were published in London.

Preface

There has been an explosion of interest in the Glorious Revolution in recent years. Long regarded as the lesser of England's revolutions of the seventeenth century, for much of the twentieth century it suffered from a relative historiographical neglect, albeit that those few studies we did possess included important works of an impressively high scholarly standard. There was a brief resurgence of interest in the Glorious Revolution at the time of the tercentenary celebrations in 1988–9, which saw a wave of fresh publications and the first serious attempt to integrate Scottish, Irish, and European perspectives into an episode that had hitherto typically been studied in an exclusively English context. But it has been in the twenty-first century that the study of the Glorious Revolution has really taken off, witnessing a spate of publications by a younger generation of scholars, most of whom were too young to have participated in the tercentenary events of the late 1980s.

It was out of an attempt further to promote this burgeoning field of historical enquiry on the later-Stuart era, and to bring to the attention of a broader audience (non-specialists as well as specialists, and in particular students coming to this period of history for the first time) some of the excellent work that was now being done in this area, that the two of us first conceived of putting together this volume some years ago. We recruited authors to write on loosely defined themes and urged them to think large, to highlight the broader implications of their research, and to write in a way that would prove accessible to a wider readership. Beyond that, however, we kept our editorial prescriptions to a minimum – believing we were likely to attain the most valuable end result if we left contributors free to address their topics in the ways that they saw fit. We knew from the start that we wanted chronological coverage, from the Restoration through to the eighteenth century, in order for the collection to address both antecedents and consequences. We wanted to make sure that this volume did full justice to the broader Britannic and international contexts, and did not have just a one essay each on Scotland and Ireland tacked on at the end almost as an afterthought. Hence we have two chapters on Scotland and two on Ireland, and they do not come at the end. Hence we also have two on the broader international contexts – one on North America, another on the European context. We wanted essays covering both the whigs and the tories in England; chapters that dealt not just with the victors of the revolutions but also those who lost out as a result of the dynastic shift that occurred in 1688–9; some that explored the political history of the period and others that tackled the history of ideas. In a volume of this size, complete coverage is inevitably difficult to attain. There are doubtless gaps, and perhaps our intention to avoid tokenism on the Britannic and international perspectives has come at the cost of allowing less room for coverage of developments in England. We think this de-centring of England justified, not because we believe England was less important within the broader Stuart multiple-kingdom context than it is typically taken to have been, but rather because England's importance has meant that its history is more fully understood. It was time, we thought, to give greater emphasis to those aspects of the story that are perhaps less familiar.

We have arranged the essays thematically. After an historiographical overview (Glassey), we have two essays on England (Goldie and Marshall), two on Scotland (Raffe and Harris), two on Ireland (Gibney and Barnard), two on the broader international context (Stanwood and Claydon), and one on Jacobitism. Given that Glassey's opening chapter provides a detailed survey of the various ways the Glorious Revolution has been classified by scholars over the generations (reminding us, in the process, just how inappropriate it is to characterize the field as being divided between 'the whigs' and 'the revisionists', as one recent controversial study has chosen to do), we have decided not to provide the traditional editors' introduction. Instead, Stephen Taylor has provided an extended 'Afterword', highlighting some neglected themes and offering a broad framework to draw the volume together.

In assembling this collection, we have incurred many debts. First and foremost, we need to thank the contributors and the press for their patience and indulgence, given the length of time it has taken us to see this venture through to completion. We would also like to thank Clare Jackson, Alexander Murdoch, and Steve Pincus, who were involved in the conceptualization of this project at the beginning. It would have been impossible to have produced this collection were it not for the support from our own institutions and from various grant-giving bodies. Tim Harris would like to thank Brown University and the Mellon Foundation for supporting two periods of extended research leave (one at the Folger Shakespeare Library in Washington, D.C., the other at the Institute for Advanced Study in Princeton, New Jersey), and the Folger, the IAS, the Cogut Humanities Center at Brown, Merton College Oxford, the Long Room Hub at Trinity College Dublin, and Emmanuel College Cambridge for providing visiting fellowships. If that sounds like a lot of support for this particular end result, he pleads in his defence that he has been working on other projects at the same time. As we are all aware, academic fellowship is vitally important to stimulating productive research, and he is extremely grateful for the wonderful home from home that these institutions provided and the friendship and support of the other fellows and the various members of staff. Stephen Taylor is likewise grateful to the Folger Shakespeare Library, the Harry Ransom Humanities Research Center at the University of Texas at

Austin, the Institute of Advanced Study at the University of Durham, and Peterhouse, Cambridge, all of which have supported his research through visiting fellowships and have contributed to this project in significant ways. For most of the prolonged genesis of the book he has been employed at the University of Reading, but it has been completed at the University of Durham in the glorious surroundings of a building named after one of the leading participants in the earlier, mid-century crisis of the Stuart monarchy, John Cosin.

1

In Search of the Mot Juste: *Characterizations of the Revolution of 1688–89**

LIONEL K. J. GLASSEY

The Revolution of 1688–9 has always had a tendency to attract adjectives. The most familiar is 'glorious', but others which have enjoyed some vogue at different times include 'bloodless', 'conservative', 'reluctant', 'accidental', 'sensible', 'aristocratic', '*élite*', 'respectable', 'bourgeois', 'popular', 'whig', 'moral' and 'modern'. Most of these words have something to offer as thumbnail definitions of the character of the Revolution. They feature prominently in examination questions; examiners commonly invite candidates to discuss how far any one of them might appropriately be employed to describe the Revolution of 1688–9. The various epithets are indeed illuminating. They constitute a sequence of mini-interpretations of a complex episode. Some of them have been fashionable, and have defined the historiography of the Revolution for a generation or more. It is instructive to consider the main arguments for and against each appellation. Inevitably, perhaps, we should start with 'glorious'.

I

The term 'the Glorious Revolution' has become formulaic. It has lost its resonances of resplendent honour, virtue, heroism and triumph. It now represents, by an accident of language and usage, the events of 1688–9 in the British Isles. The concepts embodied in the word 'glorious' were not, however, meaningless to contemporaries such as John Hampden, M.P. for Wendover in the Convention, who said in November 1689 that he thought that those who planned the Rye House plot in 1683 had laid the founda-

* I am very grateful to Tim Harris and Stephen Taylor, the editors, for their searching criticisms of an earlier draft of this essay; the remaining errors are my own.

tions of 'the glorious revolution'. The marquess of Halifax was reported as dismissing the language of Hampden's claims 'very wittily'.[1]

Those who used the word 'glorious' in the short-term aftermath of the Revolution were expressing relief at the dramatic replacement of 'popery and arbitrary government' by 'protestantism and liberty'. Back in the summer of 1688, when the seven bishops were in the Tower of London and government (both at the centre and in the localities) was exercised by catholics, dissenters and shady adventurers, the future had looked bleak to those among King James's subjects in England and Scotland who valued stability, tranquillity and the protestant religion. By the late autumn of 1688, a civil war, with one side headed by James and the other by his son-in-law William, prince of Orange, appeared imminent. But, by the spring of 1689, James had gone and his regime had been dismantled. Continuity (represented by James's elder daughter, the new Queen Mary) had been preserved after a fashion. The Declaration of Rights in England and the Claim of Right in Scotland seemed to guarantee the rule of law for the future.

This future was, admittedly, uncertain. Ireland really had descended into civil war. In Scotland, insecurity persisted as long as the catholic duke of Gordon occupied Edinburgh Castle and Viscount Dundee sustained a Jacobite presence in the Highlands. But there still seemed to be something providential, almost miraculous, about the manner in which the immediate crisis had resolved itself between William's arrival in November 1688 and his elevation (with Mary) to the thrones of England and Scotland in February and May 1689 respectively. The word 'glorious', in short, meant something like 'unexpectedly satisfactory and complete'.

There were other 'glorious' connotations as well, which cemented themselves into a national legend as the events of 1688–9 receded into the past. These connotations included: the courage of those who had organized a treasonable invitation to William in June 1688, and then prepared for his arrival; the determination of William himself, in mounting a difficult exercise in combined naval and military operations in November 1688; and the resolution of the protestants of England, Scotland and Ireland in protecting their religion. From the standpoint of the late eighteenth century, when the events of the Revolution of 1688 had passed out of living memory, its 'glory' had come to be associated with those desirable elements of the British polity which the heroes of 1688 had either upheld, or initiated: the preservation of the established Church in England; the reform of the established Church in Scotland; enough, but not too much, religious toleration; annual meet-

[1] *By Force or By Default? The Revolution of 1688–1689*, ed. Eveline Cruickshanks (Edinburgh, 1989): printed opposite the title-page under the heading 'The first mention of the words "Glorious Revolution", 18 Nov. 1689'; Lois G. Schwoerer, 'Introduction', *The Revolution of 1688–1689: Changing Perspectives*, ed. Schwoerer (Cambridge, 1992), pp. 2–4; Bodl. MS Ballard 27, ff. 88–9: Micha[e]l Theobald to Arthur Charlett, 24 Dec. 1689.

ings of parliament; the independence of the law-courts; the freedom of the press; the Union of England and Scotland; the emergence of Britain as a formidable 'great power', underpinned by the largest navy in Europe; the 'balanced' constitution.[2]

It is not difficult to challenge the concept of 'the Glorious Revolution'. Some of those who participated in it might be thought to have engaged in 'inglorious' behaviour.[3] The bishop of London was one of the seven persons whose names had been attached to the letter of 30 June 1688 suggesting that William should come to England, but he brazenly denied any involvement in a face-to-face interview with James on 1 November 1688 when William was actually at sea on the way to Torbay.[4] The desertion to the foreign invader of serving officers in the navy and the army in the weeks preceding and following William's arrival on 5 November was a breach of their oaths of allegiance and of the traditions of their service.[5] A collective national apostasy followed the Revolution early in 1689. A high proportion – not quite all – of office-holders (at every level, down to parish constables), of elected members of such bodies as corporations, guilds and livery companies, and of clergymen, abandoned the oaths of allegiance they had earlier taken to King James and took new oaths to King William and Queen Mary.

In particular, one problem with characterizing the Revolution as 'glorious' is that it depended for its credibility, to many who backed it, on the rumours surrounding the birth of the prince of Wales on 10 June 1688. Several mutually inconsistent stories were in circulation, ranging from the assertion that Queen Mary of Modena had never been pregnant at all and that the 'birth' of the prince was an elaborate deception, through the report that a stillborn baby had been replaced on 10 June by a substitute smuggled into St James's palace in a warming pan, to the supposition that an infant

2 Kathleen Wilson, 'Inventing Revolution: 1688 and Eighteenth-Century Popular Politics', *Journal of British Studies*, XXVIII (1989), 353–64.

3 Howard Nenner, 'The Traces of Shame in England's Glorious Revolution', *History*, LXXIII (1988), 238–47. Nenner principally emphasizes the callous desertion of James by his family and friends, plus the retrospective blackening of his character by Revolution propagandists to justify his overthrow.

4 Sir John Dalrymple, *Memoirs of Great Britain and Ireland* (3 vols, 1771–90), II, 2nd pagination, 228–31; Edward Carpenter, *The Protestant Bishop: Being the Life of Henry Compton, 1632–1713, Bishop of London* (1956), pp. 126–8; Andrew M. Coleby, 'Compton, Henry (1631/2–1713)', *Oxford Dictionary of National Biography* (Oxford, 2004), XII, 886–7. Compton told James that he was confident that his fellow-bishops would as readily deny inviting the prince of Orange as himself.

5 For example, the defections of the naval officers Ashby and Cornewall are described in *Memoirs Relating to the Lord Torrington*, ed. John K. Laughton (Camden Soc., new ser., XLVI, 1889), pp. 27–8; and that of Lord Cornbury, a cavalry officer, in *The Correspondence of Henry Hyde, Earl of Clarendon, and of his Brother Laurence Hyde, Earl of Rochester, with the Diary of Lord Clarendon from 1687 to 1690*, ed. Samuel W. Singer (2 vols, 1828), II, 204, 212.

prince of Wales had indeed been born on 10 June, but subsequently had fallen ill and died at Richmond in the late summer or early autumn of 1688, and was similarly replaced.[6] The rumours amount to an accusation that the king and the queen, plus (presumably) some courtiers and domestic servants in the secret, had diverted the succession to the crown to a child of unknown parentage in order to ensure a continuous line of catholic kings into the distant future. Those of James's subjects who believed this accusation must necessarily have concluded that James was not simply an ill-advised monarch pursuing unpopular policies. He was seeking to defraud Mary and Anne, his grown-up protestant daughters by his first wife, of their inheritance as first and second heirs presumptive. The belief that James was embezzling the succession convinced the credulous that he had disqualified himself from continuing to wear the crown. Such persons would not have backed a rebellion against a king who was merely misguided. They could, and did, support a rebellion against a king who had allegedly resorted to a disgraceful crime. Anne herself wondered if there might not be some truth in the coffee-house speculations about her father and stepmother which so many seemed to believe.[7] The king and queen submitted themselves to the humiliation of summoning witnesses to the birth, including midwives and washerwomen who testified among other things to the condition of the queen's underclothes during her pregnancy, before the privy council in October 1688.[8] These 'inglorious' suspicions contributed to the propaganda of the Revolution, and to its acceptability, well into the eighteenth century.[9]

The long-term developments which followed the Revolution also sometimes fell short of the criteria normally applied when contemplating the concept of 'glory'. Religious liberty was restricted: the English Toleration Act of 1689 granted liberty of conscience and freedom of worship to protestant dissenters, but it barred them from office under the crown, from elected office in municipal corporations, and from the English universities, while catholics were explicitly excluded from the Act. Patronage and privilege remained features of elections to the house of Commons and of governmental politics throughout the eighteenth century. Britain's commitments abroad in defence of the Revolution required high taxation in wartime and the creation of a large national debt, and were to be a drain on Britain's economy as long as hostile nations backed the Jacobites. Those contempo-

6 The rumours are summarized, uncritically, by Gilbert Burnet, *History of His Own Time*, ed. Martin J. Routh (2nd edn, 6 vols, Oxford, 1833), III, 244–59.

7 *The Letters and Diplomatic Instructions of Queen Anne*, ed. Beatrice Curtis Brown (2nd edn, 1968), p. 37: Anne to Mary, 18 June 1688.

8 T.N.A., PC 2/72, pp. 757–77: privy council register, 22 Oct. 1688.

9 Rachel Weil, *Political Passions: Gender, the Family and Political Argument in England, 1680–1714* (Manchester, 1999), pp. 86–101; see also the same author's essay 'The Politics of Legitimacy: Women and the Warming Pan Scandal', in *The Revolution of 1688–1689*, ed. Schwoerer, pp. 65–82.

raries who foresaw that the offer of the crown to William and Mary would entail permanent quarrels upon the nation were not wrong.[10] For example, in the early twenty-first century the clause in the Act of Settlement of 1701 that compels catholics to drop out of the hereditary line of succession to the throne remains controversial. The perception of the Revolution as 'glorious' may seem difficult to sustain.

II

The term 'the Glorious Revolution' has become neutral, but any discussion of whether the Revolution really was 'glorious' (or not) is bound to be subjective. Also implying value judgments are those phrases that carry with them some pale reflexion of the idea that the Revolution of 1688–9 was at least vaguely commendable.

One such is 'the bloodless Revolution', employed by several historians, including Stuart E. Prall in the title of a book published in 1972, to suggest that the events of 1688–9 took place with less violence than is usual in revolutions.[11] In the autumn of 1688, many private letters, public addresses, and sermons expressed concern about the prospect of 'the effusion of blood' in a civil war like that of the 1640s.[12] In England, there was correspondingly great relief as the danger of civil war receded. The casualties of the Revolution in England appear to have been approximately 50 fatalities in minor skirmishes at Cirencester, Wincanton and Reading in November and December 1688, plus a small number of persons injured in the rioting in London and elsewhere in the aftermath of James's flight on 11 December. However, the concept of a 'bloodless' Revolution of 1688 takes no account of Scotland and Ireland. The campaigns in Scotland in 1689–90 shed a good deal of blood. The war fought from 1689 to 1691 in Ireland was precisely the renewal of a civil war, with professional armies conducting sieges and battles, that had been so much dreaded in England in 1688. The combined total of casualties in Scotland and Ireland in the three years after the Revolution probably exceeded 25,000.[13]

10 An eloquent pamphlet making this prophecy was [William Sherlock], *A Letter to a Member of the Convention* (n.d. [1689]), conveniently printed in *A Collection of Scarce and Valuable Tracts ... selected from ... Public as well as Private Libraries, particularly that of the late Lord Somers*, ed. Sir Walter Scott (13 vols, 1809–15), X, 185–90.

11 Stuart E. Prall, *The Bloodless Revolution: England, 1688* (Garden City, NY, 1972).

12 Lionel K.J. Glassey, 'Introduction', in *The Reigns of Charles II and James VII & II*, ed. Glassey (Basingstoke, 1997), pp. 5–6.

13 Tim Harris, *Revolution: The Great Crisis of the British Monarchy, 1685–1720* (2006), p. 35. Historians differ on the precise numbers of casualties directly associated with the Revolution and its aftermath in each of England, Scotland and Ireland; the surviving evidence is difficult to interpret. The figures given here are conservative.

Another off-shoot of the theme of the Revolution as a worthy enterprise is the notion of a 'protective' revolution; that is, a revolution undertaken to defend the cherished liberties of the nation against ill-advised and doctrinaire reform imposed from above, or against a revival of discredited principles such as religious fanaticism and military rule from the 1650s, or against evils such as 'arbitrary government' imported from Louis XIV's France. This was the view of the Revolution taken by William's adherents. A similar interpretation was implied by a sequence of eighteenth-century historians such as White Kennett, John Oldmixon and Paul de Rapin-Thoyras. This was a 'conservative' revolution. It was necessary action undertaken, not to change anything especially, but to ensure that fundamental liberties associated with the law, the protestant religion, and the constitution were safeguarded for future generations.

This 'protective' or 'conservative' interpretation presents the events of 1688–9 as a crusade conscientiously undertaken by persons committed to the maintenance of traditions which they valued as part of the national heritage. A hundred years earlier, patriots had *resisted* a foreign invasion – the Spanish Armada – to defend this heritage; now, in 1688, their equally patriotic descendants paradoxically *welcomed* a foreign invasion for precisely the same purpose. The contemporary estimate was that 'nineteen-twentieths' of the population would welcome William's expedition.[14] This statistical guesswork reflected an assertion that William was rescuing the nation and restoring its liberties, rather than invading and conquering it.

A 'protective' Revolution was acceptable in England, where the Church of England was cherished by a majority and where James's ecclesiastical programme had aroused wide alarm; but its appeal was much less in Scotland, where William's promise to preserve the protestant religion established by law did not enthuse those who disliked the episcopalian church settlement 'established by law' in Scotland in 1660, and who wished to replace it with a presbyterian church along the lines laid down at the time of the Reformation in Scotland in the 1560s.[15] In Scotland, therefore, the Revolution was conceived to be a preliminary to change, not a guarantee of continuity; it was less a 'protective' revolution than a 'reforming' revolution.

These assessments of whether the Revolution was 'glorious' or 'inglorious', praiseworthy or reprehensible, have an unedifying flavour of 'tit-for-tat' polemic. There are better phrases, which imply interpretations of the Revolution based on evidence rather than assertions about it based on partisanship. A more profitable area of discussion is opened up by the suggestion that the Revolution was 'reluctant'.

[14] Dalrymple, *Memoirs of Great Britain*, II, 2nd pagination, 229.

[15] The prince of Orange's 'Declaration' for Scotland is printed in Robert Wodrow, *The History of the Sufferings of the Church of Scotland from the Restoration to the Revolution*, ed. Robert Burns (4 vols, Glasgow, 1828–36), IV, 470–2.

III

The notion of a 'reluctant' Revolution of 1688–9, a revolution that was regretted as an unavoidable necessity by the majority of James's comfort-loving subjects who required of their government only that it should interfere as little as possible with their local communities and with their pursuit of prosperity, was fashionable for some years after the publication of William A. Speck's *Reluctant Revolutionaries* in 1988.[16] This interpretation is persuasive. It is preferable to the idea of a 'glorious' revolution, because it incorporates into the history of 1688–9 an appreciation of widespread attitudes from 1660 onwards. These include: the loyalty shown to the Stuart monarchy since the Restoration, especially during the exclusion crisis in 1678–81; the enthusiasm for James when he became king in February 1685; and the emphatic rejection of the pretensions of Argyll and Monmouth in the summer of 1685. Those who had become disenchanted with James by the winter of 1688–9 surely experienced difficulty in overcoming what had earlier been a sincere commitment to his regime.

It cannot too often be emphasized that those who participated in moderate, respectful opposition to James's policies, and then in the confused events following William's arrival and James's flight in November and December 1688, were constrained by memories of the civil wars and the regicide in the 1640s and of the military regimes in the 1650s. How were the maverick initiatives of James and his ministers in government and religion to be countered, without risking a renewed conflict with unforeseeable consequences? The dangers were such that many who deprecated James's policies, and who lamented his apparent willingness to undermine the Church of England, were unable to translate their apprehensions into decisive action.

One who suffered genuine qualms of conscience was Lord Nottingham, who drew back from subscribing the letter of 30 June 1688 to William at the last minute. 'He was gone very far,' wrote Henry Sidney to William, 'but now his heart fails him, and he will go no further; he saith 'tis scruples of conscience, but we all conclude it is another passion.[17] Nottingham did not lack courage, as his career in politics for more than 30 years after the Revolution demonstrates; but, as he shamefacedly told another conspirator, Edward Russell, he had been advised by his clerical friends that he should not actively seek to resist a design even to destroy the nation's liberties, since resistance could not be justified by the law.[18]

16 William A. Speck, *The Reluctant Revolutionaries: Englishmen and the Revolution of 1688* (Oxford, 1988).

17 Dalrymple, *Memoirs of Great Britain*, II, 2nd pagination, 232.

18 Henry Horwitz, *Revolution Politicks: The Career of Daniel Finch, Second Earl of Nottingham, 1647–1730* (Cambridge, 1968), pp. 52–3.

Later, in the autumn of 1688, Lord Chesterfield refused to be drawn into Danby's conspiratorial activities in the north of England. Danby informed Chesterfield, in September or early October 1688, that William was preparing to invade, and that the greater part of the army and many of the nobility would join with him. Chesterfield replied that he did not wish to rebel against James, especially as he was still a privy councillor. Although he thought an insurrection would succeed, he was sure that he would always be remorseful if he participated in it.[19]

Similar opinions – a compound of prudence, conscience, and the memory of the 1640s – influenced those who were prominent in the counties and towns where they lived. Many gentlemen, invited in October 1688 to resume the local offices from which they had been dismissed earlier in James's reign for their reluctance to comply with indiscriminate toleration, expressed their duty to the king even as they politely rejected his offer to restore them to those offices. Some former justices of the peace in Norfolk articulated this attitude lucidly:

> When it was His Majesty's pleasure to honour us with his Commission we served him with loyalty and fidelity and as we were obliged by the Church of England and our allegiance. And we are steadily resolved to continue in all dutiful obedience to His Majesty and will be most willing and ready to serve His Majesty in all things which may consort with His Majesty's honour and our safety, which we cannot do by our acting in conjunction with Persons unqualified and incapacitated by the Laws of this Realm.[20]

Men such as these probably did not want a revolution. If one occurred through William's intervention while they stood on the sidelines, they might acquiesce in it; provided that, as far as possible, bloodshed and civil war did not accompany it.

Closely linked to the interpretation of the Revolution as 'reluctant' are the concepts of an 'unexpected', 'unintended' or 'accidental' Revolution. The replacement of James on the throne, the Revolution settlement, and the long-term constitutional and ecclesiastical developments which ensued, were outcomes which few of those involved had even remotely envisaged before James's decision to flee the country in mid-December 1688. What *was* foreseen, as a best-case scenario, was that James, chastened by the intervention of his son-in-law, and surrounded by responsible counsellors of the traditional type whom he would be compelled to reappoint, would resume the duties of kingship. An accommodation along these lines was foreshadowed when representatives from James and William met at Hungerford in Berkshire to open negotiations on 8–10 December 1688. There would be a general election. Some limitation of James's powers by parliamentary

19 *Letters of Philip, Second Earl of Chesterfield* (1829), pp. 336–9.

20 H.M.C., *Lothian* MSS, pp. 132–3.

statute would probably have followed, especially vis-à-vis the appointment of ministers and judges, the size of the army, and the exercise of the suspending power. Arrangements relating to the restoration of municipal charters and the privileges of colleges at the universities would presumably have been reached. It is likely that some such solution was anticipated by James's protestant subjects during the weeks immediately before and after William's arrival.[21] What prevented all this was James's flight. The form that the Revolution was eventually to take developed out of 'reluctant' ad hoc adjustments to the emergency conditions into which the nation was unexpectedly plunged on 11 December when it was learned that James had gone.

Earlier, several individuals, including Nottingham, Halifax and the former Attorney-General Sir Robert Sawyer, had believed that the acquittal of the seven bishops and the prospect of a general election meant that William's intervention in English politics was not required at all.[22] Sawyer thought that 'nothing can more dishearten the Enemyes of our religion then an Unanimous choice of members to serve in Parliament'. His expectation that the Church of England party would hold firm in the constituencies during the elections, and in the house of Commons after them, was perfectly reasonable.[23] In any case, the house of Lords would obstruct bills damaging to the Church of England proposed by a packed, subservient house of Commons. Sawyer expected that moderation and conciliation would bring about a solution. James would be made to understand his own best interests. The 'evil counsellors' who had misled him would be dismissed. The crisis in politics and religion would subside, civil war would be avoided, and life would return to normal. The Revolution was not only 'reluctant', 'unexpected', 'unintended' and 'accidental'; it was also 'unnecessary'.

These interpretations are open to criticism. Assumptions that James would remain on the throne, and that William's role would be confined to assisting his father-in-law to regain the confidence of his subjects, certainly persisted. But a vocal minority thought otherwise. There are plenty of examples of individuals who were openly hostile to James, and who pressed for a 'radical', even a 'revolutionary', outcome. William Harbord boasted in December 1688 that he conceived himself to be in rebellion against the king. Lord Delamer asserted that he no longer looked upon James as king and would no longer obey him. Clarendon noted at the conference of peers on 24 December that a group of whig lords were 'bitter and fierce' against the king. After the Convention met, Colonel Birch, the 73-year-old member for Weobley – whose military rank derived from the New Model

21 Mark Goldie, 'Thomas Erle's Instructions for the Revolution Parliament, December 1688', *Parliamentary History*, XIV (1995), 337–47.

22 Dalrymple, *Memoirs of Great Britain*, II, 2nd pagination, 235–7; *The Life and Letters of Sir George Savile, Marquis of Halifax*, ed. Helen C. Foxcroft (2 vols, 1898), I, 509–10.

23 Bodl. MS Tanner 28, f. 126: [Sir] R[obert] Sawyer to Archbishop Sancroft, 17 Sept. 1688.

Army – opened a debate on the state of the nation on 29 January 1689 in language reminiscent of Oliver Cromwell himself:

> When I consider the extraordinary hand of God that brought us hither, and the freedom we are here met in, it amazes me; and I am not able to comprehend this work of God in such an extraordinary manner; and, concerning King *James's* deposing himself, 'tis the hand of God. These forty years we have been scrambling for our Religion, and have saved but little of it. We have been striving against *Anti-Christ*, Popery and Tyranny.

In the house of Lords, on 31 January, Lord Montagu remarked that he felt himself to be absolved from all allegiance, and Lord Delamer said that if King James returned he would fight him sword in hand. Men such as these were anything but 'reluctant' revolutionaries.[24]

It is easy to identify individual examples of 'willing', 'eager' revolutionaries. But were there enough of them, and did they represent a sufficiently substantial body of wider public opinion, to challenge the interpretation of the Revolution as characteristically 'reluctant'? This question cannot readily be answered. However, if the 'enthusiastic' revolutionaries could persuade the nation that the prince of Wales was spurious, then everybody was bound to urge that James's reign be brought to an end without delay. How could James remain on the throne when his alleged crime had so completely lost him the respect of his subjects? It follows that, if this belief that there was something dubious about the baby was widespread, as contemporary propaganda indicates that it probably was, then perhaps the Revolution was less 'reluctant' than it might have appeared.[25]

Another possible weakness in the 'reluctant', 'accidental', 'unnecessary' interpretations of the Revolution is that it is difficult to apply these adjectives to the Revolution in Scotland. It is not impossible: Ian Cowan made the attempt in two essays published in 1989 and 1991.[26] Cowan argued that

24 *Correspondence of Clarendon*, II, 219, 229, 235, 257; Anchitel Grey, *Debates of the House of Commons from the Year 1667 to the Year 1694* (2nd edn, 10 vols, 1769), IX, 26; Robert A. Beddard, '"The Violent Party": The Guildhall Revolutionaries and the Growth of Opposition to James II', *The Guildhall Miscellany*, III (1970), 120–36. Beddard identifies four peers in particular (Lords Culpeper, Newport, Montagu and Wharton) as the ringleaders of the 'violent party'.

25 William's assertion in his 'Declaration' for England, that 'not only we ourselves, but all the good subjects of those kingdoms, do vehemently suspect that the pretended Prince of Wales was not born by the Queen', gave a lead to 'enthusiastic' advocates of action against James. Sir James Mackintosh, *History of the Revolution in England in 1688* (1834), p. 699.

26 Ian B. Cowan, 'The Reluctant Revolutionaries: Scotland in 1688', in *By Force or By Default?*, ed. Cruickshanks, pp. 65–77; Ian B. Cowan, 'Church and State Reformed? The Revolution of 1688–1689', in *The Anglo-Dutch Moment: Essays on the Glorious Revolution and its World Impact*, ed. Jonathan I. Israel (Cambridge, 1991), pp. 163–83.

James's indulgence was welcomed by the majority of moderate presbyterians as well as by the Scottish catholics, while the more extreme Cameronians were too insignificant in numbers to affect the issue. The venal and opportunistic politicians in Scotland were pushed into 'revolutionary' activity by James's flight and the subsequent developments in England. 'It is undeniable,' Cowan concluded, 'that the Scots had at the onset been very reluctant revolutionaries.'[27]

However, this view of the Scottish Revolution has been revised. Many Scots took an active part in opposing James's catholic regime in Scotland. They contributed to the Orangist conspiracy in the summer and autumn of 1688; they mobilized out-of-doors agitation against catholics in general, and against James's Scottish counsellors in particular; they welcomed a 'revolutionary' settlement of government and religion in Scotland in the first six months of 1689. The Scottish Convention decided, not that James had 'abdicated' the Scottish throne, but that he had 'forefaulted' it. The Scottish 'Revolution settlement' had many distinctively radical features.[28] The proposition that the Scots passively, or 'reluctantly', accepted a Revolution forced upon them by William's arrival in England, or by James's departure from England, or by the precedents set by the English Convention before the Scottish Convention even met, seems flawed.

IV

Somewhere intermediate between the concepts of a 'glorious' revolution and a 'reluctant' revolution is a 'sensible' revolution. This implies that what happened in 1688–9 owed little to doctrinaire principles and even less to the fanatical assertion of them. The Revolution was a sequence of moderate compromises arrived at by responsible persons in a spirit of pragmatism. The phrase was brought to prominence by G.M. Trevelyan in a book published for the 250th anniversary of the Revolution in 1938, and it was analysed in an essay by John Morrill in 1991.[29] Morrill found something to admire in Trevelyan's exposition, not so much for its weight of scholarship (which

27 Cowan, 'Reluctant Revolutionaries', p. 77.

28 Harris, *Revolution*, Part I, ch. 4, Part II, ch. 9; Clare Jackson, *Restoration Scotland, 1660–1690: Royalist Policies, Religion and Ideas* (Woodbridge, 2003), pp. 191–203; Ginny Gardner, *The Scottish Exile Community in the Netherlands, 1660–1690* (East Linton, 2004), pp. 178–201; Tim Harris, 'The Scots and the Revolution of 1688–1689', in *Politics and the Political Imagination in Later Stuart Britain: Essays Presented to Lois Green Schwoerer*, ed. Howard Nenner (Rochester, NY, 1997), pp. 97–113.

29 George Macaulay Trevelyan, *The English Revolution 1688–1689* (1938) – the book was reprinted into the 1970s by Oxford University Press in a popular educational series, the Home University Library; John Morrill, 'The Sensible Revolution', in *The Anglo-Dutch Moment*, ed. Israel, pp. 73–104.

was unimpressive), but rather for its consistency and elegance. The word 'sensible' avoids the triumphalist overtones of 'glorious', but still conveys the view that the Revolution was deserving of approbation. It sidesteps the implication in the word 'reluctant' that the Revolution was somehow unwanted, by hinting at intelligent solutions to difficult problems that had been squarely faced. Trevelyan suggested that the people of England and Scotland, confronted with a headstrong monarch pursuing an unconstitutional programme, gratefully accepted the opportunities offered by William's arrival and by James's folly in dethroning himself by his flight. Sensibly, responsible men took upon themselves the task of maintaining order after James's departure. Sensibly, William summoned assemblies that looked and behaved exactly like traditional parliaments in both countries. Sensibly, these assemblies, the Conventions, hammered out a political settlement that proved acceptable enough to minimize violence and civil war in the short term and which, in the medium and long term, evolved into a stable, solidly based polity, the envy of Europe in the nineteenth century. Morrill concluded that, with all the faults of his book, Trevelyan had devised a plausible interpretation of the Revolution.[30]

Morrill identified four weaknesses in Trevelyan's 'sensible' interpretation. First, he challenged the teleological aspect of Trevelyan's approach: the Revolution did not inaugurate a harmonious regime of parliamentary consensus, in which whigs and tories agreed to disagree in civilized fashion. Second, it is difficult to describe the Revolution as 'sensible' when one of its by-products was the bitter, intractable conflict between adherents of the Revolution on the one hand, and Jacobites and non-jurors on the other, which was to divide the British Isles for the following 60 years or more. Third, those admired aspects of the Revolution, 'moderation' and 'compromise', amounted to the fudging of principles of importance to seventeenth-century persons of integrity and intelligence such as Milton, Locke and Algernon Sidney: republicanism, liberty, puritanism. These principles were, through the eighteenth century, swept under the carpet. The Revolution was not 'sensible'; it was 'sanitized'.[31] Fourth, the phrase 'the sensible Revolution' contains a hint of complacency and self-congratulation, as though 'the British', unlike less enlightened nations, prefer to have gentlemanly good-natured revolutions, when they choose to have revolutions at all.

V

A different way of interpreting the Revolution of 1688–9 is to identify it with the ambitions of a particular social class. Any of the aristocracy, the country gentry, the urban bourgeoisie or the common people might

30 Morrill, 'Sensible Revolution', p. 104.

31 *Ibid.*, pp. 91–3.

have taken the lead in forcing James off the throne and placing William and Mary upon it, subsequently profiting from this change by compelling William and his successors to govern in their interests. Any of these groups in society, without necessarily coming to the fore in the events of 1688–9, might still have benefited from the working out of the Revolution settlement to the point where the Revolution might legitimately be considered as 'their' revolution.

One such interpretation is the theory that the Revolution was an 'aristocratic' revolution, even when 'the aristocracy' is defined in the limited sense of the members of the house of Lords, plus their immediate family: their wives, brothers, sisters, sons, daughters and grandchildren. All of the seven who subscribed the invitation to William were 'aristocrats'. Danby, Shrewsbury, Devonshire and Lumley were peers anyway. Henry Compton, the bishop of London, was a younger son of the earl of Northampton. Henry Sidney was a younger son of the earl of Leicester. Edward Russell was a grandson of the earl of Bedford.

The local risings against James in November 1688 were managed by 'aristocrats': the earl of Danby, assisted by Lord Willoughby d'Eresby (the heir to the earldom of Lindsey), Lord Haughton (the heir to the earldom of Clare) and Lord Fairfax of Cameron (a Scottish peer), in Yorkshire; Lord Lumley in County Durham; Lord Delamer and the earl of Derby in Lancashire and Cheshire; the earls of Devonshire, Scarsdale, Manchester and Northampton, plus Lord Grey of Ruthin, in the midlands.[32] Others who were active on William's behalf in the south of England, or who made declarations in favour of the liberties of the nation under his protection, included Lord Lovelace, Lord Herbert of Cherbury and the earl of Bath. Among the army officers who defected to William were the dukes of Grafton and Ormond, Lords Churchill and Cornbury and Viscount Colchester. The Lords' input into the Declaration of Rights and into the settlement that was eventually arrived at, especially the Toleration Act, was considerable.[33]

The peers reaped their reward. Individuals were promoted up the ranks of the peerage. Danby became successively marquess of Carmarthen in 1689 and duke of Leeds in 1694. Shrewsbury and Devonshire also became dukes in 1694. Lumley rose from a barony to the earldom of Scarborough in 1690. Henry Sidney became Viscount Sidney in 1689 and earl of Romney in 1694. Edward Russell became earl of Orford in 1697. Lord Willoughby d'Eresby, having succeeded his father as earl of Lindsey in 1701, eventually died in 1723 as duke of Ancaster. Lord Haughton succeeded his father as earl of Clare in 1689 and was created duke of Newcastle, following the extinction of the Cavendish line of dukes of Newcastle, in 1694. Lord Delamer

32 David H. Hosford, *Nottingham, Nobles and the North: Aspects of the Revolution of 1688* (Hamden, CT, 1976).

33 Lois G. Schwoerer, *The Declaration of Rights, 1689* (Baltimore, MD, 1981), pp. 232–47.

became earl of Warrington. Churchill became earl, later duke, of Marlborough. Admiral Herbert, who had commanded William's fleet, became earl of Torrington. Collectively, 'the aristocracy' embarked on that domination of politics and government in the British Isles which was to last for 150 years, until it began to be diminished in the 1830s and 1840s with the Reform Act and the repeal of the Corn Laws.

There are qualifications to this 'aristocratic' revolution as a reading of the events of the winter of 1688–9. Several aristocrats were indifferent, or hostile, to William's pretensions, and remained loyal to James. Three examples who engaged in Jacobite plots in the 1690s were the earls of Ailesbury, Clarendon and Dartmouth. The house of Lords in the Convention came close to scuppering the Revolution altogether. It doubted whether James had abdicated. It questioned whether the throne was vacant. It spent precious time in debating possible solutions to the crisis of James's flight, including two – the succession of Mary by herself, and a regency (with James remaining on the throne as titular monarch) – which found little favour in the elected chamber. Among those who voted for a regency on 29 January 1689 were Ormonde, Grafton and Scarsdale, who had all deserted James in November 1688.[34] Strenuous argument was required to bring some peers on to the side of the Revolution. The earl of Thanet, a very 'reluctant' revolutionary, confessed that he 'thought we had done ill in admitting the monarchy to be elective; for so this vote [that William and Mary be declared king and queen] had made it; but he thought there was an absolute necessity of having a Government; and he did not see it likely to be any other way than this'.[35]

The aristocracy had no especial reason to believe that its interests would be advanced by the substitution of William for James. Admittedly, every eighteenth-century cabinet would contain a majority of peers, and every house of Commons would contain numerous members (though never a majority) who had been nominated by aristocratic patrons in the constituencies. The armed services, the embryonic civil service and the Church of England would rely heavily in their appointments and promotions on aristocratic recommendation. But these developments date back at least to the Restoration of 1660. Danby, when lord treasurer in the 1670s, was already exploiting the influence of his aristocratic relations and friends in order to secure a consistent majority for the 'court party' in the house of Commons through the management of patronage. Most of Charles II's ministers were peers on their appointment, or quickly acquired a peerage in reward for their services.[36] The Revolution accelerated, rather than initiated, the growth of aristocratic power.

34 *Correspondence of Clarendon*, II, 256 n.

35 *Ibid.*, II, 261–2.

36 Some politicians in office in Charles II's reign, including Sir Orlando Bridgeman, Sir Joseph Williamson and Sir Leoline Jenkins, remained commoners; but they were

There is more mileage in the theory of an 'aristocratic' revolution if the term 'the *élite*' is substituted for 'the aristocracy'. A looser definition of 'aristocracy' incorporates all persons enjoying privilege, in the form of the ownership either of land, or of commercial or industrial wealth. The Revolution comes into focus as the revolution of the propertied classes: country gentlemen, merchants, tradesmen, lawyers and government officials, as well as noblemen.

Those who possessed estates confiscated from the Church at the time of the Reformation were apprehensive about a catholic king who might be tempted to recover them.[37] James explicitly denied that he would do this in his Declaration of Indulgence in April 1687, in which he announced '... [we] will maintain [our loving subjects] in all their properties and possessions, as well of church and abbey lands as in any other lands and properties whatsoever'.[38] But landowners, looking ahead, could not be sure that the king would be able to resist the pressure from the catholic clergy for the restoration of the Church's heritage. In the event, James never did seek to recover monastic or chantry lands. He did, however, interfere with the possessions of his subjects in a different way. The fellows of Magdalen College in Oxford held their fellowships as a freehold; in November 1687, they were ejected from them for disobedience to James's command to elect his nominee as their President.[39]

Magdalen College furnished the only real example of a direct threat from James to the property of his subjects. However, the imposition of an enormous fine of £30,000 on the earl of Devonshire for a minor brawl within the boundaries of the royal palace contributed to those clauses in the Declaration of Rights condemning the exaction of excessive bail and the imposition of excessive punishments.[40] Persons of humbler status might have anticipated financial loss as a result of James's programme of religious toleration. An attempt was made in July and August 1688 to calculate the sums exacted in fines from recusants and dissenters between 1677 and 1688. If, as is possible, the aim of this exercise was to reimburse those who had suffered because of their religion, then the wealthier inhabitants of parishes that had

exceptions to the general rule (the brothers Sir William and Henry Coventry, also ministers in Charles's reign, were aristocrats inasmuch as they were younger sons of Lord Coventry).

37 Speck, *Reluctant Revolutionaries*, pp. 144–5.

38 *English Historical Documents 1660–1714*, ed. Andrew Browning (1966), pp. 395–7.

39 *Magdalen College and King James II, 1686–1688*, ed. J. R. Bloxam (Oxford Historical Society, VI, 1886), pp. 204–5: 16 Nov. 1687; Angus Macintyre, 'The College, King James II and the Revolution 1687–1688', in Laurence Brockliss, Gerald Harriss and Angus Macintyre, *Magdalen College and the Crown: Essays for the Tercentenary of the Restoration of the College 1688* (Oxford, 1988), pp. 44–5, 64, 73.

40 Schwoerer, *Declaration of Rights*, pp. 239–40; Harris, *Revolution*, p. 344. Harris observes that there had been plenty of cases of excessive bail and fines in Charles II's time.

levied fines or distrained goods might have been obliged to contribute to repayments.[41]

James did antagonize the propertied classes in a different sense. He dismissed them in droves from the offices they held by virtue of their social status. Those affected included noblemen (who were lord lieutenants and *custodes rotulorum*) and country gentlemen (who were deputy-lieutenants and justices of the peace) in the counties; and merchants, tradesmen and lawyers (who were mayors, aldermen, common councilmen and recorders) in the towns. Between the winter of 1686–7 and the early autumn of 1688, these men of property were sacked from their local offices on an unprecedented scale. They conceived themselves to be the natural rulers of their local communities; and they resented both their own omission, and the appointment of catholic gentlemen in their places. Ex-puritans, ex-Cromwellians and obscure opportunists appeared as office-holders in those areas where suitable catholics were lacking. Bungled and incomplete attempts to restore the militia, the commissions of the peace and the corporations in October 1688 were, only too plainly, panic measures in response to the news that William was preparing his invasion.[42]

These changes among office-holders did not *cause* the Revolution, exactly. The Revolution was not a rebellion of angry squires and townsmen who were demanding to be reinstated in positions conferring power. What the changes *did* do was to create an atmosphere in which the rulers of the localities were unwilling to make much of an effort to defend the king to whom they had sworn allegiance when misfortune fell upon him. James had rejected their service. He had put his trust in persons disqualified by the law from exercising power. Disillusioned ex-office-holders, who were also property-owners, were prepared to let him take the consequences of his behaviour. This was the line taken by the gentlemen of Norfolk who are quoted above. There were, of course, many individual exceptions: Sir John Reresby in Yorkshire represents in his *Memoirs* the attitudes of a gentleman who retained his loyalty to the king, while at the same time registering disapproval of the upheavals in the personnel of the bench of magistrates in the West Riding, and also in Middlesex, on both of which he sat.[43] But the

[41] Bodl. MS Rawlinson D. 372: a volume containing the proceedings of a commission issued under the exchequer seal to inquire into money and goods levied upon recusants and dissenters in the city of Exeter and the county of Devon, 1688. It mostly consists of affidavits made on forms printed for the purpose. Presumably similar exercises took place in, or were planned for, other counties.

[42] Paul D. Halliday, *Dismembering the Body Politic: Partisan Politics in England's Towns, 1650–1730* (Cambridge, 1998), pp. 237–62; John Miller, *Cities Divided: Politics and Religion in English Provincial Towns, 1660–1722* (Oxford, 2007), pp. 228–37; Lionel K. J. Glassey, *Politics and the Appointment of Justices of the Peace, 1675–1720* (Oxford, 1979), ch. 3.

[43] *The Memoirs of Sir John Reresby*, ed. Andrew Browning (2nd edn, revised by W. A. Speck and Mary Geiter, 1991), pp. 463, 494–5, 502.

Revolution was everywhere facilitated by the sullen acquiescence in it of disconsolate men of property who had formerly been office-holders.

One contemporary contributed an important qualification to this conclusion, namely Roger Morrice, a dissenting clergyman resident in London, who described in well-informed detail the processes by which the county justices of the peace were reshuffled by the privy council in 1686–7. Morrice's account confirms that Lord Chancellor Jeffreys, technically responsible for appointing and dismissing justices of the peace, played little part, but rather that James himself made the final decisions as to who was to be added and who left out. The principal advisers of the king in this regulation were three catholic peers: Lords Arundel of Wardour, Powis and Dover. The bishop of Durham and (unexpectedly) the lord deputy of Ireland, Lord Tyrconnell, provided some help. Morrice further gives information about more changes among the justices of the peace conducted, not by the council, but by a committee of regulators in 1688.[44]

What is surprising about Morrice's account is that he wholeheartedly welcomed the changes. It would be easy to assume that the remodelling of the county commissions of the peace was resented by everybody as a breach in the traditional principle that landowners should possess authority in the communities in which they lived. Morrice introduces an unexpected point of view. He rejoiced that the 'old, mercenary Tories that have sold the Kingdome, Religion and Civill Interest' had lost office. Now the 'best men' in all the counties filled the bench, and James was king of the whole nation – 'nobility, gentry, tradesmen, freeholders, sober Churchmen and sober Dissenters' – rather than king only of a Church of England faction. Morrice believed that catholic justices of the peace were few except in a small number of counties, and that 'giddy Phanaticks' on the bench were few everywhere.[45] In short, Morrice rejoiced that the arrogant squires who had governed the counties since 1660, and who had persecuted honest dissenters during the final years of Charles II's reign, had at last been disciplined. The king was not indiscriminately humiliating the landowning gentry. He was dismissing those members of that class who had abused their powers. He was creating a harmonious, united nation. His regulation of the commissions of the peace was therefore to be approved. Morrice's opinion probably reflected that of a larger minority than has hitherto been supposed.

There is still a good deal to be said for considering the Revolution as a manifestation of the discontents of property-owners. It was frequently asserted at the time that the purpose of the Revolution had been the defence of property. One of its immediate consequences in 1689 was the

44 *The Entring Book of Roger Morrice, 1677–1691*, ed. Mark Goldie *et al.* (7 vols, Woodbridge, 2007–9), III, 273–366, especially 294–5, 301, 319; *ibid.*, IV, 226–7, 230.

45 *Ibid.*, IV, 226–7, 230–1, 234, 244, 246. Morrice also provides details of the issue of new commissions of the peace in the early months of William's reign: *ibid.*, V, 51, 54, 57, 59, 61.

reinstatement of wealthy men to the offices conferring local authority from which James had dismissed them. An epithet occasionally used to express this interpretation is 'the respectable Revolution', a phrase used by Lucile Pinkham in 1954. Pinkham did not investigate her own idea very closely; her main concern was to demonstrate William's ambitions. However, her word 'respectable' denotes a revolution conducted by responsible persons, pillars of the establishment not normally given to revolutionary activity. As property-owners, they did not intend to overthrow government or to undermine society. The 'respectable' Revolution was, rather, intended to *sustain* government and society, so that the 'respectable' classes could continue to benefit from the status quo into the future.[46]

The principal difficulty in describing the Revolution as 'respectable' is that in 1688–9 some of its more energetic exponents were raffish, disreputable figures. John Wildman, Robert Ferguson and Hugh Speke, all active in 1688–9, had been involved in either the Rye House plot or the Monmouth rebellion or both. Forty years earlier, Wildman had been a Leveller spokesmen in the Putney Debates. The aged republican and regicide Edmund Ludlow embarrassed William's friends by returning from exile in Switzerland, proclaiming the virtues of the Revolution.[47] Conversely, many of those who were either vehemently opposed to the Revolution, or who refused to accept it, *were* eminently 'respectable', such as (for example) Archbishop Sancroft of Canterbury and the other non-juring bishops. The word 'respectable' is not wholly satisfactory. Nonetheless, a revolution which owed its success and permanence to the acquiescence (however lukewarm) of 'respectable' property-owners does make sense.

Another view identifying the Revolution with a social class, now less fashionable than in the 1960s and 1970s, defines 1688 as a 'bourgeois' revolution, in the Marxist sense that it was one of the stages in the historical development of capitalism as society passed gradually from feudalism through commercialism to industrialism. A French textbook expressed this theory concisely in 1956:

> This rise [of trade] initiated a long commercial conflict with Holland and with France. The English capitalists, happy with Charles II's policy against Holland, disapproved of his attitude, and even more of that of James II, with regard to France, which had become the most formidable rival in terms of trade and the colonies … the economic struggle against France, the struggle for the religion best adapted to the capitalist spirit, provoked the Revolution of 1688. The Revolution of 1688 is the triumph of the capitalist bourgeoisie, of the merchants of

[46] Lucile Pinkham, *William III and the Respectable Revolution* (1954; repr. edn, Cambridge, MA, 1969).

[47] Barbara Taft, 'Return of a Regicide: Edmund Ludlow and the Glorious Revolution', *History*, LXXVI (1991), 197–228.

the City of London and of the country gentlemen incorporated into the bourgeoisie by agricultural capitalism.[48]

The aftermath of the Revolution of 1688–9 provides some evidence for this interpretation. The Bank of England was founded in 1694; the Bank of Scotland in 1695. The national debt originated in the mid-1690s. By the end of Anne's reign in 1714 it had swelled to approximately £35,000,000. Investment in government funds was supplying an annual income to an expanding class of *rentiers*. The growth in the number of joint-stock companies in the 1690s stimulated activity in an embryonic stock market operating in the coffee-houses of the City of London.

It is, however, difficult to establish a causal link between these 'capitalist' developments, and the political and constitutional revolution that accompanied them. The bourgeoisie, however defined, had already been prospering before 1688, during the trade expansion of the 1670s and 1680s as the Navigation Acts of the 1660s began to take belated effect.[49] The Revolution of 1688–9, unlike most revolutions, was not preceded by economic hardship or financial crisis. Overseas trade, and domestic commercial and industrial enterprise, flourished during the ten years or so before 1688. James was receiving an income averaging somewhere in the region of £2,000,000 per annum by 1688, a fortune by comparison with that of his predecessors. Possibly the Revolution was 'bourgeois' inasmuch as bankers, merchants, industrialists, shopkeepers, doctors, lawyers and schoolteachers gradually became more wealthy in its aftermath; and that eventually, much later, such persons were to perceive themselves as a consolidated 'middle class'. How much the Revolution contributed to this, and how much depended on indirect or extraneous factors (such as involvement in European wars, or participation in expanding transoceanic trade, or a growth in literacy levels) is debatable.

On the face of it, the assertion that the Revolution was a 'popular' rebellion might seem hard to justify. The proposition that James's regime was overthrown by a violent, irresistible insurrection by the 'lower orders' does not immediately convince. The opinions and attitudes of ordinary people are difficult to identify or define. Prosecutions for seditious words in the law courts are occasionally revealing, though it is hard to tell whether a prosecution meant that the words in question were regarded by everybody as scandalously improper, or whether it resulted from an attempt by an authoritarian *élite* to suppress submerged, dangerous and possibly widespread

48 Roland Mousnier, *Histoire Générale des Civilisations*, IV, *Les XVIe et XVIIe Siècles: Les Progrès de la Civilisation Européenne et le Déclin de l'Orient, 1492–1715* (Paris, 1956), pp. 292–3 (my translation). Mousnier echoed the interpretation of British Marxists such as A.L. Morton, *A People's History of England* (1938; 3rd edn, 1989), chs IX.4, X.1.

49 Joyce M. Ellis, 'Consumption and Wealth', in *Charles II and James VII & II*, ed. Glassey, pp. 191–210.

views.[50] Sometimes prosecutions were for drunkenness as much as for disaffection. In November 1687, Foster Chell of Upton-on-Severn in Worcestershire (a random example from many), said 'God Damne the King I doe not care a Turd for him'. Chell's defence was that 'he was so far gone in drink that he did not in the least remember what he did or sayd'. Sometimes opinions were described in tantalizingly imprecise terms. William Moubry or Mowbray of Castle Rising in Norfolk was accused of 'speakeing seditious, execrable and dangerous words of the King' in October 1686, but the exact nature of these words remains unknown.[51]

A more promising approach is to investigate the extent of the willingness of 'ordinary people' to volunteer for irregular service or to participate in crowd action involving demonstration or riot. Large numbers of people rallied to the various risings in the north midlands and the north of England in the autumn of 1688. It is not clear, though, that before 12 December they were backing a 'revolution', since they could not have foreseen that James would flee or that William would emerge as a candidate for the crown. They were probably expressing a mood of anxiety, frustration and resentment in the hope that manifestations of a collective dislike of James's Jesuit-inspired subversion of the Church and the laws would compel him to see reason and reverse his programme. Similar motives may have been in the minds of those who made violent attacks on catholic chapels and on the homes of catholic neighbours.

In London, there were several 'mobs' expressing different opinions at different times. All the evidence agrees that the acquittal of the seven bishops on 30 June 1688 was greeted with mass public rejoicing. But six months later a large crowd gathered to cheer James on 16 December on his forlorn return from Kent following his first, unsuccessful, attempt to escape. Then, within seven weeks or so, the Convention was besieged in late January and February 1689 by 'mobs' that seem consistently to have urged upon the members of both houses (who sometimes struggled to get into, and out of, the palace of Westminster) that the solution that they wanted was William as king as quickly as possible.[52] Anthony Rowe, M.P. for Penryn, asked leave on 2 February to present a petition 'from great numbers

[50] Numerous examples of seditious words are quoted in Harris, *Revolution*, pp. 61–5, 356–7.

[51] Worcestershire R.O., BA1/110/153/54–6: Worcestershire quarter sessions file, examination of Foster Chell and affidavit of John Woodyate, 8–12 Nov. 1687; Norfolk R.O., C/S1/10, quarter sessions book 1684–1690, unfoliated: King's Lynn sessions, 12 Oct. 1686.

[52] Tim Harris, 'London Crowds and the Revolution of 1688', in *By Force or By Default?*, ed. Cruickshanks, pp. 44–59; Harris, 'The Parties and the People: The Press, the Crowd and Politics "Out-of-doors" in Restoration England', in *Charles II and James VII & II*, ed. Glassey, pp. 125–51; Harris, 'Understanding Popular Politics in Restoration Britain', in *A Nation Transformed: England After the Restoration*, ed. Alan Houston and Steve Pincus (Cambridge, 2001), pp. 125–53; Harris, *Revolution*, pp. 290–307.

of persons', requesting that William and Mary be crowned king and queen.[53] The 'lower orders' had more impact on the course of events than perhaps used to be thought, and by the mid-eighteenth century some pamphleteers were prepared to assert that the Revolution had been conducted by 'the people'.[54]

VI

An interpretation difficult to classify under the headings so far explored is that of the 'whig' Revolution of 1688, long associated with Macaulay.[55] This seems unexceptionable. The word 'whig' came into use during the exclusion crisis to describe that body of opinion, expressed both in pamphlet literature and in political activity, which prophesied disaster in the event of the succession of a catholic monarch, and which therefore advocated the 'exclusion' of the duke of York from the hereditary succession. The original whigs of 1679–81 failed to achieve this objective, and James duly succeeded in 1685. There followed, as these original whigs had predicted, disaster; the catholic king behaved as expected. He introduced both 'popery' and 'arbitrary government'. In 1689, James was, finally, 'excluded' from the throne. Robert Beddard has emphasized that, during the interregnum following James's first flight, 'whig' politicians in London and in the provinces displayed tactical skill in outmanoeuvring the divided tories in order to accomplish this result.[56] Thereafter, they seized the opportunity to embody in the Revolution settlement principles claimed to be distinctively 'whig'. These included: a limited constitutional monarchy; the protection of the liberty of the subject; religious toleration; the freedom of the press; an independent judiciary; and a foreign policy devoted to placing restrictions on the power of France in conjunction with European allies.

In the long term, too, the whigs did well out of the Revolution. After 1714, they enjoyed a near-monopoly of high office and power. Peerages, bishoprics, wealth and privilege came their way. By the mid-eighteenth century they had been at the centre of government for so long that the

53 Grey, *Debates*, IX, 45.

54 Wilson, 'Inventing Revolution', p. 372.

55 Lord Macaulay, *The History of England from the Accession of James the Second*, ed. C.H. Firth (6 vols, 1913–15), first published between 1849 and 1865.

56 Robert Beddard, 'The Unexpected Whig Revolution of 1688', in *The Revolutions of 1688*, ed. Robert Beddard (Oxford, 1991), pp. 11–101. The word 'unexpected' in the title of this learned essay relates more to the rapid re-emergence of the whigs after a long period in the wilderness than to any unanticipated quality in the Revolution itself. The same author's 'Introduction' to *A Kingdom Without a King: The Journal of the Provisional Government in the Revolution of 1688*, ed. Beddard (Oxford, 1988), pp. 9–65, amplifies the same theme.

whig ministers of George II allegedly ceased to be that monarch's servants and became his masters. He was a 'king in chains', while the whigs were accused of exploiting his surviving powers and prerogatives to their own advantage.[57] This 'whig oligarchy' had emerged from the Revolution. Before 1688, the whig 'party' had been a 'country' party of opposition. After 1689, William was a king whom the whigs could serve.

A close inspection of the 'whig Revolution' reveals cracks in the concept. James had made overtures to former exclusionist whigs, his natural enemies, a minority of whom – such as Lord Brandon in Lancashire, Silius Titus in Huntingdonshire and William Sacheverell at Nottingham – responded to his blandishments.[58] Moreover, James had alienated the tories, his natural allies, by his concessions to dissenters in the Declarations of Indulgence, by his reshaping of local office-holding, and by his maintenance of a large army. Three of the seven subscribers to the letter of invitation to William (Danby, Lumley and the bishop of London) were more 'tory' than 'whig'. By 1688, therefore, it seemed that the whig-tory distinction had been a temporary fashion in the early 1680s, and was now obsolete. The co-operation of the ex-tories and the ex-whigs in opposition to James's programme was not to last – profound antipathies re-surfaced quickly after 1689 – but the Revolution would not have been possible without the contribution, however grudging, of these ex-tories.

Moreover, the implementation of 'whig' principles in the Revolution settlement was not achieved simply by the exertions of the whigs. For example, religious freedom in the limited form of the Toleration Act of 1689 emerged from a strategy in which it had originally been envisaged that the 'comprehension' of moderate dissenters within an elastic-sided Church of England would accompany the 'toleration' of a small remnant of intransigents. But this implied that some ex-dissenters, if 'comprehended', would no longer be subject to the Test Acts and would be eligible to hold office. The tories, alarmed at the prospect of puritans in power, rejected comprehension and voted for toleration as the lesser of two evils. Toleration was therefore achieved with tory collaboration.[59] Also, the freedom of the press, more precisely the lapse of the Licensing Act in 1695, was not expected to

[57] Benjamin Disraeli, *Coningsby* (1844), especially Book V, ch. II and Book VII, chs II and IV. Disraeli was scoring points in the context of mid-nineteenth-century politics, not writing history, but his novel brilliantly encapsulates a hostile view of 'the whig oligarchy' (which Disraeli nicknamed 'the Venetian oligarchy') of the eighteenth century. A different and more scholarly view of the 'whig oligarchy', emphasizing the continuing strength of the monarchy vis-à-vis the whig politicians, is taken by John B. Owen, 'George II Reconsidered', in *Statesmen, Scholars and Merchants: Essays in Eighteenth-Century History Presented to Dame Lucy Sutherland*, ed. Anne Whiteman, J.S. Bromley and P.G.M. Dickson (Oxford, 1973), pp. 113–34.

[58] J.R. Jones, 'James II's Whig Collaborators', *Historical Journal*, III (1960), 65–73.

[59] John Spurr, *The Restoration Church of England, 1646–1689* (New Haven, CT, 1991), pp. 102–4.

be permanent, and was not unprecedented (the Act had lapsed before, in 1679).[60] Whig claims to superior virtue in the matter of a free press seem hollow, in the light of the circumstance that in 1693 a licenser of the press, Edmund Bohun, was chastized by whigs in the Commons, and hounded from office, because he had *not* censored a tory book.[61] Furthermore, the tories had at least as much reason as the whigs to wish to limit the royal powers of William, an unknown quantity in 1689 who had not been brought up in the Church of England, who was beginning to dismantle the episcopalian Church of Scotland, and who was, above all, not 'their' king.

The whigs may have benefited ultimately from the Revolution, but before 1714 they did not have everything their own way. William distrusted the whigs. He inherited from James the idea that 'the commonwealth party' was still dangerous. In the friendly private letters James wrote to William in the aftermath of the Monmouth rebellion in 1685, James had said, more than once, that 'the presbyterian and republican party ... have as much mind to rebel again as ever'. Three years later, William repeated to Halifax that 'the commonwealth party was the strongest in England; hee had then that impression given', adding, 'hee did not come over to establish a commonwealth'.[62] William preferred to appoint as his ministers, not whigs, but men of experience in government with no doctrinaire commitment to the limitation of monarchical power. Nottingham and Godolphin were among his early choices; later, the reappearance of Sunderland as his Lord Chamberlain was equally astonishing. Throughout his reign it was William's ideal, only rarely achieved, to appoint a 'mixed' ministry with whigs and tories cancelling each other out.[63]

Queen Anne, in spite of her wish to be 'queen of all her subjects', had a temperamental preference for Church of England tories. She quarrelled with her friend of 20 years, Sarah Churchill, whose advocacy of whig men and whig measures became too exorbitant for the queen to bear. The trial of Dr Henry Sacheverell in 1710 turned into an inconclusive argument about the rights and wrongs of the Revolution.[64] The tories, not the whigs, enjoyed office and power from 1710 to 1714. The 'whig oligarchy' after 1714 was as much the product of the desertion of the Grand Alliance (of which George of Hanover was part) by tory ministers at Utrecht in 1713, as of the Revolution.

60 Hannah Barker, *Newspapers, Politics and English Society, 1695–1855* (Harlow, 2000), pp. 12–20.

61 *The Diary and Autobiography of Edmund Bohun, Esq.*, ed. S. Wilton Rix (privately printed, Beccles, 1853), pp. 101–12; Henry Horwitz, *Parliament, Policy and Politics in the Reign of William III* (Manchester, 1977), pp. 113–14.

62 Dalrymple, *Memoirs of Great Britain*, II, 2nd pagination, 137, 165: James to William, 10 Aug. 1685, 10 Sept. 1685; Foxcroft, *Life and Letters of Halifax*, II, 203.

63 Tony Claydon, *William III* (2002), pp. 106–18.

64 Geoffrey S. Holmes, *The Trial of Dr Sacheverell* (1973), pp. 179–206.

With all these weaknesses, the 'whig' Revolution is sound enough in one sense. After 1789, whigs such as Charles James Fox (whose incomplete *History* of the Revolution was printed after his death), looked back to the Revolution of 1688–9 with reverence as one of the episodes from which the 'liberty' of their own age had emerged.[65] The Bill of Rights seemed to them to rank alongside Magna Carta. It followed on from the challenge to ship money and the abolition of star chamber 50 years earlier.

The evangelicals of the early nineteenth century might have recognized one further characterization of the Revolution loosely associated with the interpretation that it was distinctively 'whig': the 'moral' Revolution of 1688. This phrase was brought to prominence by Dudley Bahlman in 1957, and the concept has been amplified by Tony Claydon and Craig Rose.[66] The Revolution incorporated a campaign for moral godliness that reflected the traditions inherited by the whigs from the puritans of the mid-seventeenth century (admittedly, some tories joined in). Societies for the Reformation of Manners were formed in London from 1691. The Society for the Promotion of Christian Knowledge was founded in 1699. Attempts were made to prosecute vices such as drunkenness and blasphemy in the courts by rewarding informers and by financing legal costs. This campaign was linked to the Revolution inasmuch as Queen Mary took a strong interest in it. The 'moral' revolution of the 1690s embraced some of the ideals of the 'puritan' revolution of the 1640s.

VII

Another perception of the events of 1688–9 is that they constituted 'the first modern revolution'. This interpretation has been articulated by Steve Pincus in a weighty book published in 2009.[67] Pincus explicitly rejects any description of the Revolution as 'consensual', 'moderate', 'conservative', 'defensive', 'bloodless', '*élite*' or 'aristocratic'. It was not a coup imposed from the top, or a foreign invasion imposed from outside.[68] Rather, it was a genuine revolution because it was caused by a process of state modernization

[65] Charles James Fox, *A History of the Early Part of the Reign of James II* (1808).

[66] Dudley W.R. Bahlman, *The Moral Revolution of 1688* (New Haven, CT, 1957); Tony Claydon, *William III and the Godly Revolution* (Cambridge, 1996); Craig Rose, 'Providence, Protestant Union and Godly Reformation in the 1690s', *Transactions of the Royal Historical Society*, 6th ser., III (1993), 151–69.

[67] Steve Pincus, *1688: The First Modern Revolution* (New Haven, CT, 2009), *passim*, especially pp. 474–86. See also S. Pincus, 'From Holy Cause to Economic Interest: The Study of Population and the Invention of the State', in *A Nation Transformed*, ed. Houston and Pincus, pp. 272–98; and S. Pincus, *England's Glorious Revolution, 1688–1689: A Brief History with Documents* (2006), 'Introduction', pp. 7–11, 21–6, 29–33.

[68] Pincus, *1688*, pp. 221–4, 278–9, 478–9.

initiated by the regime which was about to be overthrown by it, because it took place against a backdrop of commercial and industrial expansion, and because it incorporated an element of violent insurrection.

Pincus argues that the Revolution emerged out of two competing visions of a 'modern' state. On the one hand, James's government embodied bureaucratic efficiency and economic growth. It was supervised by royal direction, enforced by an enlarged army, underpinned by an ideology of Gallican (as opposed to papal or imperial) catholicism, and modelled on the archetype of a 'modern' state in late seventeenth-century Europe, namely Louis XIV's France. On the other hand, the revolutionary whigs sought to bring economic policy within the scope of parliamentary discussion influenced by pressure groups of merchants. They rejected royal direction of the economy and monopolistic trading companies. They preferred to envisage such developments as the mobilization of new forms of credit, the redistribution of the burden of taxation, and the creation of a national bank.

This interpretation of the Revolution carries with it some logical consequences, which Pincus amplifies. The Revolution could not have been 'conservative', because both sides in the conflict were looking forward to a 'modern' future rather than backward to some imagined golden age in the past. The Revolution could not have been primarily about religious differences, because James's opponents were more concerned about his modernization programme and his methods of achieving it than about his commitment to a European catholic tradition. The fiscal, governmental and commercial developments of the 1690s, conveniently described as the 'financial revolution', were projected before the 1688 Revolution and helped to cause it; they did not emerge, as somewhat unexpected consequences, after it was over.

The theme of 'the first modern revolution' has been greeted with interest, but also with less than complete approval.[69] Some criticisms relate to Pincus's interpretation of the enormous mass of primary source material he has consulted. Others relate to Pincus's omissions; aspects of the Revolution to which Pincus devotes little attention include the progress

69 The discussion has mostly taken the form of reviews: by Bernard Bailyn in *New York Review of Books*, 19 Nov. 2009; by Jonathan Clark in *Times Literary Supplement*, 15 Jan. 2010; by Jeremy Black in *American Historical Review*, CXV (2010), 486–8; by Mark Knights in an online review, 884 (April 2010) at www.history.ac.uk (accessed 12 Dec. 2011); by Warren Johnston in *English Historical Review*, CXXV (2010), 994–7; by Hamish Scott in *Journal of Interdisciplinary History*, XLI (2010), 227–42; by Melinda Zook in *Journal of British Studies*, L (2011), 206–8; by D'Maris Coffman in an online review (Feb. 2011) at www.eh.net (accessed 12 Dec. 2011); by Tony Claydon in *Journal of Modern History*, LXXXIII (2011), 160–1; by Scott Sowerby in *Parliamentary History*, XXX (2011), 236–58; by Grant Tapsell in *The Review of Politics*, LXXII (2011), 717–23; and by J.G.A. Pocock in *Common Knowledge*, XVII (2011), 186–9. In addition a colloquium with contributions by David Como, Rachel Weil and Steve Pincus is in *Huntington Library Quarterly*, LXXIII (2010), 135–62.

and distinctive character of the Revolution in Scotland, the motivation and conduct of William himself, and the contribution, first of the birth of the prince of Wales in June 1688, and then of James's own loss of nerve and psychological collapse in November and December, to the course of events. More relevant for the purposes of this essay are the possible reasons for challenging the phrase 'the first modern revolution' as a succinct summary of the nature of the Revolution of 1688–9. One cogent observation is that it would not be difficult, using similar arguments, to apply the same phrase to earlier episodes, such as the Revolt of the Netherlands in the late sixteenth century, or the War of the Three Kingdoms in the 1640s and the ensuing period of the Commonwealth and the Protectorate in the 1650s; or to later episodes, such as, most obviously, the French Revolution of 1789–95.

Another charge which might be levelled against Pincus's thesis is that he underestimates the religious dimension to the Revolution. Because issues other than religion had risen to prominence, it does not logically follow that religion had ceased to be important. The circumstance that both catholicism and protestantism had become more divided and fragmented than had been the case in the days of the confessional wars of religion did not necessarily diminish the priority of religious issues in the minds of some of those who opposed, or defended, James in 1688–9.

A different point arises from the theoretical principle that revolutions start when regimes begin the process of 'modernization'. This carries with it the implication that James must have embarked on a 'modernization' programme. The evidence that he did so is rather slight. He increased the size of the army and the navy, but it is not clear that the discipline, training, equipment, organization or infrastructure of the armed forces underwent substantial change. His ministers' techniques of surveillance, intelligence-gathering and press censorship do not seem markedly different from those employed by the ministers of Elizabeth I, Oliver Cromwell or Charles II. The purges of office-holders in local government were not efficiently executed. In the case of the corporations, they were conducted by issuing writs of *quo warranto*, hardly a 'modern' technique of management. It was not difficult for committees of regulators at some central or peripatetic headquarters to draw up lists of men to be put in and put out; the problem was to get the newly appointed men securely into office and legitimately qualified to act. For instance, new justices of the peace in the counties had to take various oaths; and a different set of persons had to be empowered to administer these oaths and to receive the appropriate fees by writs of *dedimus potestatem*. It was sometimes months before newly appointed justices could act, though the dismissal of their predecessors had taken immediate effect. The Crown Office in Chancery, where writs and commissions were manufactured, was under severe strain in the spring and summer of 1688.[70] It may

70 G.W. Sanders, *Orders of the High Court of Chancery and Statutes of the Realm relating*

be that James had in mind some 'modern' bureaucratic technique, possibly derived from French practice, for controlling the processes and personnel of local government more efficiently, and that he was thwarted by lack of time from introducing it. He did, indeed, set in motion the abolition of the archaic anomaly of the semi-independent Duchy and County Palatine of Lancaster.[71] But the Duchy and County Palatine of Lancaster survived into the eighteenth century and beyond; and, on the whole, James's credentials as a monarch with a streamlined 'modern' agenda with regard to the strengthening of royal influence in the localities seem elusive. The assertion that 'James's effort to catholicize every level of government was impressive for its thoroughness and efficiency' does not really convince.[72]

VIII

A final clutch of characterizations of the Revolution of 1688–9 includes those which imply that what happened in 1688 was not a revolution at all. It is certainly possible to argue that, the more we contemplate the events of 1688–9, the less easy it becomes to recognize a genuine 'revolution'.

To begin with, there is the theory that the Revolution was a 'mere *coup d'état*'. A *coup d'état* may be defined as an upheaval in politics which changes the individuals at the head of the government. It is both sudden, and quickly complete. There is usually some element of small-scale violence. This definition matches, superficially, the Revolution of 1688. The Revolution is occasionally described as a 'dynastic' revolution, or as a 'revolution in the family', both of which phrases convey the same sense as '*coup d'état*'.[73] There are, however, other nuances. A *coup d'état*, unlike a revolution, does not normally produce structural change in the society over which the reshaped government presides, or a new direction for long-term policies. Again, in a *coup d'état* the mass of persons who are governed are little affected by, and perhaps not much interested in, the changes at the top. Some individuals seem hardly to have noticed the Revolution. One Jack Baker wrote a 330-word letter from London dated 1 December 1688 describing the illness

to Chancery, from the Earliest Period to the Present Time (1845), pp. 381–2: order of Lord Chancellor Jeffreys to suspend Henry Barker, Clerk of the Crown, for neglecting to issue writs of *dedimus potestatem* 'soe as by reason thereof there are few justices of the peace in authority to execute the laws', 31 Mar. 1688.

71 *Calendar of Treasury Books*, VIII, 626 (3 Mar. 1686), 863 (2 Aug. 1686), 1236 (1 Mar. 1687), 1251 (8 Mar. 1687); T.N.A., DL 41/19/10: memorandum in the hand of Benjamin Ayloffe, 'Reasons against the Bill for takeing away the Dutchy and County Pallatine of Lancaster', n.d. [c. 1691], referring to proposals made in the reigns of both James II and William III.

72 Pincus, *1688*, p. 173.

73 Henri and Barbara van der Zee, *1688: Revolution in the Family* (1988).

of an uncle, which displays complete indifference to the events unfolding around him apart from a passing remark that a journey to London would be 'tedious' given the time of the year and 'this juncture of affairs'.[74]

It is hard to deny that the Revolution of 1688 was, legally, a revolution. F. W. Maitland, in lectures written in 1887–8, remarked that the English Convention was not a parliament. It had been summoned by a prince of Orange, not by a king of England. Consequently, James had not been 'deposed', nor William and Mary 'elected', by 'parliament'. The Convention, not being a parliament when it met, could not turn itself into a parliament. The statutes which purported to do this were passed by the Convention itself, and they were validated by the royal assent of William and Mary, who had become king and queen at the invitation of the Convention.[75] 'It seems to me,' concluded Maitland, 'that we must treat the Revolution as a revolution … we cannot work it into our constitutional law.' This insight has been subjected to exhaustive scrutiny by Howard Nenner, who expanded Maitland's narrow perspective into a persuasive theory of significant political change well removed from a '*coup d'état*'.[76] The fracture in the succession was accompanied by wider alterations in government. The foreign policy of William and his successors was radically different from that of James. The relationship between the monarchy and parliament, and the relationship between parliament and the monarch's ministers, were transformed. The royal finances, and the uses to which the money was put, were different in the 1690s compared to preceding decades.

The *coup d'état* interpretation of 1688 has something in common with the view that it was an 'aristocratic' revolution, and it is open to similar objections. More people were involved than a coterie of senior politicians. The cheers greeting the acquittal of the seven bishops, the risings in the north of England, the riots in London and Edinburgh, the huge quantity of pamphlet literature devoted to the political philosophy underpinning the Revolution: all weigh against the perception of a 'mere *coup d'état*'. Jack Baker, mentioned above, was unusual. Most people *were* concerned about forms of religion and techniques of government.

Next, an interpretation which was powerful in some quarters in 1688–9 and which has recently become fashionable again is that the Revolution of

74 B.L., Add. MS 30013, ff. 62–3: John, or Jack, Baker to 'Hon[oure]d Sir' [his grandfather], 1 Dec. 1688 [copy].

75 1 William and Mary, c. 1; 2 William and Mary, sess. 1, c. 1.

76 F.W. Maitland, *The Constitutional History of England* (rep. edn, Cambridge, 1920), pp. 284–5; Howard Nenner, *The Right to be King: The Succession to the Crown of England, 1603–1714* (Basingstoke, 1995), chs 7–9 and 'Conclusion'. Robert Beddard dismissed the notion of a 'parliamentary' revolution using similar arguments to Maitland: 'The Unexpected Whig Revolution of 1688', pp. 73–5. See also Lionel K.J. Glassey, 'The Lawyer, the Historian and the Glorious Revolution', in *Perspectives in Jurisprudence*, ed. E.M.M. Attwooll (Glasgow, 1977), pp. 160–74.

1688 was not a 'revolution' but a 'Dutch conquest'. This theory has two great merits. First, it sets the Revolution squarely in the context of international politics in the mid-1680s: the confrontation between France and Holland, the economic pressures on the Dutch republic, the diplomatic crisis over the archbishopric of Cologne, and the impending European war which broke out in September 1688 before William's expedition had even left port and which became the Nine Years War.[77] Second, it recognizes the circumstance that William was conducting a genuine military operation in November and December 1688. He expected to be confronted by the English navy and then by an Anglo-Scottish army. Why else should he set sail with an army of approximately 15,000 men conveyed by more than 400 transport vessels protected by about 50 men-of-war?[78] William's assertion that this army was a kind of bodyguard, 'a force sufficient, by the blessing of God, to defend us from the violence of those evil counsellors', seems disingenuous. William's priority was not protection against assassination. His 15,000 soldiers were required because he might have to overpower his father-in-law in a full-scale war.[79]

The question of whether James's navy and army were so permeated by officers and men sympathetic to William's proclaimed intentions that they would refuse combat or desert en masse was never put to the test, and is still a matter of dispute. Lord Dartmouth, in command of England's fleet, continued to think after the Revolution that his ships would have fought the Dutch. Dartmouth was over-confident before the Dutch force set sail on 1 November 1688, and then profoundly distressed at its escape on 3–5 November. He was prevented by a combination of the wrong winds, the wrong tides and the sandbanks at the mouth of the Thames estuary from engaging the Dutch ships.[80] It is fascinating to conjecture what the result might have been if circumstances had been different. The Dutch fleet, with its large number of transports, was vulnerable. November was well past the time of year deemed to be suitable for naval operations in northern Europe

77 Several of the essays in *The Anglo-Dutch Moment*, ed. Israel, address these themes, most notably two by Jonathan I. Israel, 'General Introduction', pp. 1–43, and 'The Dutch Role in the Glorious Revolution', pp. 105–62.

78 These figures vary slightly in different authorities; the estimate of 'fifteen thousand four hundred and odd Men' for William's army was made by an eyewitness who accompanied William's fleet. [John Whittle], *An Exact Diary of the Late Expedition of … the Prince of Orange* (1689), pp. 39–40.

79 Mackintosh, *History of the Revolution*, p. 700.

80 *Burnet's History of His Own Time*, III, 329; H.M.C., *11th Report, Appendix, Part VI, Dartmouth MSS I*, pp. 175–255, 260–85; H.M.C., *15th Report, Appendix I, Dartmouth* MSS *III*, pp. 54–71, 133–43. The naval campaign did not close with William's disembarkation in Devon on 5 November; Dartmouth's pursuit of the Dutch round the south coast is sometimes overlooked. On 19 November he was within sight of the Dutch ships at anchor in Torbay, and he was preparing to engage them when his fleet was dispersed by a violent storm.

in the seventeenth century. Dartmouth might have been remembered as one of Britain's great naval heroes if he had thwarted a foreign invader in home waters.[81]

Some thought at the time that the Revolution was a 'Dutch conquest'. Henry Pollexfen asserted on 15 December 1688 that James's withdrawal had forfeited his rights, and that William should simply declare himself king at the head of his army before issuing out writs for a parliament 'on Cromwell's model'.[82] Others found a parallel with Henry VII's alleged assumption of royal authority on the battlefield at Bosworth in 1485.[83] The 'Dutch conquest' theory is, however, open to an objection. The English Convention retained in theory the option of rejecting William as the replacement for James. William recognized this himself. Whatever his private intentions, which are impenetrable, William's public pronouncements, up to the time of James's first attempt to escape, were straightforward. He had not come to 'conquer' England. His purpose was to join with the leaders of responsible opinion in the protection of the protestant religion and the laws and liberties of the nation against the danger from the evil counsellors who had so fatally misled the king. After James's flight on the night of 10–11 December 1688, William's public attitudes were still clear. It was the duty of a freely elected 'parliament', even if it was not technically a parliament, to decide what to do. That 'parliament' might choose to invite James to return, or to ask William to act as regent for James, or to proclaim Mary as queen by herself with William as prince consort, or to proclaim somebody else (such as the prince of Wales, or Princess Anne) as king or queen. It was perfectly entitled to do any of these things. But, if it did anything other than invite William to accept the crown, then William would return to the Netherlands and proceed with the all-important war against Louis XIV, leaving the English to face the consequences of the Convention's decision.[84]

William was again disingenuous here. Everybody knew that if he retired to Holland with his army, then James would return and revenge himself on his now defenceless subjects. Moreover, Mary's claim to the succession would be permanently extinguished. But William did advance this solution as a hypothetical possibility. His credentials as a 'conqueror' are therefore

81 Conrad Russell, 'The Catholic Wind', in *For Want of a Horse: Choice & Chance in History*, ed. John M. Merriman (Lexington, MA, 1985), pp. 103–7, is a light-hearted exercise in counterfactual history along these lines. Russell, tongue in cheek, writes: 'the marvel is not that William failed; it is that he could ever have supposed he might succeed'.

82 *Correspondence of Clarendon*, II, 225–6.

83 *Burnet's History of His Own Time*, III, 361. A probable influence here was William Shakespeare, *The Tragedy of King Richard the Third*, V. iv. 14–20.

84 Foxcroft, *Life and Letters of Halifax*, II, 203–4; *Burnet's History of His Own Time*, III, 394–6; *The Works of John Sheffield, Earl of Mulgrave, Marquis of Normanby and Duke of Buckingham* (4th edn, 1753), II, 86–7.

diminished. Not many 'conquerors' announce at the moment of victory that they will surrender their conquests if they discover that this is what the conquered would prefer.

Another criticism of the perception of a 'Dutch conquest' relates to Scotland. There were some in the English Convention who thought that the Scots might take a different route to a solution compared to England, and that there would be little that William could do about it.[85] But when William was offered the crown of Scotland in April–May 1689, he did not have the option of refusing it. He was already king of England. It was not open to him to threaten to return to Holland. He did not win Scotland by conquest; rather, the success of William's forces at the battles of Dunkeld and Cromdale confirmed an earlier political decision.

There is a further way of looking at the Revolution without admitting that it was a revolution. There was, perhaps, a genuine 'revolution' in the British Isles in the 1680s, but it did not take place in the winter of 1688–9. It took place between 1686 and the late summer of 1688. It was a top-down revolution conducted by James himself, with the willing co-operation of his ministers. Upheavals took place in the personnel of government, at the centre and in the localities. The royal prerogatives were exploited to transform the relationship between the law and the monarch. The Church of England and the universities were subordinated to the crown. In order to implement these changes, the army was increased in size. James's revolution was resented by his subjects. At the beginning of his reign in 1685, his declaration promising to maintain liberty, property and religion had reassured those who had anticipated the prospect of a catholic king with foreboding; Henry Watkinson, the chancellor of the diocese of York, for example, remarked that 'all peoples hearts were transported with joy, thinking themselves secure enough upon his Royall Word'.[86] By 1688, the conviction that the royal word had been broken was everywhere apparent. In short, James was the *real* 'revolutionary'; and the Revolution of 1688 was not a 'revolution' but a 'counter-revolution'. It was intended, as far as possible, to restore the English nation to its condition at the end of Charles II's reign.

This theory of the Revolution as a 'counter-revolution' has something to recommend it. I have, possibly incautiously, formerly committed myself to it.[87] One objection is that most 'revolutions' undertaken before 1789 have something of the quality of a desire to return to a nostalgically imagined 'golden age' in the past. Some parliamentarians in the early 1640s thought that Charles I needed to be persuaded to govern more in the fashion of Queen Elizabeth I. Some Levellers in 1647–8 wanted to turn the clock back

[85] Grey, *Debates*, IX, 10–11 (Sir Christopher Musgrave), 55 (Sir Thomas Clarges), 56 (Sir Joseph Tredenham).

[86] B.L., Add. MS 72521, ff. 1–2: Henry Watkinson to Sir William Trumbull, 11 Feb. 1684/5.

[87] Glassey, *Politics and the Appointment of Justices of the Peace*, p. 91.

to the period before the Norman Conquest. The Restoration of 1660 was, in part, an attempt to revive what John Aubrey called the 'long peace and luxury' of the 1630s.[88] Some of the 'revolutionaries' of 1688–9, if that is what they were, hoped to revive what they idealized as prosperity and tranquillity under Charles II. If James and his counsellors were the 'real' revolutionaries of the 1680s, they presumably wished to reinstate the authority of the pope in the British Isles. If most revolutions are really counter-revolutions looking back to the past, then the idea that 1688–9 was a 'counter-revolution' does not advance discussion very profitably; it was hardly unique.

IX

No one adjective can encapsulate the complexities of the events of 1688–9, or bear the weight of interpretation that is required to define the essential character of those events or the consequences which ensued. The possibilities discussed in the preceding pages – 'reluctant', 'respectable', 'sensible' and the rest – are not mutually exclusive, and there is a good deal of overlap. The Revolution was both 'conservative' and 'revolutionary'; it was both 'respectable' and 'popular'; it was both 'accidental' and 'sensible'. It was initiated by a conspiracy, and it has something of the character of a *coup d'état*; at the same time, it marked a permanent change in the constitutional, political, governmental and religious norms of the state. The search for a single defining adjective is ultimately fruitless, since there are qualifications about all of them. We are left, however unwillingly, with 'glorious', the epithet which has somehow become inextricably associated with the Revolution.

[88] John Aubrey, *Brief Lives*, ed. Oliver L. Dick (Harmondsworth, 1972), p. 450.

2

The Damning of King Monmouth: Pulpit Toryism in the Reign of James II

MARK GOLDIE

On the field of Sedgemoor in Somerset in July 1685 the rebel army of James, duke of Monmouth, illegitimate but protestant son of Charles II, was destroyed by the professional army of the new king, James II. Monmouth was captured and executed, and those of his followers who were not butchered on the battlefield were hanged or transported into servitude by Judge Jeffreys in 'the Bloody Assize'. In later times, the Monmouth rebels have commanded a deep fund of sympathy. Harsh though judgments have been upon the duke's folly in landing with just 80 men and naive hopes of a spontaneous national uprising, his cause, and that of the artisans and farmers who rallied to his standard, has accrued three centuries of admiration.[1] Eighteenth-century whigs, nineteenth-century nonconformists, and twentieth-century socialists all celebrated the rebels as popular heroes, a pitchfork army of commoners who rose in defence of civil and religious liberty. The rebels' fate became a byword for despotic cruelty. In the 1935 film adaptation of Rafael Sabatini's *Captain Blood* (1922), one of many novels spawned by Monmouth's forlorn cause, the haughty tyrant James sends his captured nephew to the executioner's block, the duke grovelling on the floor begging for his life, a scene borrowed from Victorian genre paintings. In the long historiographical tradition of English radicalism, the rebellion was characterized as the last stand of the Good Old Cause, part of a lineage that stretched from the Levellers to the Chartists. Pro-Monmouth ballads are still sung by West Country folk groups.[2]

1 The literature is large, but see especially Iris Morley, *A Thousand Lives: An Account of the English Revolutionary Movement, 1660–1685* (1954) and Robin Clifton, *The Last Popular Rebellion* (1984). The *fons et origo* of the tradition is [John Tutchin], *The Protestant Martyrs: Or, the Bloody Assizes* [c.1689], for which see Melinda Zook, '"The Bloody Assizes": Whig Martyrdom and Memory after the Glorious Revolution', *Albion*, XXVII (1995), 373–96.

2 The album *Sedgemoor* by Strawhead: www.strawhead.org.uk. Similarly, the Monmouth display in the Blake Museum, Bridgwater, and the Monmouth mural at the Sedgemoor Service Station on the M5 motorway.

It therefore requires an effort of historical imagination to recapture the beliefs of those who were appalled by the rebellion and who damned its leader as a vile enemy of society. In the summer of 1685 the greater part of the political nation felt huge relief at Monmouth's defeat. Much as it feared popery, it more urgently feared renewal of puritan revolution, social levelling, and sectarian anarchy. From the tory elite came a chorus of condemnation. A loyal parliament rushed through an act of attainder authorizing the duke's execution without trial. Sir Edward Seymour pronounced that the crushing of 'this … rebellion has contributed to our future peace, and those [who] engaged in it have sung their penitential psalm, and their punishment [is] rejoiced at by all good persons'. The earl of Clarendon, recording Monmouth's capture, wrote, 'God be praised; it is not to be doubted but the same God, who hath put so happy and speedy an end to this rebellion, will bless the king with a long and happy reign'. There were celebrations everywhere. Sir Edward Harley reported that church bells and bonfires greeted the news of 'James Scott's rout and taking'. Daniel Defoe recorded that the rebellion was 'sung about the streets as a senseless ridiculous attempt, [and] that those who were concerned in [it] merit little but our pity as lunatics'.[3] John Selby, a veteran tory activist who kept a distiller's shop near Bishopsgate, made 'the greatest bonfire … that ever was seen about London', upon which he burnt effigies of the whig leaders, Monmouth, Argyll, Shaftesbury, Russell, Sidney, and Titus Oates. To these he added Captain Brand, innkeeper of the Red Lion six doors away, who had joined the rebels and been killed. Selby threatened to 'pull out the jade, Brand's wife, and burn her with her husband', and provided a cask of brandy for his street party, 'to drink King James's health and confusion to the whigs'.[4] Throughout England, volunteers had come forward to join loyalist militias. An address to the earl of Danby, lord lieutenant of Lancashire, offered the services of the people of Manchester. They being

> true sons of the Church of England, astonished that … our dread sovereign, the king, should be requited with an horrid rebellion, and that, too, veiled under the pretence of that religion which most strictly enjoins loyalty and allegiance, and forbids resistance and rebellion … do desire … that we may, during this most unnatural rebellion, list ourselves … in the war against the rebels.[5]

The present essay is a case study in the damning of Monmouth. It dwells on the sermons that condemned the rebels, and, through them, explores tory political homiletic at the zenith of Stuart loyalism. Monmouth staged

[3] *Parliamentary History of England*, ed. William Cobbett (36 vols, 1806–20), IV, 1374; Oxford Historical Society, *Collectanea III* (Oxford, 1896), 276; H.M.C., *Portland*, III, 385; Daniel Defoe, *Review* (1704–13), III, 402.

[4] *A London Tory Vying in Cruelty* (1691).

[5] H.M.C., *Kenyon*, p. 181.

his insurrection during the high tide of enthusiasm for James II in the early months of his reign, a seamless continuation of the 'Tory Reaction' that characterized the final years of his brother's reign. James had not yet betrayed the confidence of the Church of England and the tory gentry, and the drive to destroy the whigs and dissenters continued unabated. Loyalists regarded the rebellion as a final eruption of whig sedition, a successor to the Rye House assassination plot of 1683: it was fanatical, regicidal, an act of terrorism.

In press and pulpit, the rebellion's defeat was the occasion of the final flowering of divine right royalism in its pre-Revolution form. That ideology was an inheritance from the royalism of the 1640s, in its contest with the Parliamentarians, and in turn from the protestant monarchism of the 1600s, in its contest with Counter-Reformation catholicism. It had been rejuvenated in the early 1680s in response to the whig movement's challenge to the crown in the Exclusion Crisis, and had acquired the name 'tory'. The source literature of the tory ideology in the decade before the Revolution of 1688 is immense. Hundreds of treatises, pamphlets, sermons, newspapers, plays, and poems expressed tory ideals and sentiments. This essay aims to capture their characteristic attitudes in microcosm by selecting one representative body of texts. These are the sermons preached on or about 26 July 1685, the day appointed by the king for 'public thanksgiving for victory over the rebels', for they provide a cameo of the dominant doctrines of the moment.

Sermons of course have generic biases: they reflect the mindset of clergymen. Lawyers and laymen wrote in a different register and tended to have greater recourse to arguments from law and constitutional history and less to scripture. On the other hand, political sermons were far from anodyne, nor merely pious: they were severely dogmatic as to principles, concrete and topical as to contemporary events, savagely polemical about public enemies, scholarly in range of reference, and intricate in rhetorical construction. They were demotic, designed for wide audiences of ordinary English people, yet also sophisticated, the crafted prose of university-educated divines.[6]

6 There is a growing literature on the early modern sermon. For this period, see Tony Claydon, 'The Sermon, the Public Sphere, and the Political Culture of Late Seventeenth-Century England', and James Caudle, 'Preaching in Parliament: Patronage, Publicity, and Politics in Britain, 1701–1760', in *The English Sermon Revised*, ed. Lori Anne Ferrell and Peter McCullough (Manchester, 2000); Newton Key, 'The Political Culture and Political Rhetoric of County Feasts and Feast Sermons, 1654–1714', *Journal of British Studies*, XXXIII (1994), 223–56; Rowan Strong, 'A Vision of an Anglican Imperialism: The Annual Sermons of the Society for the Propagation of the Gospel in Foreign Parts, 1701–1714', *Journal of Religious History*, XXX (2006), 175–98; David Appleby, *Black Bartholomew's Day* (Manchester, 2007). For an earlier period: Arnold Hunt, *The Art of Hearing: English Preachers and their Audiences, 1590–1640* (Cambridge, 2010); Peter E. McCullough, *Sermons at Court: Politics and Religion in Elizabethan and Jacobean Preaching* (Cambridge, 1998); Mary Morrissey, *Politics and the Paul's Cross Sermons, 1558–1642*

Probably hundreds of sermons were preached on the day of thanksgiving in the 9,000 parishes of England; 29 are known to have been printed, about one third of all the sermons published during 1685.[7] It was a year especially thick with political sermons, for loyalist politics were preached not only on Charles the Martyr Day (30 January), Restoration Day (29 May), and Gunpowder Day (5 November), as required annually by the Prayer Book, but also on the new king's coronation day (23 April), at Monmouth's defeat, and at various other times, such as at assize court meetings. Most preachers of the surviving anti-Monmouth sermons were obscure clergymen, and this is a helpful fact: they are characteristic rather than exceptional, dealers in the common coinage of tory clerical sentiment, typical products of the Restoration universities. About one-third held posts as chaplains to the king, or noblemen, or bishops.[8] It is striking that in two-fifths of cases, the sermon was their author's sole publication in their lifetimes, a clerical parallel to those numerous tory M.P.s who sat in the parliament of 1685 for the only time in their lives. Passionate loyalism to church and crown pushed modest men to unwonted activism. In the heat of a rebellious time, the clergy, like Zadok the priest in the Book of Samuel, stepped forward to stand by King David.

Most of the Monmouth sermons, as I shall call them (they were *anti-*Monmouth sermons), were preached in ordinary parish churches, in towns like Norwich and Wakefield, or rural villages like Dedham in Essex and Chard in Somerset. A few were delivered in places of symbolic authority, such as York Minster, Westminster Abbey, or London's Guildhall. Some were preached to soldiers of the royal army or volunteer militias, others to town mayors and aldermen, county magistrates, lawyers, or university dons. One was preached to English merchants at Dordrecht in the Netherlands, in the presence of the English envoy, no doubt as an admonition to the whig exile community. In print, these sermons typically cost sixpence and filled 32 quarto pages: an hour or more's worth of spoken delivery. If we are tempted to suspect that the printed versions were longer than the spoken, it is important to note how often preachers insisted, especially in cases of controversial sermons, which were subject to gossip and criticism,

(Oxford, 2011). More generally: *The Oxford Handbook of the Early Modern Sermon*, ed. Hugh Adlington et al. (Oxford, 2011); Mary Morrissey, 'Interdisciplinarity and the Study of Early Modern Sermons', *H.J.*, XLII (1999), 1111–23.

[7] For a list of preachers and sermons, see the Appendix. As well as sermons preached on 26 July, I have included a few delivered on other days that were explicitly directed against the Rebellion.

[8] The patrons and dedicatees included the dukes of Albemarle, Beaufort and Somerset, the earls of Ailesbury and Tyrconnell, Lord Churchill, the bishops of Lincoln (Thomas Barlow), London (Henry Compton), Norwich (William Lloyd) and Salisbury (Seth Ward), and the envoy to Holland, Bevil Skelton. Three tory printers/booksellers are prominent among the publishers: Walter Davis, Joseph Hindmarsh and Walter Kettilby.

that the published version was exactly what was spoken. Even so, it is worth speculating whether these sermons were worked up for publication, with an augmentation of erudition. Did rustic audiences really hear Greek and Latin spoken, and philosophers, theologians, and classical historians cited? It is hard to say: what survives are the printed texts.

These sermons have titles like *The Wickedness and Punishment of Rebellion*, *The Damning Nature of Rebellion*, *The Character of a Rebel*, *The Loyalty of the Church of England and the Necessity of Obedience to Governors*. They carried the imprimatur of the press censors, as required by the Licensing Act; in the case of religious works, the censors being the chaplains of the archbishop of Canterbury or bishop of London. And they were adorned with dedicatory epistles, addressed to noblemen, bishops, colonels, or mayors, and often including the customary assertion that the grateful dedicatee had insisted that an otherwise self-effacing preacher should venture to publish.

It is difficult to know the reactions of congregations. A handful of preachers let slip that the tide of loyalism did not go unquestioned, and that whig recalcitrance made itself heard even at this moment of Monmouth's crushing defeat. There are reports of hostile gossip against some of these sermons.[9] One minister was even 'disturbed … in the very church'.[10] Conversely, another was criticized for not being tory enough, because he spoke too blandly about the rebels; here the preacher had chosen the ambiguous theme of not doing evil that good might come of it (Romans 3:8).[11] The diarist John Evelyn was one tory auditor. He heard two sermons on Sunday 26 July, though neither was published. A Mr Hutchins spoke on Psalm 72, 'showing from what signal dangers, God had in all ages delivered his church', while in the afternoon the curate chose Psalm 64, 'relating much of the particulars of the late rising'. Evelyn was edified, and he piously endorsed the message of these sermons:

> For my own part, I looked upon this deliverance as absolutely most signal; such an inundation of fanatics and men of impious principles, must needs have caused universal disorder, cruelty, injustice, rapine, sacrilege and confusion, an unavoidable civil war, and misery without end: but blessed be God, the knot was happily broken, and a fair prospect of tranquillity for the future likely to succeed if we reform, be thankful, and make a right use of this mercy.[12]

9 Richard Coulton, *The Loyalty of the Church of England, and the Necessity of Obedience to Governors, Delivered in a Sermon* (York, 1685), sig. A2r; Vincent Owen, *A Plain Sermon Preached to a Country Congregation in the Beginning of the Late Rebellion* (1685), ep. ded.

10 Shadrach Cooke, *A Sermon Preached at Islington upon the … Solemn Thanksgiving … for his Majestie's Late Victories over the Rebels* (1685), sig. A2v.

11 John Williams, *A Sermon Preached July 26, 1685, Being the Day of Public Thanksgiving* (1685), ep. ded.

12 John Evelyn, *Diary*, ed. E.S. De Beer (2006), p. 735.

Since this essay aims to exemplify the character of loyalist preaching, and since most of the preachers were not prominent men, the following account rarely identifies individual speakers, except in the accompanying notes. The sermons are listed in the Appendix. The focus of attention is the commonplaces of contemporary political homily. I shall, however, in the penultimate section, single out one unusual voice; and, in the final section, comment on individual preachers in order to see how they faced up to the extraordinary reversal of the fortunes of toryism in the Revolution of 1688, when James II was successfully overthrown by William of Orange.

I

Little delicacy of feeling was exhibited by pious parsons in triumphing over the rebels' defeat. They preached the sword of righteous retribution and called for national rejoicing at the Lord's display of his avenging wrath, as David rejoiced in the Psalms. 'Let all thine enemies perish, O Lord.' The crushing of the rebels by the king's forces was a 'holy violence'; the rebels were 'delivered up to slaughter or to justice'; and their defeat was a 'monument of divine vengeance'. Monmouth was assuredly damned. He failed to show penitence, for he refused to renounce the doctrine of resistance, though begged to do so by the importunate chaplains assigned to him before his execution. 'Eternal damnation is prepared for all impenitent rebels in hell.'[13]

The Monmouth preachers were, however, hesitant in claiming the immediate intervention of divine providence in securing the king's victory. Royalists had long deplored the notion that might confers right and that God hands victory to the righteous, for this was the blasphemous notion of the puritan rebels of mid-century. The usurper Cromwell had invoked providence to justify his conquests. Since the righteous royalist cause had spent 20 years in defeat and exile, circumspection was needed in handling providentialist arguments. Even so, the exhilaration of victory prompted talk of 'God's special providence … in this matter': 'providence itself seemed engaged in the fight'. The victory was a 'deliverance', 'miraculous'. Rebels, assassins, and regicides commonly meet violent deaths, for God intervenes to destroy them.[14]

[13] Charles Hutton, *The Rebels Text Opened … Being a Sermon* (1685), p. 28; Charles Allestree, *A Sermon Preach'd at Oxford* (1685), p. 6; John Hinton, *A Sermon Preached in the Parish Church of Newbury* (1685), pp. 20–2, 30; John Scott, *A Sermon Preached Before the Right Honourable the Lord Mayor* (1685), p. 25; William Jegon, *The Damning Nature of Rebellion, Or, the Universal Unlawfulness of Resistance upon Pain of Damnation … Asserted in a Sermon* (1685), p. 30.

[14] Cooke, *Sermon*, pp. 2, 5; Hinton, *Sermon*, pp. 18–19; Allestree, *Sermon*, p. 8; Augustine Frezer, *The Wickedness and Punishment of Rebellion, in a Sermon* (1685), sig. *2r,

The preachers agreed that the insurrection was the spawn of the great rebellion of mid-century. They were contemptuous of its plebeian element: 'peasants ... dregs', 'illiterates', 'mechanics', a 'rude multitude'.[15] They identified its religious ethos as nonconforming, its inspiration stemming from the puritan sects. It was noted that the rebels claimed 'conscience', but the retort was that they were in thrall to a perverted conception of conscience and to self-seeking vanity masquerading as godliness. In tory eyes, dissent coalesced with sedition. 'Persons who are members of the state are also members of the church', and if there are people who reject the second, then they reject the first, for 'schisms in the church are ... forerunners of sedition in the state', and that which is 'sown in a conventicle ... may presently reap a rebellion in a commonwealth'. Accordingly, ''tis impossible to be at peace with schismatics and fanatics'. The 'Canaanite is still in the land' and has an itch for blood, and 'our nation is not free from this vermin'. The connexion between dissent and civil rebellion was personified in Robert Ferguson, the Independent minister and whig ideologue who landed with Monmouth, preached to the rebels, proclaimed Monmouth king at Taunton, evaded capture, and escaped to Holland. The pulpit celebrants of Monmouth's defeat vilified Ferguson by name.[16]

The sermons had less to say about the rank and file than about their leader. They detected a paradox in the rebellion: whatever its pretensions to a popular or godly cause, its leader was the wayward child of the royal court, the spoiled son of Charles II. They mercilessly exposed Monmouth's nature: he was a debauched courtier and serial adulterer, unbalanced by the bitterness of rejection and dreams of revenge, seduced by flattery and beguiled by celebrity.[17] The rebellion was no noble struggle, but the petulant revenge of an unstable and witless aristocrat. The preachers depicted a tragic domestic morality play, its *mise en scène* the royal family, which carried the moral that ambition and ingratitude lead to downfall and disaster. For the tory preachers, this was no national movement for liberty, but a dismal family feud, rebellion the spasm of a parricidal rage.

pp. 1, 25; Henry Hesketh, *A Sermon Preached ... upon ... the Day of Public Thanksgiving ... for his Majesties Late Victory over the Rebels* (1685), p. 2; Edward Pelling, *A Sermon Preached at Westminster Abbey* (1685), pp. 2, 26; Scott, *Sermon*, p. 28; Richard Roberts, *A Sermon Preached ... in Bristol ... before ... the Society of the Loyal Young Men and Apprentices* (1685), p. 5.

15 Thomas Heyrick, *The Character of a Rebel: A Sermon* (1685), pp. 9, 27; John Petter, *A Sermon ... on the Occasion of the Late Rebellion* (1685), pp. 5–6.

16 Coulton, *Loyalty*, pp. 3, 11–12, 31; Stephen Willoughby, *A Scourge to the Rebellious, or, a Sermon* (1685), p. 22; Thomas Aston, *A Sermon Preached ... the Day Before the Battle and Victory over the Rebels* (1685), p. 18; Thomas Wagstaffe, *A Sermon Preached on ... the Day of Thanksgiving* (1685), p. 12; Obadiah Lee, *A Sermon ... Being the Day Appointed* (1685), p. 26.

17 Allestree, *Sermon*, p. 19; Hinton, *Sermon*, p. 6.

II

Sermons typically take the form of meditations upon a text from scripture, chosen as apposite for the occasion. The rebellion drew from the preachers a litany of biblical verses that had for generations been invoked to teach submission to rulers and confer divine sanction upon monarchy. 'Rebellion is as the sin of witchcraft' (1 Samuel 15:23); 'Who can stretch forth his hand against the Lord's anointed, and be guiltless?' (1 Samuel 26:9); 'By me kings reign, and princes decree justice' (Proverbs 8:15); 'Fear thou the Lord and the king; and meddle not with them that are given to change' (Proverbs 24:21); 'Put them in mind to be subject to principalities and powers, to obey magistrates' (Titus 3:1); 'Fear God, honour the king' (1 Peter 2:17). Most pervasive among the proof texts for loyalty was the Pauline Injunction (Romans 13:1–2), the most categorical of all biblical imperatives to obedience. 'Let every soul be subject unto the higher powers. For there is no power but of God: the powers that be are ordained of God. Whosoever therefore resisteth the power, resisteth the ordinance of God: and they that resist shall receive to themselves damnation.'

A sermon customarily involved an intricate exposition of every implication of the chosen verse. For Romans 13 there was a well established tradition of exegesis. What was it to be 'subject'? Who were the 'higher' powers, and why did St Paul pluralize 'powers'? In what sense did God 'ordain' the powers? How was the injunction inflected by verses 3–4: 'For rulers are not a terror to good works, but to the evil ... For he is the minister of God to thee for good'? What did learned exegetes like Beza and Grotius say on the subject? The preachers also commented on the historical circumstances in which St Paul had written. They agreed that he composed the epistle in the reign of Emperor Nero, the most pathologically brutal of rulers. Paul's intention therefore was clear: he did not enjoin obedience only to worthy rulers, but to *all* rulers. Not even tyranny, vice, or irreligion in a ruler provides legitimate grounds for breaching the injunction never to resist. Above all, what could be derived from Paul was the truth that sovereigns, however unworthy, are the 'deputies' and 'ministers' of God, they are 'mortal gods'.[18]

Sermons were frequently constructed around typologies. Biblical narratives or incidents were taken to be archetypal, and present-day events 'ectypal', the former symbolically foreshadowing the latter. The preachers did not claim that the Old Testament prophesied the rebellion and crushing of Monmouth, for, again, the prophetic mode had been discredited by its puritan misuse; but they did demonstrate close parallels between Monmouth and the fate of rebels in Israel. The preachers repeatedly told the story of

[18] Owen, *Sermon*, pp. 8, 11; Daniel Whitby, *Three Sermons Preach'd at Salisbury ... In Which the Doctrine of not Resisting the Higher Powers is Established from Scripture, Reason, and Antiquity* (1685), p. 10. Jegon, Owen, and Rich took Romans 13 as their text.

Absalom, a parallel whose popularity was owed to John Dryden's satirical poem *Absalom and Achitophel*, which had, in 1681, served as a brilliant rhetorical weapon in the tory onslaught on the whigs.[19] Absalom's story, declared the preachers, was 'so perfect a transcript' of our rebellion: the beautiful and indulged son of King David led 'an insurrection of the peasants'; Absalom 'affected popularity and courted the people'. To this theme was added the character of Achitophel, David's renegade counsellor who became Absalom's advisor. Achitophel's ectype was the earl of Shaftesbury, 'whose counsel ... was ... oracular among the people'.[20]

Absalom was not the only instructive parallel available. Korah, Dathan, and Abiram led an uprising against Moses and Aaron, and the earth split asunder and swallowed them up (Numbers 16). Sheba followed Absalom in rebelling against David, but loyalists cut his head off (2 Samuel 20). Adonijah, another son of David, claimed the right of succession and conspired against David's successor Solomon, who ordered his execution (1 Kings 1–2). Achan plundered what was not his; God demanded retribution, so Achan was stoned to death (Joshua 6–7). Zimri killed King Elah and usurped the throne, but his reign lasted but seven days, before a loyal general crushed him (1 Kings 16). The preachers occasionally strayed beyond the Old Testament to the pagan historians, retelling especially Sallust's account of Cataline's conspiracy. Monmouth and his cronies were said to imitate the Catalinareans: footloose and corrupt noblemen, bankrupt spendthrifts, for whom insurrection was a desperate opportunity to restore their fortunes.[21]

In earlier years, puritan and whig writers had conjured up archetypal heroes of resistance, such as Samson in Milton's *Samson Agonistes* (1671), the martyr-suicide who pulled down the pillars of the temple upon himself and his Philistine enemies (Judges 15). Tories now responded with contrasting models of militant loyalism among the people. One such was the heroine Jael. When Sisera, a wicked Canaanite, invaded Israel and was defeated, he, like Monmouth, became a fugitive – Monmouth had been captured in a ditch after an intensive search for him. On the run, Sisera was discovered by Jael, who, understanding that every citizen, in a national emergency, is an agent on behalf of the supreme magistrate, took the law into her own hands. According to an English legal commonplace, when a malefactor was at large, every citizen was a constable, a member of the *posse comitatus*. Though a woman, Jael might act the constable too:

19 On Absalom: Coulton, *Loyalty*, pp. 6–17; Frezer, *Wickedness*, pp. 14, 18; John Goodrick, *A Sermon Preached before the Honourable Society of Lincoln's Inn* (1685), p. 17; Heyrick, *Character*, *passim*; Hinton, *Sermon*, *passim*; Hutton, *Rebels*, pp. 23–5; Lee, *Sermon*, *passim*; Thomas Long, *The Unreasonableness of Rebellion, in a Sermon* (1685), p. 15; Pelling, *Sermon*, p. 7; Scott, *Sermon*, pp. 1–5; Wagstaffe, *Sermon*, p. 2. The story is in 2 Samuel 15–17.

20 Hinton, *Sermon*, pp. 5, 6, 22; Heyrick, *Character*, p. 9.

21 Frezer, *Wickedness*, pp. 15–17.

> She knew, that in extraordinary cases, every person, of whatever sex, is obliged to turn both judge and executioner too, of their enemies, and that nature invests mankind with as much authority over the lives of rebels and invaders, as over wolves and tigers and beasts of prey; and that we ought to embrace the first occasion to hunt and pursue them to death, because in these instances, every delay of justice … may be dangerous and expose government.

Accordingly, while Sisera was sleeping, Jael took a hammer and drove a nail through his temple. According to the tory preachers, her 'prowess' and 'heroic exploit' in killing Sisera were celebrated throughout Israel, and the prophetess Deborah sang in thankful praise (Judges 4:17–22; 5:24–7).[22]

The ready recourse of seventeenth-century preachers to the poetics of righteous violence is striking; as also their readiness here to applaud female violence. There is something else remarkable about the passage just quoted. It is a mirror image of a crucial precept in radical resistance theory: the right of individual self-defence against a marauder, but there the marauder is identified as an oppressive ruler. This precept is spelt out in the *Two Treatises of Government*, which John Locke, now in exile in Holland, had recently written, but could not yet publish. 'Every man hath a right to punish the offender, and be executioner of the law of nature.' For, 'every man … has a power … to secure men from the attempts of a criminal, who … hath by the unjust violence and slaughter he hath committed … declared war against all mankind, and therefore may be destroyed as a lion or a tiger'; such criminals may be treated like 'beasts of prey'.[23] Both Locke and the tory invoked the natural right to repel violators: such violators may be killed, and, in an emergency, each individual may exercise this right on the community's behalf. The crucial difference is that Locke wished to say that the violator might be the monarch himself. The tory shares the view that the citizen is always at risk of being cast into a violent state of nature – by criminals and rebels rather than by monarchs – for sovereign authority can never be ubiquitous, and it is incumbent on the citizen, *in extremis*, to act the sovereign's part, each one a constable.[24]

III

The Monmouth sermons were exercises in political theology, in the use of scripture to inculcate civil obedience. Yet, paradoxically, the preachers also sought to secularize politics. They wished to decouple civil obligation

22 Allestree, *Sermon*, pp. 6–8.

23 Locke, *Two Treatises of Government*, II, §§ 8, 11, 16.

24 Algernon Sidney cited the case of Sisera but regarded him as a tyrant whom the Israelites had a right to overthrow. *Discourses Concerning Government*, ed. Thomas West (Indianapolis, IN, 1990), p. 315.

from claims that 'true religion' or 'godly reformation' required reform of the state or the overthrow of 'ungodly' rulers. The bloodshed and anarchy of their century was, they held, the child of politicized religion. The plea of 'conscience' had licensed sedition, and the dire doctrine that 'dominion is founded in grace' had destabilized monarchs, for it made the godliness of rulers the criterion of their right to rule, and placed the judgment of that godliness in the hands of self-appointed righteous citizens.[25] Puritan sectaries had fanned the flames of rebellion with *their* chosen texts from scripture: 'Curse ye Meroz' and 'To your tents, O Israel' (Judges 5:23; 2 Samuel 20:1).[26] Royalists and tories accused puritans and whigs of antinomianism: of seeking to overrule the natural laws of civility by invoking a putative supreme law of God. The contemporary term for antinomian fanaticism was 'enthusiasm', a neologism denoting an arrogant presumption of superior divine knowledge. These were 'sick imaginations' dressed up as 'divine motions'.[27] Tory clergy used their pulpits to denounce by name the doctrinaires of seventeenth-century puritan rebellion: John Goodwin, the preacher of insurrection in the 1640s, Richard Baxter, the leading Presbyterian theologian, Algernon Sidney, the republican executed in 1683, and Robert Ferguson, Monmouth's chaplain.[28] To twist religion into a mask for rebellion was the highest blasphemy. 'Though the pretence be religion, yet the intent is rebellion.'[29] As King Charles I had remarked in his *Eikon Basilike* (1649), 'The breath of religion fills the sails of rebellion.'[30] One sermon drew the moral: 'It is the unhappy fate of the Holy Scriptures to be abused into a kind of public armoury, whence the several contending parties of the Christian world fetch weapons to arm themselves, and fight each other.'[31] Tory preachers exempted themselves from this indictment, for, they argued, their own reading of scripture endorsed, and ran with the grain, of natural law. God speaks consistently through his Word and his Works: scripture and nature cohere in teaching duties to rulers.

The preachers offered a familiar royalist account of the origins of revolutionary doctrine. They construed the Church of England's catechism of

25 Coulton, *Loyalty*, pp. 6, 28. 'Secularize' does not here refer to an historical process, but to an historically persistent argument that 'grace perfects but does not contradict nature', a position held in the Middle Ages by Aquinas and his followers.

26 Thomas Grey noted that the rebels had preached from the self-same pulpits, for he preached at Dedham in Essex, one of the old heartlands of puritan radicalism: *Loyalty Essential to Christianity, Being a Sermon* (1685), p. 25.

27 Samuel Rich, *A Sermon Preached … Before … his Majestie's Forces* (1685), p. 19.

28 Jegon, *Damning*, pp. 15, 35; Wagstaffe, *Sermon*, pp. 21–2, 24–5; Long, *Unreasonableness*, pp. 19, 21; Pelling, *Sermon*, p. 27. Other rebel authors cited in the Monmouth sermons were the Independent preachers Stephen Lobb and John Owen, the Scottish Presbyterian William Carstares and the Harringtonian republican Henry Neville.

29 Coulton, *Loyalty*, p. 26.

30 Quoted in Frezer, *Wickedness*, p. 31.

31 Hutton, *Rebels*, p. 1.

non-resistance as a *via media* between the equal and opposite extremes of the 'king-killing' doctrines of catholics and calvinists. They played on this parallel: the 'two great degeneracies of Christian religion at this day' are Rome and Geneva. The pairing could be variously symbolized: 'Jesuits and separatists', 'papists and phanaticks', 'conclaves and consistories', 'general councils and general assemblies'; the 'knife' and the 'axe'; Ravaillac and Bradshaw. (The last two pairings referred to the catholic predilection for assassination, notoriously in the killing of Henri IV of France, and the calvinist use of pseudo-judicial execution, pre-eminently in the regicide of Charles I; Ravaillac was Henri's assassin and Bradshaw Charles's judge.) Both kinds of extremist believed that 'supreme power is originally and radically seated in the people, and that if kings fail of their duty … they are … dethronable'.[32] Though the immediate threat in Monmouth's rebellion was from protestant dissidence, the preachers did not neglect this wider theme, for they found the source of whig sedition in catholicism as much as in calvinism. It was a genealogy that made plausible a charge of 'popery' against the puritan and whig sectaries. 'Jack Presbyter' was heir to Cardinal Bellarmine's doctrine that heretical princes could be overthrown by their peoples. Despite decades of puritan radicalism from 1640 onwards, royalists and tories never abandoned their intellectual anchorage in protestant anti-popery, acquired during James I's contest with the Counter-Reformation after the Gunpowder Plot.[33] Anti-popery was far from being the monopoly of puritans and whigs, for it was also a constant weapon in tory polemic.[34]

The loyal tory doctrine of 'passive obedience' was, in large measure, derived from meditation upon Christ's relationship with earthly powers. Christ had said that people should 'render under Caesar' what is Caesar's due (Matthew 22:21). The preachers pointed out that many Jews had hoped for a revolutionary Messiah who would overthrow the tyranny of the Roman Empire, whereas Christ had insisted that 'my kingdom is not of this world' (John 18:36). When, at the time of Christ's arrest, St Peter had drawn his sword to resist the magistrates, he was reprimanded by Christ: 'Put up thy sword' (Matthew 26.52). Christ did not challenge temporal institutions. Confronted by oppression or ungodliness, Christians should not resist, but should suffer for righteousness' sake. This did not mean that Christians should acquiesce in unrighteousness, for the righteous should never obey ungodly commands: but if the price of conscientious disobedience is punish-

32 Hesketh, *Sermon*, p. 23; Jegon, *Damning*, pp. 5–6, 12; Wagstaffe, *Sermon*, pp. 10–12

33 Coulton, *Loyalty*, pp. 10, 27–8; Frezer, *Wickedness*, p. 18.

34 Tim Harris, *London Crowds in the Reign of Charles II* (Cambridge, 1987), ch. 6; Tim Harris, *Politics under the Later Stuarts* (1993), pp. 98–9; Jacqueline Rose, 'Robert Brady's Intellectual History and Royalist Antipopery in Restoration England', *E.H.R.*, CXXII (2007), 1287–317. The theme is prominent, for instance, in George Hickes, *Ravillac Redivivus* (1678) and Hickes, *The Spirit of Popery Speaking out of the Mouths of Fanatical Protestants* (1680).

ment by the civil power, it must be endured without retaliation. This was the course chosen by Christ himself, in the face of barbarous treatment by his Roman and Jewish captors. Hence it was that tory pulpits described the doctrine of non-resistance as 'the doctrine of the cross'. The theory of civil subordination was not a distant extrapolation of Christian teaching, but a central message of Christ's death. 'Passive obedience' was 'a necessary and essential part of the Christian religion'.[35]

Seventeenth-century anglican clergy were impressed by the patristic era, the teachings of the Fathers of the first three centuries after Christ. The Fathers were, the preachers pointed out, closest in time and place to the teachings of Christ, and hence were the most authentic interpreters of the Christian message. In the period of the savage persecution of Christians by pagan emperors, the Fathers had unanimously counselled submission. The pulpits of 1685 rang to the names of Augustine, Tertullian, Chrysostom, Origen, Basil, Optatus, Theodoret and Oecumenius. Augustine had written of the early Christians that 'their demeanour was perpetually and invariably loyal towards their temporal governors, without the least resistance'.[36] Hence the Christian soldiers of the Theban Legion in 286 had submitted to be decimated by a tyrannical emperor. So alien were the tory divines from the ideology of armed defence of liberty, so emphatic that Christianity offered no intellectual tools for a militant politics of resistance, that they exulted in images of gruesome and self-abnegating martyrdom in the face of earthly powers. The Theban Legionaries calmly awaited their slaughter by the tyrant; their reward lay in heaven.

The preachers were on firm ground in invoking the Fathers. As with Romans 13, patristic teaching set a difficult exegetical challenge to catholic and calvinist radicals. Resistance theorists could counter-claim that the Fathers' teaching was only contingent and expedient, a prudent course at a time when Christians had no material means to resist: submission can be preferable to reckless resistance. If the Fathers' teaching was contingent, it followed that it was not universally applicable. Cardinal Bellarmine was one of those who had argued that the early Christians merely lacked the physical means to mount resistance: the tories said it was 'incredible how he is followed' by modern whigs.[37] In examining the patristic record, a test case was that of the fourth-century Emperor Julian the Apostate, who had reneged on Christianity, and was assassinated. The question of who shot the fatal arrow was hotly disputed. Whigs insisted that the assassin was a Christian. Tories hotly denied it, arguing that although most of Julian's troops were Christian – so that they had the means to overthrow him – they conscientiously chose not to. The topic was important in the 1680s,

35 Grey, *Loyalty*, p. 13.

36 Jegon, *Damning*, p. 24.

37 *Ibid.*, p. 34.

amid revelations of whig assassination plots, and when the most notorious work of contemporary whig political theory, as far as tory preachers were concerned, was Samuel Johnson's *Julian the Apostate* (1682), a veiled, allegorical meditation on the assassination of tyrants.[38] In our eyes, the whig canon is chiefly represented by Locke's *Two Treatises* and Algernon Sidney's *Discourses on Government*, but neither was published before the Revolution and, even so, the tory clerical mind would still have given weight to works couched in terms of Christian history. The clergy were especially attuned to scriptural and patristic claims: for them, nothing was so dangerous and offensive as Johnson's allegation that fourth-century Christians had assassinated their monarch.

There is a profound irony in the tory position. Much of their homiletic was preoccupied with Christian responses to kings who were tyrants or heathen idolaters. This was hardly flattering to James II and does not accord with the praise of princes that might be regarded as the stock-in-trade of 'divine right' theory. Certainly, the preachers described monarchs as God's 'vicegerents' and the 'Lord's anointed'; undoubtedly some preachers (though strikingly few) dwelt on James's personal virtues and fitness for rule;[39] and certainly they helped popularize the epithet of the moment, 'King James the Just'.[40] Yet their applause for James chiefly dwelt upon a single incident, and one that placed centre-stage the Church of England's interests rather than the monarch's: James's solemn declaration at his accession that he would be true to the Church by law established.[41] This declaration was much vaunted, a vow that loyalists took to be an impregnable guarantee of anglican security under a popish king. Though a papist, this king could be trusted. Yet the preachers made no bones: this king was an apostate; he was like Cyrus, the Persian ruler of the Jews, or Julian, the pagan emperor of Christian Rome, good monarchs but not godly monarchs.[42] Moreover, several preachers, ignoring the king's command that the clergy must avoid theological controversy, would, in the ensuing three years, prove forthright in publishing anti-catholic polemics.[43] Loyal though the Monmouth sermons

38 Richard Thompson, *A Sermon Preached in the Cathedral Church of Bristol* (1685), p. 16; Wagstaffe, *Sermon*, pp. 24–5; Whitby, *Three Sermons*, ep. ded.; Willoughby, *Scourge*, ep. ded.

39 The only unreservedly panegyrical sermon was also the sole sermon by a roman catholic, the anonymous 'E.M.', chaplain to the catholic earl of Tyrconnell, preached at Kilkenny: *A Sermon of Thanksgiving for the Happy Success of his Majesties Arms* (1685). The only extant copy is in the National Library of Ireland; my thanks to Jason McElligott for sourcing this.

40 Thompson, *Sermon*, p. 23.

41 Allestree, *Sermon*, pp. 16–17; Coulton, *Loyalty*, p. 33; Hinton, *Sermon*, p. 24; Pelling, *Sermon*, p. 28; Scott, *Sermon*, p. 28.

42 Long, *Unreasonableness*, p. 5.

43 Notably Pelling, Whitby and Williams.

were, James would have good reason to find them objectionable. These were anglican sermons mindful that the king was a papist.[44]

In their wider theology, the preachers' applause for princes, and for this particular prince, was tempered by a deeply Augustinian sense that all princes were fallible mortals. Whigs tended to accuse tory political divinity of being abjectly and naively sycophantic. Patently, the faith which tories placed in the accession vow of 'James the Just' turned out to be catastrophically naive. But on the larger canvas, tory preaching was fatalist rather than panegyrical. Earthly rulers had limited competencies, and were often morally and prudentially inept, which is why even an absolute prince needs wise counsel. For the same reason, subjects should dampen their utopian expectations of what temporal government could achieve by way of earthly felicity, righteousness and godliness. The spirit of rebellion is a spirit of childish hopefulness in the face of the fallibility of all human arrangements. 'Kings are born with the same corrupt natures, subject to the same vicious propensities and inclinations, and susceptible of the same sinful impressions with other men.'[45] The only appropriate response in the face of earthly powers was stoical resignation.

IV

The Monmouth preachers embedded their doctrine of passive obedience within the broader ambit of tory political theory. Among the theses that constituted the doctrine of 'divine right' was the claim that monarchy was the sole form of government that God ordained. 'Monarchical government was originally *jure divino*.' All other forms were deviant. God chose monarchy as most apt for earthly magistracy and he invested it with his authority. Furthermore, monarchy should be hereditary, and parliaments had no power to divert the succession. Subjects are bound to 'maintain the descent of the crown in the right line', for the king's inheritance is 'inviolable by the strictest laws of God and nature'. The Bible supported the hereditary principle, for the Lord 'showeth mercy to his anointed ... and to his seed for evermore' (2 Samuel 22:51).[46]

The sermons went on to argue that the king is above the lords and commons and not their equal, 'for monarchy admits no rivals, nor co-partners'; 'the king must be absolute and supreme'. By contrast, the rebels upheld 'pretended powers derived from lords and commons'. To plead the power of parliaments against the king is to flout the Pauline Injunction, for there was

44 William Lloyd, bishop of St Asaph, objected to one Monmouth sermon at Oxford as savouring of popery: Anthony Wood, *Life and Times*, ed. A. Clark (5 vols, Oxford, 1891–1900), III, 152, 165.

45 William Stainforth, *An Assize Sermon* (1685), p. 14.

46 Coulton, *Loyalty*, p. 6; Allestree, *Sermon*, p. 15; Cooke, *Sermon*, p. 6.

a senate in Rome, yet St Paul 'takes no notice of this senate'. To contradict this principle was to 'reduce our government to the Venetian form' – that is, one in which the monarch is a powerless Doge, the mere symbolic head of a republic. The rebels' supposition, that kings are 'of the people's creation', is 'the palladium of the republican cause'. It was a theory of pseudo-monarchy, masking republicanism, even democracy.[47]

The tory clergy were fond of repeating what absolutists had long regarded as an unanswerable argument for the doctrine that sovereign power could only have its origin in divine authority. Sovereigns, they noted, invariably claim the right of capital punishment. The hangman's gibbet, the right of the civil power to take life, was a defining characteristic of sovereignty. Since sovereigns incontrovertibly had a legitimate right to punish with death, and since the Sixth Commandment said 'thou shalt not kill', the conclusion must be that God alone authorized that right, since nobody but God could exempt a person from his own commandments. The sovereign's power of the sword 'is an essential branch of sovereignty, [and] undeniably evinces it to be originally from God, who alone could give the said power; and I would fain see it proved, that the king-creating people ever had this power: and if they never had it themselves, how they could impart it is somewhat mysterious'.[48]

As to the question of how government originally came about, the chief answer of these tory divines was patriarchalist. Monarchy had its origin in the fatherhood and husbandhood of Adam, the archetype of all monarchs. 'Adam was no sooner made, but he was an absolute monarch, and was invested with sovereignty … over his own children [and] … over his wife … here was the foundation of monarchical government.' Accordingly, submission to the monarch was the same kind of duty as that of children to fathers, wives to husbands, and servants to masters. All were encompassed by the Fifth Commandment: 'honour thy father'. As the catechisms of Stuart England explained, this commandment involves several sorts of father: natural, political, spiritual, and 'domestical' or 'oeconomick' (the father of the household). The Adamic origin of government allowed tory preachers to deny the hypothesis that government had its origin in a contract, entered into by freely consenting individuals. There could have been no such prior state of ungoverned and lawless liberty, unless it were blasphemously to be supposed that humans were not the children of Adam, but had, instead, sprung up spontaneously and without paternity. Hence it was that 'obedience to governors is not a voluntary act of the subject, in putting himself under [government], but it is a natural and necessary duty'.[49]

47 Coulton, *Loyalty*, pp. 5, 8; Lee, *Sermon*, pp. 26–7; Whitby, *Three Sermons*, p. 10; Rich, *Sermon*, p. 3; Pelling, *Sermon*, p. 27; Hesketh, *Sermon*, p. 7.

48 Jegon, *Damning*, p. 12.

49 Goodrick, *Sermon*, p. 26; Hesketh, *Sermon*, p. 7; Coulton, *Loyalty*, pp. 4–5.

Humankind is born into government, yet unruly passions prompt people to seek escape from the bridle of discipline. The preachers summoned up what might colloquially be called a 'Hobbesian' nightmare of ungoverned man, his violent passions unleashed by the absence of rule. They appealed to the proposition that anarchy was always worse than tyranny. They offered heated visions of 'boundless appetites, extravagant lusts', of lawlessness, rape, murder and plunder. Even despots provide safe streets. The mob's propensity to perpetrate mass slaughter was held to be greater than that of princes. One preacher ventured the view that more blood had been spilt by the mob *after* the fall of Nero than by the pathological butcher himself. They spoke under the profound pall of recollection of the Civil Wars: *nothing* could be worse than the savagery of such 'intestine strife' and 'popular rage'. Any survey of recent European history, from the vantage point of 1685, was apt to offer a dismal catalogue of barbarity unleashed by insurrection. The puissance of princes spelt the pleasures of peace. In the victory over Monmouth, 'righteousness and peace have kissed each other' (Psalm 85:10).[50]

These sentiments superficially resemble those of Hobbes's *Leviathan*, but they hardly needed sourcing in that book. Hobbes's ungoverned men have the capacity rationally to calculate an exit from their predicament and to act collectively to construct the artificial power of the sovereign, whom they authorize to exercise their natural powers on their behalf. This was far from the position of the tory clergy. Hobbesianism constituted only a minority tradition within absolutist thinking, for its premises were quite contrary to the Adamic patriarchalism characteristic of the pulpits.[51]

However, one Monmouth preacher did adopt the Hobbesian contract, though he preferred to cite Grotius: Hobbes was too disreputable, and Hobbes was, in any case, an English variant of a wider European tradition of natural right theory, exemplified by Grotius and Pufendorf. The exception is striking, for this preacher's perspective was alien from Adamic patriarchalism. The preacher was Daniel Whitby, who is worth quoting at length, not least because his was the most sophisticated expression of political theory among the Monmouth sermons.

> All government is for mutual defence; and for this end it is, that being free, they [the people] find it necessary to unite themselves into societies, that by united forces they may defend themselves … Men cannot thus defend themselves … but by consenting, that they shall be bound to follow the judgment or direction of some person, or persons. [Men must therefore] subject their wills unto the will of their superiors; so that the will of their superiors shall be accounted as the will of all … [This superior must judge what is] most conducing to the preservation

[50] Hutton, *Rebels*, p. 21; Grey, *Loyalty*, p. 18; Aston, *Sermon*, title page.

[51] Some preachers were explicitly anti-Hobbesian: Goodrick, *Sermon*, pp. 14, 26; Hesketh, *Sermon*, p. 7; Wagstaffe, *Sermon*, p. 21. For Hobbesian ambiguities in these sermons, see Jon Parkin, *Taming the Leviathan* (Cambridge, 2007), p. 378.

> of the common good ... They who are thus obliged to give up their wills and power to another, and have consented so to do, must be deprived of any right to revenge themselves ... It follows, that the natural right of self-defence and preservation is so far from justifying any opposition or resistance of the higher powers, or the civil government, that by endeavouring to rebel against, or overturn it, that right is also overturned, and the foundations of it are removed ... In all civil governments there must be a supreme, from whose authority lies no appeal.[52]

Whitby categorically locates the source of the legitimacy of government in the consent of individual persons, but, like Grotius and Pufendorf, he holds that there is an irrevocable transfer of right to the sovereign.[53]

It is difficult to explain Whitby's isolated position. He had been under suspicion for some time, and was nicknamed 'Whigby' for publishing a tract friendly to the dissenters in 1683.[54] For this crime he had been humiliated by the Church authorities and forced to recant, and his offending tract placed among those burnt by Oxford University in its *Judgment and Decree* against seditious works. At the time of the Monmouth rebellion, his enemies tried to have him prosecuted for sedition. His sermon, carefully emphatic in its rejection of resistance, might have flowed from genuine revulsion against the rebellion: to favour ecclesiastical accommodation with moderate dissenters was not the same as supporting insurrection. Yet it might equally have stemmed from a need to demonstrate his loyalty after two years of traumatic victimization. If the latter, he perhaps took the risk of riding two horses, applauding Monmouth's defeat, but doing so in an unorthodox way, by advancing a theory that potentially carried whiggish implications, at least if a caveat was silently implied. Several contractual absolutists, including Hobbes, had allowed that, *in extremis*, the natural right of self-defence could never be wholly alienated. Many critics of Hobbes had therefore noticed 'whiggish' implications lurking dangerously in the interstices of his doctrine. Although Whitby held that the transfer of right was irrevocable, a careful reader of his sermon might see that his doctrine was adjacent to Hobbes's. The pre-eminent patriarchalist Sir Robert Filmer had objected against his opponents that even if the people's transfer of power was ostensibly irrevocable, *any* theory of popular consent as the foundation of the state potentially undermined its superstructure.[55]

52 Whitby, *Three Sermons*, p. 16.

53 See Richard Tuck, *Natural Rights Theories* (Cambridge, 1979), ch. 5. A minority tradition within English royalism had adopted this non-patriarchalist position, notably Dudley Digges in *The Unlawfulness of Subjects Taking up Arms* (1643).

54 Daniel Whitby, *The Protestant Reconciler, Humbly Pleading for Condescention to Dissenting Brethren* (1683).

55 Sir Robert Filmer, *Patriarcha and Other Political Writings*, ed. Johann Sommerville (Cambridge, 1991), pp. 184–5.

V

With this examination of Whitby's unusual sermon we reach the end of the exposition of the Monmouth sermons. What remains is to glance forward to the responses of these preachers to the overthrow of James II in 1688.

One of the remarkable aspects of the Revolution was the high degree of acquiescence it commanded from anglican clergy. Thousands who had hitherto vociferously deplored the deposition of monarchs found ways of accepting the dethronement of James. Ninety-six per cent of Church of England clergy swore the oath of allegiance to the new regime; and 26 of the 29 Monmouth preachers did so. The careers of some throve under William. Henry Hesketh, Edward Pelling and John Williams were appointed chaplains to the new king, while John Petter served as chaplain to William's army in Flanders. Hesketh was nominated to, but declined, an Irish bishopric; John Scott was mooted for a bishopric; Williams became bishop of Chichester. The passionate loyalists of 1685 proved disloyal in 1688. Whatever casuistical means they found to persuade themselves that they were not acting inconsistently with their principles, they did not repudiate *this* revolution as an unforgivable rebellion against the Lord's anointed.

Just three of the preachers rejected the Revolution, and only two did so permanently. They were Nonjurors and Jacobites, who refused the new oath and remained loyal to the fallen House of Stuart. The most senior, Thomas Wagstaffe, became a bishop in the secessionist Nonjuror church, and was arrested on suspicion of treason in 1696. He condemned the Williamites as rebels, just as he had condemned the Monmouthites, and denounced his colleagues for apostasy and hypocrisy.[56] In at least one case, the Jacobites were able to embarrass a Revolution tory, by making a sermon of 1685 return to haunt its preacher. In 1693 an anonymous Jacobite, condemning 'these backsliding and apostate times', reprinted part of John Scott's assize sermon of August 1685, on Romans 13, in order to expose his hypocrisy in denouncing Monmouth but accepting William. Scott allegedly hurried to his bookseller to buy up old stock in order to suppress it.[57]

56 Thomas Wagstaffe, *An Answer to a Late Pamphlet, Entitled Obedience and Submission to the Present Government* (1690); *An Answer to Dr Sherlock's Vindication of The Case of Allegiance* (1692); *A Letter out of Suffolk* (1694). The other Nonjurors were Thomas Aston and Shadrach Cooke; Cooke soon conformed. Richard Thompson might have become a Nonjuror, but he died in 1685; appointed dean of Bristol in 1684, he led the tory reaction in the City. For the Revolution debate, see Mark Goldie, 'The Revolution of 1689 and the Structure of Political Argument', *Bulletin of Research in the Humanities*, LXXXIII (1980), 473–564.

57 *An Abstract (with Remarks) of Dr Scot's Sermon Preached at Chelmsford Assizes, Aug. 31 1685, Wherein the Doctor Prophetically Gives his Opinion of the Consequences of the Late Revolution* (1693).

Three of the Monmouth preachers published tracts in defence of the Revolution, seeking to rescue consistency with their former position. What two of these did *not* do was embrace whig doctrines of the consent of the people as the foundation of legitimate polities. Despite his vehement anti-Monmouth sermon, John Williams had been among those prominent in their public hostility to James's catholicism, publishing extensively against popery in 1686–8. Earlier, his strong belief in the Popish Plot was evinced by his *History of the Gunpowder Treason* (1678). As with most of the clergy, passionate hatred of catholicism and horror at James's catholic activism after 1685 alienated him from the regime. After 1689 Williams urged that *salus populi*, the public good, was the ultimate measure of allegiance. 'If a case should happen … in which the public good is so far concerned, that without some extraordinary course be presently taken, the nation and government will be destroyed, I do not question … [that] necessity, equity, and reason of state' must supervene upon ordinary principles. That which is 'a law to the law, [is the] necessity and preservation of the nation'.[58]

Likewise, Thomas Long offered a revised account of tory principles and published three tracts during 1689, now arguing that the doctrine of non-resistance contained implied exceptions: a people might preserve itself from destruction by a tyrant. For Long, tory doctrine had always contained tacit caveats in cases of tyranny, and while he accepted that some might claim that the Church had abandoned its former principles, he argued that 'those general rules might admit of just exceptions'. To this end, he offered a long list of authors who had defended royal authority yet who recognized that if a tyrant sought to destroy his people, then a nation could have recourse to self-defence. His list included the Tudor bishops George Abbot, John Jewel and Thomas Bilson, the Scottish absolutist William Barclay, the anglican moralists Henry Hammond, Robert Sanderson and Jeremy Taylor, along with Grotius and Pufendorf. Long insisted that no tory had ever argued that citizens must submit their necks to 'French dragoons or Irish cutthroats'; and, he added, no tory now argued that political power derives from the people's gift. Long protested that he had 'not changed his opinion of the doctrine of non-resistance and passive obedience, but thought it ought to be transferred' to William and Mary.[59] Thus he preserved his toryism, at least to his own satisfaction. He was certainly no convert to toleration of dissenters, for he was the first author to publish a critique of Locke's *Letter Concerning Toleration*.[60]

58 John Williams, *A Vindication of a Discourse Concerning the Unreasonableness of a New Separation, on Account of the Oaths* (1691), p. 24.

59 Thomas Long, *A Resolution of Certain Queries Concerning Submission to the Present Government* (1689; quotation at p. 24); *Reflections on a Late Book, Entituled, The Case of Allegiance* (1689); *A Full Answer to all the Popular Objections … for not Taking the Oath of Allegiance* (1689); *The Historian Unmask'd* (1689; quotation at p. 60).

60 Thomas Long, *The Letter for Toleration Decipher'd* (1689).

The third former Monmouth preacher who published in the Revolution's defence was Daniel Whitby, who ostensibly offered the most radical reversal of opinion, in now advancing the full whig case for revolution. There is, he wrote, an 'original compact' of government: monarchy is founded in the 'consent of the people'. Oaths of allegiance are conditional; if the king is despotic we are absolved from allegiance; the English monarchy is fundamentally elective, and the succession may be determined by parliament. It had, Whitby argued, hitherto been proper to preach passive obedience, out of prudence, to avoid futile bloodshed; but it was now proper to embrace the nation's deliverance.[61] When Whitby published a commentary on the Epistles in 1700, he glossed the Pauline Injunction in a manner that would have been intolerable to the preceding generation, daring to insist, in explaining this classic text of the absolutists, that political authority derives from the 'compact, consent, [and] choice of the persons governed'.[62] Whitby's conversion was perhaps not so drastic after all, for arguably it was predictable, given that his Monmouth sermon had, as we saw, been pregnant with whig possibility. In his later career, he would be yet more aberrant, supporting latitudinarian causes and theological positions of dubious orthodoxy.

Whitby is the only visible whig among the former Monmouth preachers, and whiggism remained rare among the anglican clergy for a generation after the Williamite Revolution. The Church of England shed the House of Stuart, but not toryism. Indeed, churchmen continued to vilify Monmouth. Sir Roger Manley's history of rebellions against the Stuarts, published in 1691, saw Monmouth as the last in a train of puritan rebels. James II 'was scarce settled on his throne, when the hydra of rebellion, lift[ed] up her head again, out of the lake of schism and faction'.[63] Tories deplored the work of John Dunton and John Tutchin in creating a 'Western martyrology'. A *Caveat against the Whigs* (1712) complained that 'by a dash of their pen [they] change a pernicious crew of rebels and traitors into a noble army of saints and martyrs'.[64] In a tory tract of 1704, a dialogue between 'Orthodoxus' and 'Philo-Schismaticus', Orthodoxus attacked Robert Ferguson, the ideologist of the rebellion, and vaunted 'God's avenging justice' against the rebels. The royal victory was 'a judicial decision of the controversy, and …

61 Daniel Whitby, *Considerations Humbly Offered for Taking the Oath of Allegiance* (1689); *A Letter from a City Minister* (1689); *An Historical Account of Some Things Relating to the Nature of the English Government* (1690). These tracts provide a melange of arguments, not all of them whiggish.

62 Daniel Whitby, *Paraphrase and Commentary upon all the Epistles* (1700), p. 82.

63 Sir Roger Manley, *History of the Rebellions of England, Scotland, and Ireland* (1691), pp. 335, 343. This was a translation of a Latin work of 1686, but has a continuation covering Monmouth.

64 Quoted in Stephen Parks, *John Dunton and the English Book Trade* (New York, 1976), p. 38.

an extraordinary providence'.[65] It was vital for Revolution tories to draw a categorical distinction between 1685 and 1688. They recollected that the Monmouth Rebellion was a dissenters' uprising, an assault on the Church as much as on the monarchy. 1688 was quite otherwise, a rescue of the Church. Tories needed to believe that 1688 was an anglican and not a puritan revolution.[66]

Appendix

The Monmouth sermons are as follows. Full bibliographical details can be found online in the English Short Title Catalogue. All texts are available in Early English Books Online, except the anonymous E.M.'s (for which see n. 39). Substantial collections can be found in the Bodleian Library, Oxford (Ashmole 1171–2; Pamphlets c.168), the British Library (226.i.2) and Cambridge University Library (E.10.26–7; 8.22.26). The asterisked preachers (*) have entries in the *Oxford Dictionary of National Biography*.

Preacher	**Venue**	**Date**	**Text**
Charles Allestree	Oxford	26 July	Judges 5:31
Thomas Aston	London & Hackney	1 & 5 July	Isaiah 57:21
Shadrach Cooke	Islington	26 July	Matthew 21:32
Richard Coulton	York	26 July	1 Peter 2:13–14
Augustine Frezer	Dordrecht	26 July	Psalms 24:21–2
John Goodrick	Lincoln's Inn (London)	26 July	Psalms 46:10–11
William Gostwyke	Cambridge	26 July	Proverbs 11:21
Thomas Grey	Dedham (Essex)	30 June	Titus 3:1
Henry Hesketh*	Chapel Royal (London)	26 July	1 Peter 2:13
Thomas Heyrick*	Market Harborough (Leics.)	26 July	2 Samuel 15:11
John Hinton	Newbury (Berks.)	26 July	2 Samuel 18:28
Charles Hutton	Up-Lime (Dorset)	26 July	Joshua 22:22
William Jegon	Norwich	29 May	Romans 13:2
Obadiah Lee	Wakefield (Yorks.)	26 July	2 Samuel: 18:28
Thomas Long*	Exeter	26 July	Psalms 2:1
E.M. [unidentified]	Kilkenny (Ireland)	23 Aug.	Ecclesiastes 10:17
Vincent Owen	'a country congregation'	[June]	Romans 13:1
Edward Pelling*	Westminster Abbey	26 July	Psalms 124:6
John Petter	[not stated]	5 July	John 21:22
Samuel Rich	Chard (Somerset)	21 June	Romans 13:2

65 *Animadversions on Some Passages of Mr Edmund Calamy's* (1704), pp. 47–8.

66 For commenting on a draft of this essay I am indebted to Clare Jackson and the volume editors.

Richard Roberts	Bristol	3 Sept.	1 Peter 2:17
John Scott*	London	26 July	2 Samuel 18:28
William Stainforth	York Minster	5 Aug.	1 Timothy 2:1–2
Richard Thompson	Bristol	21 July	Titus 3:1
Thomas Wagstaffe*	London	26 July	1 King's 1:5
Robert Wensley	Guildhall (London)	6 Dec.	Ezekiel 21:25–7
Daniel Whitby*	Salisbury	[June]	Titus 3:1
John Williams*	London	26 July	Romans 3:7–8
Stephen Willoughby	London	28 June	Jonah 34

3

*Whig Thought and the Revolution of 1688–91**

JOHN MARSHALL

As Charles II and James II moved towards Stuart absolutism under 'colour of law' in the 1680s, whigs lost lives, liberties and estates. After Charles dissolved Parliament in 1681 he initiated trials and executions of political opponents, commencing with the whig propagandist Stephen College in 1681 in a trial moved to Oxford in order to secure a compliant jury after one in London had refused to indict College. After a London jury similarly refused to indict Shaftesbury in late 1681, the crown initiated *quo warranto* proceedings against the charter of London and other corporation charters, to examine 'by what warrant' they held their privileges, with the ultimate objective of revoking them. In 1682 many whigs were disenfranchised in London in contested elections, and in 1683 London's charter was revoked. By such proceedings in London and other cities and towns, the crown gained control simultaneously over the electorate – and thus also over a future Parliament, should one be called – and over the appointment of sheriffs, who appointed juries, in a situation where the crown already appointed and dismissed judges. Trials and executions of leading whigs, including Algernon Sidney and William Lord Russell, followed the discovery in 1683 of plans for armed resistance, the so-called Rye House Plot, while the earl of Essex, detained on suspicion of involvement in the Plot, was alleged to have been murdered in prison. Many whigs fled into exile, were incarcerated, and had estates seized.[1]

* I am deeply indebted to Mark Goldie and John Pocock for my initial introduction to whig thought and to their works for key insights; to the members of my 2005 Folger seminar for discussions of some issues covered in this article; to the 2006 seminar in British History at Yale University which commented on a version of this essay and particularly to Steve Pincus and Keith Wrightson for the invitation and their comments; to several subsequent audiences; and to Catherine Molineux and Justin Roberts for conversations on slavery in England and its colonies and for bibliographic suggestions. On whig thought in Scotland and Ireland in 1688–91, see especially Tim Harris, *Revolution* (2006).

1 J. Marshall, *Locke, Toleration and Early Enlightenment Culture* (Cambridge, 2006); *idem*, *Locke: Resistance, Religion and Responsibility* (Cambridge, 1994); Harris, *Revolution*, ch. 5;

Still further whigs lost lives, liberties, and estates after the duke of Monmouth, Charles II's eldest illegitimate son, greeted the accession of the catholic James II in 1685 by a bloody rebellion launched in the West Country. Backed by judges whom he could dismiss at will, and whose bench he packed, James then utilized the royal prerogative to 'dispense' with and to 'suspend' laws passed by parliament which had prevented his catholic co-religionists from holding office and worshipping freely, built up a significant standing army, and appointed catholics to offices, including in the armed forces in England and in preponderantly catholic Ireland. Hoping to secure parliamentary approval, he remodelled corporation charters once again. Although he did so to seek support from whigs who desired toleration for protestant dissenters and might be persuaded to allow catholics to hold office and be tolerated, and some whigs did support him, most opposed James's efforts to increase royal power over the corporations (and thus over the electorate, parliament and legal system), his use of the dispensing and suspending power to help his co-religionists, and his granting of religious toleration to catholics, especially in the wake of the recent intense persecution of protestants in catholic France and the loss of protestant lives, liberties and estates following the Revocation of the Edict of Nantes in 1685.[2]

These many uses and extensions of royal powers in the 1680s were undertaken in a decade which witnessed the apotheosis of absolutist arguments. For tories, English monarchs possessed very extensive prerogative powers; although over the generations they may have chosen to limit themselves by concessions, England was most certainly not a 'mixed monarchy' and the English king did not share his sovereignty with parliament. Many tories also embraced the patriarchalist theories of Sir Robert Filmer (published for the first time in 1680 though penned before the English Civil War), which saw kingly authority as analogous to the authority of Adam, the 'monarch of the world', whose government began with 'dominion over his wife' and ownership of all property. Although in the later 1680s some tories were to refuse to support James's Declarations of Indulgence, by the time of James's succession there was already a powerful ideology of absolutism available, one that was to be reiterated by those who wrote in defence of James's actions, and subsequently restated after 1688 by non-jurors and Jacobites who refused to accept the legitimacy of the Revolution.[3]

idem, 'Lives, Liberties and Estates', in *The Politics of Religion in Restoration England*, ed. Tim Harris, Paul Seaward and Mark Goldie (Oxford, 1990); G.S. De Krey, *London and the Restoration* (Cambridge, 2005); P. Halliday, *Dismembering the Body Politic* (Cambridge, 1998); J. Scott, *Algernon Sidney and the Restoration Crisis* (Cambridge, 1991); J. Scott, *England's Troubles* (Cambridge, 2000).

2 Harris, *Revolution*; Marshall, *Locke, Toleration*.

3 M. Goldie, 'Restoration Political Thought', in *The Reigns of Charles II and James VII and II*, ed. L. Glassey (Basingstoke, 1997), pp. 12–35; M. Goldie, 'John Locke and Anglican Royalism', *Political Studies* (1983); T. Harris, 'Lives, Liberties and Estates';

In defending and defining the Revolution of 1688–91, whigs repeatedly attacked this combination of absolutist theory and practice under Charles and James by seeing 1680s Stuart absolutism both as already involving 'slavery' and as preparing the ground for future 'slavery'. Alleging that James intended to imitate contemporary French absolutism and persecution, and was intent on establishing slavery under 'colour of law', whigs ceaselessly reiterated that the Revolution had rescued England from 'the imminent Dangers of Popery and Slavery', and thus from 'slavery, both in body and soule'. England was thus saved from becoming contemporary France, and 'when I have named France,' as Gilbert Burnet intoned, 'I have said all that is necessary to give you a Compleat Idea of the Blackest Tyranny over Men's Consciences, Persons and Estates, that can possibly be imagined'. *A Smith and Cutler's Plain Dialogue about Whig and Tory* of 1690 declared that whigs had saved Englishmen from living as 'Slaves, as they do in France'. For whigs, Irish catholics would have aided dragoons in imposing, as Burnet's *Pastoral Letter* put it, 'Popish Tyranny, an Irish Conquest and Massacre, and French Barbarity and Cruelty'.[4]

For most whigs, James's most important 'illegal' action was his use of the 'dispensing' and 'suspending' power to remove restrictions on catholic worship and employment, the first item listed in the 'Heads of Grievances' in 1689. Thomas Comber expressed the predominant view in declaring that James had 'set up for an Arbitrary Power over the Laws, by dispensing with them', which was 'a direct Subversion of our Government'. But for the majority of whigs, James's use of the dispensing and suspending power could not be seen in isolation from his other uses of power, and they understood that lives, property and liberty had all been insecure in the face of *two* Stuart kings controlling simultaneously judges, sheriffs, juries, corporation charters and the electorate. Such issues were particularly acutely felt in London, which took a leading role in 1678–81 in support of attempts to exclude James, in 1681 in refusals of juries to convict whigs, and in 1681–3 in defence of corporation charters. In April 1689, whig M.P.s in parliament challenged the 'unjust' fines and imprisonments of whigs following the contested London elections of June 1682, and supported the petition of John Wilmore, who had been sent to the Tower and forced into exile for being a member of the London jury which refused to indict College. In debating the 'grievances of London' in May 1689, whig M.P.s stressed the 'Invasion' of 'the Rights of the City of London, in the Elections of Sheriffs for the said City, in the year 1682' and the *quo warranto* proceedings against London culminating in 1683. *The Case of Sir Thomas Pilkington* of 1689

T. Harris, *Restoration* (2005), chs 4–5; T. Harris, *Politics Under the Later Stuarts* (1993), ch. 5.

4 *The Revolutions of 1688*, ed. R. Beddard (Oxford, 1991), p. 10; G. Burnet, *Sermon … 5 November 1689*, pp. 5, 28–9; *A Smith and Cutler's Plain Dialogue* (1690), pp. 1–2; Burnet, *Pastoral Letter* (1689), p. 4; Marshall, *Locke*, *Toleration*, chs 1–2; Harris, *Restoration*, ch. 3.

spoke for many whigs in asserting that it was 'an undoubted Truth, That nothing stood more in the way of the Tyrannical and Popish Interest, than the Liberties and Privileges of the City of London; and amongst those Liberties and Privileges, the Power of Electing Sheriffs for London and Middlesex was that which chiefly obstructed their Malicious and Wicked Designs; and for that reason, their Principal Contrivance was, to subvert and destroy such Right of Election'. In 1689 whigs made Pilkington lord mayor, with a jubilee emphasizing that he had been unjustly imprisoned for defending the rights of the city.[5]

Many whig works tied the actions of James's and Charles's reigns together. *Seasonable Reflections on Dissolving Corporations in the Two Late Reigns*, for example, asserted that the attack on charters had threatened 'the utter Destruction' of England's 'Ancient, most Famous Government' and 'long enjoyed English liberties'. 'To destroy Charters', thereby undermining security of property and person, and the right of free elections, our author continued, was 'to destroy England', since 'by this late hatched Invention of getting Surrenders of and Judgments against Corporations, it is Impossible but that the King should quickly have a House of Commons absolutely at his Service and Devotion', which was tantamount to political slavery – slavery because it involved dependence on the will of another. Stressing similarly the need for judicial independence in order for political liberty to be protected, *Some Observations Concerning the Regulating of Elections* declared that parliament should 'limit and restrain the exorbitances of a Quo Warranto, so that the Electing Burroughs may have their priviledges and immunities secured, from the Judgment of a Corrupt Judge, who derives his Being, and holds his Judicial Breath only ad voluntatem Domini'. *Political Aphorisms* stressed how in Charles II's reign, 'the Charters were condemned, and seized upon in order to make us Slaves, and the Laws perverted to the loss of many innocent Lives, and many other Oppressions'.[6]

The whig M.P. John Hampden, who in the mid-1680s had been incarcerated, fined and had his estates seized, in 1689 testified that 'he looked upon himself as murdered' since he would have 'preferred death' to those 'suffer-

[5] T. Comber, *A Letter to a Bishop* (1689), pp. 6–7; De Krey, *London*; G.S. De Krey, *A Fractured Society* (Oxford, 1985), p. 53; G.S. De Krey, 'Political Radicalism in London after the Glorious Revolution', *Journal of Modern History*, LV (1983), 585–617; Harris, *London Crowds* (Cambridge, 1987); Harris, *Revolution*; Marshall, *Locke, Toleration*, chs 1–2; *idem*, *Locke: Resistance*; Scott, *England's Troubles*, pp. 85–8, 220; L. Schwoerer, *The Declaration of Rights, 1689* (Baltimore, MD, 1981); *The Case of Sir Thomas Pilkington* (1689), p. 1; M. Taubman, *London's Great Jubilee* (1689), *passim*; *The Journals of the House of Commons* (1802), X, 2 Apr. 1689, 29 May 1689.

[6] *Seasonable Reflections on Dissolving Corporations in the Late Two Reigns* (1689), pp. 2, 14, 21, 23–5 and *passim*; *Some Observations Concerning the Regulating of Elections* (1689), p. 8 ; E. Stephens, *Important Questions of State* (1689), p. 12; *Political Aphorisms* (1690), p. 31 (deploying Locke's argument); R. Ashcraft and M. Goldsmith, 'Locke, Revolution Principles and the Formation of Whig Ideology', *H.J.*, XXVI (1983), 773–800.

ings'. Sir Samuel Barnardiston, M.P. and foreman of the jury that refused to indict Shaftesbury, had been fined £10,000 for seditious libel in the wake of the Rye House Plot, was imprisoned for four years and had his estates seized to pay the fine. Thomas Papillon, whig M.P. during Exclusion and in the 1690s, had been forced into exile in 1685 after a judgment of £10,000 against him. Other leading whigs had been the defence lawyers of those who fell victim to government recrimination in 1681–5, including most famously John Somers, who had already argued in his *Security of Englishmen's Lives* of 1681 that the most essential right of Englishmen was not the right to parliament, but to a trial by jury. Reversal of the 'illegal' legal judgments against whigs formed a significant part of parliamentary business in 1689–90, and simultaneously of much whig propaganda. *Smith and Cutler's Plain Dialogue* of 1690 declared that whigs opposed 'corrupt Judges and Sheriffs and packed Juries', which had made 'the Laws a nose of wax, and every man's life precarious', with 'bloody Juries, whereby our best Protestant blood was let out', a situation where 'Every Man's Life will be at the Mercy of a packed Jury, if you have any Juries at all'. In London in 1689 a whig crowd set up a gallows at Temple Bar and executed for 'treason' effigies of the foremen of the Russell, Sidney and Cornish juries of 1683 and 1685. Whigs in 1689 issued editions of 'dying speeches' of whig 'martyrs' murdered by the government, declaring that in the 'late Violent Times' of 1683–5 'so many Excellent persons were destroyed by Forms and Subtilties of Law'. It was a result of the centrality of this issue for whigs in 1688–91 that trials and punishments were the subject of six successive provisions of the 'Heads of Grievances', which advocated reform of judges' commissions, preventing 'abuses in the appointing of sheriffs and in the execution of their office', and that juries were to 'be duly impaneled and returned, and corrupt and false verdicts prevented', together with demanding regulation of trials for treason, and prevention of excessive fines and illegal punishments. In 1701 judges' commissions were changed from appointment at royal pleasure to during good behaviour; while this fell short of the election or parliamentary appointment of judges for which some whigs campaigned in 1689–91, it was very significant indeed in restraining the royal prerogative and removing monarchs' power to execute political opponents. With reason, the eighteenth-century philosopher John Millar declared in his *Historical View of the English Government* that until these measures, judges in 'servile dependence upon the crown' had been 'the mean tools of arbitrary power' against 'the rights of the people'. Likewise Thomas Jefferson affirmed how necessary it had been 'to take out of the hands of tyrannical Kings … that deadly Weapon which constructive Treason had furnished them with, and which had drawn the Blood of the best and honestest Men in the Kingdom'.[7]

7 B. Henning, *The House of Commons 1660–1690* (1983), s.v. Barnardiston, Hampden, Papillon; M. Zook, *Radical Whigs and Conspiratorial Politics* (University Park, PA, 1999),

I

Whigs after 1688 argued not only against the many specific alleged violations of the law by James II *and* Charles II and their cumulative threat to life, liberty and estate, but also against Tory arguments for 'absolute monarchy'. They held that English government was 'mixed, not monarchical and tyrannous', as Sir John Maynard declared in the house of commons in January 1689. Burnet's *Enquiry* of 1688 stressed that legislative power was 'lodged between the King and the two Houses of Parliament; so that the power of making and Repealing Laws, is not singly in the King'. Defoe's *Reflections upon the Late Great Revolution* of 1689 depicted 'a kind of Trinity in our Government' since consent of the king and the two houses was 'necessary both to the making and abrogating a Law'. Articulating a deep, if at times malleable, 'ancient constitutionalism', many whigs insisted that England's 'mixed monarchy' was an inheritance from before the Norman Conquest, with Englishmen's rights to liberty and property likewise an inheritance of Englishmen's 'ancient liberties', protected by common law, and the English parliament a lineal descendant of Saxon representative institutions. Whigs depicted Magna Carta both as securing subjects' rights and as declarative of preceding rights to liberty and property. Such an historical case was often combined with the assertion that an 'original compact' lay at the foundation of government. Ferguson in his *Brief Justification* asserted that 'every one' was 'equally Master of his own Property and Liberty, antecedently to their Agreement with one another'. Defoe in his *Reflections* described the 'Original Contract' as having set the 'Boundary of the Prince's Authority, as also of the Subject's Submission'. For many whigs in 1689–91, resistance had been justified because James had 'subverted' the ancient constitution and fundamental laws, broken the 'original contract' and 'invaded' people's rights, thereby legitimating resistance that was not 'rebellion'. As the November 1688 Declaration at Nottingham held, 'We own it rebellion to resist a king that governs by law, but he was always accounted a tyrant that made his will his law; and to resist such an one we justly esteem no rebellion, but a necessary defence.'[8]

ch. 5; De Krey, *Fractured Society*, p. 60; Marshall, *Locke: Resistance*; *idem*, *Locke, Toleration*; *The Dying Speeches of Several Excellent Persons* (1689), 'To the Reader' and passim; *The Bloody Assizes* (1689); *Smith and Cutler's*, pp. 1–2; D. Adair, 'Rumbold's Dying Speech 1685, and Jefferson's Last Words on Democracy, 1826', *William and Mary Quarterly*, 3rd ser., IX (1952), 521–31 at 525n; Schwoerer, *Declaration*, p. 300; J. Millar, *An Historical View of the English Government* (Indianapolis, IN, 2006), pp. 652–3; *Journals of the House of Lords*, XIV, 20 Dec. 1689; H.T. Dickinson, 'How Revolutionary was the Glorious Revolution of 1688?', *Journal for Eighteenth Century Studies*, XI (1988), 125–42.

[8] G. Burnet, *Enquiry into the Measures of Submission* (Edinburgh, 1688), p. 9; D. Defoe, *Reflections upon the Late Great Revolution* (1689), pp. 29, 34, 37, 40; R. Ferguson, *Brief Justification of the Prince of Orange's Descent* (1689), pp. 6, 10–13; P. Allix, An

In January 1689, before William and Mary gained the crown, several whig authors identified various 'defects' in the constitution that needed to be remedied by the Convention in order to prevent slavery in the future. John Humfrey asserted that 'the Supreme Authority' had fallen 'to the Community' who 'must therefore choose a new Subject for that Power', and that they might choose to 'lodge it in the Lords and Commons alone, without a King, if they think that Government best' – though he accepted that it was 'most likely, that they will agree to place it again in a Monarch, Lords, and Commons according to the Ancient Constitution'. Humfrey held that the moment provided a 'Golden Opportunity' to 'bring a Crown in One hand, with Terms or Conditions in the other'. He specified that the Convention should invest in parliamentary appointment and dismissal of judges and control of the militia, and suggested the necessity of a remedy for the crown's prerogative power to call and dismiss parliaments. *A Letter to A Friend* similarly declared that power had devolved on the people to set up 'what Government they please, either the old or a new', and that placing in parliament power over the militia, judges and sheriffs would make it impossible in the future 'for the Monarch to enslave us'. Wildman's *Some Remarks* declared that 'alterations' in the 'civil government' needed to be 'very considerable', specifying as needing reform the control of the militia and of choosing judges, inter alia. Some whigs further alleged rights to annual parliaments. Ferguson's *Brief justification* declared the right 'by several positive Laws to Annual Parliaments'. Samuel Johnson declared in 1694 that he had argued 'before the coronation' that we were 'never the better for this Revolution till we had a Settlement of Parliaments, and our Ancient Right was Anniversary Parliaments, and that nothing else could set the Government to rights', and he had wished that 'all the Rights were reduced to one Line, which was our Right, To have a Parliament every Kalends [first day] of May'. Johnson's *An Argument Proving* of 1692 similarly asserted 'our right of having Stationary Parliaments, not only Annual, but Anniversary'. To whigs such as Johnson, the Revolutionary settlement was a betrayal, not a fulfilment, of whig principles.[9]

Examination of the Scruples (1689), p. 3; E. Stephens, *Important Questions of State* (1689), p. 6; E. Claridge, *A Defence of the Present Government* (1689), p. 4; Allix, *Reflections upon the Opinions of Some Modern Divines* (1689), p. 36; J. Kenyon, *Revolution Principles* (Cambridge, 1977), pp. 6–7, 35; J. Rudolph, *Revolution by Degrees* (Basingstoke, 1992), pp. 62, 70, 128; M. Goldie, 'The Roots of True Whiggism', *History of Political Thought*, I (1980),195–236; M. Goldie, 'The Revolution of 1689 and the Structure of Political Argument', *Bulletin for Research in the Humanities*, LXXXIII (1980), 473–564; J.G.A. Pocock, *The Ancient Constitution and the Feudal Law* (Cambridge, 1957); Schwoerer, *Declaration*.

9 J. Humfrey, *Advice Before it be Too Late* (1689), pp. 1–4 ; *A Letter to a Friend* (1689), p. 1; J. Wildman, *Some Remarks* (1689), pp. 5, 20–3; R. Ferguson, *Brief*, p. 14; S. Johnson, *An Essay Concerning Parliaments at a Certainty* (1694), *passim*, esp. pp. 33–4; S. Johnson, *Argument Proving* (1692), p. 30; Zook *Conspiratorial*, p. 133; Schwoerer, 'The Right to

Some whigs supporting rights of resistance possessed by the people specifically declared that right had not devolved to the people at large to reconstitute government in 1688–91. Tyrrell argued that William had a 'Right to the Crown, from that inherent power which I suppose doth still remain in the Estates of the Kingdom, as Representative of the whole Nation to bestow the Crown on every Abdication, or Forfeiture thereof', and that there was a 'tacit Contract... of maintaining the Original Constitution of great Councils' in order to avoid dissolution to 'the confused Multitude to chuse what form of government they should think fit'. William Atwood argued that a 'farther contract' beyond the 'original contract' meant that power 'devolves to the People of Legal interests in the Government, according to the Constitution' who did *not* therefore 'return to their Natural State and Anarchy'. Sir Thomas Lee MP declared in the Commons in February 1689 that there was an 'original constitution in all governments that commence by compact, that there should be a power in the States' to make provisions in 'extraordinary cases and necessities'.[10]

When published in late 1689 Locke's arguments were Janus-faced. Locke's *Second Treatise* declared that the people could choose to make a new form of government, and did not assert a 'farther contract' or residual power in the Estates, but also that people had chosen to return to the 'old Legislative of King, Lords and Commons' in previous revolutions, supported William's title to the throne, and called neither for annual parliaments nor for parliamentary control of magistrates. Locke had earlier in the year declared in correspondence about the Convention that 'the settlement of the nation upon the sure grounds of peace and security' was 'put into their hands', which could 'no way so well be done as by restoring our ancient government, the best possibly that ever was if taken and put together all of a piece in its original constitution. If this has not been invaded', he continued, 'men have done very ill to complain. And if it has, men must certainly be so wise by feeling as to know where the frame has been put out of order or is amiss and for that now they have an opportunity offered to find remedies and set up a constitution that may be lasting for the security of civil rights and the liberty and property of all the subjects of the nation'.[11]

While a significant number of whigs were willing to talk of resistance and of James as having been 'deposed' or having 'forfeited' the crown,

Resist', in *Political Discourse in Early Modern England*, ed. N. Phillipson (Cambridge, 1987), pp. 232–52; Goldie, 'Roots'; Goldie, 'Structure'; Harris, *Revolution*, ch. 8.

10 Kenyon, *Revolution*, pp. 35, 49, 150; Tyrrell, *Bibliotheca Politica*, pp. 885, 891; Rudolph, *Revolution*, pp. 104, 131, 133–5, 138–40, 150–1; J. Miller, *Glorious Revolution* (1983), pp. 112–13.

11 Locke, *Two Treatises*, 2.203–9, 220–30; *The Correspondence of John Locke*, ed. E.S. De Beer (8 vols, Oxford, 1976–89), no. 1102; Pocock, *Virtue, Commerce and History* (Cambridge, 1985), pp. 227–9; Marshall, *Locke: Resistance*; Rudolph, *Revolution*, ch. 6. On Scotland, see Harris, *Revolution*.

other whigs proposed instead that James had 'abdicated', that the throne was 'vacant', that William had attained the throne through conquest, or was in possession of the throne (however achieved), or occupied the throne providentially. Some, such as Comber, even managed to canvass all of these arguments simultaneously. Many moderate whigs spoke of abdication and vacancy, including Sir George Treby, who declared 'We have found the throne vacant ... we have not made it so.' As John Millar commented, such whigs employed (in England, although not in Scotland) a 'feigned and ridiculous pretence ... to justify a measure which they did not scruple to execute. They supposed that, by leaving the Kingdom, James had abdicated the government; instead of boldly asserting that, by his gross misbehaviour, he had forfeited his right to the crown.' Burnet quickly moved from arguments for resistance in his 1688 *Enquiry* to an argument from possession and conquest in his 1689 *Enquiry into the Present State of Affairs* and 1689 *Pastoral Letter*, to place stress on William's title as 'declared by those who only can be supposed to be the proper Judges of it', and to assert that it was the will of God 'that all Private persons ought to be subject to that authority, which is in possession'. Johnson subjected such arguments to coruscating scorn in 1692, declaring that people were then 'to venture their Lives and Fortunes in behalf of a Title which is to be sight unseen, at that ridiculous rate as no Country man will buy a pig'.[12]

There was almost no whig support for a republic or for democracy in 1688–91. A tiny number of works advocated a commonwealth in the period before the crown was conveyed to William and Mary, but when in 1690 the 'Smith' questioned if whigs desired a commonwealth, the 'Cutler' informed him that 'The Whig is for an English Monarchy, tho not a French one'. Treby declared that he would 'rather have lost a hand' than 'have a hand in anything of a republic'. Even John Hampden declared, 'I am not for a commonwealth, in the posture of affairs we are now in.' The republican Ludlow was ordered arrested. Ferguson's *Justification* declared that 'To dream of reducing England to a Democratical Republick, is incident only to persons of shallow Capacities, and such as are unacquainted with the Nature of Governments, and the Genius of Nations. For as the Mercurial and Masculine Temper of the English People is not to be moulded and accomodated to a Democracy; so it is impracticable to establish such a Commonwealth, where there is a numerous Nobility and Gentry, unless we should first destroy and extirpate them.' Weighing the evils of 'Democracy' against those of 'absolute Monarchy', Tyrrell in his *Patriarcha Non Monarcha* of 1681

12 Kenyon, *Revolution*, p. 10; E. Stillingfleet, *A Discourse Concerning the Unreasonableness of a New Separation* (1689), p. 29; Millar, *English Government*, pp. 641–2; Burnet, *Pastoral Letter* (1689), pp. 12–23; E. Fowler, *A Vindication of the Divines* (1689), pp. 7–9; S. Johnson, *Argument*, pp. 9, 12, 21; Goldie, 'Roots', p. 228.

had stated that it he knew 'not which is worst, to be knawn to death by Rats, or devoured by a Lion'.[13]

Alterations to the franchise were countenanced by a few whig works issued before William and Mary gained the crown, such as *A Letter*, which raised the possibility of representation for the Convention itself 'according to the proportion of People, and public payments'. But while several whig works suggested an extension of the franchise for underrepresented towns and cities, such works often simultaneously challenged the franchise as *too extensive* in the countryside, where whigs had won only eight of the 104 seats in 1685. Wildman's *Some Remarks* of early 1689 declared that parliament did not 'truly and fairly represent the People, the Majority and Richest of them being by such inequalities [among boroughs] excluded from an Electing Vote', while advocating *restriction* of the 40 shilling freehold in the shires to £40 to make electors 'less apt to be led aside' by 'low' means. Wildman's associate Philip, Baron Wharton, suggested that the franchise in the counties be raised to £20. *Some Observations Concerning the Regulating of Elections for Parliament* argued that 'The great number of Electors in Popular Burroughs, and in choosing Knights of the Shire' needed 'to be regulated and limited, and the power of Election to be fixed in the Optimacy only', because 'the Majority' was 'generally of a mean and abject Fortune in the World, and thereby subject not only to disorders and quarrels', but likely 'to be misguided also by their ignorance, and total want of that discerning faculty, which Electors in such weighty concerns ought to have', specifying their likelihood of being swayed by a 'Pot of Ale'. It discussed the possibilities of establishing an initial parish election of electors, and of 'Electing Votes in the County' being limited to £40 rather than 40 shillings qualification. As Mark Knights has shown recently, Edward Clarke and John Locke attempted in the later 1690s to secure legislation to regulate elections and vest the franchise in boroughs in taxpaying adult males, which in some boroughs and towns would have resulted in an expansion of the numbers who could vote but which in others would have restricted hitherto large freemen and inhabitant franchises. He suggests that this taxpayer franchise would have fulfilled Locke's expressed desire in the *Treatises* for representation to be proportioned to 'assistance' to the public; more radical in this than many whigs, Clarke and Locke were nevertheless not radical democrats. And moderate whigs in 1688–9 supported a restricted franchise. Defending against the charge that the Convention did not represent a 'fourth part of the nation', since women and non-freeholders were 'part of the Nation, and ... ought to be represented, when the Government is to be disposed of', Treby declared that the Convention represented 'the valuable

[13] *Smith and Cutler's Plain Dialogue*, p. 1; Defoe, *Reflections*, p. 36; Goldie, 'Roots', p. 216; Schwoerer *Declaration*, p. 33; Ferguson, *Brief*, pp. 22–3; Tyrrell, *Patriarcha Non Monarcha*, preface; Weil, *Political*, p. 60; Rudolph, *Revolution*.

part, and those that deserve a share in the Government'. And while some whigs pressed for increased municipal participation in some corporations, in most constituencies whigs accepted election by a very limited franchise: thus Sir Peter Colleton, M.P. for the Cornish borough of Bossiney, represented just 27 voters, whilst other whig constituencies included Tiverton with 25 voters and Truro and Andover with 24. Wildman attempted to get elected at Harwich not by challenging the electorate of 32, but by offering them a customs house. Many whigs owed seats to whig magnates. And while some whigs worried in 1689 about voters bribed by a 'pot of ale', in 1701 Sir Walter Yonge was to provide alcohol to 180 voters, claiming that the weather had forced them to shelter – in a number of inns! Three-quarters of whig MPs after 1688 were gentlemen, and many surely shared the fear expressed by Henry Ireton at Putney, that the majority of the population might wish to enact a more equitable distribution of property if enfranchised, in a nation of perhaps 180,000 freeholders, and 2.6 million people in families of labourers, out-servants, cottager, and paupers. Most whigs in 1689 desired to discipline, not to enfranchise, the poor.[14]

II

Whigs in England in 1689 united against the 'slavery' of popery as tyranny over consciences in support of toleration for orthodox protestants and widening the Church of England to comprehend presbyterians. The 'Heads of Grievances' demanded 'Effectual provision... for the liberty of Protestants in the exercise of their religion and for uniting all Protestants in the matter of public worship as far as may be possible'. Humfrey's 1689 *Comprehension with Indulgence* advocated uniting all as may be by 'farther latitude', together with liberty of conscience, 'or Toleration' for orthodox Protestant dissenters. Whigs overwhelmingly agreed with Hampden's statement that 'the Empire of Religion belongs to God; men may be forced and constrained, without other effect then to destroy the Country where it is done, and dip people in Blood'. Whigs often related argument for religious liberty to economic liberty, contending that the 'most industrious' members of the polity were not dangerous and asserting that toleration would foster

14 *A Letter to a Friend*, p. 1; J. Wildman, *Some Remarks*, pp. 24–5; *Some Observations*, pp. 10–11; Goldie, 'Roots', p. 218; A. Grey, *Debates of the House of Commons*, IX, 13; E. Cruickshanks, S. Handley and D. W. Hayton et al., *The House of Commons 1690–1715* (Cambridge, 2002), I, 46, 251–4, II–V *passim*; Harris, *Revolution*, p. 57; J. Hoppit, *A Land of Liberty?* (Oxford, 1999), pp. 28–30, 72, 145; M. Knights, 'John Locke and Post-Revolutionary Politics: Electoral Reform and the Franchise', *Past and Present*, 213 (2011), 42–86. Knights's important piece identifies Locke and Clarke with whig opposition to inequity among constituencies and electoral corruption, and with a moral campaign for electoral reform.

wealth, trade, and employment, all of which were important to the security of the nation. The reign of Charles II had involved considerable religious persecution, with the deaths of many dissenters in prison, and the loss by others of liberty and estates. The firm parliamentary provision of toleration for orthodox dissenters in 1689 supported by all whigs was thus very significant. That it did not involve full civil equality – because it retained the sacramental test for office and maintained the requirement of oaths, rejected by many quakers – set an agenda for further significant campaigns for civil and religious liberty by some whigs over the succeeding decades, as they also continued to defend that toleration which had been secured from high church tory attack. And many whigs – although not such orthodox dissenters as Humfrey – also opposed the exclusion from the toleration of 1689 of non-Trinitarian protestants, again setting an agenda for further campaigns by some whigs for religious liberty for unitarians, still denied a century after the Revolution.[15]

While thus generally and importantly supporting religious toleration, whigs often supported 'liberty' against 'libertinism', and as they did so launched campaigns against sexual non-conformity after 1688. This ethos led, inter alia, to the foundation of Societies for the Reformation of Manners by the whig divines Burnet, Tillotson, and Stephens; to the 1694 campaign against prostitution led by the lord mayor Sir William Ashurst, a dissenter who had fought for the corporation charter in 1682; to whig arguments for religious liberty not 'libertinism' calling for strict execution of laws against 'debauchery', such as Locke's *Letters Concerning Toleration*; and to increased prosecution of homosexuality in the 1690s. Some whigs tied this campaign against 'libertinism' to the defence of liberty against 'slavery'. For instance, *A Brief Collection of Some Memorandums* of 1689 declared such measures necessary because the Stuarts had sought to prepare the kingdom for popery and slavery 'by an industrious promoting of Vice and Immorality', since 'Debauchery naturally disposes to Slavery'. When men 'give up themselves to be slaves to their Lusts', it intoned, God 'will make them slaves to Rulers'.[16]

15 Wildman, *Some Remarks*, pp. 3–5; Schwoerer, *Declaration*, pp. 299–300; Goldie, 'Priestcraft and the Birth of Whiggism', in *Political Discourse*, ed. Phillipson, pp. 209–31; J. Humfrey, *Comprehension with Indulgence* [1673?], pp. 1–7; *Grey's Debates*, IX, 252; D. Lacey, *Dissent and Parliamentary Politics* (New Brunswick, NJ, 1969), pp. 225–6, 233–5, 238; Marshall, *Locke, Toleration*; Harris, *Politics*, p. 139; C. Rose, *England in the 1690s* (Oxford, 1999), pp. 108, 176; Goldie, 'Roots', p. 207; Locke, *Correspondence*, no. 2207; Marshall, *Locke*; J. Champion, *The Pillars of Priestcraft Shaken* (Cambridge, 1992); J.C.D. Clark, *English Society* (Cambridge 1985).

16 Marshall, *Locke, Toleration*; *A Brief Collection of Some Memorandums* (1689), pp. 3–4; E. Stephens, *Important Questions of State* (1689), 11; *idem*, *An Admonition to the Magistrates* (1689),pp. 1–2.

In defending 'liberty' against the 'slavery' of catholic religious persecution – which was feared from, though not practised by, James II, and which was being practised by Louis XIV and other catholic rulers – most whigs supported denying both liberty of worship and of office to catholics on the basis of their alleged political threat and commitment to intolerance. While Locke may not have meant to include all catholics in that category, he probably meant to include very many contemporary catholics (and thus exclude them from the otherwise very extensive religious toleration he supported). The *Brief Collection of Some Memorandums* of 1689 went so far as to advocate the castration of Jesuits found in England. And many whigs supported reinforcing the penal laws against catholic worship in predominantly catholic Ireland, together with the confirmation of catholics' loss of lands there, substantial further forfeiture, and other penal measures. Catholics were disarmed and banned from London in 1689. Many whigs in England maintained after 1688 the fierce and deeply prejudiced anti-catholicism which had involved, inter alia, whig-sponsored pope-burning processions in the 1670s using as an effigy 'a most costly Pope … his ears, his belly filled full of live cats who squawled most hideously when they felt the fire'. This deep anti-catholicism led in 1687–9 to attacks on catholic chapels, monasterie, and individual catholics, as in 1678–81 it had led to executions of catholics for allegedly conspiring to assassinate Charles II and massacre protestants. Some whigs, however, had served James II and had recently accepted toleration of catholics – including friends of Locke such as Yonge – and Monmouth's Declaration in 1685, penned by Ferguson, had accepted toleration for catholics. Catholics were understood by many whigs to deserve toleration for their *religious* beliefs and practices, however erroneous, even as many whigs declared that catholics political beliefs and contemporary commitment to intolerance rendered them intolerable.[17]

III

Responding to Tory patriarchalist arguments, which stressed analogies between the family and the state (and thus saw the husband and father as equivalent to an absolute monarch in the domestic sphere), many whigs argued that marriage was contractual, recognized the legitimacy of divorce, and asserted that divorce and resistance were legitimate against tyran-

17 Marshall, *Locke, Toleration* (but note that Anthony Brown, in his excellent unpublished Ph.D. thesis, 'Anglo-Irish Gallicanism c.1635–1685', University of Cambridge,1985, and John Milton, in his edition of Locke's *Essay Concerning Toleration* (Oxford, 2006), have both now shown that the 'Particular Test for Priests' was by Peter Walsh, not by Locke, a possibility canvassed by Marshall); T. Harris, *Revolution*; *idem*, *London Crowds*; *A Brief Collection of Some Memorandums* (1689), p. 2; R. Porter, *London* (1994), 157; M. Goldie, 'John Locke's Circle and James II', *H.J.*, XXXV (1992), 557–86.

nical cruelty within the family – though they did continue to stress the 'natural' superiority of husbands as men, that final decision-making power within marriage resided with husbands, and that husbands ordinarily could legitimately command and punish 'obstinate' wives. Thus although Burnet asserted that 'all Men' were 'born free' and that 'the Law of Nature' had 'put no difference nor subordination among Men', he noted the exception 'of Children to Parents' and 'of Wives to their Husbands', insisting that Scripture held that wives were to be 'subject to their Husbands, in all things', even if adultery constituted grounds for divorce. Locke's *Treatises* held that marriage was a contract, divorce legitimat, and mothers as well as fathers had authority over children; nevertheless, the husband had power to order things in the family 'as Proprietor of the Goods and Land there', and since it was inevitable that people would at times be of 'different understandings', 'the last Determination' needed to 'be placed somewhere', it 'naturally' fell 'to the Man's share, as the abler and the stronger'. Kennett in his *Dialogue* of 1689, whilst holding that every one was born free, insisted that a wife 'may not put away her Husband': 'Nay, though a very ill Husband, turn Nonthrift, spend his Estate, abuse her Person, prove unnatural to her Children, notwithstanding all this', she was nevertheless 'obliged to an entire Obedience', though he conceded that if the husband were to prove 'Tyrannically cruel' and show that 'he intends her Ruine, Destruction and Death', then laws allowed for relief as the 'Cruelties, Injustice, Violence and Irregularities of the Husband may be such, as may give just cause of Divorcement'. Tyrrell argued that in the state of nature if a husband for no crime in his wife tried to take away her life, she could resist him legitimately, and leave him if he treated her severely. Tyrrell declared that a wife could legitimately resist her husband if he went about 'to kill' her and she was unable to run away or to pacify him by tears.[18]

Lois Schwoerer has emphasized that the beneficiaries of the Revolution included Queens Mary and Anne, and that aristocratic women played roles in the Revolution. Some female printers issued whig propaganda. Many women were members of crowds supporting the Revolution. But whigs depicted political discussion as occurring solely between men, from Tyrell's 'Meanwell' and 'Freeman' to the artisanal whig 'Cutler' and 'Smith' in the *Plain Dialogue*, and whigs often stressed their 'manly' defence of liberty in works such as Ferguson's *Justification* and the *Plain Dialogue*. Even those usually identified as radical whigs typically argued for the conveyance of the crown to William alone, and many for its 'sole administration' by William.

[18] Johnson, *Of Magistracy* (1688), p. 1; Burnet, *Enquiry into the Measures of Submission*, pp. 1, 11; Locke, *Two Treatises*, 2.82, 1.48; W. Kennett, *Dialogue* (1689), pp. 17–18; Tyrrell, *Patriarcha Non Monarcha* (1681), pp. 109–11; Tyrrell, *Bibliotheca Politica* (1694), pp. 42–4; Rudolph, *Revolution*, pp. 35, 40–5; R. Weil, *Political Passions* (Manchester, 1999), pp. 62–6, 123; G. Schochet 'Significant Sounds of Silence', in *Women Writers and the Early Modern British Political Tradition*, ed. H. Smith (Cambridge, 1998), p. 230.

Ferguson pointed out that Mary, 'being the best Woman, as well as best Wife, that this or any other Age can give us an Example of', had 'sufficiently assure[d] us, that she will neither Covet, nor be willing to Accept more [than the name of Queen] ... seeing everything beyond that, would be a detracting from the Glory of her Husband'. Whig attacks on the suppositious birth of James II's son reinforced contemporary emphasis on women's sexual untrustworthiness and 'imposition' of false children on their husbands. Burnet's 1688 *Enquiry* concluded a discussion of the dissolution of the 'Branches of our Constitution' with the 'evident Indications of a base Imposture'. Sidney's *Discourses* attacked hereditary monarchy as based on the 'faith of women', 'often accused of suppositious births'. Tyrell opposed giving the vote to what he termed the 'promiscuous rabble of women'. Whig works typically presumed that women would be excluded from the vote. *Some Observations* of 1689 was explicit when it spoke of the 'natural right' of 'every individual Person' to vote, but declared that 'every Pater-Familias, or Housekeeper' was 'a Natural Prince' and 'invested with an Absolute Power over his Family, and thus had 'by necessary consequence, the votes of all his Family, Man, Woman, and Child included in his'. In the following decades, a number of women identified whig assertions of female subjection alongside male rights as inconsistent. The tory Mary Astell, for instance, wrote that 'whatever may be said against Passive-Obedience in another case, I suppose there's no Man but likes it very well in this [marriage]; how much soever Arbitrary power may be dislik'd on a Throne, not Milton himself would cry up Liberty to poor Female Slaves'. As Astell asked, 'If all men are born free, how is it that all women are born slaves?'[19]

IV

Whig argument in 1688–92 defended liberty against the political 'slavery' of absolutism and the religious 'slavery' of persecuting catholicism. Few whig works discussed civil slavery. But in the later seventeenth century, slavery was being increased massively in British colonies, and it was becoming increasingly common in England for people from Africa, bought and sold as slaves, to be held in bondage, even if they were more often referred to as 'servants' or as 'slavish servants' than as 'slaves', and even if some people from Africa in England in this period were waged servants rather than slaves. The legal

19 L. Schwoerer, 'Women and the Glorious Revolution', *Albion*, XIX (1986), 195–218; *idem*, *Lady Rachel Russell* (Baltimore, MD, 1988); *Smith and Cutler's*, pp. 1–2; Ferguson, *Brief*, pp. 11, 36; Burnet, *Enquiry into the Measures*, pp. 15–16; A. Sidney, *Discourses Concerning Government*, ed. T. West (Indianapolis, IN, 1990), p. 430; Allix, *Examination*, p. 13; Tyrrell, *Patriarcha*, p. 83; Zook, *Conspiratorial*, p. 180; *Some Observations*, p. 15; M. Astell, *Political Writings*, ed. P. Springborg (Cambridge, 1996), 46–7; Weil, *Political*, pp. 1–2, ch. 3; M. Fissell, *Vernacular Bodies* (Oxford, 2005), ch. 6.

regime of 'liberty' defended at the Revolution was not understood to end civil slavery in colonies tha were declared to be governed by separate laws, and the Revolution was followed by a series of legal decisions, several of which upheld slavery in England itself, even though others spoke of slaves as freed by coming to England as a land of liberty. In the first two decisions referring to slavery in English courts after the Revolution, slavery was upheld. In 1693, in a case concerning trover (property rights) in dogs, it was declared that 'musk-Cats and Monkeys' were 'Merchandise; and for the same reason it has been adjudged, that Trover lies of Negroes' And in 1694 it was held of 'negroes' that 'a man may have a property in them' since they were 'heathens'. Both cases cited a 1677 decision in which it had been declared that 'negroes being usually bought and sold among merchants, as merchandise, and also being infidels, there might be a property in them sufficient to maintain trover'. In 1696–7, a further court case involved a declaration that a 'slavish servant' was not 'a chattel', and in 1706 Justice Holt declared that there was 'no such thing as a slave by the law of England' while explicitly allowing slavery in English colonies. In 1729, however, the attorney general argued that slaves were not freed by being brought to England, and in 1749 Lord Hardwicke returned to the judgment of 1677 and declared that Holt had been in error in holding that a slave was 'as much property as any other thing'.[20]

It is extremely difficult to estimate the numbers of enslaved people in England around the time of the Revolution of 1688–91. The highest concentrations were probably in the port cities of London, Bristol, and Liverpool. As Catherine Molineux has recently emphasized, the fashion in England of having a 'blackamoor' servant – a slave – was spreading in the later seventeenth century. In 1690 Dryden's prologue to Fletcher's *The Prophetess* suggested that William's soldiers in Ireland should bring 'a Bogland captive home' to serve as a page 'With copper collars and with brawny backs/ Quite to put down the fashion of our blacks'. In the wake of the Revolution, William displayed a black slave at Hampton Court with a 'carved white marble collar, with a padlock, in every respect like a dog's collar'. Tim Harris has analysed the ways in which the *London Gazette* reported celebrations of popular support for William and Mary, stressing its propagandist role as official voice of the new regime. The *Gazette* also had a section of advertisements in every issue, which often advertised whig defences of the Revolution, such as Somers's *Brief History*, Tyrrell's *Bibliotheca Politica*, and Locke's *Treatises*. This section also often carried offers of rewards for runaway 'servants'. The *Gazette* for 4–7 March 1689 thus began with an address to William about the oppression of hearth money (which was abolished as 'a

[20] D.B. Davis, *The Problem of Slavery in Western Culture* (Ithaca, NY, 1966), pp. 208–9; F. Shyllon, *Black Slaves in Britain* (1974), pp. 24–5; J. Hurd, *The Law of Freedom and Bondage in the United States* (Boston, MA, 1858), I, 180–5; H. Catterall, *Judicial Cases Concerning American Slavery and the Negro* (5 vols, Washington, D.C., 1926–37), I, 1–5.

badge of slavery upon the whole people' because it had allowed surveyors to enter and search houses) and ended with an advertisement of a reward for a runaway 'Negro Man' with 'a piece of one of his Ears cut off' and a 'Brass Collar above his Neck' who spoke 'very bad English'. The *Gazette* for 7–10 October 1689 opened with various addresses from corporations celebrating the preservation of their 'Liberties' against 'Arbitrary Power'; it closed with an advertisement of a reward for a 'runaway Tawny moor'. The *Gazette* for 28–31 October 1689 advertised a reward for 'A Neager Boy, about 14 years old' run away from 'Mr Thomas Fish, Oil-Man' near Aldersgate. The *Gazette* for 27–30 October 1690 carried an advertisement for the return o 'A Negro Boy named Toney, aged about 16' as 'lost from Ratcliff the 21st of October', adding that he had 'a Brass Cholar which directs where he lived'. There were many more such advertisements in the early 1690s.[21]

The *Gazette* in these years also reported on colonial slavery by reporting on 'rebellions' planned or enacted against English settlers; the very use of the term 'rebellion' designated these actions as illegitimate resistance. Thus in December 1690 the *Gazette* reported from Jamaica that in July 'the Negroes, belonging to Mr Sutton's Plantation in the Mountains, being about 400, broke into Rebellion', stormed the house and killed 'the Man that look'd to it', 'seized upon' guns, ammunition and other provisions, and marched to 'the next Plantation, killed the Overseer, and would have persuaded the Negroes there to join with them, but they hid themselves in the Woods'. It reported that forces had then 'attacked the Negroes', killed 'divers of them' and pursued them until 'about 200 of them came in, and as many others being found dead of their wounds', 'we look upon this rebellion as quite over'. The *Gazette* in January 1693 carried a dispatch from Barbados about an alleged 'Conspiracy of the Negros of this island to destroy the English inhabitants', 'to kill the Governor' and 'to fall upon their Masters and Overseers, and after that to rendezvous with what Arms, Ammunition, and Horses they could seize, at Bridge-Town', 'to have been further supplied with Arms and Ammunition out of the Magazine, by a Negro employed there, who was to kill his Master the Keeper of the Stores … to surprise the Fort, and from thence to batter the ships in the Harbor'. According to the report,

21 C. Molineux, *Faces of Perfect Ebony* (Cambridge, MA, 2012), ch. 1; *idem*, 'The Peripheries Within', The Johns Hopkins University Ph.D., 2005; C. Tomalin, *Samuel Pepys, The Unequalled Self* (New York, 2002), pp. 123, 176–7; S. Aravamudan, *Tropicopolitans* (Durham, NC, 1999), p. 38; Shyllon, *Black Slaves*, pp. 7–8, 10; G. Gerzina, *Black London* (New Brunswick, NJ, 1995), pp. 7–10; S. Amussen, *Carribean Exchanges* (Chapel Hill, NC, 2007), pp. 221–5; M. Waller, *1700* (New York, 2000), pp. 277–81; Harris, *Revolution*, pp. 355–6; *Statues of the Realm* (1819),VI, 61–2; *London Gazette*, Jan.–Feb. 1689; 7–10, 28–31 Oct. 1689; 14–18 Nov. 1689; 5–9, 17–21, 20–4 Mar., 31 Mar.–3 Apr. 1690; 2–5 June 1690; 27–30 Oct. 1690.

their wicked Contrivances were happily brought to light by two of the Chiefest of the Conspirators, who were overheard as they were discoursing thereof, and being thereupon seized, were Condemned to be hanged in Chains till they were starved to Death, which they endured four days, and then finding they were not relieved by the Succor they hoped for from their Accomplices, they promised to declare the whole design, which they did accordingly, and made a large Confession, and discovered the Principal Conspirators, who were secured, and divers of them executed; and several Laws have been made for the future Security of this Island, against the like Attempts.[22]

Before turning to a consideration of the forms of whig support provided for the continuation and expansion of slavery after 1688, and to an analysis of several whig arguments about civil slavery in 1688–98, it is important to stress that while in the later 1680s and 1690s many tories were the leading investors in the Royal African Company, many whigs had been investors in the Company in the 1670s and 1680s, especially but not only before 1675, and that many whigs remained investors in the 1690s or became investors in plantations or trades associated with slavery. Indeed, for some whigs the overthrow of James allowed them to regain positions in the Royal African Company lost after the tory reaction after 1681. As has been emphasized recently by David Armitage, the whig M.P. Sir Peter Colleton was an absentee Barbadian planter and proprietor of the slave-owning colony of Carolina, and Shaftesbury was a Barbadian planter, an investor in the Royal African Company, and from the 1660s to the 1680s a lord proprietor of Carolina. These were but two among many whig investors in slavery. The leading London whig lord mayor Sir Robert Clayton possessed £500 of stock in the Royal African Company in 1671, and was an assistant of the company in 1681 – running its weekly business in 1681 while supporting the Exclusion of James as necessary to protect England from 'slavery'. John Bawdon, a leading London whig merchant who stood bail for the whigs

[22] *London Gazette*, 16–20 Oct., 1–4 Dec. 1690; 2–6 July, 22–6 Oct. 1691; 2–5 May 1692; 26–30 Jan. 1693; on the valences of 'rebellion', C. Condren, *The Language of Politics in Seventeenth Century England* (1994); Locke, *Two Treatises*. Earlier reports for an English audience of alleged Caribbean intended rebellions had included *Great News from the Barbadoes* (1676), which depicted a 1675 slave conspiracy to 'cut their Masters the Planters Throats' and which described their executions, with 'Six burnt alive, and Eleven beheaded' while a further five 'Hanged themselves, because they would not stand trial'. On maroon communities, revolts and alleged conspiracies, and on the many punishments being enacted by Englishmen in Barbardos, Jamaica and Antigua in the later seventeenth century, including execution by being burned alive or beheading, loss of limbs and severe floggings, see especially M. Craton, *Testing the Chains* (Ithaca, NY, 1982); D. Gaspar, *Bondmen and Rebels* (Baltimore, MD, 1985); A. Hatfield, *Atlantic Virginia* (Philadelphia, PA, 2004); G. Puckrein, *Little England* (New York, 1984); Amussen, *Caribbean Exchanges*; W. Rawlin, *The Laws of Barbadoes* (1699), pp. 186–9; A. Higginbotham, *In the Matter of Color* (New York, 1978).

Pilkington and Shute after the disputed London election in 1682, held estates in Barbados; in 1671 he owned £400 of Royal African Company stock. Richard Hawkins, scrivener and manager of the duke of Monmouth's money, was a whig common councilman in the 1680s; he had held £400 of Company stock in 1671. Benjamin Hewling, whig merchant and common councilman in London, whose two sons were executed after the Monmouth rebellion, had held £500 of stock in 1671. John Lawrence, leading London whig merchant and alderman in the 1680s, had held £1600 of stock in 1671 and was assistant of the company in 1672. Humphrey Edwin, whig merchant and alderman of London in the 1680s, had held £300 of stock in 1671. Edward Sherman, whig merchant and common councilman in the 1670s and 1689–90, had held £100 of stock in 1671. John Morrice, merchant and whig common councilman, had held £400 of stock in 1671, and was an assistant of the company in 1674–6, 1679–81, and 1689–93, and sub-governor in 1695–6. Many other whigs who were not investors in the Royal African Company were remunerated by slavery in other ways. Henry Ashurst, whig nonconformist M.P. for Truro in 1681–95 and alderman in London in 1688–9, was a merchant in the West Indies trade. Daniel Dorville, whig London common councilman in the 1680s and 1690s, was a sugar baker. Thomas Western, whig common councilman in 1680–1 and 1689–90, was an ironmonger and supplier to the Royal African Company, as were his whig son and M.P. Samuel Western and his whig M.P. son-in-law Peter Gott. Sir John Fleet, the London M.P. who stood against the 'Church party' in 1691 and had his election celebrated by Locke in 1695, was a West Indies merchant, 'sugar baker' and assistant of the company in the 1690s. Daniel Defoe was a shareholder in the Company and employed to issue propaganda on its behalf. Sir Stephen Evance, the whig M.P. and goldsmith-banker, was Shaftesbury's banker to whom Shaftesbury mortgaged his lands in England and Carolina in 1682, and banker for Locke from 1689 onwards, years during which Evance was an investor in the Royal African Company, and an assistant of the company in 1692–3, 1696, 1703, 1707 and 1710. Sir Gilbert Heathcote, whig M.P. from 1701, and, in 1690, a common councilman and supporter of the extension of the franchise in London, was a West Indies merchant, and agent for Jamaica. Heathcote advocated attacking the French West Indian islands to take control of their slaves, and thereby to promote English 'liberty' against French 'slavery'. Some of these whigs were friends or associates of Locke. As a number of scholars have emphasized, Locke was an investor in the slave trade in the 1670s, and, as David Armitage has shown, Locke was involved both in composition of the provision of the *Fundamental Constitutions of the Carolinas* that masters had 'absolute power and authority over negro slaves', and in redrafting its provisions in summer 1682 in collaboration with the Barbadian planter Colleton, while leaving that provision unchanged. And Locke served in administrative positions dealing with the colonies both in the 1670s and the 1690s, taking notes on meetings of the lords proprietors of Carolina and endorsing in the 1670s, inter alia, letters discussing bills for payment for slaves, and a report by Colleton on the condition of Barbados which included a statement about the need for more 'whites' to prevent being forced to arm 'part of their blackmen'. As secretary to the Council for Trade and Foreign Plantations in November 1674 Locke helped to arrange for a visit to the Council by officials of the Royal African Company to defend their monopoly amidst concerns that the plantations should not be 'prejudiced, by too high rates sett upon negroes' – a visit that ended with support for continued monopoly while Locke was himself a shareholder in the Royal African Company. In the 1690s, Locke was a Commissioner of the Board of Trade, whose remit included 'inspecting and improving our plantations in America'; many of its recommendations during his term of service from 1696 to 1700 were measures to facilitate slavery.[23]

[23] D. Armitage, 'Locke, Carolina and the *Two Treatises of Government*', *Political Theory*, XXXII (2004), 602–27; K.H.D. Haley, *The First Earl of Shaftesbury* (Oxford, 1968), pp. 230, 233, 246, 725; J. Woodhead, *The Rulers of London 1660–89* (1965), s.v. Henry Ashurst, John Bawdon, Robert Clayton, Daniel Dorville, Humphrey Edwin, Richard Hawkins, Gilbert Heathcote, Benjamin Hewling, John Lawrence, John Morrice, Samuel Sheppard, Edmund Sherman, Thomas Western; Cruickshanks et al., *House of Commons*, I, 993; K.G. Davies, *The Royal African Company* (1970), *passim*, esp. pp. 59, 66–9, 104; L. Stock, *Proceedings and Debates of the British Parliaments Respecting North America* (Washington, D.C., 1924), I, 422; J. Brewer, *The Sinews of Power* (London, 1988), p. 94; Bodl., MS Locke c.30, 1, 3, 8–13, 18, 33, 53, 125; *Calendar of State Papers Colonial Series, America and the West Indies (1669–74)*, pp. 19, 32, 40, 51–2, 86–9, 92, 138–40, 168–9, 209–10, 411, 493–6, 506–7, 517, 544, 578, 584; Locke, *Correspondence*, nos 1189, 1844, 1845, 1847, 1879, 1881, 1911, 2090, 2234, 2261, 2335, 2341, 2346, 2356, 2369, 2371; Library of Congress, Washington, D.C., Journals of the Council for Trade and Foreign Plantations, Phillipps MS 8539, part 1, 98–102; V. Hsueh, *Hybrid Constitutions* (Durham, NC, 2010), p. 78; R. Blackburn, *The Making of New World Slavery* (1997), pp. 263–7; De Krey, *Fractured Society*, pp. 139–40; *Journals of the House of Commons*, 17 Oct. 1690, 26 Nov. 1690, 5 Dec. 1690, 11 Mar. 1697, 18 July 1710; T. Keirn, 'Monopoly, Economic Thought, and the Royal African Company', in *Early Modern Conceptions of Property*, ed. J. Brewer and S. Staves (1995), pp. 427–66; T. Keirn, 'Daniel Defoe and the Royal African Company', *Bulletin of the Institute of Historical Research*, LXI (1988), 243–7; W. Pettigrew, 'Free to Enslave', *William and Mary Quarterly*, LXIV (2007), 3–38. On the scale of trade associated with slavery, the colonial markets, and planters' incomes from slavery, and its huge significance in Bristol, Liverpool and London by the later seventeenth century, from the creation of goods for Africa, British America and the Caribbean, and the processing of goods from these destinations, including not merely sugar and tobacco but also many other products, through the building, refitting and provisioning of ships, to the huge expansion of quays and wharves in Bristol, London and Liverpool for loading and unloading, see, inter alia, N. Zahedieh, 'Overseas Expansion and Trade', in *The Origins of Empire*, ed. N. Canny (Oxford, 1998); *idem*, *The Capital and the Colonies* (Cambridge, 2010); K. Morgan, *Slavery, Atlantic Trade and the British Economy 1660–1800* (Cambridge, 2000); *idem*, *Bristol and the Atlantic Trade in the Eighteenth Century* (Cambridge, 1993); J. Inikori, *Africans and the Industrial Revolution in Britain* (Cambridge, 2002), esp. p. 219ff; F. Knight, *The Caribbean* (New York, 1990),

V

In 1690–1 M.P.s discussed whether, for the 'benefit of the nation', trade in slaves, and other trades to Africa, should be organized through a monopoly held by the Royal African Company or by free trade. The commons' committee appointed to investigate the issue included the whigs Papillon, Barnardiston, Pope Blount, Yonge and Clarke, whilst the committee chair was Colleton, who owned 180 slaves and the fourth largest Barbadian plantation at 700 acres in 1673, was then Barbados's interim governor, was a charter member of the corporation of the Royal African Company, and was the owner of £1800 of its stock. Thus the commons was appointing as committee chair a known avid supporter of slavery who was financially supported by slavery. Colleton had testified to parliament from 1671 onwards against sugar duties, before becoming one of five members of parliament appointed to a committee to ease such duties on 9 August 1689, after James II had increased such duties significantly. In 1690 Colleton reported to parliament as committee chair the argument of opponents of monopoly that high prices hazarded 'loss of the Sugar Trade', since 'without negroes the Sugar Trade cannot be carried on', but accepted, with the committee, the central argument of the Company that the expense of maintaining forts in Africa favoured continued monopoly.[24]

Whigs repeatedly took leading roles in supporting the expansion of slavery and the slave trade in parliamentary sessions in the 1690s, whether supporting or opposing the monopoly of the Royal African Company. A committee of 1694 included Yonge, Evance and Locke's host, Sir Francis Masham, while the ailing Colleton wrote to the chair that it was essential to ensure 'sufficient care to supply the English plantations with negroes at moderate rates' or there would be 'an end of your plantation trade'. Among

p. 111; *Merchants and Merchandise in Seventeenth Century Bristol*, ed. P. McGrath (Bristol, 1955), pp. xxi, 227–93; M. Dresser, *Slavery Obscured* (London, 2001), ch. 1; E. Williams, *Capitalism and Slavery*, pp. 53, 61. On contemporary assertions of the significance of slavery in the colonies and the slave trade, see, inter alia, J. Cary, *An Essay on the State of England* (1695), preface, pp. 42–3; 47, 65, 71–86; J. Bellers, *Essays about the Poor* (1699), p. 14. Many lord mayors' shows in London in the latter half of the seventeenth century featured representations of slaves and slavery, and many lord mayors (and sheriffs) were investors in slavery; see J. Basker, *Amazing Grace* (New Haven, CT, 2002), s.v. Thomas Jordan, Elkanah Settle; De Krey, *Fractured Society*; Davies, *Royal African Company*.

24 *Journals of the House of Commons* (1803), X, 28 Feb. 1689, 16 Apr. 1689, 17, 21, 22, 30 Oct, 1690, 1, 26 Nov., 3, 5, 23, 29 Dec. 1690, 2, 7 Nov. 1691, 10 Dec. 1691; H. Thomas, *The Slave Trade* (1997), ch. 11; Keirn, 'Monopoly'; Pettigrew 'Free to Enslave'; Locke, *Correspondence*, no. 1978; Henning, *House of Commons*, s.v. Colleton; H. Beckles, *White Servitude and Black Slavery in Barbados* (Knoxville, TN, 1989), pp. 137, 147, 149–50; G. Puckrein, *Little England* (New York, 1984), p. 143; *Calendar of State Papers Colonial Series* (1669–74), pp. 141, 210–11, 493–4; Davies, *Royal African Company*, pp. 67–8.

those testifying in favour of free trade was the absentee Barbadian planter Edward Littleton, who in *The Groans of the Plantations* of 1689 had identified the defence of 'liberty' and 'property' against absolutism with a defence of the slave-holders' interests; Littleton saw James II's increase of sugar duties as aimed at crushing his 'own subjects' as a 'prelude' to establishing 'the French Government' in England. Many petitions from planters and from merchants involved in trade to Maryland, Virginia, Jamaica, Barbados, Montserrat and the Leeward Isles provoked parliamentary business throughout the 1694–8 sessions, almost all demanding opening the slave trade to ensure that plantations suffering 'discouragement and poverty' because of 'want of Negroes to carry on their work' should be 'more plentifully supplied with Negroes, and at Cheaper Rates'. By 1696, a committee of the whole house agreed 'that for the better supply of the Plantations with Negroes, all the subjects of this realm have liberty to trade to Africa for Negroes'; by 1698, with strong whig support, the monopoly of the Royal African Company was effectively ended. The result was a significant further expansion of people being enslaved.[25]

VI

Some whig works published in defence of the Revolutions in 1688–91 declared men born free, and some distinguished the relation of magistrate and subject from that of master and slave, but they generally did so in order to suggest that subjects of magistrates were not to be slaves to those magistrates, not to argue that civil slavery was illegitimate. Burnet's 1688 *Enquiry* declared men 'born free' by the law of nature, but asserted that a man 'can sell himself to be a slave', and described as legitimate a contract involving 'the total giving himself up to another, as in the case of Slavery'. Kennett's *Dialogue* of 1689 affirmed that every one was born free, but accepted that any man by 'compact or bargain' could become 'a Slave'. Johnson asserted that the 'Superiority of a Master, is an absolute Dominion over his Slave', in which the Master could lawfully sell his slaves 'like so many head of cattle, and make money of his whole stock when ever he pleases, as a Patron of Algiers does'. Stillingfleet's *Unreasonableness of a New Separation* of 1689 argued that 'when men are taken Captive by others, they are at their Mercy;

[25] *Journals of the House of Commons* (1803), XI, 24 Jan., 19 Feb., 2 Mar., 30 Nov., 10, 12 Dec. 1694, 25, 28, 30 Mar. 1695, 2, 9 Apr. 1695, 2 Jan., 28 Feb. 7, 26 Mar., 8, 11, 16 Dec. 1696, 12, 19, 21, 23, 28 Feb., 19 Mar., 13–14 May, 10 June 1698; *CSPC* (1669–74), p. 494; E. Littleton, *The Groans of the Plantations* (1689), *passim*, esp. pp. 13, 19–22; R. Blackburn, *The Making of New World Slavery* (1997), p. 420; Zahedieh, 'Overseas Expansion and Trade'; *idem*, *Capital and Colonies*; J. Inikori, *Africans and the Industrial Revolution in Britain* (Cambridge, 2002), esp. p. 219ff; Williams, *Capitalism and Slavery*, pp. 53, 61.

and the giving of life is so great a benefit, as cannot be compensated by any thing less than a perpetual Service; and in consideration of it, the Master is to afford Protection and Maintenance'. Stillingfleet noted that the 'best Writers on this subject' had held that if a slave 'be kept in Chains, he is under no obligation of Conscience to him that keeps him' and could escape, but that if he yields 'upon Terms', he was then obliged to obedient service. Allix's *Reflections* of 1689 cited the same ground as Stillingfleet for legitimate slavery in arguing that while it was legitimate for the people to resist those who attempted to change limited monarchies into tyrannies and thus 'enslave' them, Jews under Nebuchadnezzar had 'become the Slaves of that Monarch, and owed him all manner of obedience, which Bondmen do to him who has saved their lives, when it was in his power to kill them'.[26]

In arguments issued first during the Exclusion Crisis and repeated in defence of the Revolution, Tyrrell similarly depicted slavery as legitimate, while setting limits to the powers that masters could legitimately exercise over slaves. In his *Patriarcha Non Monarcha* of 1681 Tyrrell argued that a person could sell himself into perpetual service or be enslaved if captured in war. And he argued that children born to those enslaved as captives in war might themselves be enslaved. Nevertheless, someone who sold himself into slavery did not thereby give away the right to a master to kill, starve or maim him 'unjustly', could defend his life against the unjust rage of a master, and could run away if suffering perpetual hunger or cold. Even 'the worst of Slaves, that is, one taken in War', was not 'so absolutely at his Master's dispose, as that because he hath him in his power, he hath therefore a Right to use him as he will'. For Tyrrell, as long as a slave was kept a prisoner in

[26] Burnet, *Enquiry*, pp. 3,5; Kennett, *Dialogue*, p. 4 and *passim*; Johnson, *Of Magistracy* (1688), p. 1; E. Stillingfleet, *The Unreasonableness of a New Separation* (1689), p. 6; P. Allix, *Reflections* (1689), pp. 22–5; see also Molineux, *Faces*, ch. 3 on the whig John Dunton's *Athenian Mercury*. For reasons of space I cannot discuss here a small but significant number of works depicting slavery as rebarbative, and in some of these cases challenging it as illegitimate or arguing for manumission in the later seventeenth century, but in others arguing for Christianization, and not for emancipation. See, inter alia, Morgan Godwyn, *Negroes and Indians Advocate* (1680), esp. pp. 39–41; *idem*, *Supplement* (1681); T. Tryon, *Friendly Advice* (1684); F. Froger, *Relation of a Voyage* (1698), pp. 118–20; George Keith, *Exhortation and Caution to Friends Concerning Buying or Keeping of Negroes* (New York, 1693); Richard Baxter, *A Christian Directory* (1673), pp. 557–60, and Philipp Van Limborch, *Theologia Christiana* (Amsterdam, 1686) (many of these were owned by Locke). Among much scholarship on these works, see especially Molineux, *Faces*; *idem*, 'Peripheries Within', ch. 3; T. Morton, 'The Plantation of Wrath', in *Radicalism in British Literary Culture*, ed. T. Morton and N. Smith (Cambridge, 2002), pp. 64–85; N. Smith, 'Enthusiasm and Enlightenment', in *The Country and the City Revisited*, ed. G. Maclean et al. (Cambridge, 1999), pp. 106–18; P. Rosenberg, 'Thomas Tryon and the Seventeenth-Century Dimensions of Antislavery', *William and Mary Quarterly*, 3rd ser., LXI (2004), 609–42; D.B. Davis, *The Problem of Slavery*, pp. 310–11; A. Vaughn, *The Roots of American Racism* (New York, 1995), pp. 55–86; Amussen, *Caribbean Exchanges*, pp. 179–84.

fetters, there was no obligation on the part of the slave to obedience; he could run away or 'kill his Conqueror, unless he will come to other Terms with him, and make him promise him his Service and Obedience' upon granting of the 'ordinary Comforts' of life. Tyrrell then continued: 'And if he cannot enjoy these, I believe there is no sober Planter in Barbadoes (who are most of them the Assignees of Slaves taken in war) but will grant such a Slave may lawfully run away if he can.' Tyrrell criticized the 'cruelty and avarice of divers Nations' by which slaves were reckoned as among household goods or as 'beasts', and indicated that 'this is not allowed of in our Law, nor yet in France and other Countries', leaving it unclear from these words whether he thought all slavery illegitimate in England and France or whether he thought that slavery was legitimate there, but that slaves could not be classified as 'chattel'. Tyrrell's *Bibliotheca Politica* of 1692–4 contended that slavery created by one's own consent was valid, and that such servitude was lawful by the law of nations as it tended to the good and preservation of mankind, of a prisoner who would otherwise have been slain, and of those who sold themselves because compelled by external necessity. Tyrrell explicitly said, however, that there were fathers in Africa who sold their children into slavery, and that such children had the right by the law of nature to run away rather than be sold to work 'in the mines in Peru, or Sugar-works at Barbadoes'. And Tyrrell argued that if a master sought to take a slave's life due to 'Humour or passion', a slave could legitimately run away or 'resist him to save his life', even as he spoke of slaves as legitimately allowed to enjoy nothing but a 'bare subsistence'.[27]

Whig principles defending the Revolution as a revolution for 'liberty' against 'slavery', in other words, firmly opposed political slavery, but not civil slavery. Such a view was articulated strongly, but differently, in 1698 by the Scot Andrew Fletcher of Saltoun, who had joined with Monmouth's rebellion in 1685 and William's invasion in 1688. In the late 1690s Fletcher was an investor in a new Scottish company attempting to trade in slaves that was crushed by English whigs who wished to keep the profits from slavery in England. In 1698 Fletcher asked 'With what face can we oppose the tyranny of princes, and recommend such opposition as the highest virtue, if we make ourselves tyrants over the greatest part of mankind.' But he posed this question in a work advocating the re-introduction of slavery in Scotland as a cure for the problem of beggars, and suggested limiting the term 'slavery' to political slavery on the ground that a slave was one

[27] Tyrrell, *Patriarcha*, pp. 103–7 (see pp. 17, 36, 42, 48–9, 75–6, 130–1); Weil, *Political*, p. 66; J. Tyrrell, *Bibliotheca Politica* (1718), pp. 36, 78, 114–15. In Barbados, legislation allegedly prevented slaves being left to the 'arbitrary will' of masters and required that they were to provide clothes for them, but only fines were imposed for wantonly killing slaves, slaves were legally designated chattels and estates real, and it was held legitimate to kill slaves who resisted punishment: R. Dunn, *Sugar and Slaves* (Chapel Hill, NC, 1972), esp. p. 239.

who was 'absolutely subjected to the will of another without any remedy', whereas civil slavery involved 'only being subjected under certain limitations' (even though the slave could possess nothing and could be sold). Thus for Fletcher, individuals subjected under such limitations should be called servants, not slaves. Fletcher advocated the death penalty for masters who killed such 'servants', supported freedom for those mutilated or tortured by their masters and condemned cruelty by masters. By contrast, he defined men of all ranks under arbitrary government as truly slaves, indicating that while it was said that a slave setting foot in France became free, in fact in France under an absolute monarch all were slaves. He simultaneously celebrated ancient times when men were defined 'as part of the possession of another' as times when everyone had had provisions of meat, clothing and lodging. Fletcher condemned the churchmen who had ended such slavery in Europe by claiming that those baptized should be freed, and declared instead that Christianity should have opposed thus 'invading any man's property'.[28]

Sidney's *Discourses*, composed in about 1681–3 but published in 1698, declared that 'by the name of slave we understand a man, who can neither dispose of his person nor goods, but enjoys all at the will of his master'. Focusing upon political slavery, Sidney proclaimed that the English, like other classical and contemporary European nations, 'abhorred such a subjection', and were to be 'governed only by laws of their own making'. For Sidney, reiterating arguments derived originally from Aristotle, there were 'naturally base' countries whose inhabitants were 'slaves by nature' and who had 'neither the understanding nor courage… required for the constitution and management of a government within themselves'; they could 'no more subsist without a master, than a flock without a shepherd'. Sidney contrasted the 'generous' nations of ancient Britons with 'the base effeminate Asiaticks and Africans', who were 'careless of their liberty, or unable to govern themselves' and 'by Aristotle and other wise men called slaves by nature, and looked upon as little different from beasts'.[29]

The arguments of Locke's *Treatises*, also composed in about 1681–3 but published in late 1689, opposed many of these arguments said to legitimate slavery by his whig contemporaries in the 1680s and 1690s, but identified one ground for legitimate enslavement, and described the condition of those thus enslaved in the starkest terms as subjection to absolute and 'despotick' power. Unlike Sidney, Locke did not suggest that any were 'natural slaves'. Unlike Tyrrell, Burnet and Kennett, Locke denied that individuals could legitimately sell themselves into slavery in extreme necessity, arguing that

28 A. Fletcher, *Political Works*, ed. J. Robertson (Cambridge, 1997), pp. 58–67; E. Morgan, *American Slavery, American Freedom* (New York, 1975), p. 325.

29 A. Sidney, *Discourses Concerning Government*, ed. T. West (Indianapolis, IN, 1990), pp. 9, 17, 44, 343; see R. Tuck, *The Rights of War and Peace* (Oxford, 1999), pp. 35, 40–3, 65–70, 102–3; J. Milton, *Tenure of Kings and Magistrates*, in Milton, *Political Writings*, ed. M. Dzelzainis (Cambridge, 1991), p.11.

those in extreme need had rights by charity to take others' surplus in order to secure their own preservation. For Locke, 'a man, not having the Power of his own life, cannot, by Compact, or his own Consent, enslave himself to any one'. Unlike Fletcher, Locke did not propose reintroducing slavery in Britain when he proposed measures to deal with beggars in the 1690s – although he did propose working schools to inure very young children to labour, and transportation for some adults. However, Locke argued that those who used unjust force against others could be enslaved legitimately, writing that one who had by some 'fault, forfeited his own Life, by some Act that deserves Death; he, to whom he has forfeited it, may (when he has him in his Power) delay to take it, and make use of him to his own Service'. This was 'the perfect condition of Slavery, which is nothing else, but the State of War continued, between a lawful Conqueror, and a Captive'. Locke held that whenever someone thus enslaved found 'the hardship of his Slavery outweigh the value of his Life', it was 'in his power, by resisting the Will of his Master, to draw on himself the Death he desires'. For Locke, slaves were a 'sort of servants, which by a peculiar Name we call Slaves, who being Captives taken in a just War' were 'by the Right of Nature subjected to the Absolute Dominion and Arbitrary Power of their Masters'. These men having 'forfeited their Lives, and with it their Liberties, and lost their Estates; and being in the State of Slavery, not capable of any Property', they could not 'in that state be considered as any part of Civil Society', 'the chief end whereof' was 'the preservation of Property'. Such slaves were subject to 'Despotical Power', an 'Absolute Arbitrary Power one man has over another, to take away his Life, whenever he pleases'. For Locke, in a war involving 'unjust force', the king and soldiers 'who have actually assisted, concurred, or consented to that unjust force' could be enslaved legitimately. He emphasized strongly, however, that these were the only conditions under which people could justly be enslaved; 'innocent' wives and children, and men who had not concurred or assisted in unjust war, could not be made slaves, though Locke recognized that 'Conquerors… seldom trouble[d] themselves to make the distinction, but … willingly permit[ted] the Confusion of War to sweep all together'. He raised the possibility of conditions involving security of life and duties of obedience that were also discussed by Tyrrell and Stillingfleet, but argued that such terms ended slavery: that as soon as conditions were set and a compact made 'for a limited Power on the one side, and Obedience on the other', slavery itself ceased – presumably for a condition of service like that which Locke named 'Drudgery', a condition into which he held that Jews had sold themselves, and from which condition he held that maiming by masters freed them.[30]

[30] Locke, *Two Treatises*, 1.42; 1.130–1; 2.23–4; 2.85–6;2.172; 2.179; 2.183; 2.185; 2.188. Among many discussions of Locke and slavery and of the natural law contexts for these arguments, see especially J. Dunn, *The Political Thought of John Locke* (Cambridge 1969), pp. 108–10, 174–7; J. Waldron, *God, Locke and Equality* (Cambridge, 2002), pp. 141–2,

Locke's combination of arguments thus clearly rendered illegitimate *on his own principles* the contemporary enslavement and transportation to the Americas of non-combatant women and children from Africa, both of which were parts of contemporary processes of enslavement, even if the majority of those being enslaved and transported during Locke's lifetime were adult males. Locke surely intended also to render any form of hereditary slavery illegitimate when he wrote that a father justly enslaved for use of unjust force could not forfeit the lives of wife and children who 'made not the war, nor assisted in it' whose lives 'were not mine to forfeit'; that even if 'all the Men of that Community, being all Members of the same Body Politick', were 'taken to have joined in that unjust war' and so their lives were 'at the Mercy of the Conqueror', this concerned not 'their Children, who are in their Minority'; and that 'over those of the subdued Country, that opposed him not, and the Posterity even of those that did, the Conqueror, even in a just war, hath, by his Conquest, no right of Dominion'.[31]

The majority of Africans being enslaved at the time of composition of Locke's *Treatises* were captured in warfare, although some wars in Africa, conducted by Africans against other Africans, might be described as slave-raids and European demand for such slaves was encouraging these wars alongside wars fought to conquer territory, defeat rivals or gain slaves for domestic use. Locke had reason to believe that slavery was prevalent in Africa, and that warfare caused the majority of enslavement, the emphases, inter alia, in John Ogilby's 1670 *Africa*, a text with which he was familiar. In 1681 Tyrrell described the majority of slaves in Barbados as formerly prisoners of war, and the likeliest source for Tyrrell's comment was Locke, an intellectual collaborator of Tyrrell with whom Locke was staying for much of 1681. It is possible, then, that *on his own principles* Locke might have thought that a small number of those who had been enslaved might have been enslaved legitimately, but Locke's arguments suggest that *on his own principles* he would also have thought that the vast majority of Africans were being enslaved unjustly, including many non-combatant and non-

148–9, 179, 197–206; R. Tuck, *Natural Rights Theories* (Cambridge 1979), pp. 49–57; Tuck, *Rights of War and Peace*; J. Farr, 'So Vile and Miserable an Estate: The Problem of Slavery in Locke's Political Theory', *Political Theory*, XIV (1986), 263–89; J. Farr, 'Locke, Natural Law and New World Slavery', *Political Theory*, XXXVI (2008), 495–522; W. Glasser, 'Three Approaches to Locke and the Slave Trade', *Journal of the History of Ideas*, LI (1990), 199–216; W. Uzgalis, 'The Same Tyrannical Principle: Locke's Legacy on Slavery', in *Subjugation and Bondage*, ed. T. Lott (Lanham, MD, 1998), pp. 49–77; R. Bernasconi and A. Mann, 'The Contradictions of Racism: Locke, Slavery and the Two Treatises', in *Race and Racism in Modern Philosophy*, ed. A. Valls (Ithaca, NY, 2005), pp. 89–107; J. Welchman, 'Locke on Slavery and Inalienable Rights', *Canadian Journal of Philosophy*, XXV (1995), 67–81; S. Pufendorf, *Elements of Universal Jurisprudence* and *De Jure*, in *The Political Writings of Samuel Pufendorf*, ed. C. Carr and M. Seidler (Oxford, 1994), p. 38; H. Grotius, *De Jure Belli ac Pacis*, Bk III, ch. vii.

31 Locke, *Two Treatises*, 2. 183–9.

concurring women and children, and also very many males as not having '*actually assisted, concurred or consented*' in *unjust* warfare. Ogilby emphasized that many African states were absolute governments; he did not suggest that subjects would have had the choice to 'concur' in or 'consent' to decisions about warfare. Many of the wars being fought in Africa were surely, in Locke's terms, not ones with just conquerors of conquered aggressors. Locke also commented explicitly on conquerors not discriminating between those justly and unjustly enslaved among captives even when they had fought in an unjust war. Whereas Stillingfleet, Tyrrell and Allix focused on captivity in war as legitimating slavery, Locke's arguments focused on captivity in war as legitimating slavery *only* if this was the result of the use of *unjust* force wielded by individuals themselves or by their rulers with their assistance, concurrence or consent. When asked about the moral validity of Portuguese claims to have purchased slaves taken in war, the Spanish theologian Francisco de Vitoria had replied in 1546 that it was not up to slavers to discover the 'justice of the wars between barbarians' and that they may be bought 'without a qualm'. Locke's argument is clearly different, identifying only assisting, concurring or consenting combatants in an *unjust* war as legitimately enslaved. The effect is surely to limit very considerably the number of those whom Locke himself thought enslaved legitimately. At the same time, however, for those held by Locke's arguments as enslaved legitimately, his argument is unusually uncompromising about their subjection to 'despotick' authority and to 'absolute dominion and arbitrary power'. Locke emphasized that slavery involved the master's power to 'take away his [slave's] life, whenever he pleases'. Whereas Grotius cited Exodus XXI to show that under Hebraic law slaves were to be freed if maimed by their master, Locke insisted instead that the passage applied only to the condition of 'drudgery' and not 'slavery', precisely because slaves were *not* freed if maimed. Whereas Tyrrell, like Grotius, wrote of slaves as freed by maiming, and related many restrictions on how slaves could be treated by masters, and Fletcher wrote of punishments for masters who killed slaves, Locke in his *Treatises* wrote of slaves' subjection to 'absolute dominion and arbitrary power'.[32]

Locke's argument on slavery in the *Treatises* thus created a category of those justly enslaved which was much more limited in extent than that

[32] J. Thornton, *Africa and Africans in the Making of the Atlantic World 1400–1800* (Cambridge, 1992); D. Eltis, *The Rise of African Slavery in the Americas* (Cambridge, 2000); Blackburn, *New World Slavery*; Davis, *Inhuman Bondage*; J. Ogilby, *Africa* (1670), *passim*, e.g. pp. 318–20, 328, 356, 364, 434, 441, 462, 483, 487; and note also Ogilby's extremely negative portrayals of Africans as cannibals and idolators as well as his stress on war; Locke, *Treatises*, 2.179; Pagden, *Fall of Natural Man*, p. 33; Fletcher, *Political*, p. 62. Ogilby also spoke of other means than war as involved in creating slaves in Africa, including sales, punishment for crimes, the arbitrary laws of kings and great men, and kidnapping (e.g. *Africa*, pp. 360, 363, 469), as did many others in this period.

put forward by his contemporary whigs, and thereby implied clearly that very many of those then being enslaved by the English were being unjustly enslaved. While Locke seems not to have invested again in the slave trade after he sold his stock in the 1670s – at a profit – he did not change the assertion of the 'absolute power and authority' of masters when he redrafted the *Constitutions of the Carolinas* in 1682, a date close to composition of the Second Treatise. In the 1690s he lived in the house of an M.P., Francis Masham, who sat on committees helping to expand slavery; he commended the *Essay on … Trade* by the Bristol merchant John Cary, which defended the expansion of the slave trade, as the best work on trade he had ever read; and he was concerned to defend profits from the English slave trade against Scottish and other competition. And in his role on the Board of Trade in 1696–1700 Locke himself helped in various ways to reinforce or expand slavery, during years when officials and planters were demanding the expansion of slavery and the Board supported supplying the colonies 'plentifully with Negroes and at the cheapest Rates'; Locke was even on occasion assigned particular responsibility for Jamaica, Barbados and the Leeward Islands (whenever William Blathwayt was absent). Locke co-signed many memoranda to colonial governors: inter alia, he signed recommendations for defence of the Royal African Company trade in the Senegal and Gambia rivers; for control of St Lucia in order to prevent slaves running away from Barbados; for his banker Stephen Evance's petition for assistance from the governors of Barbados and Jamaica to ships engaged in importing negroes of the Spanish Asiento; and for reinforced defence of the West Indian islands by royal navy ships whose roles included protection for convoys of slaving ships. Governors were instructed to obtain laws restraining 'inhumane severities' against slaves and legal limitations on masters' powers of life and death over slaves by obtaining laws making the 'wilful' killing of slaves murder and making maiming of slaves subject to penalties. This form of instruction had commenced in royal instructions to governors in the 1680s as a challenge to the laws of Barbados and then of Jamaica which had provided respectively only fines, or fines and three months imprisonment, for wilfully killing slaves, and had been included in royal instructions to governors of Maryland, New England, New Hampshire, New York and Virginia in the 1680s and early 1690s. In the later 1690s Locke simultaneously was one of those supporting instructions to governors to find out with the assistance of councils and assemblies the 'best means' to facilitate conversion of negroes and Indians to Christianity. Once again, these instructions had direct precedents in instructions in the 1680s and early 1690s for governors of Barbados, Bermuda, Jamaica, the Leeward Islands, New England, New York, Virginia, Maryland, Massachusetts and New Hampshire (and before that in earlier royal instructions about the plantations). In 1696 the assembly in Jamaica passed legislation to make wanton killing of a negro murder, but only on the second offence; Barbados and the Leeward Islands continued to make it subject only to a fine. Jamaica passed legislation in 1696 to support

Christianization, but other governors reported the very considerable resistance of planters and assemblies to conversion. In the later 1690s, Locke very probably also advocated measures to assist the conversion of negroes and Indians to Christianity in Virginia, including recommending a law that all 'Negroes Children be baptized – catechized, and bred Christians'.

In the later 1690s, then, Locke attempted to obtain some amelioration of the conditions of slavery as he supported measures to make wilful killing of negroes murder and to obtain punishments for maiming slaves, and he proposed measures to provide slaves with what he considered the means of salvation. But for many locations in mainland America and in the Caribbean he helped during these years to reinforce and to expand slavery even as these ameliorative measures were being resisted by many planters and assemblies. Locke was thus one among many whigs after 1688 who celebrated their own victory for liberty over 'slavery', and by his practices simultaneously facilitated the enslavement of thousands of Africans.[33]

[33] Armitage, 'Locke', esp. p. 619; Cary, *Essay* (1695), preface and pp. 42–3; 47, 65, 71–86; J. Pollexfen, *A Discourse of Trade* (1697), pp. 86–7, 128–30; Locke, *Correspondence*, nos 1978, 2005, 2006, 2016, 2079, 2658, 2661; *Calendar of State Papers Colonial Series, America and the West Indies (1696–7)*, pp. 126, 167–9, 177, 202, 210–11, 531–2, 541, 567, 570, 580, 594–7, 627, 631; *(1697–8)*, 3, 19, 35, 421–2, 446, 454, 468, 519–20; *(1699)*, 250–1, 291–2, 296, 299–302, 303, 307, 329–30, 337, 350–1, 356–7, 394, 435–6, 438–9, 444, 451, 461–2, 500–1, 503–5, 510, 513–14, 519, 526, 536–7; *(1700)*, 257–9, 306, 333–6, 351; *Royal Instructions to British Colonial Governors 1670–1776*, ed. L.W. Labaree (2 vols, New York, 1967), II, 505–8; Dunn, *Sugar and Slaves*, pp. 239–46. On Locke's support for measures to Christianize slaves and Indians and some of their contexts from the 1660s to the late 1690s, see now J. Turner, 'Locke, Christian Mission and Colonial America', *Modern Intellectual History*, VIII (2011), 267–97, which also importantly discusses the undue scholarly neglect of memoranda of the Board that were signed by Locke and his role as its pre-eminent member. Holly Brewer has also indicated in an unpublished manuscript, 'Slavery, Sovereignty and Inheritable Blood', that Locke supported conversion in Virginia, and has additionally shown that Locke proposed ending grants of land by head-rights for slaves in Virginia, which she associates with his principles in the *Treatises* being opposed to slavery.

4

The Restoration, the Revolution and the Failure of Episcopacy in Scotland

ALASDAIR RAFFE

The Revolution of 1688–90 brought about the fall of King James VII and the abolition of episcopacy in the Church of Scotland. In some ways, this combination of outcomes was unsurprising. The bishops' authority had been entwined with that of the crown since the re-establishment of episcopacy in the Restoration settlement of 1661–2. Whereas government by bishops was well rooted in England, in Scotland episcopacy seemed unpopular and dependent for its survival on royal support. While Scots remained loyal to their king, as most seemed to be during the Restoration period, episcopacy could survive. But when the Restoration monarchy faced its final crisis in the Revolution, the king and bishops fell together. In the convention of estates, whose meetings in the spring of 1689 settled the fate of James VII and his style of government, the bishops' devotion to the king eroded their credibility. A minority of influential and able episcopalian clergy was willing to recognize the new monarchs, William and Mary. But the bishops' Jacobitism, and that of many of episcopacy's landed proponents, together with the presbyterianism of the Revolution's keenest supporters, left William with little choice but to accept a presbyterian settlement.[1]

Even before the opening of the convention of estates in March 1689, support was leaching away from the episcopalian Church in southern and central Scotland. Issued on 28 June 1687, James VII's second declaration of indulgence allowed presbyterians freedom of worship in meeting houses.[2] Within a month, presbyterians were organizing themselves into a rival

1 See esp. Tristram Clarke, 'The Williamite Episcopalians and the Glorious Revolution in Scotland', *Records of the Scottish Church History Society* [hereafter *RSCHS*], XXIV (1990–2), 33–51; Lionel K.J. Glassey, 'William II and the Settlement of Religion in Scotland, 1688–1690', *RSCHS*, XXIII (1987–9), 317–29; Tim Harris, *Revolution: The Great Crisis of the British Monarchy, 1685–1720* (2006), ch. 9.

2 *The Register of the Privy Council of Scotland*, 3rd ser., ed. P. Hume Brown, Henry Paton and E. Balfour-Melville (16 vols, Edinburgh, 1908–70) [hereafter *RPC*, 3rd ser.], XIII, 156–8.

national church. On 20–1 July, presbyterian clergy gathered in Edinburgh to agree measures to restore presbyterian worship, and recreate a structure of local, district and national courts.[3] Across Scotland, presbyterian ministers emerged from enforced retirement; others returned from Dutch or Irish exile. In parts of the south, dramatic change was underway, amounting in many parishes to a desertion of episcopalian worship. 'Within a few Weeks', wrote the episcopalian minister John Sage, presbyterian 'Meeting-houses were Erected in many places; especially in the Western Shires … and the Churches were drain'd.'[4] Still more damaging to the established Church were the 'rabblings', forced evictions in the winter of 1688–9 of between 200 and 300 episcopalian ministers from their parishes across southern Scotland. Though the rabblings were led by the most radical presbyterians, more moderate clergy and lay people took advantage of the situation to call for a presbyterian settlement.[5]

The revolutionary processes of 1687–90 – the revival of organized presbyterianism, rabbling and the parliamentary settlement – brought about the end of Scottish episcopacy. But why was government by bishops so vulnerable in the crisis? For generations of presbyterian historians, echoing the near-contemporary accounts by James Kirkton and Robert Wodrow, the answer was simple. Episcopacy's weakness lay in the strong commitment of the Scottish people to presbyterianism. Episcopacy was an alien form of government in Scotland, its abolition an almost inevitable outcome. Crucial to this interpretation was the Claim of Right, adopted by the convention of estates on 11 April 1689. By declaring that 'prelacy and the superiority of any office in the church above presbyters' were 'contrary to the inclinationes of the generality of the people', this document apparently revealed the true balance of support for the alternative forms of Church government.[6]

There are various problems with this argument. First, it is unclear to what extent the convention of estates represented the country at large. There was no national census of religious opinions, and elections to the convention, though more open than recent parliamentary polls, involved only a small male *élite*. Presbyterians and episcopalians made conflicting estimates of the proportion of Scots in each camp; it was clear that presbyterians were in a

[3] Robert Wodrow, *The History of the Sufferings of the Church of Scotland from the Restoration to the Revolution*, ed. Robert Burns (4 vols, Glasgow, 1828–30), IV, 428, 431–3.

[4] [Thomas Morer, John Sage and Alexander Monro], *An Account of the Present Persecution of the Church of Scotland in Several Letters* (1690), p. 11.

[5] Tim Harris, 'The People, the Law, and the Constitution in Scotland and England: A Comparative Approach to the Glorious Revolution', *Journal of British Studies*, XXXVIII (1999), 28–58, at pp. 34–7; Alasdair Raffe, *The Culture of Controversy: Religious Arguments in Scotland, 1660–1714* (Woodbridge, 2012), pp. 219–23.

[6] *Records of the Parliaments of Scotland to 1707*, ed. Keith M. Brown et al. (http://www.rps.ac.uk/) [hereafter *RPS*], 1689/3/108. See e.g. Wodrow, *History*, I, 223.

minority in much of the north and north-east.[7] But a more serious objection to the presbyterian interpretation is that it examined only one side of the problem. Concentrating on opposition to episcopacy, presbyterian historians paid insufficient attention to the Restoration Church itself. In the twentieth century, however, scholars became more interested in the Church's intrinsic strengths and weaknesses.[8] In an influential paper of 1983, Julia Buckroyd argued that government by bishops was compromised by the nobility's anticlericalism, their 'hostility to clerical pretensions of any kind'. Scotland's leaders, she showed, allowed churchmen little influence over the Restoration settlement, episcopal nominations and religious policy. Indeed, the Church had an 'emasculated episcopacy'. As Buckroyd recognized, this was the product of the settlement's erastianism, its subordination of ecclesiastical authority to secular power.[9] Investigating the settlement's theoretical dimensions, Clare Jackson has argued that 'the episcopalian establishment ... adopted a predominantly pragmatic, indifferentist and erastian attitude which ultimately undermined its own chances of survival'.[10]

Buckroyd and Jackson each give part of an explanation for the failure of episcopacy in late seventeenth-century Scotland. Building on their work, this chapter seeks to provide a fuller picture. It examines both the inherent fragility of government by bishops, and the strength of presbyterian objections to the Restoration settlement. It begins by discussing the Restoration settlement and its consequences, including the deprivation of presbyterian ministers and the emergence of nonconformity. It then turns to the Church's institutional and cultural failings. The Church lacked canons and a liturgy; there were no national synods to agree reforms. Influential episcopalians advanced an interpretation of Church government that justified the settlement's erastianism. There was some support for more robust theories of episcopacy, but their advocates were equivocal. More fundamentally, the formation of a distinct episcopalian culture, though it was underway by the time of the Revolution, was slow, hampered by the episcopalians' surprisingly limited engagement with print publication. It is impossible to say whether a stronger Church would have survived the Revolution intact.

7 Thomas Maxwell, 'Presbyterian and Episcopalian in 1688', *RSCHS*, XIII (1957–9), 25–37; Ian B. Cowan, *The Scottish Covenanters, 1660–1688* (1976), pp. 137–9; Derek J. Patrick, 'Unconventional Procedure: Scottish Electoral Politics after the Revolution', in *Parliament and Politics in Scotland, 1567–1707*, ed. Keith M. Brown and Alastair J. Mann (Edinburgh, 2005).

8 John Hunter, *The Diocese and Presbytery of Dunkeld, 1660–1689* (2 vols, [1918]) contains much undigested material; Walter R. Foster, *Bishop and Presbytery: The Church of Scotland, 1661–1688* (1958) is a useful survey.

9 Julia Buckroyd, 'Anti-clericalism in Scotland during the Restoration', in *Church, Politics and Society: Scotland, 1408–1929*, ed. Norman Macdougall (Edinburgh, 1983), quotations at pp. 168, 182.

10 Clare Jackson, *Restoration Scotland, 1660–1690: Royalist Politics, Religion and Ideas* (Woodbridge, 2003), p. 104.

But had the Church's institutional and cultural weaknesses been addressed – as many episcopalians wished – Scotland's Revolution settlement might have taken a different form.

I

The re-establishment of episcopacy was carried out in a manner both provocative and bewildering to many Scots. In August 1660, Charles II sent to the presbytery of Edinburgh a letter which most presbyterians saw as a promise to maintain their form of government. Yet when the first parliament since the Restoration met on 1 January 1661, the king's instructions to his commissioner, the earl of Middleton, contained nothing specific regarding Church government. Leading figures at court were cautious, notably the earl of Lauderdale and, to some extent, the king himself. But Middleton favoured restoring episcopacy as quickly as possible. On 28 March, therefore, parliament approved the Act Rescissory, which annulled all legislation passed since 1633, including all the current statutes in favour of presbyterianism.[11] At this stage, the king could have chosen to introduce new laws to settle presbyterian government. But in the summer, discussions at court persuaded Charles to re-establish episcopacy, a decision announced in a royal letter of 14 August.[12] Candidates were nominated to the Scottish sees, and consecrations began with a ceremony in London on 15 December.[13] On 8 May 1662, parliament restored bishops to 'their episcopall function, presidencie in the church, power of ordination, inflicting of censures and all other acts of church discipline'.[14]

The Church settlement was acceptable to much of the ruling elite, and caused minimal disturbance in northern Scotland, where most ministers and lay people were willing to conform. But the settlement was fiercely opposed by committed presbyterians, especially in the south and south-west. To understand the failure of episcopacy, we need to explain why the Restoration Church could not absorb or accommodate presbyterian ministers and lay

[11] Godfrey Davies and Paul H. Hardacre, 'The Restoration of the Scottish Episcopacy, 1660–1661', *Journal of British Studies*, I: 2 (May 1962), 32–51; Julia Buckroyd, *Church and State in Scotland, 1660–1681* (Edinburgh, 1980), pp. 26–35; Ronald Hutton, *Charles the Second: King of England, Scotland, and Ireland* (Oxford, 1989), pp. 160–2, 496; Gillian H. MacIntosh, *The Scottish Parliament under Charles II, 1660–1685* (Edinburgh, 2007), ch. 1.

[12] George Mackenzie, *Memoirs of the Affairs of Scotland from the Restoration of King Charles II* (Edinburgh, 1821), pp. 52–6; Gilbert Burnet, *Bishop Burnet's History of his own Time*, ed. Martin J. Routh (2nd edn, 6 vols, Oxford, 1833), I, 236–8; *RPC*, 3rd ser., I, 28–9.

[13] *The Diary of Alexander Brodie of Brodie, MDCLII.–MDCLXXX. and of his Son, James Brodie of Brodie, MDCLXXX.–MDCLXXXV.*, ed. David Laing (Spalding Club, 33, 1863), p. 233.

[14] *RPS*, 1662/5/9.

people, many of whom were soon worshipping illegally outwith the Church. These themes are important, partly because historians, following contemporary episcopalians, sometimes emphasize that the Restoration Church retained presbyterian structures and processes of discipline, based on parochial kirk sessions, district-level presbyteries and regional synods. According to the anglican Thomas Morer, the government of the Restoration Church was 'called *Episcopal*, tho' hardly to be discern'd for such, by Travellers who have seen what *Episcopacy* is in other places'.[15] The twentieth-century historian Walter Foster argued that there was a 'greater synthesis' of episcopacy and presbyterianism in the kirk than many scholars were willing to acknowledge.[16] The result, Henry Sefton argues, was an amalgamated ecclesiastical polity 'which worked reasonably well in some parts of the country'.[17]

In terms of ecclesiastical discipline, these judgments are reasonable. But they fail to recognize that committed presbyterians denied the legitimacy of combining bishops with presbyterian structures. The imposition of bishops, presbyterians argued, corrupted a divinely warranted Church polity. A consensus prevailed among presbyterians that, as the influential minister James Wood put it, presbyterianism was 'the ordinance of God, appointed by Jesus Christ, for governing his visible church'.[18] Because of this, presbyterian government was fixed and unalterable, regardless of political and social circumstances. Ecclesiastical polity 'may not be such as Men think fit, nor is it indifferent', explained Gilbert Rule in 1680. The names of the Church's officers were specified by the Bible, which made clear that all had equal authority. 'Christs institution is against Bishops', Rule claimed, and there 'can be no imparity of power' among churchmen.[19] According to presbyterians, then, the restoration of bishops was contrary to divine commands, and subverted true Church government.

Given the presbyterians' objections to episcopacy, the government might have sought to mitigate the offence caused by the restoration of bishops. But the crown's initial policies had the opposite effect. In the early 1670s, Archbishop Robert Leighton of Glasgow argued that the episcopalian settlement had been driven 'by too high and too hot and hasty counsels'. Had episcopacy 'bin either a litle lower modeld at first, or at least … a litle more calmly manag'd, it might likely have attained much better reception and settlement'.[20] Among the more damaging policy decisions, in Leighton's view, was a privy council act passed in Glasgow on 1 October 1662. This

15 [Thomas Morer], *A Short Account of Scotland* (1702), p. 49.

16 Foster, *Bishop and Presbytery*, pp. 170–3, quotation at p. 171.

17 Henry R. Sefton, 'Presbyterianism', in *Scottish Life and Society: A Compendium of Scottish Ethnology: Volume 12: Religion*, ed. Colin MacLean and Kenneth Veitch (Edinburgh, 2006), p. 131.

18 Wodrow, *History*, I, 404.

19 [Gilbert Rule], *A Modest Answer to Dr Stillingfleet's Irenicum* (1680), p. 16[0].

20 H.M.C., *Laing*, I, 392.

put into effect a statute of the previous June, according to which ministers settled in churches since 1649 were to receive a patron's presentation and episcopal collation to their parishes, or face deprivation. The Glasgow Act led to the ejection of over 250 presbyterian ministers, more than a quarter of the national total.[21]

The Glasgow Act converted presbyterian disaffection, which conceivably could have been contained within the Church, into outright nonconformity.[22] After the act, influential presbyterians began to argue that the episcopalian settlement had so corrupted the Church that the laity were obliged to dissent from it and adhere to the deprived presbyterian clergy, some of whom continued to preach. The proponents of nonconformity saw conforming ministers as schismatics, and claimed that many had perjured themselves by acting contrary to the National Covenant (1638) and the Solemn League and Covenant (1643), which presbyterians saw as binding oaths against episcopacy. Moreover, it was argued that new ministers admitted to parishes by the episcopalian authorities had no right to officiate in the Church. Disowning the conforming clergy was not unlawful separation, but rather a necessary duty.[23] In the face of these arguments, leading politicians recognized that the government's actions had made the worst of the situation. Thus in May 1668, the earl of Tweeddale reported that nonconformist conventicles were widespread, the result, he thought, of making the presbyterian ministers 'desperat, and turning all out at one', rather than gradually depriving the disloyal.[24]

The Glasgow Act was not the only government policy that served as a catalyst for presbyterian nonconformity. Another significant problem arose from the nature of the Church's courts. Though the re-established Church had kirk sessions, presbyteries and synods, presbyterians objected that there was no direct continuity between the courts existing at the time of the Restoration and those now functioning. Indeed, the government had ordered the courts not to meet during the months when episcopacy was being settled, before restoring them under the authority of bishops.[25] As a result, there was a period of at least nine months from January to October 1662 in which ecclesiastical discipline did not operate as normal.

The interruption of the church courts' work appalled committed presbyterian clergy. Most of these ministers suffered deprivation as a result of the Glasgow Act anyway, but those who had been settled in their parishes before 1649 faced the dilemma of whether or not to attend the courts. Some

21 *RPC*, 3rd ser., I, 269–70; *RPS*, 1662/5/15; Cowan, *Scottish Covenanters*, pp. 49–55.

22 For a useful summary, see Elizabeth Hannan Hyman, 'A Church Militant: Scotland, 1661–1690', *Sixteenth Century Journal*, XXVI (1995), 49–74.

23 Raffe, *Culture of Controversy*, pp. 182–4.

24 *The Lauderdale Papers*, ed. Osmund Airy (3 vols, Camden Society, new ser., 34, 36, 38, 1884–5), II, 104.

25 *RPC*, 3rd ser., I, 125–6, 130–1, 260–1.

objected that the constitution of the courts had changed under episcopacy. The re-established presbyteries and synods were not allowed to elect their moderators, and their actions were subject to the bishop's veto.[26] But the episcopalian apologist Andrew Honyman urged ministers to overcome their doubts and join with the courts, to avoid schism and co-operate in the exercise of discipline. As Honyman pointed out, such had been the practice of presbyterian ministers after the restoration of episcopacy in the early seventeenth-century Church.[27] This parallel with the situation under James VI was an important argument in favour of conformity, but presbyterians were unconvinced. The eminent minister Robert Douglas admitted that Jacobean presbyterians had continued to recognize the church courts after the restoration of bishops. But the circumstances were now different, he argued. Unlike the policy at the Restoration, there had not been a break in the operation of the early seventeenth-century presbyteries and synods; though they were corrupted by the introduction of episcopacy, they stood in continuity with presbyterian judicatories. Indeed, Douglas apparently advised politicians on this point before they decided to suspend meetings of the courts. 'I told [the politicians] that men would keep [i.e. attend] the [court] meetings because they were standing as they were before the Bishops tyme, but if they did discharge them, I knew no honest minister who would keep them.'[28] The exiled minister Robert McWard saw the reconstitution of the courts as symptomatic of the erastian Church settlement. James VI had superimposed an episcopate on a presbyterian system, McWard argued, but he had not insisted that the authority of the church courts derived from the bishops. By contrast, McWard complained, the policy in 1662 ensured that the courts had a 'precarious dependence on Bishops', whose power in turn rested on an illegitimate royal supremacy.[29]

Another reason to object to the re-established Church was the quality of the conforming clergy. This problem was most acute in the south and south-west, where a majority of the parishes made vacant by the Glasgow Act were located. The Church struggled to find men of high calibre to replace the deprived clergy.[30] According to Gilbert Burnet, to fill the vacancies

26 [John Brown], *An Apologeticall Relation, of the Particular Sufferings of the Faithfull Ministers & Professours of the Church of Scotland* (n.p., 1665), pp. 93–4. Bishop Robert Leighton of Dunblane apparently waived his right to appoint the moderators of presbyteries: *Register of the Diocesan Synod of Dunblane, 1662–1688*, ed. John Wilson (Edinburgh, 1877), p. ix.

27 [Andrew Honyman], *The Seasonable Case of Submission to the Church-government, as now Re-established by Law* (Edinburgh, 1662), pp. 12–13.

28 National Library of Scotland [hereafter N.L.S.], Wod. Qu. LXIII, f. 117v, [Robert Douglas], 'A Brief Narration of the Coming in of Praelacie againe within this Kirk'. See also N.L.S., MS 7024, f. 187r.

29 Robert McWard, *The Case of the Accommodation lately Proposed by the Bishop of Dumblane* (n.p., 1671), pp. 6–8, 9 (quotation), 12.

30 For the wider debate about this, see Raffe, *Culture of Controversy*, ch. 6.

there was 'a sort of an invitation sent over the kingdom, like a hue and cry'. This attracted to the west 'many very worthless persons ... who had little learning, less piety, and no sort of discretion'.[31] Archbishop Leighton was of the same view, writing that the 'filling all places with almost as much precipitancy as was usd in making them empty' was the 'great cause of all the disquiet that hath arisen in these parts'.[32] Tweeddale saw 'scandolaus or at least imprudent' episcopalian ministers as one cause of nonconformity in the west.[33] When in 1670 a commission was sent to examine religious affairs in western counties, locals called for it to investigate the faults of the clergy. The commission lacked the power to remove ministers, but politicians became aware of the most outrageous episcopalians, notably John Jaffray of Maybole in Ayrshire. He had been promoted by Archbishop Alexander Burnet of Glasgow, but had alienated his parishioners by taking legal action over the teinds (tithes) and threatening locals with violence. His parishioners' complaints were so serious that he was removed from the parish.[34]

Because nonconformity was particularly prevalent in the south-west, critics of the Church's failings attacked what they saw as the mismanagement of the diocese of Glasgow. The settling of apparently substandard clergy was one aspect of this, but another problem was that the archbishop consecrated in 1661, Andrew Fairfoul, died in November 1663. The bishopric was vacant over the following winter, and there were concerns that nonconformity was increasingly widespread.[35] In January 1664, the king responded by creating a court of high commission to enforce the laws against dissent.[36] Under Fairfoul's successor, Alexander Burnet, the Glasgow diocese's difficulties with parish vacancies and presbyterian conventicles worsened. Burnet became known for his insensitivity towards presbyterian scruples and his rigid enforcement of clerical discipline. Parish ministers who failed to attend diocesan synods and presbyteries risked being suspended or deposed from their livings. Many of the ministers concerned were committed presbyterians settled in their parishes before 1649 who, as we have seen, objected to the church courts. But it was alleged that Burnet also deposed men who might have been persuaded to attend the courts.[37] The archbishop's inflexibility was counterproductive, his critics believed, because he created more

[31] Burnet, *History*, I, 279 (quotations), 284.

[32] *Lauderdale Papers*, ed. Airy, II, 225.

[33] N.L.S., MS 7024, f. 147v; *Lauderdale Papers*, ed. Airy, II, 103.

[34] N.L.S., MS 7004, ff. 41r., 44r., 48v; 'Thirty-four Letters written to James Sharp', ed. John Dowden, *Miscellany of the Scottish History Society*, I (Scottish History Society, 15, 1893), 267–8; *RPC*, 3rd ser., III, 363–5, 451; Hew Scott, *Fasti Ecclesiae Scoticanae: the Succession of Ministers in the Church of Scotland from the Reformation* (rev. edn, 8 vols, Edinburgh, 1915–50) [hereafter *Fasti*], III, 52.

[35] *Fasti*, VII, 323; N.L.S., MS 2512, f. 25.

[36] Wodrow, *History*, I, 384–6.

[37] N.L.S., MS 7024, f. 161r.

vacant parishes and alienated potential conformists. Among the opponents of Burnet were Tweeddale and Sir Robert Moray, who with Lauderdale had great influence over the crown's policies for a few years after 1666.[38] In 1669, they persuaded the king to remove Burnet from office.[39]

While some nobles criticized the bishops for rigorously exercising ecclesiastical discipline, bishops grumbled that the criminal laws against dissent were inadequately enforced. In the winter of 1665–6, Archbishop James Sharp of St Andrews claimed that it was 'the opinion of many, that if noblemen and gentlemen did what they should and might for obedience to the Lawes, we should meet with litle trouble from the disaffected to the publick settlement'.[40] Archbishop Burnet specialized in this sort of complaint, remarking around the same time that 'we make our laws severe and strict, but punish few or none for transgressing of them'.[41] The duke of Hamilton, who as sheriff of Lanarkshire was a somewhat reluctant enforcer of the laws against dissent, reportedly wished 'that severe acts be not passed when moderate courses are to be pursued'.[42] As in England, local circumstances and national debates led to inconsistent prosecution of dissenters.[43] The distinctly Scottish dimension of this phenomenon, as Buckroyd recognized, was the noblemen's attempts to deny the bishops influence over government policy.

The politicians' disregard for bishops was especially apparent when Lauderdale, Tweeddale and Moray were pre-eminent. The group formulated two new policies, with the aim of reintroducing presbyterian ministers into parishes where dissent was most pronounced and encouraging these ministers to attend the church courts, and thus to participate fully in ecclesiastical discipline. By means of the indulgences of 1669 and 1672, the privy council settled named presbyterian ministers in specified parishes, where they were permitted to exercise their ministry subject to conditions. In 1669, it was decreed that they were not to receive the full stipends belonging to their parishes unless they accepted episcopal collation and attended presbyteries and synods. If they refused to attend the courts, they were to be confined to their parishes. Over 40 ministers accepted the indulgence of 1669, but few if any complied with these requirements, which were not reiterated in 1672.[44]

38 See Maurice Lee, Jr, *'Dearest Brother': Lauderdale, Tweeddale and Scottish Politics, 1660–1674* (Edinburgh, 2010).

39 Julia Buckroyd, 'The Dismissal of Archbishop Alexander Burnet, 1669', *RSCHS*, XVIII (1972–4), 149–55.

40 N.L.S., MS 2512, f. 235v.

41 *Lauderdale Papers*, ed. Airy, II, app., xxxii.

42 N.L.S., MS 3648, f. 10v. See Buckroyd, 'Anti-clericalism', p. 178.

43 See e.g. Anthony Fletcher, 'The Enforcement of the Conventicle Acts, 1664–1679', in *Persecution and Toleration*, ed. W. J. Sheils, Studies in Church History, 21 (Oxford, 1984); Gary S. De Krey, 'Rethinking the Restoration: Dissenting Cases for Conscience, 1667–1672', *H.J.*, XXXVIII (1995), 53–83.

44 *RPC*, 3rd ser., III, 38–40 (but cf. 47), 586–90.

The intervening years had seen the failure of a scheme to accommodate presbyterian clergy in the Church. At meetings with presbyterian ministers in December 1670 and January 1671, the acting archbishop of Glasgow, Robert Leighton, offered to forego his episcopal veto in synods, allowing business to be decided by majority vote. He was also willing that ordinations should in future take place according to the presbyterian pattern: by the presbytery acting collectively, in the specific church to which the new minister was inducted.[45] Accommodation might have integrated the indulged clergy into the Church. Rejecting the policy, the ministers became an anomalous group: they were within the Church, but not in conformity with it; they owed their positions to the privy council, and could not be persuaded to accept episcopacy.

Though the indulgences became a source of divisions among presbyterians, in the short term episcopalian clergy complained that the new policies undermined the Church. Archbishop Sharp objected that he had not been consulted about the indulgence and warned that it would compromise ecclesiastical discipline and the episcopalian clergy's authority.[46] Archbishop Burnet's synod made a formal protest against the indulgence, complaining that it overturned ecclesiastical censures against the presbyterian ministers, while exempting them from the Church's jurisdiction.[47] As well as precipitating Burnet's removal from the archbishopric, the synod's action prompted the Act of Supremacy, passed in November 1669, which made clear that 'the ordering and disposall of the externall government and policie of the church doth propperlie belong to his majestie'.[48]

The Act of Supremacy confirmed the erastian balance of authority in Restoration Scotland. But it could perhaps be argued that the bishops' political weakness resulted mostly from the dominance of Lauderdale. After his fall from power in 1679, there was scope for the bishops to have more influence. In the summer of 1680, Bishop John Paterson of Edinburgh persuaded the king to place restrictions on the new indulgence granted to presbyterians a year earlier.[49] But two developments in the period between Lauderdale's fall and the Revolution further underlined the subordination of the Church to the crown, compromising the authority of the bishops, and that of episcopacy itself. The first was the introduction in 1681 of the Test, a new oath designed to guarantee the exclusion of catholics and presbyterians from public office. All office-holders, including clergy, were required to swear. A

[45] McWard, *Case of the Accommodation*, p. 2; Wodrow, *History*, II, 179–82; Cowan, *Scottish Covenanters*, pp. 76–7, 79.

[46] H.M.C., *Laing*, I, 372; N.L.S., MS 2512, f. 130v.

[47] *Lauderdale Papers*, ed. Airy, II, app., lxv–lxvi.

[48] Buckroyd, 'Dismissal of Archbishop Burnet'; *RPS*, 1669/10/13.

[49] *A Collection of Letters Addressed by Prelates and Individuals of High Rank in Scotland and by two Bishops of Sodor and Man to Sancroft Archbishop of Canterbury*, ed. W.N. Clarke (Edinburgh, 1848), pp. 13, 22–3; *RPC*, 3rd ser., VI, 459–60.

long, complex statement, the Test combined the existing oath of allegiance and declarations against the Covenants with a new engagement to protestant orthodoxy, defined in terms of the 1560 Scots confession of faith.[50] The Test provoked unprecedented discontent among the episcopalian clergy, with much debate centring on the confession.[51] It was objected that some of the confession's articles were 'doubtful, and uncertain at least'.[52] Worse, the highly royalist Test contradicted the confession, which justified resistance to tyrannical government. It appeared that swearers were required to acknowledge principles in one breath, only to abjure them with the next.[53]

The bishops and privy council responded by arguing that swearers were not required to approve all articles of the confession, which was cited merely as an indication of protestant doctrine. Moreover, defenders of the oath insisted that it was simply a test of allegiance to the king.[54] But the most conscientious clergy complained that they were being asked 'blindly' to swear at the government's command.[55] Refusing the oath because of this and other concerns, up to 80 episcopalian ministers lost their livings, among them the eminent Edinburgh professor of divinity Laurence Charteris and many of his former students.[56] The bishops had been forced to defend a contradictory oath, and the Church had lost some of its best clergy. The government's approach had again corroded the credibility of the Church.

After his accession in 1685, James VII's campaign to repeal the penal laws against Roman catholics inflicted still more serious damage on the Church. Prior to the meeting of parliament in April 1686, James secured an undertaking to support repeal from Archbishop Arthur Ross of St Andrews and Bishop Paterson of Edinburgh. After the Revolution, defenders of episcopacy admitted that the two prelates' 'condescension' was 'very much talked of' by their critics.[57] Yet several other bishops argued against repeal. These included the ageing Bishop James Aitken of Galloway, Bishop George Haliburton of Aberdeen, whose synod demanded that he oppose the policy, and Bishop James Ramsay of Ross, who attacked repeal both privately and in a sermon before parliament.[58] But if this opposition enhanced the episcopate's

50 *RPS*, 1681/7/29.

51 See esp. Wodrow, *History*, III, 303–12; [James Steuart?], *The Case of the Earl of Argyle. Or an Exact and Full Account of his Trial, Escape, and Sentence* (n.p., 1683), pp. 26–51.

52 [Steuart?], *Case of Argyle*, p. 33.

53 *Ibid.*, pp. 33, 36, 45–6.

54 *Ibid.*, pp. 26, 27, 42, 49; *Records of the Presbyteries of Inverness and Dingwall, 1643–1688*, ed. William Mackay (Scottish History Society, 24, 1896), p. 346.

55 [Steuart?], *Case of Argyle*, p. 33.

56 Burnet, *History*, II, 314–15.

57 [Morer, Sage and Monro], *Account of the Present Persecution*, p. 9 (quotations); [Alexander Cunningham], *Some Questions Resolved concerning Episcopal and Presbyterian Government in Scotland* (1690), p. 21; cf. [John Gordon], *Plain Dealing: Being a moderate general Review of the Scots Prelatical Clergies Proceedings in the latter Reigns* (1689), p. 15.

58 Wodrow, *History*, IV, 365; Harris, *Revolution*, p. 161.

standing, James's response made the bishops appear as weak as ever. On 3 June 1686, the privy council received a royal letter depriving Andrew Bruce, an opponent of catholic toleration, of the bishopric of Dunkeld.[59] In the following January, James deprived Alexander Cairncross of the archbishopric of Glasgow. No reason was given for this action, but it was seen as a response to the archbishop's handling of James Canaries, minister of Selkirk. In 1686, Cairncross suspended Canaries for anti-catholic preaching, while secretly funding the publication of his offending sermon.[60] The king's treatment of the bishops continued the patterns of earlier anticlerical policy, proving that it was not only Lauderdale and his allies who opposed episcopal autonomy. But as the next section argues, the bishops' weakness was not simply a result of the balance of political authority. It arose also from the institutional and cultural characteristics of the Church.

II

Supporters of the Restoration Church settlement, as we have seen, thought that it revived the religious institutions and practices of the reigns of James VI and Charles I. But these kings' controversial measures – the liturgical reforms of the Five Articles of Perth (1618) and the 1637 Prayer Book, and the canons of 1636 – were tacitly laid aside. This was prudent, given the unpopularity of the Articles, canons and Prayer Book, but it encouraged committed episcopalians to regret what they saw as institutional deficiencies in the Restoration Church. Importantly, the Church was compromised by its lack of agreed ecclesiastical laws or regulations. In the absence of 'Canons to regulat' the clergy, and 'visitations to frighten' them, Gilbert Burnet lamented, many episcopalian ministers were proud and vicious.[61] No canons were adopted after the re-establishment of episcopacy in part because there was no national representative and legislative forum equivalent to the presbyterians' general assembly or the Church of England's convocation. In 1663, indeed, parliament passed an act specifying the constitution of the 'national synod', which was to assemble at royal appointment.[62] This body never met, though in the mid-1660s there were seemingly genuine preparations for it to do so. In October 1664, Charles commissioned the earl of Rothes to represent him in the synod, planned for the following May.[63]

59 John Lauder, *Historical Notices of Scotish Affairs*, ed. David Laing (2 vols, Bannatyne Club, 1848), II, 728; Hunter, *Diocese and Presbytery of Dunkeld*, I, 221–2.

60 Lauder, *Historical Notices*, II, 775–6.

61 Gilbert Burnet, 'A Memorial of Diverse Grievances and Abuses in this Church', ed. H.C. Foxcroft, *Miscellany of the Scottish History Society*, II (Scottish History Society, 44, 1904), 353.

62 *RPS*, 1663/6/39.

63 *RPC*, 3rd ser., I, 608–11.

The bishops gathered in March 1665 to plan for the meeting, 'without which', Archbishop Sharp maintained, 'we cannot have a prospect of an orderly and stable setlement'. At this point, Sharp thought that the synod could not be held before August. Archbishop Burnet was instructed to go to court to discuss the preparations with Lauderdale and the king.[64] In September, Burnet was still in England, where the king had agreed that the synod should meet in the following April.[65] The bishops considered possible canons, doctrinal articles and a liturgy in February and May 1666, but there was no full meeting of the synod. Instead, after the bishops' conference in May, Sharp went to London to speak directly to the king.[66]

There were no further steps towards the adoption of canons or a liturgy at this time, apparently because the king was cautious and the country restless. After Sharp's return home in August, there were rumours of a plan to introduce the English Book of Common Prayer in Scotland.[67] Meanwhile, the second Anglo-Dutch war had crippled the Scottish economy, exacerbating the government's fears of popular discontent.[68] In this context, Charles seems to have told Sharp that the introduction of canons or a prayer book, and possibly even a meeting of the national synod itself, would provoke disorder. At a gathering of leading politicians in August, the earl of Argyll argued that the Church's worship and discipline should be specified by law. Sharp replied that 'he knew it was his Majesties mind when he was at London that it was not a fitte time'. Argyll claimed that the naval victory in the battle of St James's Day (25 July 1666) had changed 'the face of affairs', but no other counsellor was prepared to call for reforms.[69]

Charles was unwilling to hold a national synod, and the Church continued to lack centrally agreed codes of discipline. Gilbert Burnet, perhaps ignorant of the king's reluctance, blamed this deficiency on the bishops.[70] The next attempt to introduce formal ecclesiastical rules came in July 1670, when Tweeddale, Moray, Leighton and the earl of Shaftesbury drafted a list of ecclesiastical measures including the changes to episcopal powers that were

64 N.L.S., MS 2512, ff. 68, 70r. For a longer account of the preparations in 1665 for a national synod, which plausibly emphasizes Sharp's caution and Burnet's forwardness, see John McDonnell Hintermaier, 'Power, Piety, and Polemic in the British Restorations, 1660–70', Princeton University Ph.D., 2004, pp. 211–17.

65 *Lauderdale Papers*, ed. Airy, II, app., xxvi.

66 *Ibid.*, II, app., xxx, xxxiii; Julia Buckroyd, *The Life of James Sharp, Archbishop of St Andrews, 1618–1679: A Political Biography* (Edinburgh, 1987), p. 85; Hintermaier, 'Power, Piety, and Polemic', pp. 384–426.

67 *The Life of Mr Robert Blair, Minister of St Andrews*, ed. Thomas M'Crie (Wodrow Society, 1848), p. 491.

68 Hutton, *Charles the Second*, pp. 224–5.

69 H.M.C., *Laing*, I, 353; B.L., Add. MS 23125, f. 34r.; Hintermaier, 'Power, Piety, and Polemic', pp. 426–32.

70 Burnet, *History*, I, 446; cf. John Cockburn, *A Specimen of Some Free and Impartial Remarks on Public Affairs and Particular Persons* ([1724?]), pp. 37–8.

to be proposed to the presbyterians in negotiations over accommodation. Charles was persuaded to issue an order for the implementation of the reforms, but because he left the matter to Lauderdale's discretion, nothing came of the initiative.[71] A contemporary episcopalian who became aware of the plan described it as a 'plot … to subvert Episcopacy … & to restore pr[e]sbytery under an Erastian Regulation'.[72] But even without the reforms, the Church remained structurally weak.

In 1674, calls from within the Church for a meeting of the national synod drew further attention to the lack of ecclesiastical law. The campaign was organized by Gilbert Burnet, who persuaded a group of Edinburgh clergy to draw up a petition requesting that their bishop lobby for a national synod. Lauderdale, who feared that the synod would be a platform for the government's opponents, reacted to the agitation by suppressing the petition and having its supporters disciplined.[73] The bishops responded more positively. 'Seeing it has been clamoured that there were no authorized rules for ordering the disciplin of this Church', as Archbishop Sharp put it, new canons were drafted and discussed at a meeting of the bishops in July, at which about 20 other ministers were present. There was unanimous support for the proposals, but three or four of the ministers present wanted to have the canons ratified by diocesan synods. The bishops insisted that the canons had first to receive royal approval.[74] James Ramsay, bishop of Dunblane and a supporter of the petitioning campaign, warned Sharp that unless a national synod voted for the canons, critics would see their adoption as an arbitrary reform.[75] In legal terms, the statute of 1663 constituting the national synod, to which Ramsay referred, had on this point been superseded by the 1669 Act of Supremacy.[76] But critics of Lauderdale and the management of the Church continued to complain of the lack of a national synod and the bishops' failure adequately to consult diocesan synods.[77]

Apart from in 1664–5, therefore, the government was unwilling to hold a national synod. In May 1680, indeed, Charles threatened to prosecute episcopalian clergy who would not disassociate themselves from renewed calls for a synod meeting.[78] But the king received the proposed canons

71 Thomas Stephen, *The Life and Times of Archbishop Sharp* (1839), pp. 429–39. Other copies of the royal order are at Bodl., MS Tanner 282, ff. 54–5; National Records of Scotland [hereafter N.R.S.], CH12/12/1364.

72 Bodl., MS Tanner 282, f. 56r.

73 Buckroyd, *Church and State*, pp. 108–13.

74 N.L.S., MS 2512, f. 164r.

75 H.M.C., *Laing*, I, 397–9.

76 *RPS*, 1663/6/39, 1669/10/13.

77 John Rylands U.L., Manchester, Eng. MS 43, f. 59v., 'Englands Looking Glasse Or a short account how the Kingdom of Scotland hath been dealt w[th]all and Managed by D[k] Lauderdale in these last 3 or 4 years'; [Steuart?], *Case of Argyle*, p. 30.

78 *Calendar of State Papers, Domestic Series, January 1st, 1679, to August 31st, 1680*, ed. F.H. Blackburne Daniell (1915), p. 477.

of 1674 favourably, and indicated his readiness to approve them.[79] What became of the canons is unclear: they seem neither to have been submitted to diocesan synods, nor ratified by the crown. In October 1677, the synod of Moray adopted four canons, requiring public prayers for the king and archbishops, twice-yearly sermons against rebellion, and annual administration of communion.[80] These were presumably not the 'rules and constitutions for discipline' approved by Charles,[81] and it is possible that nothing was ultimately done on a national level to regulate the Church's procedures.

Turning to the Church's ideological characteristics, it is clear that the episcopalians' ecclesiology, or theory of Church government, added to episcopacy's weaknesses. Presbyterians, as we have seen, asserted that their system had been founded by Christ and was thus an unalterable characteristic of the Church. But the main episcopalian writers made no equivalent claim for their form of government. Gilbert Burnet, perhaps the leading apologist for the Restoration Church, alleged that no form of ecclesiastical polity had particular divine warrant, and it was thus the king's responsibility to determine the government of the Church. On this interpretation, Charles II had restored bishops because he recognized that episcopacy was the system best suited to preserve monarchy and promote peace. The king's subjects had a duty to obey his laws with respect to Church government.[82] Moreover, episcopalians argued, the Covenants were no longer relevant.[83] These arguments justified the erastianism of the Church settlement, helping to perpetuate the anticlerical policy-making that undermined the bishops' authority.

The erastian interpretation of Church government became dominant because it was generally endorsed in the small number of episcopalian books in the period that seriously engaged with ecclesiology. As we shall see below, it is possible that many of the episcopalians' polemical writings resulted from a coordinated publication strategy. The effect of this campaign, if it existed, was to marginalize alternative defences of episcopacy, either because they were perceived as threatening to royal power, or because they were thought unlikely to convince presbyterian dissenters. There were two stronger episcopalian doctrines. One was that bishops were established by Christ, and

[79] *Calendar of State Papers, Domestic Series, November 1st, 1673, to February 28th, 1675*, ed. F.H. Blackburne Daniell (1904), pp. 317–18; *Calendar of State Papers, Domestic Series, March 1st, 1675, to February 29th, 1676*, ed. F.H. Blackburne Daniell (1907), p. 237. The contents of the canons are unknown, but N.L.S., Wod. Qu. XL, ff. 9–16 may be a copy: see Hintermaier, 'Power, Piety, and Polemic', pp. 566–84.

[80] N.R.S., CH2/271/3, p. 123, synod of Moray minutes, 1668–86.

[81] *Calendar of State Papers, Domestic, 1675–6*, ed. Blackburne Daniell, p. 237.

[82] Jackson, *Restoration Scotland*, pp. 110–13; Gilbert Burnet, *A Vindication of the Authority, Constitution, and Laws of the Church and State of Scotland* (Glasgow, 1673), pp. 298–362, 260–1.

[83] Raffe, *Culture of Controversy*, pp. 68–70.

governed by divine right. The other was that episcopacy had developed in the earliest age of the Church, through the conduct of the apostles, and that its authority derived from this primitive practice. In 1661, one writer claimed that some Scots were 'of perswasion, that Episcopacy is, *jure divino*'. Of all systems of government, he asserted, referring to the two possible arguments, episcopacy 'hath undoubted the best Title to Divine or Apostolical Institution'.[84] In the same year, the synod of Aberdeen addressed parliament, calling for the Church to be settled 'according to the Word of God' and 'the practise of the ancient primitive Church'.[85] Had the Church's leaders chosen to build on this sentiment, an official ecclesiology blending arguments from divine right, apostolic antiquity and monarchical authority might have emerged. In 1662, for example, Archbishop Sharp reportedly declared that the king was 'the originall of the externall exercise of all Church power', and then argued that 'Episcopall precedencie with due subordination of ministers and Clergie Is ane holy and sacred ordinance First willed and designed by God [second] actuat by Jesus C[hrist] and his Apostles [and third] owned without scruple by all Christians in all ages of the Church'.[86]

But Sharp did not publish these views, and other episcopalians seem to have been reluctant publicly to challenge the claim that Church government was indifferent and subject to the crown's determination. In a pamphlet of 1679, the episcopalian minister David Forrester set out much patristic evidence that episcopacy had 'a Divine, or Apostolical warrant at least'. Yet elsewhere in the work he argued that Church government was indifferent, perhaps in the hope of persuading presbyterians to conform.[87] Moreover, stronger episcopalian theories had the potential to question royal power. This was apparent in the controversy over the Test oath, when at least one episcopalian paper referred to episcopacy's divine right.[88] Such advocates of the divine right of episcopacy as Sir John Cunningham of Lambroughton, whom Gilbert Burnet described as 'episcopal beyond most men in Scotland', were probably in a minority.[89] But had conformists been more willing to assert the authority and antiquity of episcopacy, the Church might have been in a stronger position in the Restoration period and, indeed, at the Revolution.

[84] *Brief Resolution of the Present Case*, pp. 13, 16.

[85] *To His Grace His Majesties High Commissioner and the High Court of Parliament, the Humble Address of the Synod of Aberdeen* ([Aberdeen?], 1661), p. [iii].

[86] N.L.S., MS 597, f. 75r., 'The Apologie of M[r] J[ames] S[harp] 1 Cor. 2 :2', 20 Apr. 1662.

[87] [David Forrester], *The Differences of the Time, in Three Dialogues* (Edinburgh, 1679), pp. 115 (quotation), 4–5, 84–6, 128–31.

[88] Wodrow, *History*, III, 307.

[89] Burnet, *History*, I, 436.

The caution of divine-right ecclesiology's supporters was part of a more general problem: the excessively slow emergence of a confident episcopalian culture, distinct from presbyterianism.[90] One way of examining this process is to look at trends in the publication of religious literature. From 1662 to 1688, 247 works in English or Scots were published in Scotland, or in the Netherlands for export to Scotland, which can be classified as 'religious'.[91] Excluded from this list are Bibles, psalters and editions of apocrypha, legislation, royal and other official proclamations, addresses by non-religious corporate bodies, descriptive news reports, funeral elegies and Latin theological works. Because it is often unclear whether London publications relating to Scottish religion were exported to Scotland,[92] and because it is more difficult to identify relevant titles among the vast output of the London press, English editions have not been included in the list. It is true, of course, that London publishers produced several important works sympathetic to Scottish episcopacy.[93] It is possible that the list slightly under-represents the scale of episcopalian publication, though the overall effect is probably small. Of the 247 titles, 127 have been categorized on the basis of their authors, titles or contents as being either 'presbyterian' or 'episcopalian'.[94] The incomplete survival of printed works, the difficulties of defining 'religious' literature and of classifying presbyterian and episcopalian works, mean that these data are approximate.[95] Nevertheless, clear patterns emerge.

First, there were more apologetical and polemical titles promoting presbyterian arguments than there were supporting episcopacy, despite the considerable restrictions placed on publication by presbyterians.[96] Thirty-

90 For a longer perspective on this process, see Alasdair Raffe, 'Presbyterians and Episcopalians: The Formation of Confessional Cultures in Scotland, 1660–1715', *E.H.R.*, CXXV (2010), 570–98.

91 This list was compiled using the English Short Title Catalogue [http://estc.bl.uk/F/?func=file&file_name=login-bl-estc]; and Harry G. Aldis, *A List of Books Printed in Scotland before 1700, including those Printed Furth of the Realm for Scottish Booksellers* (rev. edn, Edinburgh, 1970). On Dutch printing of Scottish works in this period, see Alastair J. Mann, *The Scottish Book Trade, 1500–1720: Print Commerce and Print Control in Early Modern Scotland* (East Linton, 2000), pp. 84–6.

92 But a case of this was [James Gordon], *The Reformed Bishop: Or, XIX Articles* (1679): see Jackson, *Restoration Scotland*, pp. 121–2.

93 E.g. [George Hickes], *Ravillac Redivivus, being a Narrative of the Late Tryal of Mr James Mitchel* (1678); [George Hickes], *The Spirit of Popery speaking out of the Mouths of Phanatical-Protestants, or the Last Speeches of Mr John Kid and Mr John King* (1680). Also significant was John Spottiswoode, *The History of the Church of Scotland* (1655).

94 For a discussion of these definitions, see Raffe, *Culture of Controversy*, p. 34. Here I exclude the five presbyterian papers and testimonies that were published by the government for the purpose of discrediting the dissenters, but include such papers and testimonies that seem to have been published by sympathizers.

95 On these problems, see Mann, *Scottish Book Trade*, pp. 214–16; Ian Green, *Print and Protestantism in Early Modern England* (Oxford, 2000), esp. pp. 173–80.

96 See Mann, *Scottish Book Trade*, ch. 6.

four presbyterian works of a predominantly polemical nature are extant, including one arguing particularly against catholics and another attacking quaker beliefs. Though several important presbyterian apologetics were produced by Dutch printers, many other titles were published in Scotland, including one or both impressions of the two presbyterian polemical works that were printed twice in the period.[97] These pamphlets perhaps reached more readers than other presbyterian polemics, though in the absence of information about print runs, it is unclear how many copies were produced. On the episcopalian side, there were 20 essentially polemical works, of which five were anti-catholic in focus, and three targeted quakers. There were thus 12 books that served principally to criticize or ridicule presbyterians and to defend episcopalian principles; three of these titles were printed twice.[98] Most of the substantial episcopalian works shared common arguments and were written by well-connected clergy, notably Andrew Honyman, archdeacon of St Andrews and later bishop of Orkney,[99] and Gilbert Burnet, who was made professor of divinity at Glasgow in the year of his first polemical publication.[100] Later in the Restoration period, George Hickes, Lauderdale's chaplain, published forceful critiques of presbyterianism.[101] Moreover, David Forrester claimed that he published his *Differences of the Time* (1679) at the request of 'some of Note, both for Authority and Learning'.[102] It seems possible, therefore, that there was a degree of coordination, overseen by the leaders of the Church, in the episcopalians' polemical publishing. But even if this were the case, the relatively small number of episcopalian apologetics was a significant failing on the part of the establishment.

If the presbyterians had an advantage over their opponents in controversial publication, there is a more striking difference with non-polemical titles.[103] Episcopalians published 21 such works, three of which were

97 [Robert McWard], *The Poor Man's Cup of Cold Water* ([Edinburgh?], 1678), Wing M233 (also published in 1681 at Edinburgh: Wing M234); cf. Mann, *Scottish Book Trade*, p. 85; *The Last Speeches of the Two Ministers Mr. John King, and Mr. John Kid* ([Edinburgh], [1680]), Wing K508 (ESTC 006171363, 006138704).

98 *Generall Demands, concerning the late Covenant; Propounded by the Ministers and Professors of Divinity in Aberdene* (Aberdeen, 1662), Wing C4255, C4266 (first published in 1638); [Gilbert Burnet], *A Modest and Free Conference betwixt a Conformist and a Non-Conformist, about the Present Distempers of Scotland* ([Edinburgh?], 1669), Wing B5833, B5834; Burnet, *Vindication of the Authority*, Wing B5938, B5938A.

99 Honyman, *Seasonable Case of Submission*; Andrew Honyman, *A Survey of the Insolent and Infamous Libel, entituled Naphtali* (n.p., 1668); Andrew Honyman, *Survey of Naphtali. Part II* (Edinburgh, 1669).

100 See note 98.

101 Hickes's works were published in London: see note 93.

102 [Forrester], *Differences of the Time*, sig. A2v.

103 This category includes all of the 127 works not classed as 'polemical'.

reprinted.[104] In contrast, 52 presbyterian works that were not predominantly polemical were published from 1662 to 1688. Apart from the scriptures, catechisms and confessions of faith, presbyterian sermons and devotional works were the best-selling religious books in Restoration Scotland. Sixteen of the 52 titles were printed two, three or four times, and four presbyterian works were published in at least five impressions. The most successful author was the former Glasgow minister Andrew Gray, who accounted for three of the top four bestsellers, including the most reprinted work of all, *Great and Precious Promises*, which appeared in nine or ten versions from 1663 to 1686.[105] Nearly as popular were the works of another Glaswegian, James Durham: *The Law Unsealed* was published at least five times, *The Blessednesse of the Death of these that Die in the Lord* four times. Eight other works by Durham were published once or twice.[106]

Importantly, these bestselling presbyterian authors were not the dissenting activists of the Restoration period, but rather deceased worthies who had been prominent in the 1650s. Though Gray and Durham would likely have opposed the Restoration settlement, neither lived to see it. This probably explains why the government did not object to the publication of their books: indeed, the privy council granted 'particular' copyright to the printers of works by Gray, Durham and the presbyterians Hugh Binning and William Guthrie.[107] Yet the prominence of these writers in the religious book trade of Restoration Scotland was surely a reflexion of the episcopalian Church's weakness. The establishment lacked preachers of comparable stature, and its clergy produced relatively few works of popular theology or

104 William Simons, *The True Christians Path Way to Heaven* (Edinburgh, 1665), Wing S3805B, S3806 (this is rather tentatively categorized as 'episcopalian'); *Two Prayers to be Taught unto Children at School* (Edinburgh, 1672), Wing T3528A, T3528B (much of this work was then incorporated in *Morning and Evening Prayers, to be used in Families Daily* (Edinburgh, 1674)); John Menzies, *A Sermon, Preached at the Funeral of Sr. Alexander Fraiser of Doores* (Edinburgh, 1681), Wing M1728 (ESTC 006095617, 006084572).

105 Andrew Gray, *Great and Precious Promises* (Edinburgh, 1663), Wing G1608A, ESTC 006157190, Wing G1607, G1609, G1610, G1610A, G1610B, G1611 (in two versions: ESTC 006161564, 006170140), Wing G1612. The other works were Andrew Gray, *The Mystery of Faith Opened up* (Glasgow, 1668); Andrew Gray, *Directions and Instigations to the Duty of Prayer* (Glasgow, 1669).

106 James Durham, *The Law Unsealed: Or, A Practical Exposition of the Ten Commandments* (Glasgow, 1676), Wing D2817, D2817A, D2818, D2819, D2823; James Durham, *The Blessednesse of the Death of these that Die in the Lord* ([Glasgow], 1681), Wing D2795, D2796, D2796A, D2797; James Durham, *Clavis Cantici: Or, An Exposition of the Song of Solomon* (Edinburgh, 1668); James Durham, *A Commentary upon the Book of the Revelation* (Edinburgh, 1680); James Durham, *The Dying Man's Testament to the Church of Scotland* (Edinburgh, 1680); James Durham, *Christ Crucified* (Edinburgh, 1683); James Durham, *The Unsearchable Riches of Christ* (Glasgow, 1685); James Durham, *The Great Gain of Contending Godliness* (Edinburgh, 1685); James Durham, *Heaven upon Earth* (Edinburgh, 1685); James Durham, *The Great Corruption of Subtile Self* (Edinburgh, 1686).

107 Mann, *Scottish Book Trade*, pp. 244–5.

devotion. The reprinting of anglican titles – most notably works by Richard Allestree – was only a partial compensation for this deficiency.[108]

Conforming clergy made surprisingly little use of print to explain what it meant to be a Scottish episcopalian. Nor was it particularly obvious for lay people in the parish churches. Though conforming ministers accepted an ecclesiology radically different to that of the presbyterians, there was at first little to differentiate the episcopalians in terms of worship and theology. We have seen that the crown was not prepared to let the Church adopt fixed forms of prayer. Only after the Revolution were enthusiasts for liturgical forms able to use them publicly.[109] Thus while at least one synod condemned the Westminster Directory of worship, and the bishops instructed that the lord's prayer and apostles' creed should be read in churches, and the doxology sung, Restoration episcopalians' public worship was scarcely more formal than that of the presbyterians.[110]

There was likewise no immediate shift in the Church's theological tone after the re-establishment of episcopacy. The Act Rescissory of March 1661 cancelled the Westminster confession's statutory authority,[111] but this did not stop the confession and the Westminster catechisms from being reprinted four times in Latin (for educational use) after 1662, and ten times in English.[112] The Scots confession of 1560 was printed a single time (in 1681, presumably during the controversy over the Test oath).[113] The only catechism other than those of the Westminster assembly to be printed more than twice was Thomas Vincent's *Explicatory Catechism*, an elaboration of the assembly's shorter catechism.[114] By the 1680s, the episcopalians' academic theology, and probably that taught in some ministers' sermons, was becoming more Arminian in flavour.[115] Perhaps if the episcopalian Church had lasted a few decades longer, conforming lay people might have been weaned from their

108 [Richard Allestree], *The Whole Duty of Man* (Edinburgh, 1674), Wing A1178A, A1183, A1183A, A1184; [Richard Allestree], *The Ladies Calling* (Edinburgh, 1675), Wing A1143A, A1143B, A1143C. See Raffe, 'Presbyterians and Episcopalians', pp. 582–3.

109 Raffe, 'Presbyterians and Episcopalians', p. 594.

110 *Selections from the Records of the Kirk Session, Presbytery, and Synod of Aberdeen* (Spalding Club, 15, 1846), pp. 262–4; *Register of the Diocesan Synod of Dunblane*, pp. 2, 10, 13, 33, 62.

111 *RPS*, 1661/1/158.

112 *Confessio Fidei in Conventu Theologorum Authoritate Parliamenti Anglicani Indicto, Elaborata* (Edinburgh, 1670), Wing C5740, C5741, C5742, C5743; *The Confession of Faith, and the Larger and Shorter Catechism* (Glasgow, 1669), Wing C5768D, C5769, C5769A, C5770, C5770aA, C5770A, C5770AB, C5771, C5772, C5773.

113 *The Confession of Faith and Doctrine, Beleeved and Professed be the Protestantes of Scotland* (Edinburgh, 1681).

114 Thomas Vincent, *An Explicatory Catechism* (Glasgow, 1674), Wing V433, V433A, V434A, V435, V435A.

115 Raffe, 'Presbyterians and Episcopalians', pp. 583–6.

habitual Calvinism. But the episcopalians' political pragmatism and intellectual compromises prevented them, during the Restoration period, from developing the sort of strong religious culture that had come to characterize the Church of England. The reaction of mid-seventeenth-century English episcopalians to rampant puritanism shaped what would be called anglicanism: episcopacy and the fixed liturgies of the Book of Common Prayer were crucial; Reformed theology lost the hegemony it had enjoyed earlier in the century. In Scotland, where the comparable dimensions of episcopalian culture were in an early stage of development at the Revolution, it was much easier for lay people – and for some episcopalian clergy – to transfer their allegiance to presbyterianism after 1687.

III

The weaknesses of the Restoration Church in Scotland and the strength of presbyterian opposition to bishops were closely entwined. In what ways do these factors explain the failure of Scottish episcopacy? Several decisions made during the re-establishment of episcopacy ensured that the settlement was highly unpalatable for presbyterians. By requiring a majority of clergy to recognize the new bishops or face deprivation, the government brought about the sudden ejection of more than a quarter of Scottish clergy, mostly concentrated in the south. By interrupting and changing the character of the church courts, the crown stimulated further presbyterian objections. Both policies suggest that Scotland's leaders paid insufficient attention to presbyterians' scruples. Drawing on their strong ecclesiological objections to the settlement, deprived ministers soon formulated compelling arguments in favour of nonconformity. This seriously compromised the effectiveness of the established Church, notably in the large diocese of Glasgow. Presbyterians' continuing hostility towards erastianism prevented the indulgences and accommodation scheme from bringing about a more comprehensive Church. Meanwhile, the government refused to allow the national synod to develop, thus denying the Church an administrative and legislative forum and a source of institutional self-confidence.

In spite of these problems, most Scots conformed to the episcopalian Church. No doubt many did so because of obedience, indifference or the government's coercive enforcement of religious uniformity. But some preferred episcopacy to presbyterianism. During the Restoration period, the conforming clergy gained followers who would remain committed to episcopacy after its abolition. Many were in the Highlands and north-east, but there were pockets of strong support in southern and central Scotland.[116] Yet in terms of religious culture, presbyterians had an advantage over the

116 See Raffe, *Culture of Controversy*, esp. chs. 7–8.

episcopalians. The Restoration Church was slow to distance itself from presbyterian theology, worship and piety. Episcopalian clergy published fewer sermons, theological and devotional works than their presbyterian rivals. Though an episcopalian alternative was emerging by the 1680s, therefore, presbyterians dominated the traditional Scottish protestant culture, with its Calvinist theology and extemporary piety. At the Revolution, resurgent presbyterianism seemed more orthodox and sincere – and a better bulwark against popery – than the weak and unreliable Restoration Church. James VII's indulgences, the rabblings and the bishops' political allegiances guaranteed episcopacy's downfall, but its failure was as much cultural as political.

5

Scotland under Charles II and James VII and II: In Search of the British Causes of the Glorious Revolution

TIM HARRIS

One of the most exciting historiographical developments in early Stuart studies over the last couple of decades has been the rise of the 'New British History'. In order to understand the outbreak of the English Civil War in 1642, it has been shown, we must recognize that James I and Charles I ruled over a multiple-kingdom inheritance that was inherently unstable, that the policies they pursued in any one kingdom inevitably had reverberations in the other two (making it extremely difficult to rule all three kingdoms at once in a harmonious way), and that Charles I's inability to manage his problematic multiple-kingdom inheritance effectively played a large part in his downfall. We have also been reminded that Scotland and Ireland revolted against Charles I before England did, and thus that the causes of the English Civil War need to be sought, at least in part, in external and contingent factors, rather than solely within England. As Conrad Russell argued: 'the Civil War is not an enclosed English subject. It cannot be understood in any purely English context'; 'the problem of multiple kingdoms had a major influence on the daily developments of the crisis which led to the English Civil War'.[1] The New British History has proved controversial: Scottish and Irish historians have criticized the anglocentric bias that seemed inherent in Russell's approach, whilst many English historians would question whether England should be de-centred so much in accounts seeking to explain the origins of the English Civil War. Nevertheless, there can be no doubting that the Britannic perspective has proved to be a fruitful stimulus to Civil War scholarship, raising new questions, engendering new debates and generating (as even its sternest critics would concede) valuable interpretative insights.[2]

1 Conrad Russell, *The Fall of the British Monarchies 1637–1642* (Oxford, 1991), p. 525; *idem*, *The Causes of the English Civil War* (Oxford, 1990), p. 28.

2 The pros and cons of the New British History are discussed in *The New British History: Founding a Modern State 1603–1715*, ed. Glenn Burgess (1999).

The value of the three-kingdoms approach for the later-Stuart period, however, is less readily apparent. In the words of one sceptic, although it might allow us to trace 'parallel developments across Britain and Ireland', it 'does not show that Ireland and Scotland were instrumental in bringing about the decisive cause of the Glorious Revolution'.[3] Similarly the authors of one recent survey, whilst broadly sympathetic to the Britannic approach, have nevertheless cautioned that 'it would be implausible to claim that the key political event of the period – the overthrow of James II from December 1688 – was driven by "British" concerns. As at other points in the seventeenth century, the Scots and Irish functioned mainly as awkward adjuncts to a ferocious English drama.'[4] There is a recognizable sense in which the prior revolts in Scotland and Ireland might be said to have *caused* the English Civil War. The Covenanter rebellion of 1638–40 forced Charles I to recall parliament in England in 1640 and subsequently to agree to the passage of an act whereby the Long Parliament could not be dissolved without its own consent, thereby denying Charles the means whereby he would have been able to free himself from a confrontation with parliament. The Irish Rebellion of 1641 prompted the crisis in England over whether parliament or the crown was to control the forces needed to suppress it, thereby dividing the political nation into the two sides that were to go to war in 1642. By contrast, the Glorious Revolution in England of 1688–9 was triggered by William of Orange's decision to invade England from Holland, one he made out of a concern about Louis XIV's aggression towards the Low Countries. Thus it might be suggested that one is better off looking to Holland and France for the causes of the Glorious Revolution, rather than to Scotland and Ireland, and that after James VII and II had been overthrown in England the revolution was simply exported into Scotland and Ireland.

Several large questions, then, confront would-be practitioners of the New British History for the later-Stuart period. Why did Scotland and Ireland not cause the same sort of trouble for Charles II or James VII and II as they had for Charles I, given that these two kingdoms appear at this time to have been intrinsically more unstable than England? Why were there no prior revolts in Scotland or Ireland? And given that there were none, what explanatory force, if any, does the British approach possess for the later-Stuart period? Since two other chapters in this volume deal with Ireland, here my focus will be on Scotland, though Ireland will intrude occasionally into the discussion. This essay will seek to show that political developments in the period from the Restoration to the Glorious Revolution cannot be fully understood in purely an English context and that the need for Charles II and James VII and II to manage multiple kingdoms did have

[3] Julian Hoppit, 'Dutch Comfort', *Times Literary Supplement*, 17 Feb. 2006, p. 14.

[4] George Southcombe and Grant Tapsell, *Restoration Politics, Religion, and Culture: Britain and Ireland, 1660–1714* (Basingstoke, 2010), p. 103.

a major influence on how events came to play themselves out in England. However, our impression of what the New British History can offer has been distorted by the early Stuart historiographical fixation with explaining the causes of the English Civil War. The tendency of early Stuart Revisionist historians to stress that there was no high road to civil war in England and that even in the 1630s England remained most 'unrevolutionary'[5] made it difficult to find compelling internalist explanations for the breakdown that eventually did occur and thus prompted the need to search for contingent and external factors. Yet British History should not just be about the search for the *causes* of great events, and it should certainly not just be about blaming Scotland and Ireland for things going wrong in England. It must also be about providing appropriate contexts for our analysis, without which historical understanding would be incomplete. What is meant by this will become clear as this chapter unfolds.

I

Let us start by briefly considering why there was no Scottish rebellion against the crown in the later-seventeenth century on a par with that which occurred in Scotland in 1638–40. There were, of course, two rebellions in Scotland during the Restoration – the Pentland Hills uprising of 1666 and the Bothwell Bridge rebellion of 1679. Both were rebellions of covenanters, who were bitterly aggrieved at the religious policies pursued in Scotland by their absentee monarch resident in England. However, both were easily contained by the English crown.[6] One obvious question to ask, then, is why was it that the covenanter rebellions of 1666 or 1679 came nowhere near as close to causing the same sorts of problem for the crown as did that of 1638–40.

The answer has many dimensions. Part of the explanation lies in England. Given the greater wealth and resources of England, and its much larger population, Charles I should have been able to defeat the Scots in the two Bishops' Wars of 1639–40. The fact that he could not hints at the fragile state of his regime in England by the end of the 1630s. Charles's refusal to call a parliament in England prior to the first war, and then his failure to obtain funding from the Short Parliament for the second, left him stretched financially, a situation that grew worse as the collection of ship money began to break down and people refused to pay coat and conduct money. There was considerable alienation from the crown in England as a result of the policies Charles I had pursued in England (particularly his

5 Conrad Russell, *Unrevolutionary England, 1603–1642* (1990).

6 I.B. Cowan, *The Scottish Covenanters 1660–88* (1976); Richard L. Greaves, *Enemies under His Feet* (Stanford, CA, 1990), ch, 2, and *Secrets of the Kingdom* (Stanford, CA, 1992), ch. 2.

religious policies) during his personal rule. Shortage of money and lack of public support in turn undermined the government's efforts to recruit an effective army to fight the Scots.[7] Charles II, for all the difficulties he faced during his reign, never got into quite such a desperate situation in England. He managed to maintain a sufficient degree of public support, even during the Exclusion Crisis and especially during the ensuing Tory Reaction, whilst with royal finances being boosted towards the end of his reign by a combination of subsidies from Louis XIV and improved revenues from customs and excise he was even able to avoid having to call parliament again after 1681.[8]

Part of the answer to our question lies in Scotland. Although there were rebellions in Scotland under Charles II, in fact only a minority of Scots rebelled – the more extreme and desperate lower-class presbyterians concentrated in the Scottish south-west. The Scottish *élite* did not lend their support to either Pentland Hills or Bothwell Bridge. The Covenanter Rebellion that began in 1638, by contrast, was a national revolt and *élite*-led. Several factors help explain why the Scottish *élite* was not willing to countenance rebellion under Charles II when they had been under Charles I, including the memory of what had happened in the 1640s and 1650s, which made the *élite* wary of countenancing any active resistance, aware now of where this could lead; a certain disillusionment with presbyterian extremism and clericism after the experiences of the 1640s and 1650s; and an anxiety about the antics of the more radical field conventiclers in Restoration Scotland, especially in the aftermath of the assassination attempts on the archbishop of St Andrews – the first, in 1668, unsuccessful; the second, in 1679, seeing the archbishop brutally stabbed to death in front of his own daughter. Another crucial difference between the covenanter unrest under Charles I and Charles II is the fact that the revolt of 1638 had not been purely about religion. The *élite* had become alienated as a result of Charles I's Revocation scheme of 1625 (which posed a serious threat their economic interests), his high-handed efforts to manage the Scottish parliament in 1633, and his reckless attempt to silence noble discontent by having the opposition peer Lord Balmerino convicted of treason, as well as by his attempt to impose religious reforms on Scotland in 1636–7 without working through either the Scottish General Assembly or the Scottish parliament. A

7 J.S. Morrill, *The Revolt in the Provinces: The People of England and the Tragedies of War, 1630–1648* (1999), ch. 1; Henrik Langelüddecke, '"I Finde all Men and My Officers All Soe Unwilling": The Collection of Ship Money, 1635–1640', *Journal of British Studies*, XLVI (2007), 509–42; Henrik Langelüddecke, 'Preparing for the Scots' Wars, 1638 to 1640', in his 'Secular Policy Enforcement During the Personal Rule of Charles I: The Administrative Work of Parish Officers in the 1630s', Oxford D. Phil (1995), pp. 282–307 (esp. 306); Michael Braddick, *God's Fury, England's Fire: A New History of the English Civil Wars* (2008), chs 2, 3; Clive Holmes, *Why Charles I was Executed?* (2006), ch. 1.

8 Tim Harris, *Restoration; Charles II and His Kingdoms, 1660–1685* (2005), esp. chs 4, 5.

mixture of economic, political and constitutional grievances, alongside class self-interest, growing resentment at absentee monarchy and deep-seated religious grievances explains why the Scottish *élite* were willing to lead the resistance to Charles I after 1638.[9]

Yet if the Scottish *élite* were not willing to countenance rebellion under Charles II, this does not mean that all members of the Scottish *élite* were totally happy with developments during Charles II's reign. The Scottish presbyterians suffered brutal persecution under the Restoration penal code and many landlords sympathized with the plight of their tenants, even doing their bit to shield them from the full rigour of the law, hence why the government issued its infamous Bond in 1674, and again in 1677, making landlords responsible if they failed to stop their tenants from attending conventicles. The landed classes of Scotland's presbyterian south-west bitterly resented this initiative. The duke of Hamilton led resistance to the Bond, encouraging the heritors of Lanarkshire to refuse to comply, setting a precedent for landowners elsewhere to follow. The earl of Cassilis was a leading figure in opposing the government's decision to use the Highland Host to enforce the bond in 1678. Likewise, there was significant opposition from the Scottish political *élite* to the Scottish Test Act of 1681, which required office-holders to testify both their religious conformity and their political loyalty. A number of leading figures refused the Test. One such was the ninth earl of Argyll, who fled to the continent and who was to launch his own, unsuccessful, rebellion in 1685 in an effort to unseat James VII and II. Another was Sir James Dalrymple of Stair, who was to be part of William of Orange's invasion force from Holland in 1688. More members of the Scottish *élite* were to become alienated as a result of James VII and II's policies of 1685–8 – so much so, that very few were to stand by him and attempt to secure Scotland on his behalf in the wake of William's invasion. The alienation of the Scottish *élite*, in other words, clearly was a factor in explaining the success of the Glorious Revolution in both England and Scotland. It is a point to which we shall return.[10]

II

Let us now turn to the question of causes. Although there were no prior revolts in Scotland or Ireland which can be said to have triggered the Glorious Revolution in England, prior revolts in Scotland and Ireland did play a significant role in helping to bring about the restoration of monarchy

9 Allan Macinnes, *Charles I and the Making of the Covenanter Movement* (Edinburgh, 1991); John Stevenson, *The Scottish Revolution 1637–1644: The Triumph of the Covenanters* (Newton Abbot, 1973).
10 Harris, *Restoration*, chs 2, 6; Tim Harris, *Revolution: The Great Crisis of the British Monarchy, 1685–1720* (2006), chs 2, 4, 9.

in England in 1660. In December 1659 a group of army officers in Ireland backed by gentry of old protestant stock, alarmed by the recent dissolution of the Rump in England and the seizure of power by the English army, instigated a coup whereby they seized control of Dublin Castle and other garrisons, purged the army of radicals, and called an Irish parliament to meet in Dublin on 27 February 1660; this parliament in turn then proceeded to call for the restoration of monarchy. As the second earl of Clarendon was later to recall, it was the English in Ireland who 'made the Earliest advances towards his Majestie's Restoration when the 3 Kingdoms were Governed by Usurpers'.[11] It was ultimately the invasion of England in early 1660 by an army from Scotland under the control of George Monck that paved the way for the return of the monarchy: Monck forced the Rump Parliament to dissolve itself and call fresh elections for a 'full and free' parliament, a body which once assembled decided to call back Charles II (as everyone knew it would). Yet according to Anthony Ashley Cooper, the future earl of Shaftesbury, Monck would never have done what he did without knowing that he had the support of the army in Ireland.[12] In short, the Restoration must be seen as a Britannic event – and with Britannic causes.

Moreover, although prior revolts in Scotland and Ireland did not trigger the Glorious Revolution in England, a prior revolution in England did trigger – and indeed necessitate – subsequent revolutions in Scotland and Ireland. It is surely peculiarly anglocentric to insist that three-kingdoms history has merit only if it shows how events in Scotland and Ireland directly caused events in England, but not the other way around. William of Orange certainly made it clear in his invasion manifestos that it was his intention to secure protestant liberties in all three kingdoms.[13] The very fact that a dynastic shift in one kingdom led inevitably to a dynastic shift in the other two (even though in Ireland it required a lengthy war with extensive loss of life to secure it), and that it was the self-professed intention of those who overthrew James VII and II's regime in England to overthrow it also in Scotland and Ireland, surely underscores the explanatory force of a three-kingdoms approach to the Glorious Revolution.

In short, even if we limit ourselves to considerations of direct causation of landmark events such as the Restoration and the Glorious Revolution,

[11] B.L., Add. MS 28,085, f. 217.

[12] W.D. Christie, *A Life of Anthony Ashley Cooper, First Earl of Shaftesbury. 1621–1683* (2 vols, 1871), I, 210. For a full narrative of events in England and Wales, see: Ronald Hutton, *The Restoration: A Political and Religious History of England and Wales, 1658–1667* (Oxford, 1987); Neil H. Keeble, *The Restoration: England in the 1660s* (Oxford, 2002).

[13] *The Declaration of His Highnes William Henry … Prince of Orange, etc. Of the Reasons Inducing him to Appear in Armes in the Kingdome of England* (The Hague, 1688); *The Declaration of His Highness William … Prince of Orange, etc. of the Reasons Inducing Him, To Appear in Armes for Preserving of the Protestant Religion, and for Restoring the Lawes and Liberties of the Ancient Kingdome of Scotland* (The Hague, 1688).

the three-kingdoms approach appears to have much to recommend it. Yet explanatory force for historians does not lie solely in the pursuit of direct causal factors. As Richard Evans has observed, 'historical explanation is not just about finding causes for discrete events… Historians can explain something by putting it into context.'[14] It is thus not necessary to establish that events in Scotland directly *caused* those in England, or vice versa, for a British perspective to be of analytical value. The British perspective can offer insight into why political actors came to understand political developments in the way that they did, even if how they responded as a result had direct causal significance only for the history of their own political nation. Russell appreciated as much in his own work on the outbreak of the Civil War, which was never just about causes. Here we might note, as one example, his well-known contention that 'The Royalist party was an anti-Scottish party before it was a Royalist party.' It was fear of what the Covenanters were up to in Scotland that first persuaded some of those who had been unhappy with the personal rule in England to rally behind Charles I and to oppose the initiatives of John Pym and the political and religious opposition in the Long Parliament. This upsurge of loyalist sentiment in England had little if any discernible impact on Scottish affairs, but of course it was to have an enormous impact on affairs in England.[15]

There is an obvious parallel here with the late-seventeenth century. For example, the English whigs' concern about the threat of popery and arbitrary government during the Exclusion Crisis was informed not just by their anxiety over the prospect of the catholic duke of York inheriting the English throne but also by their perception of what was going on in Ireland and Scotland under Charles II, where the threat of popery and arbitrary government to them did appear very real. In contrast, the tories sought to discredit the English whigs in the eyes of the public by comparing them to radical Scottish presbyterian rebels: both, they alleged, preached resistance theory, advocated popular sovereignty, and sought to undermine the political authority of the crown and the existing establishment in the Church.[16] Hence, of course, why the whigs and the tories called each other tories and whigs in the first place (the party labels started as terms of abuse): tories were Irish catholic cattle thieves, and whigs Scottish presbyterian rebels.[17] In other words, the Scottish and Irish contexts help explain developments in England under Charles II. Indeed, without appreciating these contexts our understanding of the English situation is seriously incomplete, even

14 Richard J. Evans, *In Defence of History* (1997), p. 135.

15 Russell, *Causes*, p. 15.

16 Tim Harris, 'The British Dimension, Religion, and the Shaping of Political Identities during the Reign of Charles II', in *Protestantism and National Identity: Britain and Ireland, c. 1650–c.1850*, ed. Tony Claydon and Ian McBride (Cambridge, 1998), pp. 131–56.

17 Robert Willman, 'The Origins of "Whig" and "Tory" in English Political Language', *H.J.*, XVII (1974), 247–64.

though it is clear that developments in Scotland and Ireland did not *cause* the Exclusion Crisis in England.

We must further recognize that the policies pursued by both Charles II and James VII and II were at times crucially affected by their awareness that they ruled over three kingdoms. The royal brothers often self-consciously pursued Britannic policies, and on occasion sought to play their different kingdoms off against each other in an effort to attain particular desired results (sometimes successfully, at other times less so). For this reason, only an historical analysis that is Britannic in scope can fully explain why things transpired in the ways that they did. It is in this sense that the three-kingdoms perspective carries considerable explanatory force not only contextually but also causally.

Let us take the Restoration ecclesiastical settlement as an example. It is undoubtedly the case that an internal English dynamic alone would suffice to explain the restoration of episcopacy in England. There appears to have been quite widespread support for the return of the bishops after 1660, not just amongst the parliamentary classes but also the nation at large, and the cavalier anglicans who came to dominate the parliament that met in 1661 succeeded in forging an ecclesiastical settlement which was less eirenic and far more intolerant than Charles II had initially intended.[18] Likewise an internal Irish dynamic is sufficient to explain the restoration of an episcopalian Church of Ireland (apart from the fact that under Poynings' Law all Irish legislation had first to be approved by the Privy Council in England). The priority that the protestant political classes in Ireland placed on securing their estates meant that they were willing to compromise with Charles II on the issue of episcopacy, and besides many of the leading Irish protestants appear to have favoured a return to that 'forme of church government and divine worshipp' used under Charles I and James I.[19] However, an internal Scottish dynamic does not so readily explain the restoration of episcopacy north of the border. Episcopacy had much shallower roots in Scotland than it did in either England or Ireland, and although (as mentioned earlier) there was some lay reaction against the excesses of presbyterian clericism at the time of the Restoration, there was clearly nowhere near the same support in Scotland for the return of the bishops as there was in England

[18] R.S. Bosher, *The Making of the Restoration Settlement: The Influence of the Laudians, 1649–1662* (1951); I.M. Green, *The Re-establishment of the Church of England, 1660–1663* (Oxford, 1978); Paul Seaward, *The Cavalier Parliament and the Reconstruction of the Old Regime, 1661–1667* (Cambridge, 1989).

[19] Trinity College Dublin, MS 808, f. 156; J.I. McGuire, 'The Dublin Convention, the Protestant Community and the Emergence of an Ecclesiastical Settlement in 1660', in *Parliament and Community*, ed. Art Cosgrove and J.I. McGuire (Belfast, 1983), pp. 121–46; Aidan Clarke, *Prelude to Restoration in Ireland: The End of the Commonwealth, 1659–1660* (Cambridge, 1999), chs 7, 8; *Calendar of the Ancient Records of Dublin*, ed. John T. Gilbert (16 vols, Dublin, 1889–1913), IV, 185–6.

or Ireland. Bishops were restored in Scotland by royal fiat – by Charles II himself, in part because he loathed the Scottish presbyterians (holding them responsible for what had happened to his father and resenting the fact that they had forced him to sign the covenant in 1650), but also because he wanted the ecclesiastical settlement north of the border to be in line with the respective settlements in England and Ireland. With the Scottish parliament having acknowledged in March 1661 the king's right to settle a frame of Church government that was 'most agreeable to the word of God, most suteable to monarchicall government, and most complying with the publict peace ... of the Kingdome', in August 1661 Charles simply informed his Scottish privy council that he intended to restore 'government by bishops, as it was by law before the late troubles', in order to promote 'its better harmony with the government of the churches of England and Ireland'. It was not until the late spring of 1662 that a legislative package was enacted formally re-establishing episcopacy.[20]

Charles II's decision to opt for an episcopalian settlement in Scotland, backed up – as it was soon to be – by a fierce penal code striking at presbyterian dissent, proved highly contentious and was the source of many of the problems that were to bedevil Scottish politics after the Restoration. Legislation enacted in 1662–3 obliged all university teachers and ministers to comply with the Church under episcopacy or face deprivation (about a third of the established ministry in the Church were driven out as a result), declared private meetings and house conventicles illegal, required anyone who held office under the crown to sign a declaration renouncing the covenant, and laid down stiff fines for those who withdrew themselves from church.[21] The government's decision to send troops to the presbyterian heartland of the south-west to suppress conventicling activity and collect fines from those who refused to come to church further exacerbated the problem, eventually prompting the Pentland Hills rebellion of 1666. Although a couple of attempts were made to 'indulge' moderate presbyterians in the late 1660s and early 1670s, the more radical presbyterians – and especially those who met in field conventicles – were targeted with increasingly brutal legislation. In 1670 deprived ministers who continued to hold meetings were to be imprisoned until they posted bonds for their good behaviour or else agreed to leave the kingdom and never return; those

20 *The Records of the Parliaments of Scotland to 1707* [hereafter *RPS*], ed. K.M. Brown et al. (St Andrews, 2007–2012), 1661/1/159, 1662/5/4, 1662/5/9; *The Register of the Privy Council of Scotland. Third Series, 1661–1691* [hereafter *RPCS*], ed. P.H. Brown et al. (16 vols, Edinburgh, 1908–70), 1661–4, pp. 28–9, 30–2; Robert Wodrow, *History of the Sufferings of the Church of Scotland, from the Restauration to the Revolution* (2 vols, Edinburgh, 1721–2), I, 96–8, 115; Robert Steele, *A Bibliography of Royal Proclamations of the Tudor and Stuart Sovereigns and of others Published under Authority 1485–1714* (3 vols in 2, New York, 1967), III, no. 2210.

21 *RPS*, 1662/5/20, 1662/5/21, 1662/5/70, 1663/6/19.

who attended conventicles were to be subject to a sliding scale of fines (with those who owned the houses where the conventicles were held being subject to double the fine); and any unlicensed minister who preached at a field conventicle was to be sentenced to death.[22] The turning of the screws from the mid-1670s, with the imposition of the Bond of 1674 and 1677, the government's decision to send a Highland Host to the Scottish south-west in early 1678 to enforce the Bond, and the increasingly severe policing of field conventicles, prompted discontented and oppressed elements in the south-west to rise again in rebellion in 1679. The final years of Charles II's reign brought even harsher measures against presbyterian dissent, including the royal government's decision to allow military commissions to try summarily and execute radical covenanters in the field, resulting in some 100 such covenanters being executed during what is known to Scottish history as 'the killing times'. In 1685, at the beginning of James VII and II's reign, the Scottish parliament made it treason either to write or speak in defence of the covenants and made it a capital offence either to preach at a house conventicle or merely to be present at a field conventicle.[23]

The attempt to enforce episcopacy on the Scots, then, came at a huge cost, both politically and in terms of human suffering. It also ultimately proved unworkable, and when the Scottish whigs and presbyterians found themselves in a position of political dominance in the Scottish Convention that met in the early months of 1689, in the wake of James VII and II's flight to France, they moved quickly to overturn episcopacy and subsequently restored a presbyterian polity in the Church. And all of this seemingly deriving from Charles II's initial desire to keep the Church of Scotland in 'better harmony with the government of the churches of England and Ireland'. It would be wrong, of course, to imply that the religious problems in Scotland stemmed solely from the decision Charles II took in August 1661. To understand why religious peace proved so elusive in Scotland requires a detailed examination of Scottish affairs and the Scottish context. Yet it seems clear that Charles II felt that he could not act in Scotland without regard for England and Ireland. His policy for one kingdom was shaped, at least in part, by his own awareness of the implications of the fact that he ruled three kingdoms at the same time. It is conceivable that if Charles II had been king of Scotland alone, and not also king of England and Ireland, he might have acted differently in Scotland; he certainly would have been freer to have done so had he so desired. Yet that is not really the point. History is about explaining what did happen given contemporary realities, not about what might have happened had the contemporary realities been different. Charles II's situation was such that he could not act other than as

22 *RPS*, 1670/7/11.

23 *RPS*, 1685/4/22, 1685/4/28; Harris, *Restoration*, pp. 104–29, 329–76; *idem*, *Revolution*, pp. 69–70.

a king who simultaneously ruled three kingdoms of very different political and religious complexions, a historical reality that was never lost on him and which oftentimes shaped the courses of action he chose to take.

III

Let us now explore in a little more detail two particular occasions when the later Stuarts sought to play the British card in politics, in order to illustrate the ways in which developments in Scotland did have a significant impact on affairs in England. The first relates to the Exclusion Crisis and how Charles II successfully used Scotland to help defeat the Exclusionist movement in England. The second concerns the attempt by James VII and II to establish toleration for catholics in Scotland and England, and how in the summer of 1686 he tried but failed to exploit the greater control the crown enjoyed over the Scottish parliament to bring pressure to bear on the English parliament to grant catholics relief. The two are related because James VII and II's decision to try to play Scotland off against England was shaped by his awareness of his brother's previous success in doing so. Yet the fact that James's attempt to play the British card backfired forced him into a change of strategy, thus directly affecting the course of history not just in Scotland but also in England. It led him into a course of action that was to result in the alienation of considerable sections of the political classes and the general public in both kingdoms, an alienation which in turn was to prove a crucial factor in explaining why James VII and II's regime was to crumble so easily in the wake of William of Orange's invasion. In short, James's failure in Scotland in 1686 is a vital part of the explanation of why he was ultimately to fail in England.

The reason why both Charles II and James VII and II thought they might be able to play Scotland off against England was because they believed the authority of the crown was stronger in Scotland than in England and that the Scottish parliament was potentially more susceptible to royal influence. In England, parliament had shown that it could prove a significant restraint on the crown's independence, given its control over the purse strings and the fact that any royal initiatives had to be approved by both a House of Commons and a House of Lords, neither of which was particularly easy to control. Although the crown's interest amongst the unelected peers and the bishops who sat in the upper house could provide a safeguard against legislative initiatives pursued by the opposition in the elected lower chamber (note the Lords defeat of the Commons' Exclusion Bill in November 1680),[24] it was also the case that the upper chamber could prove

24 Richard Ashcraft, *Revolutionary Politics and Locke's 'Two Treatises of Government* (Princeton, NJ, 1986), pp. 289–90.

a check on policies promoted by the government interest in the lower house (note the Lords' defeat of Danby's Test Bill of 1675).[25] The Scottish parliament, by contrast, was a unicameral body, where the clergy, hereditary lords, shire representatives and burgesses all sat together. The electorate was small, even in the counties, where the vote was vested in tenants-in-chief holding lands with an annual value of 40 shillings: the average number of voters in shire elections in the Restoration period may have been as low as 16. In the burghs the electorate typically comprised members of the town council. Thus not only were elections easier for the government to influence (through bringing pressure to bear on the landed *élite* or interfering with burgh elections), but those elected members of the Scottish parliament did not feel the same dependency upon (or obligation to) those whom they represented as did M.P.s in England. Furthermore, legislative initiatives in Scotland were controlled by a select steering committee known as the Lords of the Articles, comprising eight bishops, eight nobles, eight shire and eight burgh commissioners, and eight privy councillors. The bench of bishops chose the nobles who were to serve, who in turn chose the bishops, and the elected bishops and nobles then chose the burgh and shire representatives: since bishops were royal appointees, this effectively gave the king control over the composition of the articles. It would be wrong to imply that the seventeenth-century Scottish parliament was merely a rubber stamp; recent scholarship has shown that it was nowhere near as easy for the king to control as was once thought, something which James VII and II found out to his cost. Nevertheless, the Stuarts certainly seemed to believe that was easier to manage the Scottish parliament than its English counterpart, and that the odds were tipped in its favour when it came to getting the legislation it wanted enacted.[26]

Having two very different types of parliament in the two kingdoms afforded the crown certain tactical advantages, as was made clear to Charles II in 1669–70 when the possibility of a political union between England and Scotland was briefly under consideration. The staunchest royalists in Scotland vehemently opposed the idea, insisting that 'whilst the Kingdoms stood divided' and 'his Majesty had two parliaments … one might always be exemplary to the other', and they 'might, by loyal emulation, excite one another to an entire obedience'; alternatively, 'if either should invade the royal prerogative, or oppose unjustly their Prince's just

[25] K.H.D. Haley, *The First Earl of Shaftesbury* (Oxford, 1968), ch. 18; Mark Goldie, 'Danby, the Bishops and the Whigs', in *The Politics of Religion in Restoration England*, ed. Tim Harris, Paul Seaward and Mark Goldie (Oxford, 1990), pp. 82–3.

[26] Harris, *Restoration*, pp. 23–5. For works that emphasize that the Scottish parliament was not as easy to control as once thought, see *The History of the Scottish Parliament Volume 2: Parliament and Politics in Scotland 1567–1707*, ed. Keith M. Brown and Alastair J. Mann (Edinburgh, 2005); Gillian H. MacIntosh, *The Scottish Parliament under Charles II, 1660–1685* (Edinburgh, 2007).

commands', then 'one might prove a curb to the other's insolence.' It would be foolish for the king, they felt, to 'extinguish a Kingdom' which could prove 'so serviceable to him', and where he had 'more influence upon our Parliaments than in England'.[27]

Charles II came to appreciate how serviceable the Scottish parliament could be to him during the Exclusion Crisis. It was a central argument of the English opponents of Exclusion that if the whigs forced an Exclusion Bill through the English parliament, neither the Scots nor the Irish would accept it and thus war between the three kingdoms would likely result.[28] Whig M.P.s were of course quick to deny such a doomsday scenario; it became one party's prediction against another's. Hence why the government decided it needed to show the English, quite unequivocally, that Scotland would not accept Exclusion. Following the dissolution of the Oxford Parliament at the end of March 1681, Charles II opted to call a parliament to meet in Edinburgh that summer, as part of his strategy for neutralizing the Exclusionist challenge.

This was not the first time the Stuarts had tried such a tactic. In between the two sessions of the English Parliament of 1621, James VI and I convened a parliament to meet in Scotland in the hope that the Scots, by doing their best to help financially, 'may giue an exemple to [their] neighboures of grater wealthe, to doe the lyke in ther dew proportione'.[29] In similar fashion, albeit with a different kingdom, Charles I decided to call a parliament first in Ireland in 1640, prior to the meeting of what became known as the Short Parliament in England, in the hope that taxes raised in Ireland would decrease his dependence on the English parliament and that an appropriate show of loyalty from the Irish parliament might cajole the English into compliance with the king's demands.[30] On neither occasion did the ploy prove successful. This did not mean that it could not succeed, in a different context. The idea of calling a parliament in Scotland in 1681 appears to have originated within Scotland: it was purportedly some of the 'chief men' of that kingdom who convinced Charles that 'the loyal disposition of the greatest part of the [Scottish] nobilitie and Gentrie' would 'make

27 Sir George Mackenzie, *Memoirs of the Affairs of Scotland from the Restoration* (Edinburgh, 1821), pp. 138–9.

28 Anchitell Grey, *Debates of the House of Commons, from the Year 1667 to the Year 1694* (10 vols, 1763), VII, 248, 408; *The Parliamentary History of England from the earliest Period to the Year 1803*, ed. William Cobbett (36 vols, 1806–20), IV, 1185–6.

29 *The Historical Works of Sir James Balfour*, ed. J. Haig (4 vols, Edinburgh, 1825), II, 89–90; Julian Goodare, 'The Scottish Parliament of 1621', *H.J.*, XXXVIII (1995), 31–2. The idea had first been suggested by the English privy councillor Edward Lord Wotton in September 1615: *The Letters and the Life of Francis Bacon*, ed. James Spedding (5 vols, 1861–9), V, 201; *The House of Commons, 1604–1629*, ed. Andrew Thrush (5 vols, Cambridge, 2010), I, 399–400.

30 B.L., Add. MS 11,045, f. 82r. For the Irish Parliament of 1640, see Michael Perceval-Maxwell, *The Outbreak of the Irish Rebellion of 1641* (Montreal, 1994), ch. 3.

a Parliament not only contribute to the quiet and advantage of Scotland, but by running counter to that of England, be a check and bar to such violent proceedings as hitherto distracted that Nation'.[31] As one Edinburgh newswriter put it, a parliament was 'to be called in Scotland' so that 'by their good example' they might 'mother the English to a better compliance with the counsel'.[32] The crucial difference between 1621 or 1640 and 1681 was that on the last occasion Charles II was able to avoid having to meet a parliament again in England. His calling a parliament in Scotland therefore was not part of a strategy for influencing the parliament in England; rather, it was part of a strategy for neutralizing the Exclusionist challenge, which involved both trying to sway opinion in England (convincing the English that Exclusion would be unworkable) *and* denying the English whigs a forum through which they could continue to bring pressure on the crown to change the succession.

The Scottish parliament met at Edinburgh on 28 July 1681. The duke of York served as high commissioner and Charles gave his brother specific instructions not to let any business be transacted that had not passed through the Lords of the Articles. Although not everything went smoothly for the government, the crown did succeed in getting the parliament to pass a Succession Act on 13 August, asserting that kings of Scotland derived 'their royall power from God Almightie alone' and that upon the death of the monarch, the right and administration of the government devolved immediately upon 'the nixt immediat and laufull heir, either male or female', irrespective of religion. Not only did the act stipulate that parliament could not 'alter or divert the right of succession and lineal descent of the croun', it even made it high treason for any subject to endeavour to alter the succession or debar 'the nixt laufull successor'. The measure was intended both to ensure York's succession to the Scottish crown and to make it impossible to contemplate excluding him in England, unless the king's subjects wanted to expose themselves, as the act put it, 'to all the fatall and dreadfull consequences of a civil war'. To make sure the English got the point, what the Scottish parliament had done was reported in the *London Gazette* and the Succession Act duly published in London.[33] The 1681 Parliament also passed a Test Act requiring all public officials, including those who sat in parliament, to swear unconditional loyalty to the king, 'his heirs and laufull successors', to renounce resistance, and to promise to uphold 'the true protestant religion'.[34]

The fact that the duke of York had presided over the Scottish parliament of 1681 meant that he was fully aware of how the Scottish parliament might

31 *The Life of James II*, ed. J.S. Clarke (2 vols, 1816), I, 683.

32 National Library of Scotland, Wod. MSS Qu. XXX, f. 94.

33 *RPS*, 1681/7/18; *An Act Acknowledging and Asserting the Right of Succession to the Imperial Crown of Scotland* (1681); *London Gazette*, no. 1644, 18–22 Aug. 1681.

34 *RPS*, 1681/7/29.

be used to mother the English into 'a better compliance'. As he put it in a letter written from Scotland in September 1681 to the duke of Ormonde in Ireland, he hoped that 'what has been done here' might 'encourage people there [in England]'.[35] And the swing of public opinion in England in favour of the hereditary succession during the final years of Charles II's seemed to confirm the impression that the English had been encouraged in their loyalty. Hence upon his accession in 1685 James decided that his Scottish parliament should meet before the English one, so that its 'loyalty' could serve as 'a good example' for English M.P.s to emulate.[36] The Scottish parliament proved true to its trust. On 28 April it passed a remarkable Excise Act, permanently annexing the excise to the crown for all time coming, and also proclaiming in its preamble that 'by the first and fundamental Law of our Monarchy' Scottish kings were invested with 'Sacred, Supreme, Absolute Power and Authority'.[37] It must be noted that at the beginning of the session James also agreed to the passage of an act ratifying all laws in favour of the established religion, in order to alleviate any concerns members might have had about a catholic king.[38] Yet it certainly did the trick, since this parliament proceeded to give James all he asked for: money, to meet the threat of the earl of Argyll's rebellion, and a series of savage measures against the Scottish presbyterians.[39]

Despite the fact that the parliament which met in England in May 1685 was an overwhelmingly tory body (only 57 of the 513 available seats went to known whigs), James found that English M.P.s were not as eager to emulate the loyalty of the Scots as he had hoped. Even in its opening session, the Commons agreed to address the king asking for a strict enforcement of the laws against all dissenters from the Church of England (catholic as well as protestant), although in the face of royal displeasure MPs eventually backed down. However, when James boldly announced at the opening of the second session in November that he had given dispensations to catholics to enable them to hold commissions in the army in violation of the English Test Act, both houses took exception. Furious, James decided to prorogue parliament on 20 November, before even obtaining a grant of taxation.[40]

35 Bodl., MS Eng. c. 5237, f. 21.

36 Sir John Lauder of Fountainhall, *The Decisions of the Lords of Council and Session from June 6th, 1678, to July 30th, 1713* (2 vols, Edinburgh, 1759–61), I, 342; *Life of James II*, II, 13–14.

37 *RPS*, 1685/4/16.

38 *RPS*, 1685/4/15.

39 *RPS*, 1685/4/16, 21, 22, 23, 28, 33.

40 *Parl. Hist.*, IV, 1357–8, 1367–88; *L.J.*, XIV, 73–4, 85; Grey, *Debates*, VIII, 353–72; Bodl., Eng. hist. d. 210, pp. 1–9; *The Entring Book of Roger Morrice 1677–1691*, ed. Mark Goldie, John Spurr, Tim Harris, Stephen Taylor, Mark Knights and Jason McElligott, with the assistance of Francis Henderson (7 vols, 2007–9), III, 54–64; *The Several Debates of the House of Commons Pro and Contra Relating to the Establishment of the Militia* (1689).

James therefore had to rethink his next step. Although he had been able to help catholics evade the provisions of the penal laws by issuing them dispensations by dint of the royal prerogative, without as yet a catholic heir to the throne he needed to achieve some degree of formal toleration if anything he did to help his co-religionists were to stand a chance of surviving his reign. Following the difficulties he had encountered with the English parliament in November, he decided his best bet now lay in pushing for catholic toleration first in Scotland, in the belief that the Scottish parliament would 'cast England a good copie and example', as they 'had done in 1681, in declaring the right of succession'.[41] James had every reason to feel confident, given the loyalty the Scottish parliament had demonstrated the previous year (since the parliament had been prorogued, not dissolved, he would be dealing with the same body of men), and given the government's control of the composition of the Lords of the Articles.[42]

Leaving nothing to chance, the government engaged in a public relations campaign to explain why James wanted catholic toleration, seeking to get the message across through a combination of personal communication, public sermons and printed propaganda. Those who defended the proposed toleration emphasized that the king's desire to help the catholics stemmed merely from the fatherly care he had for the concerns of all this subjects; at the same time they warned Scottish M.P.s that the king could grant catholics toleration without parliament, if he so desired, by dint of the powers he enjoyed under the terms of the Scottish Supremacy Act of 1669, implying that it would be a mistake not to cooperate.[43] The government also tried to make sure that nothing was published 'against the King's favourite design'.[44] Nevertheless, a number of works critical of the proposed toleration did circulate in manuscript. These took the line that although James, as 'our supreme Ruler', might not be tied to the laws, his subjects nevertheless were, and M.P.s were not free to support catholic relief because in doing so they would be in violation of the Test Oath of 1681, a measure which had indeed been ratified by James himself at the beginning of his reign when

[41] Sir John Lauder of Fountainhall, *Historical Observes of Memorable Occurrents in Church and State from October 1680 to April 1686*, ed. David Laing and A. Urquhart (Edinburgh, 1840), p. 234.

[42] Sir John Lauder of Fountainhall, *Historical Notices of Scotish [sic] Affairs*, ed. David Laing (2 vols, Edinburgh, 1848), II, 712, 736. The 1686 session is discussed from a different perspective by Alastair J. Mann, 'James VII, King of the Articles: Political Management and Parliamentary Failure', in *Parliament and Politics in Scotland*, ed. Brown and Mann, pp. 184–207.

[43] Wodrow, *Sufferings*, II, 594; 'Reasons for Abrogating the Penal Statutes', in Wodrow, *Sufferings*, II, Appendix II, pp. 163–7; Thomas Burnet, *Theses Philosophicae* (Aberdeen, 1686); Fountainhall, *Decisions*, I, 415–16.

[44] Wodrow, *Sufferings*, II, 594.

he had agreed to the passage of an act in 1685 'confirming all Laws for the protestant Religion'.[45]

James formally asked his Scottish parliament to grant catholics toleration in a letter read to the assembly on 29 April, promising free trade with England and a full indemnity for all crimes committed against the crown in return. He chose the earl of Moray, a recent catholic convert, as his high commissioner to push through the royal agenda.[46] Yet parliament proved not to be in a compliant mood. A motion was made to prevent anyone who had not taken the Test from sitting in the house, and Moray was only able to prevent a vote by threatening to have anyone who supported it arrested.[47] In reply to the king's letter, parliament promised to go to 'as great lengths' in helping the catholics as 'conscience will allow', presuming that James would also 'be carefull to secure the protestant religion established by law', though some were heard to observe in private that 'they had fully examined the case, and found they could goe no lenth at all'.[48] After much heated debate, the Lords of the Articles eventually agreed, by a vote of 18 to 14, to a draft bill granting catholics immunity from prosecution under the penal laws provided they met certain conditions. The proposed bill, however, was so unfavourably worded that Moray refused to accept it: it merely provided that catholics should not incur punishment 'for the Exercise of their Religion in their private Houses', but it did not allow catholics to worship in public and it further affirmed that 'this Immunity' should in no way 'infringe... the Laws and Acts of Parliament made against Popery, or in favour of the protestant Religion', including the Test Act.[49] In effect, the proposed measure confirmed that all catholics who had been given public office by James – including those in the highest level of the Scottish government – were in violation of the law. When the king suggested modifications, these were deemed unacceptable.[50] A frustrated James prorogued parliament on 15 June, astonished 'that considering the former good disposition of the

45 Wodrow, *History*, II, App. nos. 117, 119 and 120, pp. 161–3, 168–77; H.M.C., *Earl of Mar*, p. 217.

46 *His Majesties Most Gracious Letter to the Parliament of Scotland* (Edinburgh, 1686), quote on p. 2; *RPS*, 1686/4/6.

47 *Entring Book of Roger Morrice 1677–1691*, III, 127.

48 James II, *His Majesties Most Gracious Letter* (Edinburgh, 1686), p. 4; *RPS*, 1686/4/11; Fountainhall, *Historical Notices*, II, 721; *The Flemings in Oxford, Being Documents Selected from the Rydal Papers in Illustration of the Lives and Ways of Oxford Men 1650–1700*, ed. John Richard Magrath (3 vols, Oxford Historical Society, Oxford, 1904–24), II, 158–9.

49 Wodrow, *History*, II, App. no. 116, pp. 160–1; *Entring Book of Roger Morrice*, III, 143; H.M.C., *Laing*, I, 446–7.

50 *Entring Book of Roger Morrice*, III, 139; Narcissus Luttrell, *A Brief Historical Relation of State Affairs from September, 1678, to April, 1714* (6 vols, Oxford, 1857), I, 378, 381; H.M.C., *Hamilton*, p. 173; H.M.C., *Earl of Mar*, pp. 218–19; *C.S.P.D., 1686–7*, nos 619, 620, pp. 151–2; James King Hewison, *The Covenanters: A History of the Church of Scotland from the Reformation to the Revolution* (2 vols, 1908), II, 498–9.

Scotch Nobility and Gentry, they should demur to so modest a request'.[51] What had gone wrong?

There was a spectrum of opinion in parliament over the repeal of the penal statutes. Some maintained that parliament should simply acquiesce in whatever the king demanded: in a sermon preached before parliament on its opening day Bishop Paterson of Edinburgh, for example, informed members it was 'their duty' to comply.[52] Others, who 'were for pleasing the Court', were far from endorsing the logic of the crown's position, proposing that the indulgence should last only during the king's lifetime and maintaining that they could safely yield to the king's demands because 'a protestant successor would rescind all'.[53] On the sub-committee of the Lords of the Articles set up to draft the toleration bill, Sir George Lockhart moved not only that catholics should be allowed the freedom to worship only in their private houses and should continue to be barred from public office but also that any who took office should be deemed guilty of treason.[54] A significant number of members – including key lay episcopalians and 11 of the 14 bishops – opposed any measure of relief for catholics, even with the limitations which the bill provided, believing it to be a violation of the Test.[55]

The failure to get catholic relief through the Scottish parliament proved a serious blow to the crown. As one pro-government newsletter writer reported on 3 June, 'The affaires of Scotland have not succeeded as was wished and hop'd at Court.'[56] James himself confessed to the French ambassador that 'the affairs of Scotland had not taken the turn he at first expected'.[57] Instead of casting England 'a good copie and example', it had cast a very bad copy and example indeed. There was no logic now in reconvening the English parliament, until James had achieved what he wanted through other means. In fact, the English parliament was never to be reconvened; it was finally dissolved on 2 July 1687.

If James had succeeded in getting catholic toleration through the Scottish parliament in 1686, the subsequent history of the reign – not just in Scotland but also in England – would have been different. Failure meant that he was left with little option but to pursue catholic relief through his royal prerogative. Again he began with Scotland. Not least, there was the

51 *Life of James II*, II, 68.

52 *Entring Book of Roger Morrice*, III, 122.

53 Fountainhall, *Decisions*, I, 416.

54 *Entring Book of Roger Morrice*, III, 131, 139; Fountainhall, *Decisions*, I, 415.

55 *Entring Book of Roger Morrice*, III, 118, 122, 124; H.M.C., *Hamilton*, p. 173; Fountainhall, *Decisions*, I, 415; Fountainhall, *Historical Notices*, II, 726, 735; Rait, *Parliament of Scotland*, pp. 93, 306; Hewison, *Covenanters*, II, 498.

56 Folger Shakespeare Library, V. b. 287, no. 18. Cf. *Entring Book of Roger Morrice*, III, 221.

57 Sir John Dalrymple, *Memoirs of Great Britain and Ireland … A New Edition, in Three Volumes; With Appendices Complete* (1790), II, 'Part I. Continued, Appendix to Books II and IV', pp. 109–10.

need for a face-saving exercise, given that the Scottish parliament had already confirmed by statute that the king of Scotland was absolute and given that the government's line all along had been that the king could grant catholic toleration in Scotland by dint of his prerogative alone if he so wanted. On 21 August James therefore wrote to his Scottish council informing them that he had decided to grant catholics the freedom to exercise their religion in private, indemnifying them against all the penal laws, although he had to undertake a purge of the council to ensure that it would agree to his request.[58] On 12 February 1687 James took the bolder step of issuing a Declaration of Indulgence for Scotland, granting by his 'Soveraign Authority, Prerogative Royal, and Absolute Power' (which, the Declaration insisted, all subjects were 'to obey without Reserve') his 'Royall Tolleration' to moderate presbyterians (provided that they met in private houses and said or did nothing seditious or treasonable), quakers and catholics (both of whom were allowed to hold public meetings). It also annulled all existing oaths of loyalty (including the Test Oath) and instead required office-holders to take an oath of non-resistance and to promise to 'assist, defend, and maintain' the king, his heirs and lawful successors 'in the Exercise of Their absolute Power and Authority'.[59]

The Indulgence proved controversial in Scotland. It further alienated the episcopal establishment, whilst failing to win over the presbyterians; James had to issue a revised Indulgence that summer, offering them the same liberties as catholics, before the presbyterians were prepared to avail themselves of the toleration.[60] It also set off alarm bells in England, especially when it was followed by an English Declaration of Indulgence on 4 April. The language of the English Indulgence was more moderate than its Scottish counterpart: it did not use the language of royal absolutism nor require subjects to take an oath to defend the king and his successors 'in the Exercise of Their absolute Power'. Yet it was clear that the policy of Indulgence was part of a coordinated British strategy. As Gilbert Burnet, writing from exile in the Low Countries, observed in a tract condemning the Scottish Indulgence and its designation of the king's 'Absolute Power': 'we here in England' could now 'see what we must look for'.[61]

58 Wodrow, *Sufferings*, II, 598–9; *RPCS*, *1686*, pp. xii, 425, 435, 454; Fountainhall, *Historical Notices*, II, 740–1, 748, 750.

59 James VII, *By the King. A Proclamation* (Edinburgh, 1687).

60 *RPCS*, *1686–9*, pp. xvii, 156–8; Steele, III, no. 2693.

61 [Gilbert Burnet], *Some Reflections on His Majesty's Proclamation of the 12th February 1686/7 for a Toleration in Scotland* [Amsterdam?, 1687], p. 5.

IV

It is worth pausing to re-cap. Both Charles II and James VII and II did, at times, self-consciously play the British card. Charles did so with considerable success, but for James the strategy backfired disastrously. The explanation for James's failure is a story that belongs to Scottish history. The arguments were about the powers of the crown in Scotland, and an understanding of the allegiances that developed in the Scottish parliamentary session of 1686 can only be derived from a consideration of political developments in Scotland. There is no evidence to suggest that Scottish M.P.s acted in the way that they did because they were concerned what implications their actions might have for England. However, James's failure changed what he was able to do next not just in Scotland but also in England. The implications of his failure, moreover, proved to be far-reaching. In his pursuit of the policy of indulgence for catholics, James managed to alienate the traditional supporters of the crown in both Scotland and England – the anglican/episcopalian interest in Church and state. As Charles II's final years had shown, if the crown worked with this interest, it could establish a remarkably strong position for itself, even in the face of quite widespread religious and political dissent.[62] James VII and II's regime was to show that losing the support of this interest could make the crown extremely vulnerable indeed.

It was the issuance of a second Declaration of Indulgence in England in April 1688 and the subsequent resistance of the Seven Bishops, whose arrest and trial came in the same month (June) as the birth of prince of Wales (which in turn raised the prospect of a never-ending catholic succession in England, Scotland and Ireland), which set in motion the train of events that was to lead ultimately to the Glorious Revolution. Why James came to pursue catholic toleration in England by means of the suspending power was the result of a British strategy for achieving toleration in a parliamentary way that had gone wrong. Why the English came to be so alarmed by James's English Declarations of Indulgence was at least in part conditioned by the more blatant way in which James had flaunted his prerogative – and his absolutism – in Scotland. In this sense, an understanding of what was going on in Scotland must factor into our explanation of what went wrong in England. One might engage in counter-factual parlour games and speculate whether or not James might have been forced to act the same way in England even if he had not also been king of Scotland. Being also king of Scotland, one might suggest, at most only gave James a further opportunity to try to induce his English parliament to be more sympathetic to catholic toleration, and there might have been little likelihood that the English parliament would have proved sympathetic even if the Scottish had been

62 Harris, *Restoration*, part II; Grant Tapsell, *The Personal Rule of Charles II 1681–85* (Woodbridge, 2007).

willing to do his bidding in 1686. Yet again, this is not really the point. The simple fact is that James *was* also king of Scotland. As king of both England and Scotland he saw the potential to achieve what he desired by playing the two kingdoms off against each other. He deliberately and quite self-consciously pursued a British strategy which ended up not panning out as expected and which led him in turn to adjust the policies he was pursuing in England, forcing him down a path that was ultimately to generate sufficient opposition to his rule in England as to cost him his throne.

It was, of course, the English who invited William of Orange to invade, not the Scots. And William invaded England, not Scotland. (By contrast, when the Jacobites attempted to effect a regime change in England 1715 and 1745, they launched their rebellions in Scotland.) William's mission proved so successful, so quickly, because very few people in England were willing to rush to James's defence. William was doubtless taking a huge gamble when he launched an invasion fleet so late in the season, and he came over with a large army of 15,000 trained professionals to give him a fighting chance of success. But he had been assured in advance of support from sections of the English army and navy, the English landed and mercantile *élite*, and significant cross-sections of the population. His invasion in November 1688, in other words, was predicated upon an informed belief that James's regime was already collapsing from within. Framed like this, there is doubtless still room for debate as to which weighed more, Dutch or English factors, in bringing about the Glorious Revolution – or French factors for that matter (we have to ask why Louis XIV was not in a position to prevent William's invasion of England) – but we might question whether any significant explanatory force should be attributed to developments in Scotland.

Again, this is something we need to rethink. As mentioned already, William invaded with the explicit intention of rescuing protestant liberties in Scotland (and, for that matter, in Ireland), as well as in England. He even issued a separate invasion manifesto specifically for a Scottish audience.[63] In advance of his invasion he sent over a number of agents to Scotland both to gather news and to distribute propaganda, in the hope of making sure the Scots would support his enterprise. There were a number of Scots in Holland (many of whom had been forced into exile in the final years of Charles II's reign) who were influential in William's entourage at the Hague, and who joined with his invasion force – amongst them Sir James Dalrymple of Stair, William Carstares, the tenth earl of Argyll, Andrew Fletcher of Saltoun, Sir Patrick Hume, Lord Cardross and the earl of Leven (Leven's father, the earl of Melville, was also at the Hague, but unable to join the invasion force due to health). The man who commanded the English and Scottish squadron in William's invasion force was a Scot, Major-General Hugh Mackay. Within

[63] *Declaration of His Highness William … Prince of Orange, etc. of the Reasons Inducing Him, To Appear in Armes for … Scotland.*

Britain, two Scots undertook to manage the Scottish dimension of William's campaign: Sir John Dalrymple who sat on the Scottish privy council in Edinburgh, and the earl of Drumlanrig in London. William had the backing of Scots (and some important Scots at that, who were to play an important part in the post-Revolution government north of the border), and he believed that he had backing within Scotland.[64] It would thus be incorrect to paint a picture of William invading England blithely unconcerned about what was going on in Scotland. One might wonder whether he would have gone ahead and invaded England even if he had had no Scottish backing and been led to believe that Scotland would remain firmly loyal to James; perhaps the stakes he was playing for in his struggle against Louis XIV were so high that the gamble would have been worth it. But again the exercise in counter-factual history does not really get us very far, since the ultimate task of the historian is to explain things as they were, not as they might otherwise have been. The simple fact is that Scotland did factor into William's decision to invade, and the information he had received pointed in the direction that there was considerable disaffection north of the border and that a significant number of Scots would welcome his efforts to free them from popery and arbitrary government. In that sense, explaining why the situation in Scotland had come to that pass whereby it could factor into William's decision in the way that it did must, in turn, be part of the explanation of why the Glorious Revolution was to come about.

An assessment of the situation in Scotland also factored into James VII and II's decision-making process. So confident was James of his power-base in Scotland that, in the face of William's invasion, he ordered the standing army in Scotland to march south to help defend his regime in England.[65] It proved a serious miscalculation. Not only did it do little to strengthen his ability to stop William in England, but it also made it difficult to police the mass of the population north of the border, hence the outbreak of anti-catholic disturbances in Scotland in the autumn of 1688, with assaults on catholic chapels and orchestrated pope-burning processions in Edinburgh, Glasgow and elsewhere. It was also why the earl of Perth, James's right-hand man in Scotland, was unable to hold Edinburgh for the king as William continued his march towards London: anti-catholic riots in Edinburgh were to force Perth to flee the Scottish capital on 10 December, a day before James was to flee England. Hence also the 'rabbling' of episcopalian ministers, which began on Christmas day and continued over the next couple of months, as angry crowds of presbyterians in various communities across Scotland (particularly in the south-west) sought to avenge their sufferings at the hands of the episcopalian establishment since the Restoration by driving orthodox ministers from their livings. Tellingly, these forcible ejections were

64 Harris, *Revolution*, p. 368.

65 John Childs, *The Army, James II, and the Glorious Revolution* (1980), p. 180.

subsequently sanctioned by the Scottish Convention which met in March 1689, thus having a crucial impact on the settlement in the Church that came with the Glorious Revolution in Scotland.[66]

The inability to police Scotland effectively also had a significant impact on the composition of the Scottish Convention. It is true that the catholic duke of Gordon continued for a while to hold Edinburgh Castle for the crown, but there was little he could do to secure the city. His presence also prompted a volunteer force of some 2,000 men from the south-western shires, mostly radical presbyterians (or Cameronians), to march on Edinburgh to provide a guard for the Convention. Their presence created an extremely hostile environment for open supporters of James VII and II in the Convention, who found themselves shouted at and threatened whenever they appeared in public. Hence the decision of so many open Jacobites to leave Edinburgh, thereby leaving control of the Scottish Convention in the hands of the Scottish whigs and presbyterians, and thus why the revolution settlement north of the border came to be framed by whigs and presbyterians – and was not the bi-partisan compromise that it was to be in England.

V

This chapter has sought to demonstrate what the British perspective can offer with regard to enhancing our understanding of the later-Stuart period. It is not the intention, however, to downplay the importance of the continental European contexts. English perceptions of Louis XIV's France are vital to understanding English politics under both Charles II and James VII and II, from the level of high politics down to the level of the crowd, as I have shown myself in earlier work. Likewise, the Dutch context remains crucial to understanding the causes of the Glorious Revolution: that is something no one could ever question. Nor is it being suggested here that British history (or British and Irish or Britannic history) should supplant the separate national histories of the constituent kingdoms of the Stuart multiple-kingdom inheritance. To glean the full insights that a multiple-kingdom perspective might have to offer us, we actually need to have a deep understanding of the separate national histories of the three kingdoms. Indeed, a fuller understanding of the British and Irish contexts can actually serve to strengthen the autonomy of English, Scottish or Irish history.

Let me illustrate once more with regard to Scotland. For a long time Scottish historians tended to assume that the Scots played little part in bringing about the Glorious Revolution: they 'remained passive', at best they were 'reluctant revolutionaries', and 'the Revolution was made in England and

66 For this and the following paragraph, see Harris, *Revolution*, ch. 9.

imported into Scotland'.[67] In fact, a consideration of the Glorious Revolution from a British perspective makes us appreciate how misleading such assumptions are. It is by no means apparent that the Scots were any more passive, reluctant, or less revolutionary than the English. Not only did some Scots actively intrigue with William, but they seized the opportunity afforded by the overthrow of the Jacobite regime to forge a Revolution settlement that addressed their concerns and grievances. However, the concerns and grievances addressed in the Scottish Claim of Right and Articles of Grievances of 1689 were Scottish ones. The Scots did not simply import a ready-made revolution from England; they took the opportunity provided by the overthrow of James VII and II to address issues that were peculiar to the Scottish context. Thus in 1689 the Scottish revolutionaries sought to undo the entire Restoration settlement in Church and State, resenting not only the forcible imposition of episcopacy and the resulting brutal persecution of presbyterians but also the peculiar nature of the powers of the monarchy in Scotland (which, as we have seen, were different from England). The Claim of Right condemned the absolute powers that the Scottish crown was acknowledged to possess by the Scottish Supremacy Act of 1669 and the Excise Act of 1685; it condemned the ways in which military force had been used against presbyterians in the Scottish south-west; it condemned abuses of Scottish law and legal procedure; and it condemned prelacy as 'a great and insupportable greivance and trouble to this nation, and contrary to the inclinationes of the generality of the people', which ought to be abolished. The Articles of Grievances called for the abolition of the Lords of the Articles (no committee like this had ever existed in England) and demanded the repeal of the Scottish Supremacy Act, an act of 1663 giving the kings of Scotland the power to impose customs on foreign trade, the Cumulative Jurisdictions Act of 1681 (a measure designed to restrict the independence of the Highland clan chiefs, but because of loose wording gave the Scottish vast discretionary legal powers which had paved the way for the Killing Times of the 1680s), and most of the legislation enacted by the Scottish parliament of 1685. The search for why the priorities of the Scottish revolutionaries were what they were requires us to look into the Scottish past. The answer is to be found in Scottish history, not in English history.[68]

67 Gordon Donaldson, *Scotland: James V to James VII* (Edinburgh, 1965), p. 383; Rosalind Mitchison, *Lordship to Patronage: Scotland, 1603–1745* (1983), p. 116; Ian B. Cowan, 'The Reluctant Revolutionaries: Scotland in 1688', in *By Force or By Default?*, ed. Cruickshanks, pp. 65–81.

68 *RPS*, 1689/3/108; Harris, *Revolution*, pp. 391–409; Clare Jackson, *Restoration Scotland, 1660–1690: Royalist Politics, Religion and Ideas* (Woodbridge, 2003), esp. pp. 191–215; Jeffrey Stephen, 'Defending the Revolution: The Church of Scotland and the Scottish Parliament, 1689–95', *S.H.R.*, LXXXIX (2010), 19–53.

6

*Ireland's Restoration Crisis**

JOHN GIBNEY

The defining issues in Irish political and social life from the Restoration to the Revolution were, essentially, the unresolved legacies of the Confederate wars and Cromwellian conquest of the 1640s and 1650s. This continuity was not lost on those who sought to use those conflicts as a benchmark by which to gauge later events. In January 1689 William of Orange was presented with an assessment of the condition of Ireland in which the catholic Irish of the later 1680s were depicted as a far more formidable enemy than their predecessors in the 1640s. For

> now they have the Government, the Garrisons all the ports, and a vast Number of Men in Arms and some of them of Experience. They have the Kings Authority added to the Fury of their priests. They have Interests and Councills of France to abett them, and the Kings Authority will be now so much at the mercy of France, that in effect the King of France, will be now King of Ireland. Nor will a Popes Nuntio be long wanting thence, to unite the minds of the Clergy in this War of Religion.[1]

It is striking that the crisis of the 1640s was still an obvious point of reference over four decades later. This analysis was provided to William as he prepared to deal conclusively with a crucial loose end of the so-called 'Glorious Revolution': the fact that James II, despite having lost his English throne, remained king of Ireland with the support of both the catholic Irish and the French. Consequently, after attempts at a diplomatic solution to this impasse failed, 'it became clear that military force would be needed to

* Earlier versions of this chapter were presented before audiences at both the 'Restoration Ireland' conference held at Trinity College Dublin, on 10 September 2004, and the Keough-Naughton Institute for Irish Studies at the University of Notre Dame, Indiana, on 23 February 2007. I would like to thank those present on both occasions for their comments and suggestions. In quotations from primary sources, spelling, punctuation and capitalization remain unchanged; interpolations and uncertain words are indicated in square brackets.

1 Royal Irish Academy, MS 24. G. 2, fos 1v–r.

establish William's authority in Ireland'.[2] In August 1689 the first military expedition to be sent to Ireland since that of Oliver Cromwell in 1649 was dispatched under the command of Friedrich Herman, duke of Schomberg. But there the comparison ended: Schomberg's expedition was a disastrous failure, and in 1690 William himself led a far more ambitious and (from his perspective) far more successful invasion of Ireland, embarking on a campaign that saw both the symbolic victory at the Boyne in July 1690 and the decisive military victory at Aughrim in July 1691.

The Williamite invasions were intended to break, swiftly and decisively, Jacobite resistance in Ireland and end the prospect of a second, western theatre of war being opened with the French at a time when William was already fighting Louis XIV on the continent.[3] Given his wider preoccupations, William was present in Ireland only for the early stages of his campaign (an ironic fact in the light of his enduring reputation as the saviour of Ireland's protestants). After all, these events took place upon a broader canvas, against the backdrop of British dynastic change and European conflict. But ultimately, they had local implications. And after the defeat of the Jacobite cause in Ireland, members of the Irish catholic intelligentsia retained their long-standing loyalty to the Stuarts and continued to devote time to their particular version of the recent past.[4]

According to the Jacobite Charles O'Kelly, the Irish had expected the accession of the catholic James, duke of York, to the throne as James II to be the prelude to the restoration of their religion, and of the lands that they had lost in the seventeenth century; sufferings they had endured despite their proclaimed loyalty to the crown, a loyalty which, according to O'Kelly, was not necessarily shared by those protestants who had benefited from their dispossession.[5] The theme of loyalty versus disloyalty was also taken up in the monumental Jacobite history entitled 'A light to the blind', in which 1678, the year when the Popish Plot had first come to light in England, was perceived by the Old English author (most likely Nicholas Plunkett) as 'the famous year, wherein the Monumental troubles of his Royal Highness began'.[6] The subsequent opposition to the prospect of York succeeding his brother Charles (the 'Exclusion Crisis') was prompted by anti-catholicism, which in turn had led to a number of plots aimed at destroying catholi-

[2] J.G. Simms, *Jacobite Ireland, 1685–91* (1969), p. 120.

[3] Jonathan Israel, 'The Dutch Role in the Glorious Revolution', in *The Anglo-Dutch Moment*, ed. Jonathan Israel (Cambridge, 1991), pp. 147–59.

[4] Breandán Ó Buachalla, 'James our True King: The Ideology of Irish Royalism in the Seventeenth Century', in *Political Thought in Ireland since the Seventeenth-Century*, ed. D. George Boyce, Robert Eccleshall and Vincent Geoghegan (1993), pp. 7–35; Breandán Ó Buachalla, *Aisling ghéar: na Stíobhartaigh agus an t-aos léinn* (Dublin, 1996); Éamonn Ó Ciardha, *Ireland and the Jacobite Cause, 1686–1766* (Dublin, 2002).

[5] Charles O'Kelly, *Macariae Excidium*, ed. J.C.O'Callaghan (Dublin, 1850), pp. 13–15.

[6] N.L.I., MS 476, f. 275.

cism in the Stuart kingdoms and disinheriting the rightful king.[7] The rule of James in England did indeed attract odium for its authoritarian nature, but according to the author of 'A light to the blind' the clear disloyalty of protestants in Britain and Ireland proved that it was necessary to rule them with a strong hand. Ample evidence of that disloyalty was provided by the 'exclusion' campaign of 1679–81, depicted here as the first in the sequence of rebellions – the others were those of Argyll and Monmouth – that had their ultimate success in the Glorious Revolution.[8] For the anonymous author of 'A light to the blind', the continuity between 1678 and 1688 was obvious.[9] One had served as a prelude to the other. Yet from a Williamite perspective, as revealed in the memorandum drafted for the benefit of William himself, there were other continuities that were of more pressing relevance, in the form of other unresolved questions from Ireland's recent history. This chapter is concerned with how the various institutional, political, religious, and social tensions that were the legacy of that recent past retained their potency throughout the 1660s and 1670s, and how, in the 1680s, they set the stage for the inglorious Irish consequences of the Glorious Revolution.

I

The relative neglect of Restoration Ireland by Irish historians arises from the assumption that it was little more than 'an interim between upheavals'.[10] J. C. Beckett eloquently conceptualized it as:

> A period of transition, in a more direct and genuine sense than that overworked phrase commonly implies. By the 1660s the basis of the 'Protestant Ascendancy' that was to dominate the eighteenth century had already been laid; but it was not until after the wars of the Revolution that Irish Protestants acquired the arrogant self-confidence that became one of their main characteristics. In the interval, they still felt insecure; they still feared that the dispossessed Roman

7 N.L.I., MS 476, f. 277.

8 N.L.I., MS 476, fos 282–3; Patrick Kelly, '"A Light to the Blind": The Voice of the Dispossessed Élite in the Generation after the Defeat at Limerick', *Irish Historical Studies*, XXIV (1985), 448.

9 Tim Harris, 'The British Dimension, Religion, and the Shaping of Political Identities during the Reign of Charles II', in *Protestantism and National Identity: Britain and Ireland, c. 1650–c.1850*, ed. Tony Claydon and Ian McBride (Cambridge, 1998), pp. 131–56; Vincent Morley, 'The idea of Britain in Eighteenth-Century Ireland and Scotland', *Studia Hibernica*, XXXIII (2004–5), 101–24.

10 R.F. Foster, *Modern Ireland, 1600–1972* (1988), p. 117. For general accounts of restoration Ireland, see the relevant sections of Tim Harris, *Restoration: Charles II and his Kingdoms, 1660–1685* (2005), and S.J. Connolly, *Divided Kingdom: Ireland, 1630–1800* (Oxford, 2008). More specific studies of various aspects of the period are to be found in *Restoration Ireland*, ed. Coleman A. Dennehy (2008).

> catholics might strike a blow to recover their estates and their power; and they watched anxiously the course of events in England, lest some change of policy there should weaken or destroy their position.[11]

The notion of 'transition' implies a degree of continuity with what came before and after the reign of Charles II. Beckett was looking forward, to the dominance of the protestant 'ascendancy' whose status was secured in this period, and whose descendants 'were to dominate Irish society for the greater part of the next two centuries'.[12] But to make sense of what energized the 'period of transition' of which Beckett wrote one needs to look backwards, and in doing so there is an obvious concept that can be borrowed from Jonathan Scott: the notion of a 'restoration crisis'.[13]

In its initial formulation, Scott's argument was specifically related to the period of the Popish Plot and Exclusion Crisis (1678–81) in England. The bedrock of his argument was that these years witnessed a political crisis that was seen to echo, and to have the potential to replicate, the events of the early 1640s; furthermore, this was merely part of a 'connected sequence of instability' throughout the seventeenth century that persisted up to (and beyond) 1688.[14] Scott placed a great emphasis on such continuity. The connected crises that he wrote of were the outbreak of the Civil Wars, the Popish Plot and Exclusion Crisis, and the Glorious Revolution itself, along with the various settlements that followed them and which were, he argued, best seen as attempts to resolve the issues these crises had highlighted in the first place. Scott's analysis focused on England, but if one looks at the broad continuum of Irish history in the same period, the relevance of his interpretive model becomes obvious.

Throughout the early seventeenth century Ireland was colonized by predominantly protestant British settlers, with the northern province of Ulster experiencing the densest settlement.[15] The process of colonization and plantation precipitated a broad range of grievances and resentments on the part of the native Irish whom the colonists had supplanted. The brutal rebellion against the colonists that eventually erupted in Ulster in October 1641, and which ushered in the equally brutal warfare of the 1640s, was in large part driven by these grievances and the insecurities that followed in

[11] J.C. Beckett, 'The Irish Armed Forces, 1660–1685', in *Essays Presented to Michael Roberts*, ed. John Bossy and Peter Jupp (Belfast, 1976), p. 41.

[12] Connolly, *Divided Kingdom*, p. 139.

[13] Jonathan Scott, *Algernon Sidney and the Restoration Crisis, 1677–1683* (Cambridge, 1991), pp. 1–49; *idem*, *England's Troubles* (Cambridge, 2000).

[14] Scott, *England's Troubles*, p. 5.

[15] The most comprehensive extant accounts of this process of colonization are Nicholas Canny, *Making Ireland British, 1580–1650* (Oxford, 2001), and William J. Smyth, *Map-Making, Landscapes and Memory: A Geography of Colonial and Early Modern Ireland, c.1530–1750* (Cork, 2006).

their wake. But the 1641 rebellion was also part of a sequence of events intimately linked to the parallel civil wars that broke out in Britain: the conflict in Ireland eventually culminated in the parliamentarian reconquest of 1649–53.

This invasion was initially led by Oliver Cromwell himself and was undertaken for a number of reasons: to punish Irish catholics for their rebellion in 1641, which had generally been interpreted in purely sectarian terms as a concerted and horrifically cruel attempt to exterminate protestants; to secure England's security from a potential challenge to the west; and finally to pay off the debts accrued from the war against the crown.[16] The ultimate means of securing these goals came in the aftermath of the war, as the parliamentarian regime sought to strip the Irish catholic elite of their lands and compensate them with smaller and inferior holdings in the western province of Connacht. Given that they were collectively assumed to have been rebels, catholics had technically forfeited their lands, which had in turn been used as collateral by parliament to fund its war against the king. Now these debts were to be collected. The critical issue that shaped the Restoration in Ireland was the fact that these huge land transfers remained largely intact, despite the legislative and political eradication of the commonwealth after 1660. The calamitous events of the 1640s and 1650s had transformed the island of Ireland in ways that were maintained beyond the Restoration at the expense of a diverse, disgruntled and dispossessed catholic community.[17] The persistence of this anomaly defined Restoration Ireland, and was ultimately the basis for the crisis that Irish protestants seemed to be presented with in the reign of James II. What had also persisted was a lingering uncertainty as to whether the changes wrought in the 1650s and confirmed in the 1660s would be permanent, or might yet be reversed. Herein lies the fundamental nature of Beckett's 'transition'. Later events would dictate the eventual outcome.

II

In December 1659 Dublin Castle was seized in a coup that presaged the Restoration of the Stuart monarchy: a pre-emptive strike by a coalition of Cromwellian grantees and older protestant settlers who perceived a poten-

16 The origins, course and aftermath of the Cromwellian campaign in Ireland are detailed in Micheál Ó Siochrú, *God's Executioner: Oliver Cromwell and the Conquest of Ireland* (2008).

17 The Irish catholic community was, broadly speaking, composed of two distinct ethnic groups: the indigenous ('Gaelic') Irish, and the 'Old English', the descendents of those colonists of British extraction who had settled in Ireland after the Anglo-Norman invasion of the twelfth century.

tial threat to their newly found (or newly enhanced) status.[18] The Restoration period in Ireland therefore opened on the basis of a straightforward question: who were to be the masters of Ireland? In the later seventeenth century, the initial answer seemed obvious: British protestant colonists. In the early 1660s the twin pillars of the monarchy and the established church had been restored, and the contentious land settlement – the Acts of Settlement and Explanation of 1662 and 1665 – had been implemented in Ireland. According to the most recent estimate, in 1641 catholics owned 66 per cent of Irish land, predominantly outside Ulster; by 1675 this percentage had been denuded across the island to 29 per cent.[19] Despite some limited redress, the bulk of the lands confiscated from catholics during the 1650s remained in protestant hands, and the protestant 'interest' was thereby secured.

But there was a price to be paid for this. According to Aidan Clarke, 'it was essential that the land settlement should survive, in short, not merely because individuals had profited, but because it was the basis of a reconfiguration of power which excluded catholic competition in a new colonial Ireland. The condition of protestant survival was that the community should be made invulnerable to the forces that had almost destroyed it in the 1640'.'[20] The settlement in Ireland rested upon this fact, and it was maintained by force through a 5–7,000-strong army, which had the dual (and interrelated) function of defending Ireland against internal and external threats, and the various local militias organised by local protestant grandees.[21] The imperative to uphold this new dispensation was strengthened by the basic numerical fact that in Ireland catholics vastly outnumbered protestants of all denominations. In 1672 Sir William Petty had estimated the Irish population to consist of 200,000 English (deemed anglican), 100,000 Scots (deemed presbyterian) and 800,000 Irish (deemed catholic, and assumed hostile).[22] The anxieties of Irish protestants were heightened by this sectarian arithmetic. The substantive preservation of the Cromwellian settlement remained inextricably linked to the exclusion of catholics from the power and influence they had expected to regain after 1660. As a result

[18] Aidan Clarke, *Prelude to Restoration in Ireland* (Cambridge, 1999).

[19] These conclusions are stated in Kevin McKenny, 'The Restoration Land Settlement in Ireland: A Statistical Interpretation', in *Restoration Ireland*, ed. Dennehy, pp. 35–52. This challenges the previous estimate of J.G. Simms, who argued that the share of catholic owned land in Ireland had declined from 59 per cent in 1641 to 22 per cent by 1688: *A New History of Ireland: Volume IX: Maps, Geneologies, Lists*, ed. T.W. Moody, F.X. Martin and F.J. Byrne (Oxford, 1984), p. 57.

[20] Clarke, *Prelude to Restoration*, p. 317. See also Robert Armstrong, *Protestant War: The 'British' of Ireland and the Wars of the Three Kingdoms* (Manchester, 2005), pp. 230–4.

[21] Beckett, 'Irish Armed Forces', p. 45; Aidan Clarke, 'Restoration Ireland', in *Encylopedia of Irish History and Culture*, ed. J.S. Donnelly (2 vols, Farmington Hills, 2004), II, 626–7.

[22] William Petty, 'The Political Anatomy of Ireland', in *The Economic Writings of Sir William Petty*, ed. C. H. Hull (2 vols, 1899), II, 141.

of this catholic discontent was inevitable, and would be articulated: after all, they had been the losers and, naturally, both ethnic catholic groups on the island – Irish and Old English – wanted the unappealing reality of their dispossession reversed.

The case against Irish catholics after the Restoration rested on the crucial assumption that, having rebelled in 1641, they had brutally attempted to exterminate British protestants in the process. Even aside from its punitive purpose, the continued dispossession of catholics was justified as a necessary measure for the preservation of the protestant interest; it was intended to insulate the future from the past.[23] On the other hand, catholic claims to redress after 1660 largely rested upon the peace treaty signed between the king's representative, the then viceroy James Butler, earl of Ormond, and the Confederate catholics in 1649, which offered significant concessions in terms of both religious toleration and security of land tenure, and which had, theoretically, also been restored with the monarchy.

Such claims also rested on the technical illegality of the confiscations sanctioned by the Cromwellians. It was anticipated that these would be reversed after the Restoration of the monarchy, but the newly restored Charles II remained wary of the consequences of doing this, and so the land settlement offered only partial redress. Even then it was the Old English who benefited most from such adjustments as were facilitated.[24] For many other catholics, their grievances remained unresolved.

As a consequence Irish catholic spokesmen sought to redress this imbalance. There were two intertwined strategies by which they attempted to do so. One was to refute the allegation that catholics carried out brutal atrocities against protestants during the 1641 rebellion, given that this had been used to justify their dispossession; the other was to demonstrate their continued (and unrewarded) loyalty to the crown.[25] The early 1670s seemed to offer Irish catholics some hope of redress, as Charles II moved into an alliance with France, with the possibility of a review of the land settlement in 1670–1, and the prospect of greater toleration of the catholic church. But by 1673 the intensification of anti-catholic attitudes in the Cavalier parliament had put a halt to such developments and catholic writers, both Irish and Old English, continued to bemoan the reality of their community's dispossession. Yet these sentiments did not automatically equate with actively attempting to undo that dispossession. For example, during the hysteria of the Popish Plot at the end of the 1670s the Dublin administra-

23 'An Act for the better Execution of his Majesties gracious Declaration for the Settlement of his Kingdom of Ireland' (14 & 15 Cha. II), *The Statutes at Large, Passed in the Parliaments Held in Ireland* (13 vols, Dublin, 1786), II, 239–45.

24 Karl Bottigheimer, 'The Restoration Land Settlement in Ireland: A Structural View', *Irish Historical Studies*, XVIII (1972), 19–20.

25 This is a key theme of Anne Creighton, 'The Catholic Interest in Irish Politics in the Reign of Charles II, 1660–85', Queen's University, Belfast Ph.D., 2000.

tion, while sharing the wariness and fear of catholics held by many amongst the protestant community, accepted that catholic discontent was in no immediate danger of turning into outright rebellion.[26]

Equally, the government also accepted that such discontent remained very much alive. Irish catholics were by no means reconciled to the dashed expectations of the 1660s and 1670s; the reign of James II eventually offered them another chance of restitution. By then the Irish army's purpose was no longer to defend the protestant interest; quite the opposite. The reasons why this shift took place had been foreshadowed in the writings of the Irish catholic literati and intelligentsia over the previous three decades.

III

Perhaps the most far-reaching consequence of the 1640s and 1650s in Ireland was the crystallization of distinct sectarian identities that soon took precedence over ethnicity. For Irish catholics this process was accelerated by the fact that, irrespective of the latent tensions between the Irish and Old English, their protestant enemies had simply lumped them together as catholics. It was perhaps inevitable in such circumstances that representatives of both catholic communities came to articulate a common rhetoric of dispossession. The Irish poet Seán Ó Connaill apparently wrote *Tuireamh na hÉireann* ('Ireland's dirge') in Munster in the latter half of the 1650s. Its commentary on the devastation wreaked in the course of the Cromwellian conquest had an enduring valency beyond 1660, as it was copied and disseminated for generations.

'S iad do chríochnaig *conquest* Éireann,
do ghabh a ndaingin 's a mbailte le chéile
ó Inis Bó Finne go Binn Éadair
's ó Chloich an Stacáin go Baoi Béarra.
...
Cá ngeabham anois nó créad do dhéanfam?
Ní díon dúinn cnoc ná coill ná caolta.
Níl ár leigheas as liaig í n-Éirinn
Acht Dia do ghuí 's na naoimh i n-aonacht.

(It was they who completed the *conquest* of Ireland,
and seized its fortresses and towns together,
from Inishbofin [west] to Howth [east]
and from the White Lady [north] to Dursey [south]
...

[26] H.M.C., *Ormonde*, old ser., II, 279.

Where will we go now or what will we do?
We have no shelter from hill, wood or marshes.
The physicians of Ireland cannot heal us
we can only pray to God and the saints in unison.)[27]

Similar attitudes found expression in the immediate aftermath of the Restoration settlement. After all, it had done little to change the circumstances that had originally given rise to Ó Connaill's lament. One of the more notable representatives of the Old English was Nicholas French, the catholic bishop of Ferns who, having been active in the Confederate Association in the 1640s, was vehemently opposed to the price later paid by catholics whose dispossession was confirmed by the Restoration settlement. In *A Narrative of the Earl of Clarendon's Settlement and Sale of Ireland* (1668) he readily identified those whom he deemed responsible for 'the sad and deplorable state of the Irish Nation, and the apparent Injustice, and inequality used in the present Settlement of that Kingdom'.[28] French blamed leading protestant grandees in Ireland for forcing the king to maintain the dispossessions of the 1650s, for 'the Cromwellian Party in Ireland hath no more power than what his Majesty hitherto is pleased to grant them'.[29] This was perhaps an optimistic view of the situation, but within French's reading of the settlement of the 1660s was a very clear implication. If the Restoration settlement was inherently unstable, then it could potentially be altered; and the catholic Irish were the most likely candidates to do so. Perhaps in an effort to deflect attention away from this rather obvious fact, French also dwelt upon the loyalty of the Irish to the crown in defeat, which served in turn to highlight their continued suffering.[30] He also suggested that the continued dispossession of the Irish, and their alienation from the crown, might open the door to the lurking threat posed by Scottish presbyterians in Ireland by negating a potentially alliance between Irish catholics and the English anglican interest. The common bond of protestantism had not fully obscured the tensions that existed between presbyterians of Scottish extraction and anglicans of English descent; and after all, 'the English of Ireland

27 The verse extract and translation are cited in Vincent Morley, 'Views of the Past in Irish Vernacular Literature, 1650–1850', in *Unity and Diversity in European Culture c. 1650–1850*, ed. Tim Blanning and Hagen Schulze (Oxford, 2006), pp. 180–1. This study largely concerns itself with the poem's influence and dissemination. For an additional exegesis, along with the complete Irish text, see *Five Seventeenth-Century Political Poems*, ed. Cecile O'Rahilly (Dublin, 1952), pp. 50–82.
28 [Nicholas French], 'A Narrative of the Earl of Clarendon's Settlement and Sale of Ireland' (Louvain, c.1667–8), in *The Historical Works of the Right Rev. Nicholas French, D.D.*, ed. S. H. Bindon (2 vols, Dublin, 1846), I, 77.
29 *Ibid.*, 99–100.
30 *Ibid.*, 121.

are not able to defend themselves against the Scots in that Country; if the Irish be Neuters'.[31]

This was, however, one perspective. If French voiced the concerns of the dispossessed, one should not forget the concerns of the possessor. The writer and diplomat Sir William Temple was born in Ireland, and his unpublished 'Essay on the present state and settlement of Ireland' was, like French's first work, composed *circa* 1668, and also dealt with the settlement of the 1660s and its flaws.[32] But it did so in order to determine how best 'to own and support upon all occasions that which is truly a Loyal English Protestant Interest, and to make it as comprehensive as can be'.[33] On the other hand, Petty, in his *Political Anatomy of Ireland* (1672), thought that while the 'English' in Ireland were drastically outnumbered, they might not necessarily be the victims of another rebellion. In an interpretation that was the polar opposite to that presented to William of Orange less than two decades later, he argued that the 'English Protestant interest' had, at this juncture, a strategic and military advantage in Ireland, and could probably survive as they could almost certainly depend upon further support from England itself.[34] But this could, in principle, be balanced out by the reality that Irish catholics also had recourse to an external power: the catholic church.[35] Crucially, Petty perceived the land settlement to be the key source of division on the island.[36] The Irish may well have had valid grievances (which implied that they were not inherently degenerate, and were therefore capable of being reformed), but this was a moot point: they fully expected the restitution of what they had lost in the 1650s.[37] The 'loyal English Protestant interest' of whom Temple had written were unlikely to have been oblivious to such matters.

There were therefore a number of immediate issues that arose from the settlement of the 1660s, and that ultimately had their origins in the early decades of the seventeenth century. The Restoration settlement in Ireland rested upon the narrow foundation of the anglican community. It was legitimized under the auspices of the monarchy and established church, and was underpinned by the anomaly of the land settlement. Prudence and self-interest ensured that former Cromwellians such as Roger Boyle, created earl of Orrery at the Restoration, swiftly reconciled themselves to the monarchy. Despite what Nicholas French may have thought, Charles II was not in a position to oppose such manoeuvring, even had he been inclined to do

31 *Ibid.*, 121.

32 Sir William Temple, 'An Essay on the Present State and Condition of Ireland', in his *Select Letters to the Prince of Orange* (1701), III, 197–216.

33 Temple, 'Essay on the Present State and Condition of Ireland', p. 213.

34 Petty, 'Political Anatomy', pp. 155–7.

35 *Ibid.*, p. 164.

36 *Ibid.*, p. 167.

37 *Ibid.*, pp. 201–3.

so. The protestant elite were strongly opposed to any alteration in their recently acquired status, a stance forcefully articulated by figures such as Sir Audley Mervyn, the speaker of the Irish house of commons.[38] But the renewed anglican ascendancy had weaknesses of its own, and fears that fed on such weaknesses. Despite their occasional pretensions, the protestants of Ireland were essentially a colonial community who remained painfully aware that, just as Temple had argued, the ultimate basis of their safety and security lay in their links to the mother country.[39]

There was, however, a potential enemy other than catholicism: the substantial Scottish dissenter population in the north of Ireland.[40] Protestant dissent had arrived in Ireland with Scottish settlers in the 1630s and Cromwell's army in the 1650s: presbyterians, quakers, baptists and independents, all of whom stood outside the established church. The creation of a distinct presbyterian identity in the area of Scottish settlement in Ulster had been evident prior to the watershed of 1641; this combination of settler society and religious institution proved extremely difficult to suppress after 1660.[41] Throughout the Restoration period, dissenters were discriminated against and viewed with distrust by both the Dublin administration and the established church (sometimes with good reason). Scottish presbyterians, the strongest and most significant group in Ulster, were a source of particular concern. Covenanter activity in Scotland could have a resonance in the north of Ireland troops were often sent to Ulster to deal with potential unrest.[42] Yet equally, by 1672 many dissenters were seeking to demonstrate their loyalty to the crown and to come to an accommodation with a government that was in no position to take too severe a line with them. Covenanters remained a concern, but a discreet level of tolerance could be permitted to other non-conformists: witness, for instance, the financial assistance provided to non-conforming ministers by the government in the form

38 *The Speech of Sir Audley Mervyn, Knight … Containing the Sum of Affairs in Ireland* (Dublin, 1663).

39 Jim Smyth, 'The Communities of Ireland and the British State, 1660–1707', in *The British Problem, c. 1534–1707*, ed. Brendan Bradshaw and John Morrill (Basingstoke, 1996), pp. 246–9.

40 Phil Kilroy, *Protestant Dissent and Controversy in Ireland, 1660–1714* (Cork, 1994), pp. 225–43; Richard L. Greaves, '"That's No Good Religion that Disturbs Government": The Church of Ireland and the Nonconformist Challenge, 1660–88', in *As by Law Established: The Church of Ireland since the Reformation*, ed. Alan Ford, Kenneth Milne and James McGuire (Dublin, 1995), pp. 120–35; Toby Barnard, 'Enforcing the Reformation in Ireland, 1660–1704', in *Enforcing Reformation in Ireland and Scotland, 1550–1700*, ed. Elizabethann Boran and Crawford Gribben (2005), pp. 202–27.

41 Raymond Gillespie, 'The Presbyterian Revolution in Ulster, 1660–1690', in *The Churches, Ireland and the Irish*, ed. W.J. Sheils and Diana Wood (Oxford, 1989), pp. 159–70.

42 J.C. Beckett, 'Irish-Scottish Relations in the Seventeenth-Century', in *Confrontations: Studies in Irish History* (Plymouth, 1972), pp. 37–8.

of the *regium donum*. In October 1673, following complaints from Scots in Ulster about their 'persecution (as they terme it)', the viceroy Arthur Capel, earl of Essex, defused the prospect of mounting tension by permitting them to worship on Sundays, provided that they did so unobtrusively; there were limits to such tolerance.[43] In a neat reversal of Nicholas French's suggestion, a potential catholic threat allowed for solidarity between denominations at times: presbyterians may not have been the right kind of protestants, but at least they were protestants. In 1689–91 the awareness of a common enemy would permit a short-lived protestant unity in the face of the Jacobite threat.

This was short-lived precisely because hostility towards dissenters had become ingrained: both the catholic church and the anglican Church of Ireland remained wary of what they perceived to be the latent danger of presbyterianism. While presbyterians in Ulster, like catholics in the 1660s, were often preoccupied with proving their loyalty to a sceptical government, it was impossible for such efforts to be fully representative, or indeed comprehensive. Thus they remained suspect, but they were not necessarily the most pressing concern faced by the Irish government and the anglican interest. For protestants of all denominations, danger was most likely to be posed to them by the disgruntled and dispossessed catholic Irish. They were rendered even more dangerous by the religion they shared with England's enemies in catholic Europe and the relationships forged between them: most especially catholic Ireland's clerical, commercial and military links with catholic France.[44] In January 1678 the Munster landowner and politician Sir Robert Southwell had observed that war with France seemed imminent, and 'it is manifest that our enemy will do his best to excite troubles both in Scotland and Ireland, and in this latter especially where all places lie naked to his invasion… all who have their estates lying in that kingdom have reason to be alarmed'.[45] The anglican interest in particular remained acutely aware of that fact.

IV

This is not to say, however, that attempts were not made to secure their position. Through the 1670s successive governments in Ireland sought to restore stability and security after decades of warfare and instability.[46]

43 *Essex Papers, vol. I: 1672–1679*, ed. Osmond Airy (1890), I, 124.

44 Eamon O'Ciosain, 'The Irish in France, 1660–90: The Point of No Return', in *Irish Communities in Early Modern Europe*, ed. Thomas O'Connor and Mary Ann Lyons (Dublin, 2006), pp. 85–102.

45 H.M.C., *Egmont*, II, 70.

46 J.C. Beckett, 'The Irish Viceroyalty in the Restoration Period', in his *Confrontations*, pp. 67–86; James Ernest Aydelotte, 'The Duke of Ormond and the English Government of Ireland, 1677–85', University of Iowa Ph.D., 2 vols., 1975.

Ireland remained deeply unsettled. Catholic grievances generated by the land settlement raised the spectre of subversion and rebellion. Such protestant anxieties were accentuated still further both by memories of the wars of mid-century and by the unsettling reality that the catholic population vastly outnumbered them. On the other hand, the existence of large numbers of non-conformists in Ulster offered potential threat from the other end of the denominational spectrum. But the Dublin administration was in no position comprehensively to address these issues or their implications. It lacked the money and resources to do so. Their inability to fully implement the policies deemed necessary fully to secure Ireland to the crown ensured that a degree of uncertainty about Irish affairs would remain evident amongst the ruling elites in both Dublin and London. The persistence of such uncertainty meant that the Irish governments of this period were continually tasked with attempting to overhaul the administrative structures that overlay and sought to manage the country that they sought to control.

Having overseen the implementation of the land settlement in the 1660s (and having being damned by Nicholas French for so doing), Ormond was replaced as viceroy in May 1669, thus drawing to an end the first phase of the Restoration in Ireland.[47] He was reappointed in August 1677, and was forced to deal with many of the issues with which his successors had sought to grapple during the 1670s. The primary task of Ormond's immediate replacement, John, baron Robartes of Truro (1669–70), was to address two intertwined problems of reform: an exchequer that was running a continual deficit and a dilapidated and unpaid army that was potentially unable to fulfil its official functions. Robartes' tenure was too brief to have any real impact, but fiscal and military reform would be on the agendas of his successors: Sir John Berkeley, Baron Berkeley of Stratton (1670–2), and Essex (1672–7). In Berkeley's case, his appointment was accompanied by instructions to revitalize the structure of the Church of Ireland in an attempt further to bolster the English protestant interest. Berkeley was also rumoured to be a catholic. Whether this was true or not, he was seen to be in a position to seek some kind of *modus vivendi* with the catholic clergy, and would enjoy good relations with the catholic primate and archbishop of Armagh, Oliver Plunkett (who was later executed during the Popish Plot). But his authority was eventually rendered irrelevant by an altogether less exalted factor: the financial 'undertaking' of Richard Jones, earl of Ranelagh.

In March 1671 a consortium headed by Ranelagh proposed to Charles II that they could pay for the government of Ireland between December 1670 and December 1675 whilst also providing him with £80,000 directly into the Privy Purse for two years; the condition was that the consortium would pocket whatever proceeds remained. Charles was in no position to refuse

47 James McGuire, 'Why was Ormond Dismissed in 1669?', *Irish Historical Studies*, XVIII (1973), 295–312.

a seemingly alluring offer that also provided a licence for corruption on a huge scale, and which would come to haunt both Essex and Ormond. In more immediate terms, the undertaking undermined Berkeley's administration by effectively stripping it of control of Ireland's revenues and Essex replaced him in May 1672.

Once again, fiscal and military reforms were firmly on Essex's agenda, but his instructions also had a marked emphasis on religious matters: the king had privately authorized Essex to dispense with the oaths of allegiance and supremacy should the situation warrant it. This was consistent with the Declaration of Indulgence issued by Charles in March 1672, the implications of which, in terms of tolerating catholicism, prompted great unease in England. But it was restricted to England: the text of the declaration made no reference to Ireland, and so the instructions given to Essex were perhaps an attempt to extend its range to Ireland.[48] Essex was to determine 'what are the properest ways to give Satisfaction to all Our subjects in that Our Kingdome, in the point of Liberty of Conscience, without distinction of Parties, what Numbers of Severall Perswasions there are & by what proper means each Party may best have its Satisfaction': this naturally, and explicitly, was to apply to Irish catholics.[49]

The catholic church in Ireland had been devastated during the 1650s. The inevitable attempts to rebuild it after the Restoration culminated, in 1669, in three new appointments to vacant bishoprics (one of these was Plunkett). By 1672 the catholic church was undoubtedly active again, and Essex was prepared to reach an unofficial accommodation with it through an ostensibly severe but actually moderate policy. There was an element of *realpolitik* to such a stance. More repressive measures directed at the catholics, such as actively disarming them, could prove problematic; after all, 'the Crown had other enemies in Ireland & 'twould be hard to fix such a mark of distrust upon the papists, & have the other sort uncensored who had been equally obnoxious', namely militant presbyterians. But in strategic terms there were important distinctions to be made between catholics and dissenters: the courtier and diplomat Sir Sidney Goldolphin argued that catholics, 'being poor & dispossest of their estates were desperate & more likely therefore to take violent courses for the righting themselves', whereas the *de facto* loyalty of presbyterians would be guaranteed by self-interest.[50] Irrespective of this latter assessment, there remained obvious concerns about the potential for unrest amongst presbyterians in the north, especially as 'the seditious Preachers of Scotland' often absconded to Ulster.[51] It was obvious that the security of one Stuart kingdom could impinge upon that

48 The text of the declaration is reproduced in *English Historical Documents, 1660–1714*, ed. Andrew Browning and David Charles (2nd edn, 1996), pp. 387–8.

49 B.L., Add MS 21,505, f. 29v–r.

50 B.L., Stowe MS 201, f. 349.

51 *Essex Papers*, I, 14–16, 34.

of another; here was another echo of the 1640s. Presbyterians, however, were not the only community that were viewed with suspicion. In March 1673, amidst the furore that forced the revocation of the Declaration of Indulgence, the English house of commons resolved to prepare an address to the king 'to represent to him the State and Condition of the Kingdom of *Ireland*; and the Danger of the English Protestant interest'.[52] When this was finally produced it outlined a variety of measures to protect the protestant interest and facilitate 'the suppression of the Insolencies and Disorders of the *Irish* Papists'.[53]A surprising response to this came from Orrery, who could usually be relied upon to advocate stern measures against catholics. In this instance he bemoaned the weakened condition of the Irish army, for

> I cannot say this they will doe, but I can say to yor Exce only, that 'tis likelyer they [catholics] should doe somthinge now than yt they should atempt what they did [in] 1641; & what they did then atempt we shall not easily forget. Then they had noe Provocation; now they will beleeve they have.[54]

But to raise the issue of security in Ireland, explicitly or otherwise, posed two questions: what was the priority of the Irish government, and how was it going to pay for such security?

For Essex, the first question had an obvious answer: he was in Ireland in order to maintain the protestant interest whose newly entrenched status rested upon the Act of Settlement.[55]

> Tho' I have ever since my coming into this Countrie made it my business to confirm all men in the belief that these Acts would never be in the least measure violated, yet have I allwaies found that the generalitie of the English who enjoy their estates upon these new titles could not shake off their apprehensions of loosing them again.[56]

After all, he observed, 'the Irish doe almost universally discours that they will have their lands agen'.[57] The uncertainties that this bred had economic implications:

> The truth is, the lands of Ireland have been a mere scramble, and the least done by way of orderly distribution of them as perhaps hath ever been known, which makes all men so unsettled in their estates and so unquiet in their possessions. And this hath been a ground for projectors to work upon; which, considering

52 C.J., IX, 270.
53 *Ibid.*, 277.
54 *Essex Papers*, I, 66.
55 *Ibid.*, pp. 49–50.
56 *Ibid.*, p. 50.
57 *Ibid*, p. 52.

> Ireland as a plantation (for in reality it is little other), cannot but be so great a discouragement to all people from coming hither, and to those who are here from laying out moneys on improvement.[58]

Hence the relevance of the second question: the security of the protestant interest might have been his priority, but it would also have to be paid for.

An obvious means of providing funds with which to do this was by calling a parliament in Ireland, but the collection of the revenue doggedly remained in private hands; Ranelagh's. The corrupt nature of his 'undertaking' ensured that Ireland's defences and military establishment remained underfunded and inadequate, and Ranelagh's influence with the king meant that he was in a strong position to deflect the unwelcome scrutiny of viceroys. Berkeley's downfall served to confirm this.[59] Yet it was impossible for Essex to disregard the question of finance, especially with regard to the penury of the army, which was 'really in a worse condition than ever they were since his Majesties Restauration'.[60] The lack of money for the military had allegedly been an issue in 1641; had the army in Ireland been properly funded then, the initial rebellion (and by implication all that had stemmed from it) could supposedly have been crushed with ease.

This potential vulnerability to internal and external threats was accentuated by other, more traditional concerns. In July 1676 the catholic clergy were apparently 'very indiscreet, and over busy', and a watching brief was to be maintained upon them 'especially in these times, the Irish being so big with expectations of a change in Religion'. In July 1676 copies of Nicholas French's *Bleeding Iphigenia* (another work from his pen that railed against the dispossession of the Irish) were reportedly circulating in Connacht; Essex thought that 'the people are so taken with y^{t} that … if 20000 volumes had come over they would all have been bought up', such was its attraction to those who had been dispossessed.[61] Alongside murmurs of catholic discontent came rumours of Presbyterian unrest. In late 1676 Essex received reports that the covenant had been revived in County Derry; he was unable to confirm this ('so true are the brethren one to another') but was convinced it was true.[62] A more concrete manifestation of such concerns came in January 1677, when the Church of Ireland bishop of Killala, Thomas Otway, told Essex of his intention to crack down on wandering Presbyterian preachers in his diocese who 'ride up and down the country like martiall Evangelists with sword and pistolls, as if they came not to prate down; but storm our

58 *Ibid.*, pp. 200–2.

59 Sean Egan, 'Finance and the Government of Ireland, 1660–85', Trinity College, Dublin, Ph.D., 2 vols, 1983.

60 *Selections from the Correspondence of Arthur Capel, Earl of Essex, 1675–1677*, ed. C. E. Pike (1913), pp. 56–8.

61 *Ibid.*, pp. 66–9.

62 *Ibid.*, p. 93.

Religion'.[63] Vigilance remained necessary, as the weakness of the colonial state in Ireland ensured that these problems, as yet, defied resolution. Such difficulties soon intermeshed with the more fundamental issues highlighted by the crisis of 1678–81. When Titus Oates made his revelations about the existence of a catholic plot directed against protestants across the Stuart kingdoms in autumn 1678, the fact that Ireland was the most catholic of those kingdoms guaranteed that it had a very specific role to play.

V

The events of 1678–81 do not usually loom large in Irish historiography.[64] Admittedly, the Popish Plot had a greater resonance in Ireland than the subsequent crisis over the succession. The general neglect of both arises from the basic fact that they had little *overt* effect on Ireland; little actually happened. But in terms of expectations, it is another matter entirely. The Popish Plot is traditionally interpreted by Irish historians in terms set by Thomas Carte almost 300 years ago: that it was of little significance in Irish terms because Ormond, as viceroy, essentially kept Ireland under control and thus guaranteed its stability.[65] Yet this suggests that there was a potential for instability, for given the overwhelmingly catholic composition of the island, allegations of catholic plotting were bound to have a resonance.

And they did. According to Oates, the catholic Irish were ready to rise with the aid of the papacy, 'for the Defence of their Liberty and Religion, and to recover their Estates'.[66] Irish assassins were to murder the king, and the rebellion was to facilitate a French invasion of Ireland; ultimately, the Irish intended 'to cut the Protestants Throats again, when once they rise'.[67] It was inevitable that the Irish government under Ormond (who was also to have been murdered by the plotters) would be forced to deal with this. In subsequent months they arrested and interrogated suspects, and sought

63 *Ibid.*, p. 95.

64 For the impact of the Popish plot and exclusion crisis on Ireland, see John Gibney, *Ireland and the Popish Plot* (Basingstoke, 2009).

65 For examples see Thomas Carte, *History of the Life of James, First Duke of Ormond* (2nd edn, 6 vols, Oxford, 1851), IV, 542–638; Richard Bagwell, *Ireland under the Stuarts* (3 vols, Dublin, 1909–16), III, 127–140; Aydelotte, 'The Duke of Ormond and the English Government of Ireland', I, 24–9; *A New History of Ireland, vol. III: Early Modern Ireland, 1534–1691*, ed. T.W. Moody, F.X. Martin and F.J. Byrne (Oxford, 1976), pp. 432–33; J.C. Beckett, *The Cavalier Duke: A Life of James Butler First Duke of Ormond, 1610–88* (Belfast, 1990), pp. 115–22; S.J. Connolly, *Religion Law and Power: The Making of Protestant Ireland, 1660–1760* (Oxford, 1992), pp. 24–32; David Dickson, *New Foundations: Ireland 1660–1800* (2nd edn, Dublin, 2000), pp. 19–21.

66 *L.J.*, XIII, 315.

67 *Ibid.*, 317.

to ensure the expulsion of catholic clergy from Ireland, the disarmament of the catholic laity and the strengthening of protestant Ireland's defences.[68]

The threat perceived in Ireland during the Popish Plot derived strength and credence from memory (fears of a repeat of the perceived atrocities of the 1641 rebellion), and contemporary reality, given that protestants were, as Petty had previously noted, vastly outnumbered by the catholic community that was deemed collectively responsible for the original rebellion. The crisis was seen to echo the events of the 1640s, and the dark allegations of a catholic conspiracy could be interpreted as the prelude to a repeat of 1641. The crisis was exacerbated by material concerns. The land settlement was under review by Ormond's government when the plot allegations emerged. Their priority at the time was to get Irish defences onto a secure footing through a radical restructuring of its financial base. The ultimate means of providing money for this was a parliament – none had met since 1666 – that would almost certainly be composed of protestant landowners who were unlikely to be tractable without having something to show for it. The sweetener was to be full and unchallenged confirmation of the estates held by so many since the 1650s, but for many in both Ireland and England this was a crucial sticking point, given the automatic favour it indicated to existing catholic landowners and the implicit closure of the land settlement to outstanding and future claims.[69] But the heightened fears engendered by the plot ensured that this prospective parliament never sat.[70] Consequently, the state of Ireland's defences remained largely unchanged.

No hard evidence came to light that might prove the existence of any plot in Ireland, and Ormond remained largely unconvinced of its reality. Inclined to discount such concerns, after the first few months he did not pursue an active policy against catholics. If no rebellion was stirring stringent action was superfluous, and, like Orrery in 1673, Ormond argued that stringent action was both unrealistic and provocative, for even a small insurrection might attract the attention and involvement of the French.[71] True, the Irish might launch attacks upon colonists, but they knew that retaliation was inevitable.[72] Thus, the official line in Ireland was prudence.

The undercurrent of fear was nonetheless real: plenty of sinister reports found their way to Dublin. For Ormond, his chosen policy of moderation, amongst other things, ensured that he himself became a subject of a whispering campaign in Ireland and England claiming him to be a covert catholic, intimately involved in plans to orchestrate an uprising.[73] Fears of

[68] Gibney, *Ireland and the Popish Plot*, pp. 28–65.

[69] Aydelotte, 'The Duke of Ormond and the English Government of Ireland', I, 30–98.

[70] N.L.I., MS 11971, fos 53–4.

[71] Bodl., Carte MS 38, f. 659.

[72] H.M.C., *Leyborne-Popham*, pp. 242–3.

[73] N.L.I., MS 13014: 'A Coppy of Som Discovery of ye Plott', 5 Feb. 1679; *Ireland's Sad Lamentation* (1680).

catholics were bolstered by the fact that throughout the crisis references to the template of 1641 were never far away: the pedigree of Ormond's relative Colonel John Fitzpatrick, for instance, was that *'His Father [was] a hainous Rebel, and his Mother Hanged for making Candles of Englishmen's Grease in the time of the late Rebellion'*.[74]

While the possibility of another Irish rebellion eventually became an adjunct to the exclusion campaign in England, dubious Irish informers (amongst others) were co-opted into swearing to the existence of an 'Irish plot' before the English parliament, in order bolster the whig campaign to exclude the catholic York from the succession.[75] The continuing attempts to procure evidence in Ireland to prove the existence of such a plot were driven by the requirements of the whig opposition: it was at this juncture that the word 'tory' began its long journey through English political history. Originally a term for an Irish catholic outlaw or bandit (themselves often drawn from the ranks of the dispossessed), it was soon deployed as a term of abuse directed at supporters of the ostensibly pro-catholic court.[76]

Ormond and his administration were obliged to facilitate the supply of such evidence as was sought in England, and had little control over what was demanded of them. No concrete fears of any catholic plot emerged in Ireland during the crisis. Yet the fears that underpinned it had been evident since the Restoration. While they may have been highlighted and accentuated during the Popish Plot, they were nothing new. And they survived. In May 1682 Sir Robert Southwell was of the opinion that

> You will find in Ireland a profound quiet, as it has lately been, when Scotland had in it an actual rebellion, and England been filled and disquieted about the plot. I cannot impute this under God to anything but the conduct of the Duke of Ormond, for he, having by long experience knowledge of the kingdom, and all men in it, having a large fortune, and, consequently, many dependents scattered into its several parts, and being also related in blood to great number of the Irish papists, the discontented had either dread to begin, or he presently knew and suppressed whatever was contriving. Thus, knowing what security the kingdom was in he had the courage to undergo all those calumnies and accusations thrown upon him in the heat of the plot, whereas if a stranger had there governed, who must have been influenced by the general outcry, the Irish had certainly been driven into desperation, and when the number is (as some think) ten to one, that could not have produced good.[77]

74 *Ireland's Sad Lamentation* (n.p.).

75 Gibney, *Ireland and the Popish Plot*, pp. 99–114.

76 Robert Willman, 'The Origins of "Whig" and "Tory" in English Political Language', *H.J.*, XVII (1974), 247–64. For an important study of Tory activity in Ireland, see Éamonn Ó Ciardha, 'Toryism and Rappareeism in County Armagh in the Late Seventeenth Century', in *Armagh: History & Society*, ed. A.J. Hughes and William Nolan (Dublin, 2001), pp. 381–412.

77 H.M.C., *Egmont*, II, 111–12.

The suggestion that Ormond's prudence ensured that matters did not come to a head implies that there were indeed tensions within the Irish polity that could yet prove disastrous. The emphasis on the supposed existence of a catholic plot ignored the continual (and more real) fears of unrest among Scots presbyterians in Ulster, which had been simmering since the onset of the Popish Plot. On 3 May 1679 Archbishop James Sharp was assassinated outside St Andrews by disaffected presbyterians. The subsequent Covenanter rebellion ended at Bothwell Brig on 22 June but fears that it might spill over into Ulster had been heightened as 'fanatic' preachers arrived there in the aftermath of Sharp's murder.[78] Ironically, fears about the security of protestant Ireland highlighted by the Popish Plot may well have been heightened by a protestant rebellion: as Ormond noted, events 'such as those were the beginning of our troubles before 1641'.[79]

The wider implications of this crisis were obvious, as both catholic and presbyterian insurrection could easily be encouraged by events elsewhere.[80] Given Ormond's scepticism about the existence of an Irish plot, not to mention his longstanding distrust of dissenters, the reality of the Scottish rebellion was bound to take precedence. Complaints about troops from Ireland being deployed to deal with the Scottish rebellion were deemed to stem

> from such as would not have the Rebellion in Scotland supprest too Soone, or from such as do not consider how much better it is to meet a growing Enemy [illegible] & at a distance from home than to stay till he got to his full strength & comes to Our doores.[81]

Rumours persisted that presbyterians in Ulster were emboldened by events in Scotland, though at least some dissenting ministers were prepared to pledge their loyalty to the government.[82] But the actuality of presbyterian unrest was more immediately problematic than notions of a catholic conspiracy.

This inevitably brought Ireland's finances to the fore. Military forces cost money. The lack of one hamstrung the other and ensured 'the danger of this Kingdome to it selfe, and in consequence to the rest of his Dominions to his Matie'. While the eventual successes against the Scottish rebels ostensibly justified measures to prevent 'Insurrection or Invasion', the lack of money to do so adequately remained a running sore, despite the rebellion having highlighted the problem. Again, an Irish parliament was the obvious means of raising funds, and Ormond bemoaned his inability to call one without prior approval from London at a time when English politics was preoccupied

78 T.N.A., PC/2/68, 53 (23 May 1679).
79 H.M.C., *Ormonde*, new ser., V, 131.
80 Bodl., Carte MS 146, p. 188.
81 N.L.I., Ormond MS 2388, p. 279.
82 Bodl.,Carte MS 45, fos 431–4, 529.

by the popish plot and exclusion crisis.[83] It seems that the English government did not automatically prioritize the overhaul of Ireland's defences, which suggests that they did not view Ireland as a pressing problem at this time. If this was indeed the case, it was a stance that was the polar opposite to that taken by William of Orange at the end of the 1680s.

VI

A persistent concern in Restoration Ireland was the considerable fear amongst protestants there as to whether they would survive and prosper, or whether they would fall victim to another onslaught along the lines of what 1641 was believed to have been. These fears had been highlighted during the Popish Plot. There is a striking contrast, after all, between the perceived stability of Ireland in 1678–81 and the crippling warfare of 1689–91. With hindsight, the prevailing fears of 1678–81 – the rumours of an imminent French invasion and a catholic assault upon protestants – resemble the reality of events in 1689–91. Thus, the crisis of 1678–81 stretched the fragile fabric of a post-war society to reveal the tensions that wracked it. In a manner reminiscent to that suggested by 'A light to the blind', the spectre of a catholic threat to protestants in 1678–81 foreshadowed the Jacobite era.

In the years after the crisis Ireland seemed to remain stable. In April 1682 the Dublin corporation offered a petition of loyalty to both Ormond and the king.[84] Throughout 1682–3 similar petitions were drawn up across Ireland, perhaps in a similar vein to the English petitions issued during the so-called 'tory revenge', as the king and court sought to consolidate their position across the three kingdoms whilst avenging themselves upon their opponents.[85] The majority of the Irish petitions assured Charles of the support of his loyal protestant subjects there. It remains virtually impossible to gauge whether the English political divisions of 1679–81 were replicated in Ireland: the absence of an Irish parliament ensured that there was no forum in which such beliefs could find expression. But some common ground can be discerned. Just as in England and Scotland, by the final years of Charles II's reign the danger to the Stuart dynasty in Ireland was seen to have passed, and the succession had been secured.

Despite this, there was still an occasional resonance accorded to the specific concerns highlighted by the Popish Plot in Ireland, and which had never been satisfactorily resolved. At some point in the early 1680s William Petty once again turned his attention to the condition of Ireland in general, and its defences in particular.

83 N.L.I., MS 802, f. 11.

84 *Calendar of the Ancient Records of Dublin*, ed. J.T. Gilbert (16 vols, Dublin, 1889–1913), V, 232–4.

85 Harris, *Restoration*, pp. 390–5.

> Suppose [the] ports and garisons of Dublin, Wexford, Waterford, Youghall, Corke, Kinsale, Dingle, Trallee, Lymerick, Galaway, Sligo, Derry, Carryckfergus & Drogheda to be in the hands of Catholique officers, under one Catholique Generall, who comands perhaps 15 Garisons and 15 regiments; It is manifest that the sd Generall and 30 officers can if they agree let in the French.[86]

It followed, then, that the catholic Irish

> would triumph in full splendor of Religion, the Protection of the mightiest Prince, the exercise of all offices, the merit of extirpating heresy, and revenge even by massacre upon the Brittish and Protestant interest, and to be delivered from the fear of a Protestant successor.[87]

The invocation of a catholic Irish 'massacre' in this context ('revenge') was deeply suggestive. The passing of the Popish Plot did not alter the reality that protestant Ireland was seen to be vulnerable to attack, and if catholic France was an enemy without, catholic Ireland remained an enemy within. The concerns that Petty gave expression to – of internal subversion assisting a catholic invasion – were reminiscence of the allegations made during the earlier crisis, and indeed since the Restoration itself.

The undercurrent of unease that characterized much of the 1680s was facilitated by uncertainty about the present and certainty about the past. Ireland retained its large and disgruntled catholic majority, and its small and wary protestant interest. When Nicholas French's *Narrative of the Earl of Clarendon's Settlement and Sale of Ireland* was reprinted in 1685, an 'English Protestant' offered a riposte: its subject matter remained relevant and contentious, for the legitimacy of the Restoration settlement remained at stake.[88] In July 1686 the chief secretary, Sir Paul Rycaut, observed that 'the Irish talk of nothing now but recovering their lands and bringing the English under their subjection, which they who have been the masters for above 400 years know not how well to bear'.[89] Unsurprisingly, given the catholic revival of the 1680s (especially the danger to the land settlement posed by the 1689 Jacobite parliament), and the stark fact that French forces were in Ireland supporting a catholic monarch, the Williamite war triggered an outburst of printed material similar in tone to that employed in previous generations.[90]

86 B.L., Add MS 72881, f. 23.

87 B.L., Add MS 72881, f. 24.

88 *Calendar of the Clarendon State Papers*, ed. W.H. Bliss, W. Dunn Macray, O. Ogle and F.J. Routledge (5 vols, Oxford, 1872–1970), V, 657.

89 'Sir Paul Rycaut's Memoranda and Letters from Ireland, 1686–1687', ed. Patrick Melvin, *Analecta Hibernica*, XXVII (1972), 157.

90 Gibney, *Ireland and the Popish Plot*, pp. 161–5.

During the reign of James II the Popish Plot in Ireland could arguably be seen to be on the verge of coming true. Enduring fears of the catholic Irish, as reflected through the lens of 1641, ensured that when the same fears seemed to be on the brink of realization after 1685, the response of the protestant interest would have enormous consequences. The Popish Plot had been a prelude, a shadow version of what might yet happen as the catholic Irish returned to power and influence after the accession of York as James II in 1685: the expulsion of protestants from civil and military office; the reversal of the land settlement; and, eventually, the arrival of the French in Ireland. The spectre of 1641 would be invoked again as Irish protestants of all denominations briefly smothered their differences and sought relief from England that came in the form of a Dutch king for whom such relief was but a minor detail. Their salvation would be one of the principal local implications of the war of 1690–1. The other would be the *de facto* destruction of the catholic political interest on the island of Ireland, and its subsequent exile to the continent. 'A light to the blind' would not be the only version of these events, or of their prelude; there would be other histories that would correspond to, and crystallize, the racial and sectarian divisions that underpinned and almost undermined Restoration Ireland.[91] Having shaped the nature of the Glorious Revolution in Ireland, such divisions would ultimately shape its legacy.

91 Patrick Kelly, 'Nationalism and the Contemporary Historians of the Jacobite War in Ireland', in *Nations and Nationalism: France, Britain and the Eighteenth-Century Context*, ed. Michael O'Dea and Kevin Whelan (Oxford, 1995), pp. 89–102.

During the [illegible]
thought to be [illegible]
[illegible]

7

Ireland, 1688–91

TOBY BARNARD

On 21 March 1688 a new charter was borne into the borough of Galway, in the westerly province of Connacht. Galway, a last redoubt of the catholics during the Confederate War, had surrendered to the Cromwellian forces only in 1652. Thereafter, protestants were intruded into its government and trade, as in all boroughs throughout Ireland. After Charles II's return in 1660, the protestant monopoly was eroded, especially in places such as Galway where protestants were few. The reinstatement of catholics, first as traders and craft-workers, then as freemen and civic functionaries, gathered momentum after the accession of James VII and II in 1685. The personnel and programme of the government in Ireland changed dramatically. Events in Galway in 1688 were part of a process that exhilarated the catholic inhabitants of Ireland in a way not felt since the heady 1640s. Indeed, optimists hoped that the exclusions and discriminations of the past century would soon be reversed.

Three hundred townspeople prepared to welcome the town clerk returning with the precious document. A detachment of 50 rode to Loughreagh on the border of County Galway, whence it processed back to the borough itself. The charter was placed on a horse, richly caparisoned in crimson and silver. A dozen footboys all in white were followed by six horses led by pages. Four young gentlemen mounted on horses preceded the sergeant of the mace, who was succeeded immediately by the horse carrying the charter. A young gentleman bore the king's sword sheathed in a red velvet scabbard ornamented with silver plates on which were engraved several mottoes. (Similar, but earlier swords are preserved among the remarkable civic regalia of Waterford.) More mounted gentlemen with drawn swords rode in front of the mayor himself, who, for whatever reason, was flanked by a pair of blackamoors. Other functionaries such as the recorder, sheriffs, justices of the peace and local gentlemen completed a panoply totalling 400, 'all in due order'. At the approaches to the city, the parade was greeted by local delegations: about 120 apprentice merchants, 'with their colours flying … well clothed'; next, the town's seamen, also with colours fluttering in the breeze; then about 100 young scholars all clad in white; the members of the several guilds, they too with banners and music. Finally, as the crowd entered the borough, 120 virgins and the children of the townsfolk, 'neatly and richly dressed', strewed garlands of flowers and herbs in the path. The subsequent festivities were presided over by the mayor's wife, helped by matrons. The garrison and trades-people were feasted.[1]

The description of the ceremonies was intended to be published in a newspaper, and may therefore have exaggerated numbers and delight.[2] Much in this celebration drew on the pageantry which customarily marked the passage of the year in larger municipalities. The only difference was the substitution of catholics for protestants as the chief participants. Otherwise, the account was free from any suggestion of menace or indeed any clear confessional dimension. However, private comments on events immediately following the reception did spell out implications more ominous to the local protestants. An abstract of the Galway charter had been read aloud from the tholsel (or town hall), and revealed that the mayor was to have the right to nominate the warden and eight vicars in the college. A priest was heard to remark that the college should be seized. More worrying – and an augury of events to come – was the suggestion that the parish church should be repossessed by the catholics.[3]

Several elements in the account of the Galway celebrations are worth isolating, since they have implications for what was happening – or would soon happen – elsewhere in Ireland. Galway was one of 105 corporations, the charters of which were recalled and re-issued between 1687 and 1688. The return of most boroughs to the control of a catholic majority, sometimes in partnership with docile protestants, was important both in itself and as a preliminary to the summoning of a parliament in Dublin.[4] A majority of its members sat for the borough constituencies. If, for the first time since 1634, they were overwhelmingly catholics, then an assembly summoned by King James might dismantle the recent settlement. The most offensive feature so far as catholics were concerned was the transfer of so much of their land to protestants. As a result of measures in the 1650s, the catholics' share

[1] N.L.I., de Vesci MSS, G7: 'The reception of the charter of Galway to be put into the gazette', 21 Mar. 1687[8]; M. Coen, *The Wardenship of Galway* (Galway, 1984), pp. 21–4; E. MacLysaght, 'Report on Documents Relating to the Wardenship of Galway', *Analecta Hibernica*, XIV (1944), 148–56; S.J. Rabbitte, 'Galway Corporation MS C', *Journal of the Galway Archaeological and Historical Society*, XIII (1927), 73.

[2] No newspaper from Ireland of the date is known to survive. R.L. Munter, *A Handlist of Irish Newspapers, 1685–1750* (Cambridge, 1960); *idem*, *The Irish Newspaper, 1685–1760* (Cambridge, 1967), pp. 11–13.

[3] N.L.I., de Vesci MSS: Fielding Shawe to Abp. J. Vesey, 23 Mar. 1687[8]; Rabbitte, 'Galway Corporation MS C', pp. 73–4.

[4] T.C. Barnard, 'Conclusion: Settling and Unsettling Ireland: The Cromwellian and Williamite Revolutions', in *Ireland from Independence to Occupation, 1640–1660*, ed. Jane H. Ohlmeyer (Cambridge, 1995), 275–6; W. Harris, *The History of the Life and Reign of William-Henry Prince of Orange* (Dublin, 1749), Appendix, pp. iv–xvi.

of land in Ireland had plummeted from 59 to 22 per cent. After 1660, the trend towards a protestant ascendancy over power and property was modified but not reversed. Catholics hoped and protestants feared that once a parliament convened, the full implications of the accession of a catholic monarch would become clear. By the time that it was elected – in 1689 – the situation had changed. James had abandoned and been abandoned by England and Scotland. Ireland in consequence assumed a new importance in his plans: so much so, that he came there. He was the first king since Richard II to do so.

Festivities in Galway emphasized one important change: the catholics' recovery of municipal office. A second – the remodelling of the army in order to make it predominantly a catholic force – was not disclosed in the account from the west. However, a third source of mounting protestant unease was mentioned: the catholic ambition to recover ecclesiastical revenues and church buildings, which, since the sixteenth-century reformation, had been occupied by the protestants of the established Church of Ireland. During the 1640s, in the extensive areas controlled by the catholics, the older churches again accommodated catholic worship. Inevitably, once the Cromwellians reconquered the island, the buildings were returned to protestant custody, in which they stayed even when first Charles II and then James VII and II showed greater generosity towards the catholics. The importance with which the catholics regarded the recovery of the property of the Church is one theme that will be explored in what follows. A second is the forwardness of the protestant clergy in resisting both the specific demand and the larger hopes of the catholics.

I

Interpretations of James's reign in Ireland vary chiefly in emphases. Among the catholic majority, differences in tactic – between patience and aggression – have sometimes been traced back to the similar disagreements of the 1640s and earlier. The varied approaches might reflect geography. Palesmen in the east of the Ireland were allegedly more temperate in opinions and tactics than those remote in Connacht or displaced by the recent protestant settlements of Ulster and Munster. Ethnicity, too, was thought to colour attitudes: those claiming English lineage (often described as 'the Old English') were identified with political moderation, whereas those who proclaimed Irish descent were said to be impatient with diplomacy. Friction over strategy has been discerned between 1685 and 1691, yet there is general agreement that it was less acrimonious and debilitating than in the 1640s. The contrast can be explained partly by the fact that, once Ireland became a theatre of a European war between 1689 and 1691, the Irish catholic commanders needed to unite lest they be pushed aside by their continental allies, notably the French. Back in the 1640s, although foreign aid had been sought, it had not materialized other than in the contentious interventions of successive papal nuncios sent to Ireland.

The responses of the protestant minority to James VII and II have excited only mild disagreements among historians. The protestants in Ireland constituted a minority of the inhabitants – at most 20 per cent of the population. In this numerical inferiority, they differed strikingly from their counterparts in England, Wales and Scotland. Being so small a proportion of the inhabitants of Ireland, the protestants were vulnerable to any withdrawal of official favour. Moreover, the protestants were themselves divided: between conformist members of the established Church and dissenters. The latter were especially strong in areas of Scottish settlement concentrated in Ulster. In politics, too, protestant opinion ranged from a passionate and passive loyalism towards the Stuart dynasty to nostalgia for the achievements of the Cromwellian interregnum. If not yet in name, then certainly in attitudes, the distinctive beliefs of Tories and Whigs could be detected. Most protestants responded cautiously to royal policies, rather than showing early or intransigent opposition. In support of this interpretation, it is possible to find prominent protestants who submitted without public complaint to, or even co-operated with, James's and his agents' policies for Ireland.[5] Undoubtedly, some out of favour throughout much of Charles II's reign under the high anglican regime of the duke of Ormond welcomed the accession of James. A notable example was Sir William Petty, whose endless projects for advancing the public good had been as frustrated as his personal hopes of aggrandisement and advancement. Petty looked to James to reverse his neglect.[6] Enthusiasts like Petty were rarer than the merely compliant, but both groups deferred to the new monarch.

All writers, despite differences in emphasis, agree that the dangers facing the protestants in the later 1680s did not match those of the 1640s. Massacres of the sort popularly supposed to have disfigured the earlier

[5] Barnard, 'Settling and Unsettling Ireland', pp. 265–91; A.I. Carpenter, 'William King and the Threats to the Church of Ireland during the Reign of James II', *Irish Historical Studies*, XVIII (1972–3), 22–8; R. Gillespie, 'The Irish Protestants and James II, 1688–1690', *Irish Historical Studies*, XXVIII (1992), 124–33; J. Miller, 'The Earl of Tyrconnell and James II's Irish Policy, 1685–1688', *H.J.*, XX (1977); J.G. Simms, *Jacobite Ireland, 1685–1691* (1969, repr. Dublin, 2000); *idem*, 'The War of the Two Kings', in *A New History of Ireland. III*, ed. T.W. Moody, F.J. Byrne and F.X. Martin (Oxford, 1975), pp. 478–508.

[6] T.C. Barnard, 'Sir William Petty, Irish Landowner', in *History and Imagination: Essays in Honour of H.R. Trevor-Roper*, ed. H. Lloyd-Jones, V. Pearl and A.B. Worden (1981), pp. 201–17; *The British Library Catalogue to the Additions to the Manuscripts. The Petty Papers* (2000), pp. xvii–xx; *The Petty-Southwell Correspondence, 1676–1687*, ed. H.W.E. Petty-Fitzmaurice, marquess of Lansdowne (1928), pp. 207, 213, 215, 233, 279, 283; F. Harris, 'Ireland as a Laboratory: The Archive of Sir William Petty', in *Archives of the Scientific Revolution*, ed. M. Hunter (Woodbridge, 1998), pp. 73–90.

decade were rumoured, but they did not happen.[7] Above all, nervous protestants had several years in which to contemplate what their fate might be. As a Cork resident observed in 1686, when he reported the quickening pace of change, it was better to foresee than be surprised by events.[8] The lengthy wait alarmed some; others were enabled to prepare for whatever might come. Many of substance had ample time to remove their effects, families and even themselves to the safety of Britain.

The ingenious or unscrupulous tried to devise a propaganda campaign comparable to that of their forbears immediately after October 1641. Yet, it lacked the conviction and desperation of the earlier efforts. William III came to the aid of Ireland much more quickly than the English parliament after 1641. He did nothing to attract the opprobrium heaped on Cromwell after Drogheda and Wexford. Violence and fatalities were inevitable in any war, but the conflict ended more quickly and less bloodily than its predecessor. Beleaguered protestants were intimidated and humiliated, but nothing akin to the 'massacres' in and after 1641 occurred. A pamphlet of 1690 issued in London, which claimed that Athlone had been captured and its garrison put to the sword, proved a work of fiction.[9] Disease and famine following the war did not cause the levels of mortality suffered in the early 1650s. Even the political and legal impact can be played down. The catholic defeat merely allowed the completion of the exclusions long under contemplation. The catholics' share of land fell further: from 22 per cent in 1688 to 14 per cent as a result of fresh confiscations of the 1690s. But this was not such a dramatic decline as had occurred in the aftermath of the Cromwellian victories.[10] There was an exodus of the vanquished and dispossessed, but again these movements, both enforced and voluntary, were hardly new.

II

Two threads running through evaluations of the events in Ireland between 1685 and 1691 are worth re-examining. One is the unease of the protestants as they were stripped quickly of their military powers. The second is the place of confessional strife in the developing crisis. In relation to the role of religious competition, there are two issues that deserve greater notice than they have usually received: wrangling over physical possession of churches; and clerical leadership of the protestant interest.

7 Cambridge U.L., Baumgartner MSS, Add. MS 1/60; Royal Irish Academy, MS 24 G 2/3: letters of information from Cork, 3, 5, 10 Jan. 1688[9].

8 Hovell letter-book, Farmar MSS: W. Hovell to J. Putland, 18 May 1686.

9 *Great News from Athlone and Waterford* (1690); H. Murtagh, *Athlone: History and Settlement to 1800* (Athlone, 2000), p. 149.

10 J.G. Simms, *The Williamite Confiscation in Ireland, 1690–1703* (1956).

Under Charles II and James II, protestants in Ireland had good reason to be both alarmed and embarrassed. The protestants' past record was not one of unswerving loyalty to the Stuarts. Even a perfunctory glance at recent history challenged the common equation of protestantism with political fidelity and catholicism with subversion. Apprehensive that catholics' protestations of devotion would be believed by Charles and James, the protestants of Ireland varied between trying to exhibit an almost servile loyalty and working to discredit their catholic rivals. Thereby the protestants were liable to tarnish further their already spotted reputations with the monarch. In 1686, one protestant bishop wrote irritably of how the catholics 'pretend to be the greatest, if not only king's men'.[11]

The protestants' fears of a loss of power were well-founded. It made sense for a regime, struggling to find adequate representatives to fill local offices, such as the shrievalty and magistracy, to turn to reliable and substantial catholics. Already, in the 1670s, there were complaints that the employment of catholics was being sanctioned by the lord chancellor. Indeed, it was alleged that a third of the 900 justices of the peace were 'Irish', and therefore by implication catholic or sympathetic to catholicism.[12] Early in the 1680s, opinion moved strongly in favour of the king as he navigated the hazards of the Popish Plot and the Exclusion Crisis.[13] In Ireland, the inclination to turn to the dependable regardless of confession was strengthened. An abundance of willing catholics there compared well with the paucity of suitable protestants. Accordingly, the policies that had been tried in the 1670s were more enthusiastically and less equivocally adopted in the following decade. The decision to rely yet more heavily on catholics whose forbears had last held important local and national offices during the catholic ascendancy of the 1640s, but before that not since the 1620s, seems to have been taken before Charles II died. To clear the way, a chief obstacle, the incumbent lord lieutenant, the duke of Ormond, had to be removed. Ormond, although passionate in his allegiance to the Stuarts, shared the anxieties of the protestants, into whom he (although by ancestry catholic) had been assimilated. He communicated some of his own, and his co-religionists', alarm to his masters in Whitehall. But Ormond belonged now to a generation apparently out of touch with the flexible approach to confessional affiliation and state-craft. In consequence, it was agreed that Ormond must go, although he was able to prevent a humiliating dismissal. Ardent

[11] E. Wetenhall, 'The Christian Law of the Sword. Both as to its Publick & Private Use, Briefly Stated in a Sermon at Christchurch in the city of Cork' (Dublin, 1686), in E. Wetenhall, *Hexapla Jacobae* (Dublin, 1686), p. 35.

[12] N.L.I., MSS 17,845.

[13] P.D. Halliday, *Dismembering the Body Politic: Partisan Politics in England's Towns, 1650–1730* (Cambridge, 1998); Tim Harris, *Restoration: Charles II and his Kingdoms, 1660–1685* (2005), part II; Grant Tapsell, *The Personal Rule of Charles II, 1681–85* (Woodbridge, 2007).

catholics had long reviled Ormond as a formidable adversary whose influence at the Stuart court largely explained why the dispossessed Irish had not been recompensed adequately. Ormond, following his departure from the viceroyalty and his retirement to England, was still blamed for his malign advice. But this was to credit him with an influence over the king that he no longer possessed.[14]

Ormond's immediate replacement as lord lieutenant in 1685 was the second earl of Clarendon. Although Clarendon, unlike Ormond, was English-born, he personified continuity, since he breathed the same anglican royalism that Ormond himself had long exhaled. Clarendon was appointed to reassure the Irish protestants as the pace of the catholic re-entry into the government and army quickened. However, 'in his ticklish station', he could not altogether allay protestant worries. In part, this was because he lacked the instinctive and long-standing connections with the propertied protestants that Ormond had built up since the 1630s. Then, too, it was embarrassingly clear that Clarendon had little power to direct policy. Soon after his installation in Dublin, a whispering campaign against him started in England, where he was spoken of 'disadvantageously'.[15] He was seen as a brake on the implementation of 'the intended total discarding of the Whigs in Ireland, and putting the catholics of that country into civil and military employments'.[16] Even more galling to the disgruntled catholics was Clarendon's reassurance, shortly after he landed in Dublin in January 1686, that the land settlement would not be tampered with. This refusal to reverse the massive transfers of land from catholics to protestants since the 1650s, ultimately traced back to the king, gravely disappointed catholics and, for a time at least, calmed protestant nerves.[17]

In one particularly sensitive area, the army, Clarendon was speedily bypassed. In the summer of 1686, Richard Talbot, earl of Tyrconnell, was commissioned as commander in chief in Ireland. Hitherto, command of the army had been coupled with the headship of civil government. By uncoupling them, James showed both his scant confidence in Clarendon and the priority that he gave to the rapid remodelling of the Irish army. Talbot had been a companion of the king when they shared exile in the Low Countries in the later 1650s. Thereafter, Talbot, member of a prominent and prolific family of the Pale, emerged as a leader of the Irish catholics, especially those

14 'A Series of Eight Anonymous and Confidential Letters to James II about the State of Ireland', *Notes and Queries*, 6th ser., V and VI (1882), V, 363; É. Ó Ciardha, '"The Unkinde Deserter" and "The Bright Duke": Contrasting Views of the Dukes of Ormonde in Irish Royalist Tradition', in *The Dukes of Ormonde, 1610–1745*, ed. T. Barnard and J. Fenlon (Woodbridge, 2000), pp. 177–94.

15 Somerset R.O., DD/BR/ely, C/1509, 3/9.

16 'Eight Anonymous and Confidential Letters to James II', V, 361; VI, 3.

17 Petworth House, West Sussex, Orrery MSS, general series, 30: Lord Inchiquin to the Dowager Countess of Orrery, 23 Jan. 1685[6].

(like him) of Old English lineage, as they campaigned to recover the possessions and power lost since 1641. At the court of Charles II, he had swung in and out of favour.[18] The accession of James heralded Tyrconnell's return to power. However, he was a figure who aroused strong feelings, and was not admired universally even by English catholics. Some hoped that the king would soon grow tired 'of having so many of the Irish hanging about him'.[19]

It was in the military sphere that the impact of a catholic monarch became visible most rapidly and dramatically. A reason for replacing Ormond with Clarendon was that the former had intimate and ancient ties with many of the officers in the Irish military establishment and was prepared to take up their causes when they were threatened with dismissal. In contrast, Clarendon had no such ties, so that, while alive to the distress and anger of disbanded veterans, he was less assertive about bringing their grievances to the attention of the government in London. In practice, Clarendon, denied the command of the Irish army, was powerless to stop Tyrconnell's swift moves to turn the force from a protestant into a catholic body. One in Clarendon's entourage reported the numbers of the dismissed at 2,500. There would not be enough space for them in the newly built hospital on the outskirts of Dublin for military veterans, an equivalent of Les Invalides in Paris.[20]

The plight 'of old cavaliers or the sons of those gentlemen eminent for their loyal services' elicited sympathy which could be expected to be shared by connections and comrades in England.[21] Others might fear that they would soon be treated in the same summary way. Yet, not all were. Tyrconnell was politic enough to see the undesirability of alarming too many influential protestants. Also, some of the social connections and friendships that he had formed earlier with members of the Irish protestant élite came into play. One beneficiary was Henry Boyle, the younger son of the first earl of Orrery, one of the most strident and unscrupulous champions of Irish protestant rule over Ireland. At first glance, this was an improbable relationship. Boyle acknowledged that his father had been motivated by religious ideology (and self-interest) to oppose Tyrconnell's efforts to recover more of what his co-religionists had forfeited during the 1650s. Despite this sharp divergence over confessional politics, Tyrconnell still professed respect for Orrery and his family, and retained Boyle in his military command. Tyrconnell's calculation was that Boyle's influence in south Munster could help

[18] A. Creighton, 'The Catholic Interest in Irish Politics in the Reign of Charles II', Queen's University Belfast Ph.D., 2000.

[19] *The Correspondence of Henry Hyde, Earl of Clarendon*, ed. S.W. Singer (2 vols 1828), I, 276.

[20] 'Sir Paul Rycaut's Memoranda and Letters from Ireland, 1686–1687', ed. P. Melvin, *Analecta Hibernica*, XXVII (1972), 153.

[21] J.P. Kenyon, *Robert Spencer, Earl of Sunderland, 1641–1702* (1958), pp. 136–7; 'Rycaut's Memoranda', pp. 144–5, 147, 149, 153.

to reconcile the substantial protestant population there to the projected changes. Boyle suspected that Tyrconnell might prefer to use him rather than a catholic from the area, such as Justin McCarthy, to 'disoblige your friends, neighbours and father's followers' by disarming them. Boyle was deputed to command the garrison at Bandon in County Cork: a borough that belonged to his uncle, the second earl of Cork, and which had a reputation for being 'very stubborn and like to be more so', owing to the high concentration of protestants there. Boyle did what Tyrconnell wanted: he persuaded the Bandonians to send a loyal address to the king; they also surrendered the keys of the recently walled town.[22]

In 1686, Henry Boyle was mollified and flattered. Tyrconnell sought but hardly followed his advice. Boyle urged Tyrconnell to treat as loyal all who were prepared to take communion according to the rites of the Church of Ireland, and to swear the oaths of allegiance and supremacy. In this way, Boyle strove to shield his own community of protestants in Munster, for the most part conformable to the established Church, and to distinguish them from the settler population of Ulster, a substantial section of which adhered to presbyterianism. However, Boyle admitted that Tyrconnell was sceptical about the likelihood of oaths constraining dissidents. Moreover, his optimism about Tyrconnell's reasonableness disappeared when he and his regiment were ordered from Bandon to the northern garrison of Lisburn. He was further dismayed to hear from Tyrconnell, as he left a military review at Kilkenny in the summer of 1686, that the displaced officers were to be replaced only by 'natives and those too of the Romish religion'. These were instructions to which (he believed) the lord lieutenant, Clarendon, had not been privy.[23] Again the powerlessness of Clarendon in the vital sphere of the army was revealed. As the catholic takeover gathered momentum, Boyle himself was dismissed. Neither the links between Tyrconnell and his father and uncle nor his being the senior captain in the force prevented this fate.[24]

Some of Boyle's dismissed comrades accepted service in the Low Countries, thereby forging an early and useful link with William. Others took their complaints to the authorities in Dublin and London.[25] Boyle, in contrast, remained at his south Munster seat. He claimed still to be exercising a moderating influence. Like his ancestors in the 1640s and canny contemporaries, he was biding his time to see when best to act against

22 Petworth House, West Sussex, Orrery MSS, general series, 30: H. Boyle to unknown, undated [1686]; 'Rycaut's Memoranda', p. 132.

23 Petworth House, West Sussex, Orrery MSS, general series, 30: H. Boyle to Dowager Countess of Orrery, 21 July 1686; Surrey R.O., Midleton MSS, 1248/1, f. 204; *Calendar of the Orrery papers Papers*, ed. E. MacLysaght (Dublin, 1941), pp. 319–20.

24 Petworth House, West Sussex, Orrery MSS, general series, 30: H. Boyle to an unknown peer, 14 Jan. 1688[9]; *Calendar of the Orrery Papers*, p. 322.

25 BL, Add. MS 28,938, fos. 289, 314; J. Child, *The Army, James II and the Glorious Revolution* (Manchester, 1980), p. 74; *Petty-Southwell Correspondence*, pp. 301–3.

the catholic advance. He declared, early in 1689, 'I have inclinations and interest enough here to serve the English interest and the protestant religion': a credo echoing that of his father.[26] With a kinsman, Lord Inchiquin, Boyle organized a defensive association of the protestants in County Cork. Not all his co-religionists approved his initiative. In addition to objections that such action was incompatible with allegiance to James, there were warnings that it was impolitic since it might provoke greater violence from the local catholics.[27]

More were affected by changes in the army than by the advancement of catholics into the magistracy, shrievalty and privy council, or onto the judicial bench. Furthermore, as the cashiered crowded into the cities, flash-points were created. Relations between the dismissed and their supplanters, seen by contemporaries as distinct in race and confession, were not improved by the evident contempt with which the displaced regarded the newcomers. In 1686, it was predicted that the projected remodelling of the Royal Regiment would fill it 'with poor silly cowkeepers and wretched creatures out of the countries, who will give the officers trouble sufficient before they learn their right hand from their left'. The animosity recurred. Talk of 'raw, silly Irishmen' hardly conduced to amicable dealings.[28] In other spheres, where catholics were advanced rapidly in the places of protestants, similar disdain was expressed.[29]

The army in Ireland had long concerned the Stuarts and their advisers. In the 1620s, late 1630s and 1640s, it was seen as a potential source of support against both foreign and local adversaries. Accordingly, there was strong interest in ensuring that the force was reliable and, better still, available for service outside the kingdom of Ireland. Towards the end of Charles II's reign, a more integrated approach to the business of defence and warfare encouraged the shifting of regiments between the three kingdoms and overseas stations, such as Tangiers. The dramatic changes instituted by Tyrconnell could be justified as a continuation (and intensification) of long-standing schemes.[30] The numbers of catholics, and the absence of more attractive employments for many of them, made it easy enough to achieve a rapid transformation in the personnel of the army. It was alleged that in preparation for the changes, priests had returned numbers of fit males in their parishes. They were said to total 54,000. Once the catholics had taken over the army, the report was that the wealth of the established Church would be returned to them. The property of the protestant laity would

26 Petworth House, West Sussex, Orrery MSS, general series, 30: H. Boyle to an unknown peer, 14 Jan. 1688[9].

27 Lambeth Palace Library, MS 3152, fos 20, 21v, 24, 26.

28 'Rycaut's Memoranda', pp. 152–3.

29 'Rycaut's Memoranda', p. 153.

30 'Eight Anonymous and Confidential Letters to James II', V, 401.

soon follow.[31] Changes in the army occasioned localized clashes. Soldiers, unhappy at the developments, had the means to protest, and sometimes did so, thereby provoking reprisals from those now entrusted with arms.[32] Even more offensive to the protestant inhabitants were the orders that those who served in the county militias should hand in their arms. There were moves to resist the proclamation: for example, in County Cork. But, for the moment, obedience prevailed. Yet, the disarmament offended the protestant settlers' strong military traditions. It was the prelude to the abolition of the protestant militia, and left the protestants exposed – so they believed – to the depredations of their neighbours.[33]

Inevitably in this confused situation, where rumours abounded, defensive steps were easily mistaken for offensive ones. Each side accused the other of provocations. A notable in Kilkenny collected and annotated the proclamations issued during James's reign. The annotations frequently amounted to nothing more than hearsay. Nevertheless, they show what stories were current and how terrors gripped small communities. The published version, edited in the nineteenth century by Sir John Gilbert, an eminent but partisan scholar, suppressed the most unpleasant passages. In doing so, Gilbert spared the squeamish, and sought to protect the reputations of James's catholic subjects.[34] News reached Kilkenny that in Naas, soldiers, incited by their aggressive commander Lord Galmoy, 'went from house to house and made every one, men and women, show their nakedness and some they assaulted with other vile actions not fit to mention'. Other 'vile actions' were reported from Trim, where a female servant was abused by soldiers as 'an English bitch'. The assailants 'forced her and lay with her and then took a stick and cutting nicks in it thrust it into her body which could not be got out so she died'. The reports may have owed more to accounts from the 1640s than to accurate information about the current situation. The law intervened, and – it was said – four were hanged and quartered for the crime.[35] Inadvertently, in noting that the miscreants were tried, the Kilkenny collector attested to the discipline that still prevailed.

31 Armagh Public Library, Dopping MSS, 1/53, 54, 56.

32 T.C. Barnard, 'Athlone, 1685; Limerick, 1710: Religious Riots or Charivaris?', *Studia Hibernica*, XXVII (1993), 61–75.

33 T.N.A.,, P.R.O., SP 63/351, 91, 143; Hovell letter-book, Farmar MSS: W. Hovell to W. Houblon, 25 May 1686; Barnard, 'Athlone, 1685; Limerick, 1710', pp. 66–71; H.M.C., *Egmont*, II, 154, 157–8, 164; H.M.C., *Egmont Diary*, III, 354–5; R.T. Steele, *Bibliotheca Lindesiana: A Bibliography of Royal Proclamations* (2 vols, Oxford, 1912), II, nos. 947, 958 (Ireland).

34 For Gilbert's *parti pris*, see T.C. Barnard, 'Sir John Gilbert and Irish History', in *Sir John Gilbert 1829–1898: Historian, Archivist and Librarian*, ed. M. Clark, Y. Desmond and N.P. Hardiman (Dublin, 1999), pp. 91–110.

35 Collection of proclamations annotated by Colles in N.L.I., MS 1793. The expurgated version is in H.M.C., *Ormonde* MSS, new ser., VIII, 346.

III

In this jumpy atmosphere, inevitably rumours circulated and panics occurred. For substantial protestants, the overriding worry was that they might be stripped of their recently acquired properties. Ironically, James continued to disappoint his most zealous Irish catholic backers by the caution with which he approached the controversial topic. However, once Tyrconnell replaced Clarendon in January 1687, albeit with the inferior title and more modest powers as lord deputy, the expectation increased that a parliament would be summoned, and that its members would tackle the knotty matter. Already, in June 1686, it was reported that 'we are in miserable fear of our act of settlement, which is the only stay of the English of this kingdom'.[36] Soon, a veteran observer of the Irish protestant scene concluded, that 'the settlement like St Sebastian is stuck full of arrows'.[37]

In preparation for the parliamentary elections, the boroughs were remodelled. catholics were not only readmitted to trade, but also to civic government. Since the franchise in most boroughs was confined to small groups of municipal functionaries or to the freemen, these changes brought closer the prospect of a parliament in which a majority was catholic. More than two-thirds of the members of the Commons were elected for borough constituencies. Even in the counties, with more catholics with freeholds and with many sheriffs also catholic (the sheriffs acted as returning officers), here too the likelihood of the return of catholics improved. Nervous protestant observers might comfort themselves that whatever happened in Ireland would be achieved 'in a parliamentary way'.[38] In practice, it was scant comfort, since an Irish catholic parliament was likely to hesitate less than an English king, even when catholic, about dispossessing the protestants of Ireland. This, indeed, proved to be the case when such a parliament assembled in Dublin during 1689.

Responses among the protestants of Ireland, as has been stressed often, varied.[39] Although they had good reasons to be disquieted by what the preparations presaged, in contrast to 1641 they were not taken by surprise. Those who retained interests and connections in Britain could remove themselves without too much trouble. Most, lacking such links, had little option but to

[36] Hovell letter-book, Farmar MSS: W. Hovell to J. Putland, 16 July 1686; see, too: *Petty-Southwell Correspondence*, p. 140

[37] *Petty-Southwell Correspondence*, p. 264.

[38] Petworth House, West Sussex, Orrery MSS, general series, 30: J. Hall to dowager countess of Orrery, 22 Jan. 1686[7]; *Petty-Southwell Correspondence*, pp. 249, 251.

[39] Gillespie, 'Irish Protestants and James II', pp. 124–33; D.W. Hayton, 'The Williamite Revolution in Ireland, 1688–1691', in *The Anglo-Dutch Moment: Essays on the Glorious Revolution and its World Impact*, ed. J.I. Israel (Cambridge, 1991); P.H. Kelly, 'Ireland and the Glorious Revolution: From Kingdom to Colony', in *The Revolutions of 1688*, ed. R. Beddard (Oxford, 1991).

stay. But there were, too, differences in outlook, based on experience and ideology, comparable with and sometimes influenced directly by attitudes among the Stuarts' subjects in Scotland and England. Correspondents wrote of their faith in the king's good intentions towards the protestants of Ireland and of their confidence that nothing untoward would befall them. Fearful that letters might be intercepted, it may be doubted that the writers always committed their real views to paper.[40] Government censorship blacked out potentially unsettling information.[41] As a result, greater credence was accorded to rumours, hearsay and imported news. Some calculated that, so long as they exhibited a complete and almost craven loyalty, they would be spared from any serious harm. Yet the extent to which cautious protestants took preventative measures, notably by shipping moveables and valuables from Ireland, although it may have been exaggerated, can hardly be gainsaid.[42] Officials, such as Sir John Temple, long settled in Ireland, arranged for his family to return permanently to England in May 1687.[43] By June 1687, it was noted that several prominent merchants from Cork and Youghal had migrated to Somerset, where they retained family and trading links.[44] The following month there were reports of a dramatic drop in the customs revenue collected in the port of Dublin, easily read as a sign of the contraction in trade, and of the closure of 30 shops in two of the city's smartest thoroughfares.[45]

It suited some correspondents in Ireland to dramatize their predicament. Indeed, 'the consternation of the times' proved a plausible excuse for not remitting money from Ireland to landlords and creditors in England.[46] Accounts were also designed to engage the sympathy and support of protestants elsewhere for 'the poor English of Ireland'.[47] Not the least of the

40 Hovell letter-book, Farmar MSS: W. Hovell to W. Houblon, 23 July 1686, 2 Nov. 1686; T.C. Barnard, 'The Political, Material and Mental Culture of the Cork Settlers, c. 1650–1700', in T.C. Barnard, *Irish Protestant Ascents and Descents* (Dublin, 2003), pp. 78–9.

41 M. Pollard, 'Control of the Press in Ireland through the King's Printer's Patent', *Irish Booklore*, IV (1980), 79–95.

42 Hovell letter-book, Farmar MSS: W. Hovell to W. Houblon, 7 Dec. 1686, 7 Jan. 1686[7]; Petworth House, West Sussex, Orrery MSS, general series, 30: J. Hall to dowager countess of Orrery, 11, 18 and 22 Jan. 1686[7], 9 Feb. 1687[8]; Bowood House, Petty MSS, 18, now BL, Add. MS 72,864: T. Dance to J. Waller, 15 Jan. 1686[7]; *Petty-Southwell Correspondence*, p. 251.

43 Southampton U.L., BR 7A/1, f. 93: Account book of Sir John Temple, s.d. 20 April 1687, May 1687, 17 May 1687.

44 *Calendar of the Orrery Papers*, p. 330.

45 Bowood House, Petty Papers, 18, now BL, Add. MS 72,864: B. Cadogan to Sir W. Petty, 9 and 16 July 1687; T. Dance to J. Waller, 26 July 1687.

46 Bowood House, Petty Papers, 18, now BL, Add. MS 72,864: T. Dance to J. Waller, 29 Jan. 1686[7]. Cf. Petty's scepticism in *Petty-Southwell Correspondence*, pp. 280–1.

47 Boole Library, NUI, Cork, Southwell shrievalty papers, MS U/55: C. Crofts to Sir R. Southwell, 8 Jan. 1686[7].

implicit messages was that soon it would be the turn of the English and Scots to suffer comparable assaults. The temptation to over-egg the pudding persisted into the war and its aftermath. Still the motive was the need to elicit British and Dutch help. One lobbyist candidly stated early in 1691 that 'it is the duty of every body that is concerned in Ireland to use their endeavour and interest to get those poor protestants that have suffered so much to be in some way considered and countenanced by the government'.[48] Agents in Ulster in 1690 and 1691 excused their failure to remit rents to absentee landlords in England with harrowing tales of depopulation and destruction.[49]

A further factor adding to the opacity of Irish protestant responses was the absence of lay leaders of stature or eloquence. The first earl of Orrery died in 1679. Lord Anglesey, another owner of large Irish properties and capable of operating as a politician on both sides of the Irish Sea, went to his grave in 1686. Even before that, he had loosened his ties with Ireland, where he was born and retained estates. In addition, his strident anti-catholic sentiments and a personal quarrel with Ormond left him without official influence. Ormond himself, retired in England and restless about James's policies for Ireland, survived until 1688, but waned in power. Local heroes would emerge in provincial Ireland: among them Orrery's son, Henry Boyle, as well as Sir Thomas Southwell and (in the north) Frederick, Hans and Gustavus Hamilton. However, these younger leaders were thrown up by the events of 1689, by which time the choices for the protestant proprietors had been simplified.

IV

Because of feeble lay leadership, the clergy of the Church of Ireland did what they could to steady the members of their congregations, revive drooping morale and allay fears. In common with their counterparts in England, the protestant clerics in Ireland were reluctant to depart from unquestioning obedience towards the monarch. The clerics deposited in Irish bishoprics after 1660 were required to sedate rather than excite by their preaching and teaching. Most fulfilled, indeed frequently surpassed, the expectations. Only a few who themselves bore the scars of past encounters with local adversaries, such as Henry Jones, from 1661 to 1682 bishop of Meath, preferred vitriol to balm. But beneath the torpid episcopate, composed predominantly of weary English and Welsh 'sufferers' foisted on Ireland by the English administration, there developed an indigenous protestant clergy who shared

[48] N.L.I., MS 13,230: Lord Clifford to W. Congreve, 25 Jan. 1690[1].

[49] Private collection, Co. Down: W. Waring to W. Layfield, 5 Sep. 1690, 9 July 1691, 25 Sep. 1691.

the experiences and outlooks of their congregations. In their minds, history united with dogma to suggest the incompatibility of catholic with protestant beliefs. Accommodations were uneasy, and, so experience taught, might be superseded by violence and intolerance, as throughout the 1640s and 1650s.

Younger clerics, many of them trained in the local protestant seminary of Trinity College in Dublin, spoke against their catholic rivals with a vehemence that protestant laymen generally avoided. With no newspapers produced in Ireland and with the reticence of correspondents, the pulpit became a platform from which royal policies could be criticized covertly and openly. In the first year of his reign, James upbraided the Irish viceroy about the indiscretions of some protestant preachers in Dublin. Like their colleagues in London, the clerics had had the effrontery to meddle 'with controversy more than was necessary or expedient'. Specifically, they had inveighed against popery. The bishop of Meath, Anthony Dopping, was said to have preached in this manner before the viceroy himself. Lord-Lieutenant Clarendon answered diplomatically that Dopping was a dull preacher, so that he had not taken much notice of what the bishop said. However, Clarendon could not deny that a problem existed. 'The inferior clergy in most places', he confided, 'are unruly, and not so apt to take advice as to give it.' A second protestant prelate, Edward Wetenhall, the bishop of Cork and Ross, scandalized some by decrying 'popish' doctrines, while 'preaching loyalty and allegiance'. He chose sensitive moments for his outbursts: church services at Christ Church cathedral in Dublin when the lords justice (the local substitutes for the lord lieutenant) were present and the occasion of Ormond's final departure from Ireland in March 1685 after he had been superseded as viceroy.[50] Wetenhall prided himself on preaching in language that was 'plain, honest and strong'. Admirable as the intention was, when sermons attacked catholic writers as 'those chieftains whose spittle other less people lick up and vent', they were calculated to inflame confessional animosities.[51] Clarendon was relaxed enough to appeal to the good manners of the Dublin preachers. At the same time, he repeated instructions that the clergy, including the bishops, were to reside on their livings and to discontinue their frequent journeys and 'unnecessary stays' in Dublin. The injunctions told of fears lest the clergy coordinate opposition by meeting in the capital.[52]

Most protestant preachers did not comment publicly on or dissent openly from current events in the hope of averting the impending trouble. Clear statements were few, making it tricky to decide whether the overt loyalism to or the covert criticism of the Stuart monarchy more accurately repre-

50 Wetenhall, *Hexapla Jacobae*, sig. [*5], [*8–*8v], †[1]–[†2]. This work was reissued as *Six Sermons Preached in Ireland, in Difficult Times* (1695). For more on reactions to it, see: Cambridge U.L., Baumgartner MSS, Add. MSS. 1/57, 58.

51 Wetenhall, *Hexapla Jacobae*, [†1v], [†8].

52 N.L.I., PC 436; *Correspondence of Clarendon*, I, 258, 282–3.

sented their opinions. In a tense atmosphere, merely to attend protestant worship could announce certain solidarities. In March 1685, the churches of Dublin were said to have been thronged immediately after news broke that Ormond was to be superseded as viceroy.[53] One incumbent in County Cork typified the ambivalences and awkwardnesses of the Church of Ireland clergy. At the end of 1683, Archdeacon Richard Synge, eager to uphold the divine right of the Stuart dynasty to rule, cautioned against 'distracting our thoughts with fears and jealousies, with succession and popery and arbitrary government and commonwealths, all which are made use of as so many bugbears to frighten the nations into rebellion'. Yet, Synge could not forbear reminding his auditors that the characteristic doctrines of the Church of Rome – itself 'the scarlet whore and mother of all abominations' – amounted to 'sugar plums for children'.[54] By 1687, Archdeacon Synge acknowledged the apprehensions arising from Tyrconnell's recent appointment as lord deputy. He admitted that some now feared a repetition of the 1641 massacre. Still, he counselled fortitude. Synge reminded a congregation in the heavily protestant town of Bandon that God sometimes allowed enemies to triumph in order to chastise and test the patience of the faithful, as had happened in the aftermath of 1641.[55]

Protestants, led by their clergy, were encouraged to remember what they had undergone and achieved. Some of these recollections, such as the annual celebration of 23 October 1641 as the occasion when they had faced and survived catholic insurrection, entailed mutual hatreds on the two confessions. The government throughout the 1660s and 1670s discouraged all from dwelling too long on these events, fearing rightly that the ruminations would wreck inclusive policies whereby both protestants and catholics should share the government of Ireland. Despite what the authorities in Dublin and London decreed, the liturgy, preaching and popular traditions of the established (and protestant dissenting) churches kept alive often lurid recollections of what the previous generation had endured. Protestants, conditioned by sermons and accounts of recent Irish and European history to expect the worst, were ready to believe that new massacres were in the offing.[56]

If protestants had solid as well as irrational grounds for worrying about their catholic neighbours' intentions, the latter had even stronger reasons to question the protestants' stance towards them. Without delving back as far as the horrific 1650s, catholics knew how fragile were the foundations

53 *Petty-Southwell Correspondence*, p. 136.

54 Private collection, Greenwich: R. Synge, sermons on Matthew, 6, v. 34 (2 Dec. 1683); on Ephesians, 5, v. 15 (30 March 1684).

55 *Ibid.*: R. Synge, 'A Sermon Preach[ed] at Bandon when People were under Great Fears upon Tyrconnell's coming over Lord Lieut[enant] of Ireland', 13 Feb. 1686[7].

56 T.C. Barnard, 'The Uses of 23 October 1641 and Irish Protestant Celebrations', *E.H.R.*, CVI (1991), 889–920, reprinted in Barnard, *Irish Protestant Ascents and Descents*.

on which their own more indulgent treatment rested. They remained prey to sudden panics and reprisals. Protestant governors, headed by the lord lieutenant, Ormond, congratulated themselves that Ireland had not been seriously unsettled by the Popish Plot. Nevertheless, the alarms claimed one conspicuous victim: none other than the catholic primate, Oliver Plunkett. Set-backs of this kind, although they indicated the vulnerability of catholics to vindictive protestants (and also vicious feuding among the catholics), did not wholly mask the steady improvement in the structures and morale of the catholic church throughout much of Ireland. The laity was cheered as the generally occluded sympathy of Charles II gave way to the open friendship of his brother. Events on the continent also raised catholic hopes, while news of the harshness towards the Huguenots depressed the protestants. French protestant refugees gradually found their way to Ireland, and told grim stories of the *dragonnades* to which they had been subjected. Indeed, such was the sympathy in protestant Dublin for their sufferings that the city was derided as 'Geneva-Dublin'.[57]

In some areas, catholic expectations of improvements in their condition ran ahead of royal actions. The eagerness of a few catholic clergy and laypeople to reclaim what they felt rightly belonged to them put at risk the personnel and property of the Church of Ireland. The clergy of the established Church sought to balance their loyalist instincts with defence of their endangered privileges. Ardent protestants strove, as catholics had in previous reigns, to display their unquestioning obedience to the sovereign while refuting the religious doctrines to which James subscribed. The sincerity of the clerical protestations in the secular sphere never altogether masked the unease of the adherents of the Church of Ireland at the prospects that they must face under a catholic sovereign. Like the catholics in England since the protestant reformation, indeed like catholics in early Stuart Ireland, protestants had to convince their rulers that they were obedient subjects even while differing in religion. After 1685, the clergy, no less than the laity, faced a more alarming prospect than that which confronted their brethren in England. Because Ireland was peopled overwhelmingly with catholics, the argument for restoring catholicism as the official cult was more compelling than it could be in late seventeenth-century England.

Occasional hints reveal how the rising confidence of their catholic adversaries disquieted the protestant clergy. John Vesey, the protestant archbishop of Tuam, attested to the anxieties. Vesey, hitherto fervently loyal towards the Stuart monarchy, believed as early as the summer of 1687 that the catholic clergy had the church buildings in their sights. 'We are taking care for our churches. God knows how long we may keep them.'[58] Others within

57 *Correspondence of Clarendon*, I, 189.

58 Petworth House, West Sussex, Orrery MSS, general series, 30: Abp J. Vesey to dowager countess of Orrery, 9 July 1687. For Vesey's political opinions: J. Vesey, *A Sermon Preached at Clonmell, on Sunday the Sixteenth of September, 1683. At the Assizes*

protestant Ireland appreciated that the church lands, whether alienated to protestant laypeople or to the Church establishment, would be a prime target of catholic ambitions.[59] Yet, in this matter, as in that of secular land, James seemed loath to act. He and his advisers were content to leave vacant bishoprics and dignities unfilled, so that the revenues might replenish the depleted Irish treasury. But it was still protestant not catholic bishops who received writs of summons to the Dublin parliament in 1689. Nor were any official orders issued to transfer church buildings to the catholics.

Protestant incumbents were grateful for the king's restraint. Even so, they knew that royal forbearance might not last indefinitely. Alongside the tangible challenges to the precarious ascendancy of the Church of Ireland, more shadowy threats were spotted. An experienced protestant observer surmised that 'the care and culture of catholic religion' underlay James's plans. The monarch, it was thought, by 'giving it such growth, vigour and authority by wealth and acres' would oblige his successors 'to be friends with them [the catholics] upon fair and equal terms'.[60] The thinking behind the scheme eluded some of the king's most exuberant catholic supporters, while the gradualism irritated others. They took matters into their own hands, confident that first Tyrconnell and then James would approve their actions. An early example of how destructive confessional rivalries could prove occurred in 1685. At Kilmallock, the Church of Ireland vicar, Hugh Anderton, previously a chaplain to Ormond, was assaulted as he read the burial service. When Anderton died from his injuries, protestants were alarmed. The violence was traced to 'an ignorant young priest, newly ordained'.[61] News of further disturbances in County Tipperary circulated. The neighbourhood of Borrisokane had been terrified by stories that the catholics were about to rise and kill the protestants. Those under threat crowded into Borrisokane only to be prosecuted for an unlawful assembly.[62]

In this edgy mood, the separate confessional communities suspected each other of plotting aggression. As in the past, measures planned for defence were interpreted by the hostile as belligerence. Rumours of affronts and affrays rumbled around the provinces. Late in 1686 it was alleged that the protestants of Westmeath and Longford – not a numerous company – were intending to massacre their catholic neighbours.[63] At Lismore in County Waterford, worshippers in the recently rebuilt cathedral of St Carthage

held for the County Palatine of Tipperary (Dublin, 1683); J. Vesey, *A Sermon Preached at Windsor before His Majesty, the Second Sunday after Easter, 1684* (1684).

59 T.C. Barnard, 'Land and the Limits of Loyalty: The Second Earl of Cork and First Earl of Burlington (1612–1698)', in Barnard, *Irish Protestant Ascents and Descents*, p. 101.

60 *Petty-Southwell Correspondence*, p. 264.

61 H.M.C., *Ormonde MSS*, new ser., VII, 346, 347, 355, 364, 370.

62 H.M.C., *Ormonde MSS*, new ser., VII, pp. 365–7, 371, 373, 378, 381, 387, 394, 399.

63 *Correspondence of Clarendon*, II, 105.

were interrupted by a hail of stones on the building.[64] In Kerry, another area where protestants were few, it is possible that dispossessed catholics re-entered properties that had once been theirs, confident that the local authorities would not interfere. Protestants, discomposed by this reversal of fortune, moaned that they could no longer expect justice from local courts.[65] With the judicial bench and magistracy largely manned by catholics and with catholics empanelled as jurors, protestants knew that the legal system was slipping from their control. The appointment of four catholics as judges in 1686 was said to have depressed the value of lands owned by the protestants.[66] A sardonic observer commented on this rapid bouleversement: 'it is ill for any that have controversies at law, the courts and juries favouring one side now, as much as heretofore they did the other'.[67] In Dublin, a spate of robberies was reported in the winter evenings of 1687. For protestants, it seemed further testimony to the lawlessness of the poorer catholics, emboldened by the dramatic improvement in their condition.[68]

These incidents, coupled with the undeniable evidence of the rapid advancement of catholics into public offices, did not conduce to calm appraisals of the situation, and revealed deep-rooted fears. In 1685, protestants had grasped eagerly at assurances from first the king and then from Clarendon that there would be no sudden changes in Ireland. By May 1686, a Cork merchant wrote that 'fear [is] so epidemical on the minds of both the protestant gentry and traders that improvements and commerce move very faintly'.[69] Frequently, it was the expectation not the occurrence of trouble that depressed the protestants. Confidence was hard to maintain in the face of the high spirits of catholic neighbours. If the lengthy overture allowed the protestants to prepare for the drama in a way that had been denied in 1641, the uncertainties caused a malaise, especially among those reluctant or unable to quit the island.[70] One correspondent abandoned circumspection when he wrote – early in 1688 – of the 'English' in Ireland, meaning the protestant settlers, as being 'terribly frightened'.[71] The source of their

64 St Carthage's cathedral, chapter act book, 1663–1829, s.d. 2 Dec. 1686, Lismore, Co. Waterford, fo. 23v.

65 H.M.C., *Ormonde* MSS, new ser., VII, 399.

66 Hovell letter-book, Farmar MSS: W. Hovell to ?W. Houblon, 19 March 1685[6], 27 Apr. 1686.

67 Cambridge U.L., Add MSS. 1/59; Bodl., Clarendon MS 89, fo. 102.

68 Bowood House, Petty MSS, 18, now in BL, Add. MS 72,864: T. Dance to J. Waller, 15 Jan. 1686[7].

69 Hovell letter-book, Farmar MSS: W. Hovell to W. Houblon, 4 May 1686.

70 Hovell letter-book, Farmar MSS: W. Hovell to J. Putland, 26 Oct. 1686; Bowood House, Petty MSS, 18, now BL, Add. MS 72,864: T. Dance to Sir W. Petty, 12 Nov. 1687.

71 Bowood House, Petty MSS, 18, now BL, Add. MS 72,684: T. Dance to J. Waller, 25 Feb. 1687[8].

fear was not, on this occasion, the aggression of new recruits in the army, but the numerous cases depending in the Dublin and local courts.

V

Alarmist stories fed on traditions of antagonism and indeed of atrocities that had been strengthened by the differing confessional memories of the events since (and before) 1641. Anderton's death at Kilmallock remained exceptional. Nevertheless, disturbing undercurrents flowed through protestant communities, especially in those outside eastern Ulster and remote from Dublin where catholics easily outnumbered protestants. The lands and livelihoods, not the lives of the protestants, were the prime objects of catholic desire. Among the properties that the catholics wished to recover were the church buildings. Sacred spaces, both the pre-reformation churches and the burial grounds adjacent to them, had been commandeered by the established protestant church. In many cases, although proprietorship had passed to the new establishment, and the rites officially celebrated within them were protestant ones, the places retained their importance for catholics. The latter, enjoying rights of sepulture, continued to bury their dead in spots nominally controlled by the newer confession. The grievance about the loss of these holy places was taken up by the clergy during the 1640s. Then, throughout much of the kingdom, physical control of churches had been regained by the catholics. Clerics wished to put this occupation on a secure legal footing. Lay colleagues, gathered at Kilkenny, did not give the same priority to the question.[72] Soon enough, the opportunity of widespread repossessions ended. Defeat deprived the catholics once more of the buildings. They were obliged to use makeshifts. Even in the more permissive 1680s, when, as one outraged protestant in Cork complained, 'idolatrous mass' was celebrated publicly in the city, catholic churches hardly matched the grandeur or solemnity of the older buildings, now occupied by the protestants.[73] Nor indeed did they approach the splendour, externally or internally, of catholic churches in continental Europe, with which many priests and monks and some laypeople were familiar.

Only in 1689 and 1690 were there numerous reports of churches being wrested from the protestants. As will be shown, the accounts were chiefly directed to and preserved by the bishop of Meath, Anthony Dopping. Throughout the 1680s, Dopping earned respect for his endeavours to animate the comatose Church of Ireland. First at Trinity College, next in the Dublin parish of St Andrew and ultimately as a bishop, he was active. He investigated the rights and history of both his church and the Irish parlia-

72 Tadgh Ó hAnnracháin, *Catholic Reformation in Ireland* (Oxford, 2002), pp. 77–8.

73 Hovell letter-book, Farmar MSS: W. Hovell to W. Houblon, 25 May 1686.

ment. Through intellect and exertions he was the obvious person to rally protestants at an ominous time. In 1688, he may well have been behind the decision to authorize the publication of a narrative of a catholic priest's conversion to protestantism. Dopping possessed a manuscript version of the text.[74] In its timing, it was a singularly provocative and defiant gesture.

Dopping's activities during James's reign established him as pastor and controversialist, and, as such, a leader for both younger clergy and anxious laypeople. Dopping and most of his clerical acolytes had been trained in a rigorous theological school – Trinity College Dublin – by Henry Dodwell and successive provosts, Richard Lingard, Robert Huntington and Narcissus Marsh. The academic training combined with a sharp awareness of the exposed situation of the protestant minority within Ireland. Several of these strenuous divines joined the Dublin Philosophical Society, started in 1684. Alongside the Philosophical Society, dedicated to scientific experiment and speculation, a theological discussion group flourished. Here, several who soon rose to prominence within the Church of Ireland extended their knowledge and refined their dialectical skills.[75] Arguments learnt in the circle were directed in turn on catholics, notably a defector from the Church of Ireland, Peter Manby, and then onto Presbyterians, like Joseph Boyse.[76] Leading figures from this company, Dopping himself, Nathanael Foy, Samuel Foley, William King and John Stearne, after serving as fellows of the college for a spell, were beneficed in Dublin.[77] The challenge of sizeable congregations in the capital, and from both protestant dissent and catholicism, encouraged a strict economy of prayer, catechesis and administration of the sacraments. Through these devices, it was hoped that the faith of the minority already within the state Church would be fortified and protected against attack.[78]

74 N.L.I., PC 519, Dopping-Heppenstall MSS; Neal Carolan, *Motives of a Conversion to the Catholic Faith* (Dublin, 1688).

75 Bodl., MS Eng. Lett. C. 29, fos 2, 4, 6b.

76 Cambridge U.L., Add. MS 1/58, 78; [J. Boyse], *Some Impartial Reflections on D[r] Manby's Considerations, &c. and Dr. King's Answer* (Dublin, 1687); W. King, *An Answer to the Considerations which Obliged Peter Manby, Dean of Londonderry … to Embrace what he calls the Catholique Religion* (Dublin, 1687); *idem*, *A Vindication of an Answer to the Considerations* (Dublin, 1688); *idem*, *A Vindication of the Christian Religion and Reformation against the Attempts of a Late Letter wrote by Peter Manby* (Dublin, 1688); P. Manby, *The Considerations which Obliged Peter Manby, Dean of Derry, to Embrace the Catholique Religion* (Dublin, 1687); *idem*, *A Letter to a Friend Showing the Vanity of the Opinion that Every Man's Sense and Reason is to Guide Him in Matters of Faith* (Dublin, 1688); R. Gillespie, 'Print and Protestant Identity: William King's Pamphlet Wars, 1687–1697', in *Taking Sides? Colonial and Confessional Mentalities in Early Modern Ireland. Essays in Honour of Karl S. Bottigheimer*, ed. V. Carey and U. Lötz-Heumann (Dublin, 2003), pp. 231–50.

77 Bodl., Tanner MS 36, fo. 135.

78 T.C.D., MSS. 1995–2008/ 75 and 76; Cambridge U.L., Add. MS 1/68, 82; Lambeth Palace Library, MS 942/96; *An Address to Absenters from the Publick Worship of God* (3rd edn, Dublin, 1719).

In 1689, Dopping obeyed a summons to James's Dublin parliament. There he distinguished himself as a champion of protestant concerns by speaking and voting against the repeal of the Act of Settlement.[79] Yet, soon, his mere presence in the largely catholic assembly would damage his reputation. However, in 1689, with the increased assertiveness of the catholics, apprehensive protestants looked to Dopping for a lead. From the provinces arrived detailed accounts of the protestants' privations. Other bishops, notably Edward Wetenhall in Cork and Simon Digby at Limerick, noted the affronts offered to the protestants, and the increasing obstacles put in the way of their worshipping in church.[80] However, neither Wetenhall nor Digby was treated as a suitable recipient for information about happenings outside their own dioceses. Dopping, thanks to his seniority and his being for much of time in or near Dublin, was best placed to amass and distribute the news. Moreover, he, in tandem with his junior, King, the dean of St Patrick's in Dublin, was entrusted with oversight of the archdiocese of Dublin when the archbishop skipped over to England. The legal powers buttressed the moral authority which led subordinates to venerate Dopping and King almost 'as oracles'. They were deluged with 'whatever news they either heard or learned... Whatever evil had happened to them, or was feared, they opened to us.'[81]

Descriptions of protestant tribulations in 1689 and 1690 hardly dropped unbidden onto Dopping's desk. His role was not a purely passive one. It resembled that of his immediate predecessor in the diocese of Meath, Henry Jones, who, during the 1640s, collected and collated accounts of what had befallen the protestants of Ireland. Even without the link of the diocese, Dopping could hardly have been ignorant of Jones's energy in cherishing and publicizing protestant sufferings and eventual deliverance. Dopping's own concern to draw together information about the new troubles suggests that eventual publication may have been in his mind. In the event, the materials were not printed. Yet, they were preserved carefully, in much the same manner as the depositions recounting the losses in and after 1641. In the early 1640s, Jones and his adjutants had been motivated by the need to persuade the sluggish English to rescue an endangered protestant Ireland. The mass of evidence that purported to show catholic perfidy and brutality belonged to a systematic campaign to discredit all catholics and to grab their properties. Jones's efforts succeeded, but only after more than a decade had

[79] The fullest account of his career is M.E. Gilmore, 'Anthony Dopping and the Church of Ireland, 1685–1695', Queen's University Belfast M.A. thesis, 1988.

[80] Lambeth Palace Library, MS 3152: Diary of Bp. S. Digby of Limerick; E. Wetenhall, *Pastoral Admonitions Directed by the Bishop of Cork to all under his Charge* (Cork, 1691).

[81] C.S. King, *A Great Archbishop of Dublin, William King, D.D., 1650–1720* (1906), pp. 23–5; *A True and Perfect Journal of the Affairs in Ireland* (1690). Cf. T.C.D., MSS. 1995–2008/63, 66, 70.

elapsed.[82] How far Dopping intended consciously to imitate Jones's design cannot be ascertained. A crucial reason for the uncertainty about intentions is that the two episodes – the Confederate and Williamite Wars – differed from, far more than they resembled, one another. Accordingly, the reports received by Dopping were fewer and (in general) less brutal than those from the 1640s.[83]

Wary and wily protestants had been conditioned to expect 1641 to be repeated. It was not. The disorders, destruction and deaths between 1689 and 1691 had been foreseen at least since 1685. In the spring of 1688, one protestant wrote from Ireland that, were the king to die, protestants would be killed.[84] Apparently authoritative warnings of a massacre planned for 8 December 1688 precipitated an exodus, particularly from Dublin.[85] The panic spread to Cork. An observer wrote, 'you cannot imagine what a fright and confusion it put all into, all running out with their swords in their hands and breaking the church windows to get out'. Catholics jeered, but the wary repeated the adage, 'the burnt child dreads the fire, and have not forgot'.[86] Elsewhere in Munster, would-be worshippers were intimidated as they came to their churches. In December 1688, the bishop of Limerick was angered to find catholics from the garrison exercising in the precincts of St Mary's cathedral. The dean was unable to persuade them to stop. The garrison commander, Lord Clare, told that the martial display 'frighted the people from coming to church', was apparently unsympathetic. Early in February 1689, a moment of deteriorating relations between catholics and protestants, the churchyard at Kilmallock again saw trouble. The minister and his congregation discovered that there were soldiers waiting to take them hostage.[87] In the western counties of Mayo and Galway, where prot-

82 T.C. Barnard, 'Crises of Identity among Irish Protestants, 1641–1685', *Past & Present*, CXXVII (1990), 39–83; *idem*, '1641: Bibliographical Essay' in *Ulster 1641: Aspects of the Rising*, ed. B. MacCuarta (Belfast, 1993), pp. 173–86; A. Clarke, 'The 1641 Depositions', in *Treasures of the Library, Trinity College Dublin*, ed. P. Fox (Dublin, 1986), pp. 111–22; J. Cope, 'Fashioning Victims: Dr Henry Jones and the Plight of Irish Protestants, 1642', *Historical Research*, LXXIV (2002), 370–91.

83 A further link may be suspected through John Stearne, eventually bishop of Clogher. To Stearne belonged responsibility for acquiring the depositions relating to the 1641 uprising that Jones had collected. Stearne ensured their preservation by presenting them to Trinity College Dublin. Stearne was a protégé of Dopping, to whom he owed early preferment. Stearne also acquired some manuscripts that had belonged to Dopping, which he later gave to Marsh's Library in Dublin. T.C. Barnard, 'A Bishop and his Books: John Stearne', in *Marsh's Library: A Mirror on the World: Law, Learning and Libraries, 1650–1750*, ed. M. McCarthy and A. Simmons (Dublin, 2009), pp. 185–202; W. O'Sullivan, 'John Madden's Manuscripts', in *Essays on the History of Trinity College Library Dublin*, ed. V. Kinane and A. Walsh (Dublin, 2000), pp. 104–113.

84 Cambridge U.L., Baumgartner MSS, I/60.

85 T.C.D., MSS. 1995–2008/61; [W. Hamilton], *Life of James Bonnell*, pp. 46, 47.

86 Surrey R.O., MS 1248/1, fo. 227.

87 Lambeth Palace Library, MS 3152, fos 14, 22.

estants were few, alarm intensified. By January 1689, Archbishop Vesey of Tuam reported that most protestants of consequence had left the region and he himself was concluding reluctantly that 'this province [is] no place for us'. Vesey left Connacht for Dublin on 29 January 1689. Within a week, he wrote later, the ways were impassable 'by the multitude of skein men and half pikemen called raparees'. [88] In County Monaghan, in the town of Clones, the conforming protestants were forced from the parish church on 19 March 1689. This presaged the seizures in Leinster and Munster at the close of the year, and at the start of the next. The protestants of Bandon, notwithstanding the efforts of preachers like Wetenhall and Synge and of Henry Boyle to calm them, were victimized. Sections of the town's walls were demolished.[89]

Incidents like these alarmed the protestant historians of 1688–91, but, hard as they might try, they could not be fashioned into anything comparable to 1641 and its aftermath. The most that could be done was to insist that the protestants had been at risk, but that the risk had providentially been averted by the arrival of William and his forces. The belief persisted that the speed with which catholics coordinated their activities could be traced to instructions from the catholic priesthood, often issued at mass. Frequently the stories were merely hearsay: what an unnamed friar was alleged to have said or anonymous reports of what had been heard in church. In the latter genre, the bishop of Killaloe was informed of a priest, who, at Sunday mass, 'told the people that they were obliged to destroy all the enemies of God and ought to cut them off even to the suckling child'. Around Athlacca in County Limerick, it was thought that great numbers of catholics had been – and were still being – raised and armed 'by the assistance of the popish priests, who at mass enjoined the young men and such were fit for service to enlist themselves in the army and the rest to arm themselves with half pikes and skeins'.[90] In some aspects, this alarmism continued traditions in which the friars were viewed as particularly dangerous. It also revealed how readily unsubstantiated stories could circulate. Yet, not all the apprehensions were invented. Especially with the cycle of observances in the darkening days of late autumn, protestants were reminded of what their forebears had recently suffered. Dealings between the distinct confessional communities had not altogether ceased, although each perhaps had become more wary of the other. Just as notables such as Boyle had confidently addressed Tyrconnell, so protestant grandees in the provinces complained to the catholics newly installed as governors and commanders and to ecclesiastical dignitaries about alleged maltreatment of the protestants. By 1689, there were increasing signs that at best the catholics in power listened courteously,

[88] T.C.D., MSS. 1995–2008/63, 66; N.L.I., de Vesci MSS, G5: journal of Abp. J. Vesey.
[89] N.L.I., MS 13,226: Lord Cork and Burlington to W. Congreve, 4 Oct. 1690, 4 Dec. 1690, 30 May 1691.
[90] Lambeth Palace Library, MS 3152, fos 7v, 11, 19.

but did little. Some did not even observe the courtesies.[91] Early in 1690, Lord Barrymore complained that his intervention with Lord Clare, now the governor in Cork, had failed to secure the restitution of the church at Great Island to the protestant congregation.[92]

Many of the letters preserved by Dopping were written by parish and cathedral clergy. Some came from his own diocese of Meath, which straddled the territory contested by James's and William's armies. Common themes recurred. From Lynally (King's County), it was reported how the parish priest had demanded the key to the church. When refused it, the priest entered with a dragoon and began to celebrate mass there. Also in Dopping's diocese, the church at Balliboy had been seized. In both cases, the ejected incumbent professed concern about the safety of monuments to local notables. In Lynally, part of the memorial to John Forth had been taken down to serve as an altar.[93] Bishop Wetenhall told how two of the churches in Cork city had been made over to the catholics, notwithstanding petitions that they be restored to the protestants. In nearby Cloyne, the protestants had managed to regain use of the parish church – the seat of a bishop who had fled – but no clergy were willing to read services there.[94] The few protestants of the vicinity were subjected to abuse. The sister of the local priest apparently egged on catholics to curse, rail and hoot at protestant worshippers, who were also pelted with stones and called 'ruffians, devils and other vile names'.[95] In another parish on the edge of Cork, catholics demanded the keys of the church. The incumbent insisted on how few of his congregation had left. This was to emphasize the need for a building in which to conduct services, but it also reminded that poorer protestants could not so easily as their well-to-do neighbours quit their homes in Ireland.[96]

In the heartlands of the protestant plantation of Munster, one rector, Francis Beecher, was troubled. He professed good affection to King James, taking as his text St Paul's admonition 'to fear God and honour the king'. Early in 1690, he was commanded by a friar to deliver the keys to the church at Tallow (County Waterford). The friar, it was said, made the request in the name of the pope. Beecher demurred. On entering Tallow, he found the streets 'full of men armed with staves, swords, and raparees or half pikes, guarding the way to the churchyard', where the friar (in the absence of the parish priest still in Dublin) waited with a great multitude. Beecher invoked the king's recent declaration of liberty of conscience to loyal protestants. However, the friar and his supporters took control of the church and Beecher

91 Lambeth Palace Library, MS 3152, fos 10–11, 13–14, 20, 25.

92 Armagh Public Library, Dopping MSS, 1/82, 83, 85.

93 *Ibid.*, 1/84.

94 *Ibid.*, 1/87. For the absent bishop, see D.R. Hainsworth, *Stewards, Lords and People: The Estate Steward and his World in Late Stuart England* (Cambridge, 1992), p. 163.

95 Armagh Public Library, Dopping MSS, 1/98.

96 *Ibid.*, 1/91.

retired from the fray. Interestingly, Beecher's complaint reached James, then in Dublin. The king seemed to promise redress if Beecher's allegations were verified. However, James could no more bring his catholic supporters in the localities to heel than could the protestants their supporters.[97] Beecher, like others, stressed that these unruly catholics obeyed not the king but the pope. In this way, the protestant prepared to counter the charge that they were fickle in their political allegiances. It picked up the theme of how the secular and regular clergy, with their ultramontane allegiances, had organized and excited their congregations even before 1688. It implied that 'popery' with its political connotations could be distinguished from the theological error of catholicism.

From the city of Waterford, further troubles were reported. The dean of the cathedral expressed sorrow that King James was not prepared to entrust the building to the loyal protestants, but insisted that they would not repine.[98] Afternoon service in the cathedral was disrupted, with attempts to force open the locked door and stones flung at the windows. The mêlée was traced to French sailors who had landed nearby and who were to assist James II. Efforts to punish the miscreants brought Irish catholics in the garrison to their defence. Meanwhile, the unruly sailors were said also to have broken into another church, and desecrated its furnishings, pulpit, prayer-books and bible. Dean Wallis felt intimidated, but did not leave. Frightening as the incidents were, they stopped short of the humiliations of the 1640s when protestants were forced to eat their holy books.[99] Many left churches physically scarred, furnishings damaged and protestants indignant but unharmed.[100] In Athlone, the protestant incumbent was denied his tithes: a financial sanction which had been feared for some time.[101] The town, of great strategic value as a crossing of the River Shannon between the provinces of Connacht and Leinster, was garrisoned with 3,000 soldiers under Sarsfield. One hundred of the troops joined women and children to abuse the protestants when they assembled for worship. The congregation was taunted with cries of 'come out you rebels and we will tear you in pieces'. The liturgy was ridiculed and windows broken. Rather tamely, given this ferocity, it was allowed that no one had been injured. A leading protestant layman, William Jones, complained to the garrison commander, but unavailingly. Jones, recorder of the borough, would later represent it in the

97 P.R.O.N.I., DIO 4/15/2/1 & 2. Cf. Armagh Public Library, Dopping correspondence, 1/136, 137.

98 *Ibid.*, 1/89.

99 *Ibid.*, 1/92, 94.

100 Cambridge U.L., Baumgartner MSS, Add. MS 1/95.

101 Armagh Public Library, Dopping MSS, 1/108. For Wallen, a Trinity graduate, see: H. Murtagh, *Athlone: History and Settlement to 1800* (Athlone, 2000), pp. 139, 200.

Dublin parliament. No doubt his local reputation had been enhanced by his resistance to the Jacobites.[102]

Carlow, like Athlone and Waterford, was a borough with a sizeable protestant minority. All had been disturbed by rising tensions in the past few years as the protestant governors resisted the demands of assertive catholics.[103] Some at least of the initiative to take back churches which had formerly belonged to the catholics came from laypeople prominent in the communal life of their towns. The mayor of Carlow demanded the key of the parish church, lately rebuilt by the protestants, so that it could be conferred on the catholics. It was noted that the catholics already possessed two chapels in the town. The protestant incumbent was driven to preach in an inn. So great was the throng that it was feared that the floor might give way. The preacher was imprisoned for his pains.[104] Waterford and Kilkenny saw similar developments. In November 1689, Dean Wallis told Dopping how one Saturday the mayor and sheriffs had appeared with 'a great rabble' and taken possession of Waterford cathedral. However, Wallis had to concede that one sheriff had intervened to protect him, and that he had suffered nothing worse than a torn gown.[105] Subsequently, the civic authorities were berated for ignoring an order from the king reinstating the protestants in Waterford cathedral. This defiance was supported by the local Jacobite commander, Lord Tyrone.[106] From Kilkenny, the bishop, Thomas Otway, wrote of the mayor taking St Mary's church from the protestants in the same month. He too complained that soldiers had assisted.[107]

The full implications of the catholics' reinstatement in more than a hundred municipalities, memorably recorded at Galway in March 1688, were becoming clear. In many towns, parish churches were linked to the rituals of the municipality. In some, the office-holders and members of the corporation processed each Sunday through the streets to church, where they were seated in designated and prominent places. It is unclear whether, once the government of towns was restored to catholics from 1687, civic rituals were transferred to the catholic chapels in the back streets. Certainly it becomes more comprehensible that catholics should seek to regain the parish churches in order more appropriately to accommodate services attended by the municipal dignitaries. A powerful lead in public ceremony

102 E. M. Johnston-Liik, *History of the Irish Parliament* (6 vols, Belfast, 2002), IV, 507–8; Murtagh, *Athlone*, pp. 143–4, 189, 192–5.

103 H.M.C., *Ormonde* MSS, new ser., VIII, 346.

104 Armagh Public Library, Dopping MSS, 1/115. Cf. R.C.B., P. 317/5.1, p. 31: Carlow vestry book, 1669–1762; T. King, *Carlow, the Manor and Town* (Dublin, 1997).

105 Armagh Public Library, Dopping MSS, 1/116.

106 *Ibid.*, 1/125, 127.

107 *Ibid.*, 1/123, 128.

came when Christ Church in Dublin was used, with James II attending one service in November 1689.[108]

Violence intimidated, but as often through words as by blows, and seldom resulted in any serious hurt. Weight of numbers reminded of the catholic superiority over the protestants. The latter indicted the catholics for acts of desecration similar to those for which in the past – especially in the 1650s – the protestants had been blamed.[109] At Lanesborough, Captain Oliver Fitzgerald had bedded down his men in the church, allowed them to drink there and even had a sheep slaughtered.[110] From Athlone, it was reported that oxen were driven into the building at service time. There, soon enough, the general, Sarsfield, authorized catholic use of the parish church.[111] Control of the church buildings had symbolic resonances, but important practical consequences as well. In most settlements, the church was the only edifice of any size. Protestants, when ejected from it, had to resort either to barns, inns or the open air: the expedients to which previously the catholics had been reduced, and for which they, together with protestant dissenters, were derided. The protestants of Waterford city, expelled from the cathedral, had no option but to walk the streets and shelter in alleys until they saw the minister. They had lost control of the bell which hitherto had summoned them to services. Loitering and meeting in the streets aroused suspicions that they were 'caballing and plotting', and brought new reprisals from the city authorities.[112] At Clones, the Church of Ireland congregation, expelled from its customary venue, was not able to use the building again until April 1692, and then had to repair it extensively.[113]

VI

Neither protestants nor catholics united in their respective response to the challenges and opportunities presented by James VII and II. In a rapidly changing situation, individuals and groups had to assess how best to react. Many found it hard to reconcile ideological imperatives with those of self- and family preservation. In each camp, it was recognized that help from outside Ireland was essential. Arguments had to be made to convince the sceptical English, Dutch and French, that the outcome of the struggles in Ireland mattered to their own plans. In the interval before the help arrived,

108 T.C.D., MSS 1995–2008/76; K. Milne, 'Restoration and Reorganization, 1660–1830', in *Christ Church Cathedral Dublin: A History*, ed. K. Milne (Dublin, 2000), pp. 270–3.

109 Armagh Public Library, Dopping MSS, 1/117.

110 *Ibid.*, 2/146.

111 *Ibid.*, 1/108, 114.

112 *Ibid.*, 2/142.

113 R.C.B., P. 804.1.1, p. 183: Vestry book, Clones, s.d. 15 Apr. 1692.

groups in Ireland had to fend for themselves. Some, including a majority of the bishops and prosperous dignitaries of the established Church, fled to Britain. The ingenious justified flight in disinterested or desperate terms.[114] Sensitive to charges of cowardice, the refugees traduced those who stayed in their Irish dioceses and parishes as quislings willing to collaborate with James, now deposed or abdicated from his English and Scottish thrones.[115] In persuading William to mount an invasion of Ireland, clerical urgings probably carried less weight than the military and political arguments. But the exiled bishops and ministers, in addition to furthering their own claims to preferment, protected the established Church against the consequences of William's inclinations towards toleration.

Ecclesiastical politicians came fully into their own once the war in Ireland was won and when a protestant parliament again assembled in 1692. By then, rivalries and disagreements, sometimes originating in differences in politics and churchmanship, were worsened by recollections of behaviour during the recent war. Dopping, as the senior bishop to have stayed in Ireland throughout the war, found that his conduct was either misunderstood or misrepresented deliberately. In consequence, any further advance in his career was blocked.[116] In contrast, an adjutant who had also stayed, William King, transformed himself into the most eloquent exponent of the Irish protestants' predicament and their reasons for accepting William and Mary. Already in 1687, King was hailed 'a sound scholar and a sounder head; one of the greatest men we [the Irish protestants] have here'.[117] So, despite the fact that Dopping had proved the most effective protestant leader during James's reign, it was King with his *State of the Protestants* that riveted Irish protestants to William.[118] In addition, the tract reminded of the prominence, ingenuity and courage of the clergy of the Church of Ireland in responding to a catholic monarch in a catholic kingdom. The clerics saw themselves as having been principal targets of the catholics' aggression and to the fore in resisting it. Dopping assembled the documentation to prove these points, and the dangers that had beset small communities of protestants scattered across Ireland in 1689 and 1690. Yet, King, in writing about the troubled times, hardly needed Dopping's evidence. He, too, knew

114 N.L.I., de Vesci MSS, G5: Journal of Abp. J. Vesey; R. Caulfield (ed.), *Journal of the Very Rev. Rowland Davies*, Camden Society, 1st ser., LXVIII (1857).

115 Cambridge U.L., Baumgartner MSS, Add. MS 1/8.

116 Cambridge U.L., Baumgartner MSS, Add. MS 1/68; Armagh Public Library, Dopping MSS, 2/211, 214; Gilmore, 'Anthony Dopping and the Church of Ireland', pp. 122–35.

117 Cambridge U.L., Baumgartner MSS, Add. MS 1/58.

118 W. King, *The State of the Protestants of Ireland under the late King James's Government* (1691). Cf. Carpenter, 'William King and the Threats to the Church of Ireland', pp. 22–8; J.I. McGuire, 'A Remora to King James' Affairs: William King's Defence of Protestant Office-Holders, 1689–90', in *Archbishop William King and the Anglican Irish Context, 1688–1729*, ed. C. Fauske (Dublin, 2003), pp. 36–46.

at first hand from his ministry in Dublin what difficulties had been placed in the way of the free exercise of protestant worship. King was the more agile ideological contortionist; or, as a sympathizer expressed it, he 'managed himself with great wariness'.[119] He adjusted more nimbly than Dopping to the facts of William's and Mary's enthronement and William's victories. Later, he warned a sceptic that the protestant gentlemen of Ireland, having been reinstated thanks to William's intervention, 'can't with patience bear any doubt to be made of the lawfulness of it'.[120]

Even in the era ushered in by William, the leaders of the Church of Ireland did not adopt a single policy. How best to treat the defeated catholics and to guard against any future resurgence provoked contradictory proposals. As in the past, so in the 1690s and thereafter, some clergy urged generosity and others severity. A preference either for coercion or for conciliation did not reflect the simple fact of whether or not an individual had stayed in Ireland between 1688 and 1691. Dopping, it is true, lost faith in some constructive measures, such as preaching in the Irish language, that he had backed in the 1680s.[121] To that degree, he had been hardened by living at close quarters to the resurgent catholics. In contrast, King, imprisoned for a time in Jacobite Dublin, dissociated himself from the vindictive and vicious triumphalism that gripped many colleagues and co-religionists. In the immediate wake of victory, protestants in the Irish parliament saw to it that the mistakes of the past were not to be repeated. Catholics were to be disabled from ever again endangering the incipient protestant ascendancy. Not only were remnants of property and power stripped from the defeated, measures were enacted to ensure that the catholic religion itself would within a generation shrivel and die. The hope was that, once the catholic church was starved of its social, economic and intellectual leaders, it would wither away. Moreover, a weather eye had to be kept on catholic neighbours who had so recently reclaimed and (it was frequently claimed) ransacked parish churches. The buildings were brought back into firm and exclusive protestant control, and the catholics (and dissenters) were forced into humiliating makeshifts.

King, in common with others such as Foy and Foley, who had endured the trials in Dublin as catholic confidence mounted, pondered the lessons. A common conclusion was that the protestants' own failings had provoked divine rebukes. The failings had now to be corrected through personal and collective reformations and through institutional regeneration. Thinking of this sort did not lead to total introspection. However, it was a more manageable objective to try to overhaul protestant communities than to launch

119 Cambridge U.L., Baumgartner MSS, Add. MS 1/8.

120 Bodl., MS Eng. Lett. C. 29, fos 126, 132.

121 'Remedies proposed for the Church of Ireland (1697)', ed. J. Brady, *Archivium Hibernicum*, XXII (1959), 163–73.

offensives against catholicism.[122] Just as the preachers who reflected on the lessons of the shocks and shame of 1641 concluded that the protestants of Ireland had learnt little and forgotten much, so the celebrants of the protestant deliverer, William, annexed the more recent history to their particular causes. Recriminations were directed at protestant dissenters, who, despite the forwardness of the presbyterians at Derry and Enniskillen in resisting the Jacobites, were accused of pusillanimity or compliance. Even more ferocious were the invectives against the alleged Jacobites, such as Dopping and Wetenhall, who had not deserted their flocks.[123] The new divisions disheartened those who had hoped that in the fiery furnace of the Jacobite experience a union of all Irish protestants would be forged. Instead disunity, apparent in responses during 1685 to 1691, remained the bane of the protestant interest in Ireland.

122 T.C. Barnard, 'Reforming Irish Manners: The Religious Societies in Dublin during the 1690s', *H.J.*, XXXV (1992), 805–38; *idem*, 'Protestants and the Irish Language, c. 1675–1725', *Journal of Ecclesiastical History*, XLIV (1993), 243–72, both reprinted in *Irish Protestant Ascents and Descents*, pp. 143–207; D.W. Hayton, 'Did Protestantism Fail in Early Eighteenth-Century Ireland? Charity Schools and the Enterprise of Religious and Social Reformation, c.1690–1730', in *As by Law Established: The Church of Ireland Since the Reformation*, ed. A. Ford, K. Milne and J.I. McGuire (Dublin, 1995), pp. 166–86.

123 Cambridge U.L., Baumgartner MSS, Add. MS 1/65, 67, 70.

8

Rumours and Rebellions in the English Atlantic World, 1688–9

Owen Stanwood

In the last months of 1688 a wave of fear swept England's American colonies. In Barbados, planters believed themselves to be targets of a vast design by popish recusants, French Jesuits and Irish servants to reduce the island to 'popery and slavery' and perhaps deliver it to France. In January 1689 almost identical rumours appeared in New England, where Indians joined the list of enemies, and two months later settlers on the frontier of Maryland and Virginia began whispering of the same plot. At the same time, rumours of a different sort arrived from Europe, telling of William of Orange's invasion, James II's flight to France, and a possible change of government. This combination of fears and great expectations pushed matters to a crisis. In April colonists in Boston took to the streets demanding a change of government, and before the summer's end political strife had spread to many, if not all, of the colonies. By now one former governor languished in prison, two more had been forced to resign, and a fourth had surreptitiously abandoned his post, sailing for England. All told, the rebellions of 1689 marked the most dramatic political disturbance in the colonies before the next revolution a century later.[1]

The colonial extension of England's revolution of 1688–9 has received ample attention from historians. Nonetheless, no single consensus has emerged on the revolution's impact on the colonies or the empire. Indeed, historians have looked at the same sources and reached almost opposite conclusions, some arguing that the revolution provided for greater cohesion and centralization, others contending that it led to greater colonial autonomy. Most scholars of the events have agreed on only one thing: there was little coherence in colonial reactions to the events of 1688–9. Each of the regional crises developed out of a local context, and had little relation

1 Another version of this chapter appears in Owen Stanwood, *The Empire Reformed* (Philadelphia, PA, 2011), pp. 85–112.

to happenings in other parts of England's far-flung empire.[2] In the meantime, scholars of contemporaneous events in England have barely considered the disturbances across the Atlantic, preferring to view the revolution as a British or European event rather than an Atlantic one.[3]

This essay rethinks this old subject by simultaneously looking closer and stepping back. My chronological span is narrow, focusing only on the 12 months following the summer of 1688. I make no effort to deal with the complicated aftermath of the rebellions.[4] This emphasis allows a more detailed look at how colonial subjects dealt with the complicated and uncertain news coming from England and Europe over the course of the revolution. Within this short time period I have adopted a comparative approach, examining not the whole empire, but three very different parts of it: Barbados, New England and the Chesapeake colonies. This approach reveals that despite their very real differences, colonists in the various parts of the empire interpreted the revolution in broadly similar ways. Everywhere, colonial subjects believed themselves to be targets of a vast popish plot, and everywhere as well, they demanded that their leaders protect them from the threat. It was this fear of the dark forces of 'popery', and the consequent desire for protection, that shaped the outcome of the revolution in the colonies. Differing reactions of local leaders, rather than among colonial subjects, determined how the revolution turned out in the various parts of the empire. This suggests, in turn, that the revolution did more to bring the empire together than to break it apart: not by constructing institutions but

2 Previous overviews include Jack P. Greene, 'The Glorious Revolution and the British Empire, 1688–1783', in *The Revolution of 1688–89*, ed. Lois G. Schwoerer (Cambridge, 1992), pp. 260–71; Richard R. Johnson, 'The Revolution of 1688–9 in the American Colonies', in *The Anglo-Dutch Moment*, ed. Jonathan I. Israel (Cambridge, 1991), pp. 215–40; K.G. Davies, 'The Revolutions in America', in *The Revolutions of 1688*, ed. Robert Beddard (Oxford, 1991), pp. 246–70; Richard S. Dunn, 'The Glorious Revolution and America', in *The Oxford History of the British Empire. Volume 1: The Origins of Empire*, ed. Nicholas Canny (Oxford, 1998), pp. 445–66. Relevant book-length studies include David Lovejoy, *The Glorious Revolution in America* (New York, 1972); Stephen Saunders Webb, *Lord Churchill's Coup* (New York, 1995); Richard R. Johnson, *Adjustment to Empire: The New England Colonies, 1675–1715* (New Brunswick, NJ, 1981); David William Voorhees, '"In Behalf of the True Protestants Religion": The Glorious Revolution in New York', New York University Ph.D., 1988; Lois Green Carr and David W. Jordan, *Maryland's Revolution of Government, 1689–1692* (Ithaca, NY, 1974).

3 For a British approach to the revolution, see Tim Harris, *Revolution: The Great Crisis of the British Monarchy, 1685–1715* (2006), which does not consider the colonies. For a European approach, see Steve Pincus, *1688: The First Modern Revolution* (New Haven, CT, 2009), which does briefly touch on American events (pp. 246–7), claiming that the revolution fundamentally altered the management of the empire, though with few specifics. In contrast, Tony Claydon, *Europe and the Making of England, 1660–1760* (Cambridge, 2007) overtly rejects an Atlantic approach: see esp. pp. 10–11.

4 For the aftermath, see Stanwood, *The Empire Reformed*, pp. 112–39.

by revealing an imperial ideology, an anti-catholic nationalism that could bind the colonies together with their new protestant monarchs. This revolutionary legacy paved the way for Britain's massive expansion during the next century.[5]

This chapter builds on two strands of scholarship in early modern history. On the one hand, I take seriously the role of rumour and innuendo in inspiring grassroots political change. Previous historians have spent a lot of time trying to figure out when English colonists learned of the cataclysmic events in England during 1688 and 1689. What they have missed, however, is that the unrest in the colonies was based not on the availability of reliable news, but on the circulation of rumours – unlikely reports of vague conspiracies that were almost invariably false, but that most people at the time believed to be true. This essay traces these rumours and tries to figure out why people believed them, and what they reveal about popular political beliefs.[6]

On the other hand, the content of the rumours, which all related to a vast popish conspiracy, call for specific attention to the role of anti-popery in the formation of imperial political culture. As scholars of early modern Britain have made clear, anti-popery constituted more than prejudice against or fear of Roman catholics. It was a complex political language used by protestants to understand their place in the world. Popery represented the opposite of true religion, a vague but frightening force that aimed to promote superstition, arbitrary authority and violence. The forces of popery included actual catholics – especially the terrifying French monarch Louis XIV – but the definition was capacious enough to include anyone who seemed not to be staying true to the global protestant cause. As officials in both Britain and America learned, rumours of popish plots had the potential to inspire political unrest, but they could also bring subjects together. Just as the whigs who participated in the London pope-burning processions of the 1680s did not oppose monarchy per se, so frightened colonists did not necessarily oppose the empire. Rather, they expected imperial officials to be good protestants

5 Historians of eighteenth-century Britain have also argued for the importance of anti-Catholicism to British nationalism, especially Linda Colley, *Britons: Forging the Nation, 1707–1837* (New Haven, CT, 1991). For America, see Brendan McConville, *The King's Three Faces* (Chapel Hill, NC, 2006).

6 On rumours in early modern politics, see for example, Ethan H. Shagan, 'Rumours and Popular Politics during the Reign of Henry VIII', in *The Politics of the Excluded, c. 1500–1850*, ed. Tim Harris (Basingstoke, 2001), pp. 30–66; Adam Fox, 'Rumour, News, and Popular Political Opinion in Elizabethan and Early Stuart England', *H.J.*, XL (1997), 597–620; Arlette Farge and Jacques Revel, *The Vanishing Children of Paris* (Cambridge, MA, 1991); Gregory Evans Dowd, 'The Panic of 1751: Rumors on the Cherokee-South Carolina Frontier', *William and Mary Quarterly*, 3rd ser., LIII (1996), 527–60. The pioneering analysis of communication in 1688 is Ian K. Steele, 'Communicating an English Revolution to the Colonies, 1688–89', *Journal of British Studies*, XXIV (1985), 333–57; and *The English Atlantic, 1675–1740* (New York, 1986).

and protect the people from popish enemies – especially during times of crisis. Once imperial officials learned this lesson, they could get on with the task of reforming the empire, which they did in the eighteenth century, usually with the cooperation of American subjects who were proud to define themselves as partners in a potent protestant union.[7]

I

In August 1688 the people of Barbados witnessed one of the most extravagant displays of loyalty ever to appear in the English colonies. Lieutenant Governor Edwyn Stede had recently received word of the birth of a male heir to James II, and he was not content for a simple day of thanksgiving or firing of the fort's cannon. In addition to those ordinary measures, he organized a vast procession of all the island's prominent people dressed in their finery, followed by hundreds of horse and foot soldiers, and punctuated by the 'most magnificent Entertainment, such as the present state of the West-Indies never Saw & the future age will admire', a feast for over 2,000 people with enough wine to drink the health of the entire royal family. The whole display demonstrated, in Stede's view, the great loyalty that the people of Barbados showed to their monarch.[8] Nonetheless, the first stirrings of trouble in the colonies in 1688 came not from a den of sedition and puritanism like New England or Bermuda, but from this cradle of monarchism.

Despite their longstanding loyalty, people in Barbados and the king's neighbouring island colonies had good reasons to be afraid in 1688. Beyond the constant fear of slave conspiracies, the islanders also lived in close proximity to two groups of strangers whom they did not entirely trust. The first were their indentured servants, many of Irish catholic origin, a fact that proved particularly vexing in the years after the Irish Rebellion of 1641.[9] The second threat came from another variety of papist, the French. The two nations had coexisted in the region, not always peacefully, for decades, even sharing the small island of St Christopher, but after Louis XIV's rise to power the French menace became a preoccupation both of English gover-

[7] My definition of anti-popery follows that of Peter Lake, 'Anti-Popery: The Structure of a Prejudice', in *Conflict in Early Stuart England*, ed. Richard Cust and Ann Hughes (1989), pp. 79–106. For the pope-burnings, see Tim Harris, *London Crowds in the Reign of Charles II* (Cambridge, 1987), pp. 96–129. For a recent analysis of the character, and limits of anti-Catholicism during this period, see Scott Sowerby, 'Opposition to Anti-Popery in Restoration England', *Journal of British Studies*, LI (2012), 26–49.

[8] T.N.A., P.R.O., CO 1/65/50.iii.

[9] On the Irish, see Hilary McD. Beckles, 'A "Riotous and Unruly Lot": Irish Indentured Servants and Freemen in the English West Indies, 1644–1713', *William and Mary Quarterly*, 3rd ser., XLVII (1990), 503–22; Donald Akenson, *If the Irish Ran the World* (Montreal, 1997); Jenny Shaw, 'Island Purgatory: Irish Catholics and the Reconfiguring of the English Caribbean, 1650–1700', New York University Ph.D., 2009.

nors in the region and ordinary people – especially since Irish servants had shown a willingness to defect to catholic enemies in previous wars. By 1688 Stede had taken on the role of the foremost challenger of the French in the islands. His main focus was on the islands of St Lucia, St Vincent and Dominica – thinly inhabited, mountainous bastions that lay within the official bounds of Stede's commission but which contained only a few French and Carib Indian inhabitants. Stede forcefully ejected the islands' French residents on several occasions, sending a clear message that he would not tolerate interlopers. In his estimation, the French were bad neighbours, enemies to the king's interest, despite the official peace in Europe.[10]

During this period of fear and uncertainty several questionable visitors arrived on Barbados. One was Sir Thomas Montgomery, James II's choice for attorney general in 1687. Like other officials on the island, he was fanatically loyal – but with a difference, as he was also Irish and allegedly a catholic convert.[11] This meant that Montgomery favoured royal policies – in particular, religious toleration – that many of the king's tory supporters could not completely endorse, and as the king's legal representative he felt compelled to promote them. In addition, he appealed to a new constituency: the catholic servants who, despite their chequered pasts, appeared to Montgomery as dependable subjects of the catholic king. Early in his tenure Montgomery complained to the lords of trade that Barbadian servants were 'used with more barbarous Cruelty then if in Algiers … as if Hell Commenced here and but continued in the world to come'.[12] Such sentiments could only serve to alienate the planter *élite*, who quickly came to see the attorney general as a particular enemy, a threat to both their profits and their safety.

The second unwelcome visitor caused much more alarm: sometime during the summer of 1688 a French Jesuit priest arrived in Barbados from Martinique. The Jesuit, named Father Michel, seemed to have come with the support or at least connivance of English authorities. Lieutenant Governor Stede promised the president of the Committee on Trade and Plantations that he would not allow anyone to 'molest, affront, abuse or scoff at him', though he noted that the presence of a French man on the island at that time of tension 'made the People here to Conclude him Rather a Spye than a Priest'. Montgomery took a more active approach, offering the priest lodging in his house, though he later claimed he did so out of obligation

10 For Stede's challenge to the French, see T.N.A., P.R.O., CO 1/61/3.

11 The Montgomerys were a prominent Ulster Scot Protestant family with strong ties to the Stuart dynasty and the Church of Ireland, though I have not been able to trace Sir Thomas's particular genealogy. In general, see William Montgomery, *The Montgomery Manuscripts (1603–1706)* (Belfast, 1869).

12 T.N.A., P.R.O., CO 29/4/6–7.

rather than pure charity. It was at this time, according to his enemies, that Montgomery formally converted to catholicism.[13]

The priest's activities during his six months in Barbados remain uncertain, but he seems to have spent most of his time ministering to the colony's substantial Irish catholic population. He held mass both at Montgomery's house and the dwelling of another prominent planter named Willoughby Chamberlain. Later investigations revealed the names of at least 44 people who attended the services, but rumour had it that some services attracted more than 200 Barbadians, most 'Irish men, and them of the poorer sort, and many of them Servants'. Chamberlain and Montgomery allegedly scoured the countryside to inform the colony's catholics of the rare opportunity to receive genuine religious instruction, and even offered 'treats' to entice them to attend. The depositions of Irish servants who attended the services hint at a brief golden age for the island's catholics, a time when the combination of a catholic monarch and relaxation of the penal laws provided new opportunities for public expression of faith. And many catholics evidently embraced the new freedom, as political and religious arguments moved out of the council chamber and coffeehouse into the island's fields and curing houses.[14]

To the island's respectable protestants, it appeared that Montgomery and the Jesuit had emboldened Barbados's unruly Irish population. For instance, in September 1688 a labourer named William Kelly charged the minister of St Lucy's parish, John Wilson, with 'Uttering or Speakeing of Treasonable words'. The incident occurred early in the morning on 2 September after Wilson awoke to the sounds of Kelly beating one of the minister's servants. When Wilson confronted the intruder Kelly accused him of threatening to chase all Roman catholics out of his parish, after which the minister allegedly made some unkind comments about the catholic king – charges that he vehemently denied. Kelly could find no one to back up his story, and he did not help his case when he claimed to be the disinherited son of Irish nobility, but the fact that the court heard his testimony at all demonstrates the strange state of colonial politics in 1688. One fellow servant testified that Kelly told him 'you will see an alteracon of affaires in a short time and that he himselfe should be a great man', and that 'two Preists' had confirmed that dramatic changes were imminent.[15]

Such evidence begged for a conspiratorial interpretation. All of the pieces were there: the scheming, foreign Jesuit; the turncoat recusant; and the Irish shock troops that would provide the manpower to bring the plot to its conclusion. But in November 1688 it was still dangerous to speak out loud about a popish plot, so most prominent Barbadians expressed themselves

13 T.N.A., P.R.O., CO 1/65/54.

14 T.N.A., P.R.O., CO 31/4/121–2. On the numbers of attendees, see T.N.A., P.R.O., CO 28/37/7.xxx; CO 28/37/7.xlvi.

15 T.N.A., P.R.O., CO 31/4/96–7; CO 1/65/65.xxi; CO 1/65/65.xxii; CO 1/65/65.xxiv.

with great care. Stede, for example, denounced Montgomery to authorities in Whitehall, but he couched his criticism in language calculated not to offend his royal master. Stede had no problem with catholicism, he pledged, nor did anyone else in Barbados, but Montgomery had shown an immoderate zeal in promoting his new faith. The attorney general 'makes it his buisness to quarrill with every body about it', Stede wrote, '& Not Onely threaten them with Law & his Ma[jes]ties Displeasure, but upon Suprise falls upon them … which breeds much heart burning with the People'.[16] The problem lay with Montgomery and not the people of Barbados, who remained loyal subjects of their catholic king. But one could sense the uneasiness in Stede's writing: he knew that it might become difficult to remain loyal to the king and also maintain order among nervous colonists.

As if the king's representatives in the West Indies did not have enough problems, they soon began to hear rumours of a different sort. There was trouble at home, though the exact dimensions of the crisis remained unclear. By 20 November, word of an impending Dutch invasion of England had reached the neighbouring Leeward Islands – just two weeks after William of Orange's landing at Torbay. The news, vague as it was, caused a great deal of consternation. Already in late November one inhabitant of the Leewards named Colonel Beach spread rumours – which no one dared to repeat in print – that King James may have lost the throne. When the assembly of Nevis declined to affix their names to a late declaration expressing joy over the birth of the prince of Wales, Governor Nathaniel Johnson accused them of giving too much credence to the rumours.[17]

As autumn turned to winter Barbadians received more news, but none of it official or particularly reliable. Various reports arrived of William of Orange's landing, his triumphant march toward London, and James II's flight to France, but it was impossible to know for sure if William had really defeated James, and if so, whether or not he could hold onto power. In some ways, the reliable communication links between the islands and England were harmful rather than helpful: by February most people knew at least something of the revolutions at home, but their leaders did not have enough information to take any definite action. Official correspondence from this time contained more than a little desperation – Thomas Montgomery and Nathaniel Johnson even took the step of writing to the French governor in Martinique to try to find more reliable news. The results must have only added to the confusion, since the comte de Blenac assured Montgomery in

16 John D. Rockefeller Library, Colonial Williamsburg [hereafter CW], Blathwayt Papers, vol. 31, folder 4: Stede to Blathwayt, 16 Aug. 1688; *ibid.*, vol. 32, folder 5: Stede to Blathwayt, 23 Oct. 1688; T.N.A., P.R.O., CO 1/65/54.

17 T.N.A., P.R.O., CO 153/1/107–8.

early January that William of Orange's invasion force had returned to the Netherlands in disgrace.[18]

The frequency of communication meant that Stede had to act in order to maintain stability, but he faced a terrible choice. Choosing the wrong side would mark his political downfall in the best of circumstances, and could lead to charges of treason. But if he stayed neutral others with more strident beliefs, like Montgomery, would undoubtedly fill the vacuum, perhaps pulling the island toward civil war. Faced with this dilemma, Stede decided to cast his lot with William of Orange – sort of. At the end of February he called the council together to consider the island's security during these times of troubles, and they produced a document that was at once an act of incredible daring and a study in vagueness and equivocation. It saved Stede's career, ended Montgomery's, and could have stood as a model for how colonial governors could deal with such crises.

The stated reason for the council's emergency session was the danger of a French invasion. Several reports of a French fleet in Martinique had circulated around the island, and Stede argued that the colony must put itself in a better posture of defence against the enemy. Nonetheless, the council did little to prepare for an invasion; instead, it turned against the island's catholics. Stede and his councillors must have had access to official justifications of William of Orange's invasion, as they consciously adopted much of the anti-catholic language that had become fashionable in England. They blamed all of the king's problems on 'the subtile, wicked, horrid and abominable contrivances of Popish Recusants, and more particularly those called Jesuits, who goeing about with their head & father the devil ... have for many years been undermindeing and Endeavouring to destroy, overturne, and utterly abolish the truely antient, Catholicke and apostolicke Protestant faith'. The wording of the declaration was curious in that it adopted an anti-catholic interpretation of the Glorious Revolution but also studiously avoided any acknowledgment of the revolution itself – just vaguely thanking God for preserving the laws, liberties and religion of England in the face of the catholic menace. The text even implied that England's catholic king was himself a victim of popish plotting – merely tricked by the machinations of recusants and Jesuits.[19]

Yet Stede and the council did more than just yoke Barbados's fortune to the protestant revolution at home. They also illustrated how the problems plaguing Europe, caused by recusants and crafty Jesuits, had come to the

[18] CW, Blathwayt Papers, vol. 32, folder 5: Stede to Blathwayt, 16 Mar. 1689; T.N.A., P.R.O., CO 28/1/1; CO 153/4/119. Ian K. Steele stresses the active lines of communication between Barbados and England: *The English Atlantic*, p. 97. While true, even the news that was reliable was rarely current, which caused much consternation since the political situation in England seemed to change so fast during 1688–9.

[19] T.N.A., P.R.O., CO 28/1/6. See also CW, Blathwayt Papers, vol. 32, folder 5: Stede to Blathwayt, 16 Mar. 1689.

plantations as well. There was indeed a popish plot against Barbados and all of the English empire, a design to replace the perfect English system with 'popery and slavery' and to subvert the protestant faith. Its champion was the convert Thomas Montgomery, aided by another convert, the planter Willoughby Chamberlain. Stede urged the council to act quickly against the threat, not only by disenfranchising catholics, which they did, but also by imprisoning the two ringleaders (the Jesuit had wisely left Barbados in January). The council concurred, charging that Montgomery and Chamberlain had 'suffered themselves to be perverted, & reconsoled to the Popish Religion', helped a Jesuit priest proselytize contrary to the law, and attempted to 'subvert the Government, and change the true, and Established Protestant Religion' to popery.[20]

The actions of the lieutenant governor and council were both dramatic and politically astute. They had received no official word of any change in government at home, but they acted anyway, essentially undoing James II's decree of religious toleration and throwing his appointed legal representative in jail. Some would have interpreted it as an act of rebellion against authority, albeit one championed by the executive. But it was also a necessary rebellion. Stede and the councillors surely knew that their past loyalty to James II would not serve them well with their subjects or the people who were likely to wield power in the new government. They needed to shield themselves from both popular rage and recrimination from their new masters, and they did so by presenting themselves, rather incredibly, as the saviours of protestantism. They also created a scapegoat, Montgomery, whom they could paint as the real Jacobite in their midst.

In order to do this Governor Stede gathered nearly a hundred pages of evidence against Montgomery and his accomplice Chamberlain that related 'their popish tricks and Evill Corrispondencies'.[21] The collected material, which included incriminating letters to the attorney general as well as numerous depositions about him and other Barbadian catholics, constitutes one of the most stunning examples of how protestants could imagine popish plots even without the benefit of much solid evidence, especially as Stede provided extensive commentary on many of the documents telling his readers in Whitehall exactly how to interpret them.[22]

The primary charge against Montgomery and Chamberlain was that they harboured the Jesuit priest, who had come to the island with the diabolical goal of undermining the true protestant church and establishing popery in its place. One of Montgomery's servants provided the corroborating details, confirming that Father Michel made 'his Generall abode' at Montgomery's

20 T.N.A., P.R.O., CO 28/1/6.

21 CW, Blathwayt Papers, vol. 32, folder 5: Stede to Blathwayt, 16 Mar. 1689.

22 The documents are in two different places in the Colonial Office Papers: T.N.A., P.R.O., CO 28/37/7 and CO 28/1. I am grateful to Jenny Shaw for bringing these sources to my attention.

house 'and read and said Mass Publiquely'. The attorney general, meanwhile, not only countenanced such activities but 'officiated at the service thereof', even though he required lessons in Roman catholic liturgical practice from his own servants. This was one of the central pieces of evidence for the assertion, which Montgomery always denied, that he had abandoned the Church of England and turned to popery. Stede gathered similar evidence against Chamberlain, taking depositions from numerous servants and neighbours who either witnessed the frequent masses held at his house or heard about them from others. Many of these same witnesses also testified that Chamberlain frequently declared his catholic faith: even the minister of St Philip's parish declared that the planter had pledged to 'spill the last dropp of his Blood' for the Roman catholic church.[23]

Stede presented this evidence as proof that Montgomery and Chamberlain had violated English laws against recusancy and the harbouring of popish priests. To do so required the governor and council to make a novel argument about the strength and limits of English law in the colonies. They contended that English laws had equal force in Barbados as in England, even if they had never been officially endorsed by the local legislature. Furthermore, they declared invalid James II's toleration decrees, depending as they did on the dispensation or suspension of parliamentary statute. Montgomery responded that some degree of religious toleration had always applied in the colonies, 'whose fundamentalls are upon much different grounds than those of England', and that at any rate he was obligated as a servant of the king to obey his master's directives. Few unbiased observers could have failed to see the hypocrisy in Stede's arguments, since the lieutenant governor had pledged himself to enforce liberty of conscience and protect the visiting priest only five months earlier.[24]

The authorities charged the two men with far more ominous crimes than simply harbouring the Jesuit. In particular, Stede argued that after their plan to promote the catholic faith had failed, Montgomery and Chamberlain had resolved to betray Barbados to the French, paving the way for an invasion that would accomplish by force what the Jesuit could not by persuasion. The main evidence for this charge came from several letters from French correspondents that Stede's men found after Montgomery's arrest. It was the very existence of these letters, rather than their contents, that most impressed Stede. The comte de Blenac, French governor of Martinique, simply passed on some false reports from Europe in a January letter, probably responding to queries from Montgomery before he had reliable news of what had happened in England, but this was enough evidence for Stede that Montgomery was 'frenchified' as well as catholic. Along with Blenac's letter

23 T.N.A., P.R.O., CO 31/4/121–2; CO 28/37/7.xix; CO 28/37/7.liii.

24 T.N.A., P.R.O., CO 28/37/7.xx. Stede offered no philosophical or legal justification for the applicability of the penal laws in Barbados. For his earlier pledge to protect the priest, see T.N.A., P.R.O., CO 1/65/54.

were three from ecclesiastical officials: Latin letters from the Jesuit superior on Martinique as well as one from the lady superior of the island's Ursuline nuns. Stede appeared not to have read the Latin letters, but he speculated that they were part of a design to have more Jesuits sent to Barbados 'by which our protestant religion would be weakened, & the French intrest strengthened'.[25] At any rate, the fact that priests and nuns considered him a friend seemed further to establish Montgomery as an internal enemy.

The next plank in the plot involved the 'rude debauched, drunken swearing hactoring Irish papists' whom Montgomery and Chamberlain had entertained at their houses. These were the shock troops that would allow the French to conquer the island, rising up as one when their master Montgomery directed them. Most of the evidence of the Irish uprising bore little or no relation to the case against the attorney general, but Stede included it in the same packet – with very little commentary – in order to underscore the connection between Montgomery's intrigues and the Irish threat. For example, he included several depositions concerning an Irish servant named James Jordan who 'had spoken very Irreverently and prophanely of the holy Bible and other bad Expressions of Englishmen', as well as a man named Dominick Rice who assaulted a neighbour for refusing to drink the pope's health. Both incidents appeared to be the result of mixing drink and politics during a tense time, but their accumulated effect was to ratchet up the level of fear in the colony.[26]

Despite their marginal relevance, these documents spoke very clearly to the level of panic in Barbados in the early months of 1689. If Stede was taking advantage of an opportunity to destroy a political rival, he also responded to real alarm on the part of subjects, who were conditioned both by upbringing and experience to fear the Irish. As rumours travelled, each auditor added or changed details to increase the sense of alarm. This appeared most clearly in the case of Cork Farley. In November 1688 this former servant was at the house of Tom and Martha Custley, where a third 'young man' was reading a popular protestant devotional tract, and commented to the catholic Farley that 'he Must not Worship Images', at which Farley replied 'angerly that Bibles were Bookes that Caused a great Deall of differences, & that the Roman Religion was the first Religion that was Upon the earth & that it would be the Last'. This was how the incident appeared to an eyewitness, but, by the time Tom Custley told a neighbour, the story had a new wrinkle, that Farley had also pressured the young protestant to turn catholic '& told him if he did not turn to that Religion he [would] repent it for that he hoped to see the blood of the Protestants swim on the ground'. As they heard reports of these everyday arguments about politics and religion,

25 T.N.A., P.R.O., CO 28/1/1; CO 28/1/3; CO 28/37/7.iv; CO 28/37/7.ii. I am grateful to Mary Zito for translating the three Latin letters, which like the French ones contained mostly European news.

26 T.N.A., P.R.O., CO 28/1/5; CO 31/4/114–15; CO 28/37/7.lxiv.

people added gory details that happened to adopt the same language of Irish atrocities popularized by Sir John Temple in his famous book about the Irish Rebellion of 1641.[27]

If fears of the Irish depended very much on Old World prejudices, another element of the plot was distinctly American. At a dinner of the leading gentlemen of Christchurch parish on 25 February, after the quarter sessions, conversation turned to fears of a French invasion. One planter observed that if the French did invade they would have a difficult time as 'there was severall good trusty negroes' that would gladly fight and 'venter their lives' to defend the island. At this Sir Thomas Montgomery was incredulous: he speculated that as soon as the French arrived on the island they 'would give all the Negroes their freedomes' and the slaves would desert en masse to the enemy, joining the island's servants who 'would fall upon us first'. Apparently the planters had never considered that their slaves might join an invading army: they upbraided Montgomery for even voicing such a thought, especially since several black slaves were in the room at the time, and they suspected him of trying to inflate the strength of the French and dissuade his neighbours from resisting them. With his comment, Montgomery connected the long-time fears of French and Irish catholics with homegrown anxieties over slave insurrections. Within a week he was in prison.[28]

The final set of charges against Montgomery involved his designs on the governorship. Along with plotting a bloody invasion, the attorney general had also supposedly attempted to bring about regime change in a more traditional way, by complaining to superiors in England about Stede's conduct and urging Whitehall to appoint a new governor – perhaps Montgomery himself. Of all the charges, this was the least serious and also the least supported by evidence. There was hardly a royal appointee in the colony who did not angle for a promotion, but Stede's only evidence was the fact that Montgomery had corresponded with several members of James II's privy council, including his hated confessor Fr Edward Petre, in what could only have been another round of popish intrigue. In fact, Stede turned Montgomery's possible attempt to secure a promotion into an act of treason by connecting it with the larger popish plot. Montgomery opposed Stede, the lieutenant governor argued, because the attorney general considered Stede to be an 'obstinat heritick' who 'opposed them and their popish Supersti-

[27] T.N.A., P.R.O., CO 28/37/7.xvii; CO 28/37/7.xvi. Temple published *The Irish Rebellion* in 1646, but editions appeared throughout the Restoration period. The same phenomenon appeared in the 1641 rebellion itself, in which reports of catholic violence multiplied and increased in intensity as they travelled through the countryside. See Nicholas Canny, *Making Ireland British, 1580–1660* (Oxford, 2001), ch. 8.

[28] T.N.A., P.R.O., CO 28/37/7.xl; CO 28/37/7.xli. Barbados had experienced several recent insurrection scares, though incredibly this was the first speculation that slaves could provide aid to catholic enemies. In general, see Michael Craton, *Testing the Chains: Resistance to Slavery in the British West Indies* (Ithaca, NY, 1982), pp. 105–14.

tions and Idolatrus religion' and resisted their campaign for 'Setting up popery in this Island'.[29]

Taken as a whole, Stede's campaign against Montgomery aimed to discredit his rival and save himself and the council from the taint of their past loyalty to James II. In both goals he succeeded admirably, simultaneously defining himself as a loyal subject of the new king and a zealous protestant who would protect the island from popery. Events over the course of the summer only strengthened his position, when the French attacked and conquered St Christopher with the help of the island's Irish servants. Stede was the first colonial official to use fear of catholics to buttress state authority, and as a result Barbados managed to avoid any major political strife. In other parts of the king's dominions rulers were not so astute.[30]

II

If Barbadians had a reputation for loyalty, their counterparts in New England were, in the minds of most royal officials, the most refractory of subjects: they harboured several regicides after the Restoration, ignored economic regulations and repeatedly asserted their independence from royal authority. The customs agent William Dyre described this independent spirit in colourful terms: New Englanders were 'raging furious fanatick whiggs ... Rebellious & unnatural hators & warr[i]ors Ag[ain]st the true mother church'. The proclamation of James II as king, Dyre added, was 'Cold & heartlessly performed, Coursly, and Carelesly Slubber'd over in that place ... which is a shame to Relate.'[31] Dyre had a particular grudge – his mother had been one of the quaker missionaries executed by Massachusetts authorities in 1660 – but he was not alone in his sentiments. It was this reputation for disloyalty and irregularity, along with the region's strategic position alongside New France, that prompted royal officials first to revoke the Massachusetts charter, and then to create the Dominion of New England, an experiment in absolute rule that united all the colonies from Maine to New Jersey under a single governor-general, an appointed council and no assembly. Such a potent

29 T.N.A., P.R.O., CO 28/37/7.xx; CW, Blathwayt Papers, vol. 32, folder 5: Stede to Blathwayt, 28 May 1689. One of Montgomery's servants witnessed his master writing letters to Petre and other prominent allies of James II, which he allegedly sent to England with the Jesuit Michel in January 1689, but may have been lost at sea. T.N.A., P.R.O., CO 28/37/7.xix.

30 On the invasion of St Christopher, see T.N.A., P.R.O., CO 29/4/120; CO 153/4/158–70. The situation was slightly more complicated in the neighbouring, but separate Leeward Islands, where Nathaniel Johnson resigned his position rather than accept the new monarchs.

31 CW, Blathwayt Papers, vol. 4, folder 3: William Dyre to William Blathwayt, 5 Mar. 1685, 12 June 1685.

union, officials believed, would force New Englanders to behave, while also defending the colonies from foreign designs.[32]

Given the region's history, therefore, one would almost expect that it would experience troubles as word of unrest at home crossed the ocean. And indeed, news of the revolution did convulse the region, eventually leading to an uprising nearly as dramatic as the one at home. It is tempting to blame this crisis, as royalist officials did, on the region's peculiar principles, had not the rumours that inspired colonists to rise up against the Dominion of New England been almost identical to the ones circulating in the West Indies. The main difference was the reaction of royal officials, who uniformly rejected popular fears of a popish design. This was the central lesson of the rebellion of 1689 in New England: not that New Englanders were impossible to govern, but that they had to be governed in a particular way.

During the first months of 1689 New Englanders suspected that dramatic events were occurring in England, but had no reliable information about them. While the Gulf Stream and the moderate weather allowed information to travel quickly from England to the West Indies, the voyage across the North Atlantic was nearly impossible during the winter months, and as a result New Englanders received much of their news from the Caribbean rather than Europe. What they received in 1689, therefore, was recycled news – probably variations on the rumours spread by Colonel Beach in the islands in November – along with the occasional newsletter or reprint of a pamphlet or newspaper. Only in January did New England officials learn of the impending Dutch invasion, and it was not until 11 February that New Yorkers received 'a flying reporte from Virginia; that the Prince of Orange was landed in Tarrbay'. Around the same time a ship from Nevis brought similar news to Boston, along with the Prince of Orange's Declaration. Within a few months more ships had spread news of William's victory, but the details remained unclear. Even as late as April a Boston merchant complained to a business partner in Rotterdam that while 'we have heard by way of Virginia of strange & great Revolutiones In England ... we doe all Long for a Shipe directly from England', and could not be sure exactly what had transpired.[33]

Just as in the islands, these rumours landed in a place already primed to fear the worst. In the summer of 1688 a series of Indian attacks claimed a few

[32] The definitive account of this period in New England's political development is Johnson, *Adjustment to Empire*, but see also Viola Barnes, *The Dominion of New England* (New Haven, CT, 1923); and T.H. Breen, *The Character of the Good Ruler: Puritan Political Thought in New England, 1620–1720* (New Haven, CT, 1970).

[33] Massachusetts Historical Society, Boston [hereafter MHS], Winthrop Family Papers: Francis Nicholson to Fitz John Winthrop, 16 Feb. 1689; Massachusetts Archives Collection, Columbia Point, Boston [hereafter Mass. Arch.], 35: 216: John West to Fitz John Winthrop, 23 Feb. 1689; National Archives of Scotland, Edinburgh, RH 15/106/690, #39; NAS, RH 15/106/801, #2.

lives and caused great consternation around New England, especially when colonists learned that French authorities in Canada may have authorized the attacks. Moreover, when the governor, Sir Edmund Andros, impressed hundreds of men from Massachusetts towns to raise an army to fight the natives, this only increased suspicions, as it seemed that the governor was leaving the towns defenceless just at the time they needed their young men most. As summer turned to autumn, many ordinary New Englanders came to believe the alarmist rhetoric of Andros's enemies, who claimed that the governor and his cronies were crypto-catholics whose sympathies lay not with the protestant colonists, but with the French enemy.

As soon as news of a possible revolution at home reached New England, colonists began to integrate their own troubles into the larger story. The first rumours probably came from discontented soldiers in Maine, who overheard and repeated a number of odd comments and behaviours on the part of their officers. When two men suggested to the governor that he should hire the Mohawks – New England's fiercest Indian allies – to fight the Abenakis, Andros cryptically objected, saying 'they may be [of use] to me another time'. To the two men, this comment indicated that Andros intended to hire the Mohawks for a later assault on New England – a rumour soon confirmed by reports of two local Indians who had spoken with a Mohawk messenger. Soldiers who returned from the frontier brought these reports home to Massachusetts. William Sargeant told his Amesbury neighbours that 'the great man', meaning the governor, 'had hired the Indians to come downe on the English, to destroy them, & had given some Coats & some money'.[34]

These reports became fodder for the governor's enemies. According to one official, 'some Ill Spiritts' in New England persisted in 'Scattering & publishing Seditious & Rebellious Libells'.[35] While the official did not relate the contents of these libels, he may have referred to the 'paper' found by the side of the highway in Newbury by Joseph Bayley. While walking down the road in January 1689, Bayley discovered a handwritten tract in verse that warned New England to 'rise and be armed' and 'let not Papist you charme'. The anonymous author claimed the war against the Abenakis was merely a ruse to drain New England towns of their young men, leaving them vulnerable to an attack by 'Indians french and papist[s]'. Unfortunately no copy of the paper itself has survived, and its provenance and authorship remain unclear, but it points to an inclination among some New Englanders to interpret their troubles in light of a global catholic conspiracy just like the

34 *Documentary History of the State of Maine*, ed. James Phinney Baxter (24 vols, Portland, ME, 1869–1916) [hereafter *DHSM*], V, 36: Deposition of Thomas Jentt and William Willcott, 27 Jan. 1689; Mass. Arch., 107: 29: Testimony of Waterman and David, 4 May 1689; *DHSM*, VI, 472–3: Testimony of Stephen Greenleafe, Jr., 9 Apr. 1689; ibid., VI, 473: Testimony of George Little.

35 MHS, Winthrop Family Papers: John West to Fitz John Winthrop, 23 Feb. 1689.

one that had recently struck Barbados, as well as a communication network that sought to spread the alarm around the countryside by an interesting combination of print and word of mouth.[36]

Evidence from local Indians provided more specific revelations about the plot. In the town of Sudbury, for example, a Christian Indian named Solomon Thomas told some English neighbours that Governor Andros had visited the 'praying Indians' of Natick and told them of a plan for a catholic and Indian force to overtake New England. If the English army proved victorious against the enemy Indians, the governor had supposedly claimed, 'in the spring french and Irish would Com to Boston' with a large number of Indians, and after destroying the capital, the popish army would continue to 'the Countery townes'. To remove any doubt about his motives, Andros had given the Indian 'a booke that was better than the bible' that contained pictures of the Virgin Mary and the 12 apostles, and claimed that 'all that would not turn to the governor['s] reledgon and owne that booke should be destroyed'.[37]

Rumours of the governor's misconduct circulated beyond Massachusetts. In New York, which James II had added to the Dominion of New England in 1688, Dutch and English inhabitants of Westchester County heard of a plan by Andros to invade Manhattan at the same time of the alleged expedition against Boston. A local sachem told a Dutch colonist named Barent Witt that the governor 'did promise him a brib of twelf pounds to be ready with a Company of Indians so many as he could get at Manhatans Island in the month of April'. In addition, Witt also spoke to some Frenchmen who passed though the region who confirmed that 'some ships were arrived' in Canada that would soon set out to conquer New York – again, a rumour almost identical to the one circulating in Barbados, with New France substituted for Martinique. When Witt brought his concerns to the leading landowner in the region, a prominent merchant and member of the Dominion's council named Frederick Philipse, the councillor laughed and said 'it was foolish to be afraid', which led Witt and his neighbours to suspect Philipse as well. They also connected their anxieties with the sanguine imagery common to protestant propaganda. Barent Witt's wife believed that 'she would be the first which should be burnt in case the French should take the place', probably because she was a French protestant. New York had a large Huguenot population, and these recent refugees from Louis XIV's regime feared that the Sun King would deal with them cruelly if he gained control

36 *DHSM*, V, 28–9: Deposition of Caleb Moody, 9 Jan. 1690; Mass. Arch., 35: 166: Deposition of Joseph Bayley, 9 Jan. 1690. The surviving fragments of the poem suggest parallels to the famous anti-catholic tract, [Charles Blount], *An Appeal from the Country to the City* (1679), whose publisher, Benjamin Harris, was living in Boston at the time.

37 *DHSM*, IV, 446–7: Testimonies of Joseph Graves, Mary Graves and John Rutter, 3 Jan. 1689; *ibid.*, IV, 448–9: Depositions of Thomas Browne, John Grout, Sr, John Goodenow, Jonathan Stanhope and John Parmenter, 22 Mar. 1689.

of the colony. New Yorkers had shown little resistance to imperial reforms in the years immediately before 1689, but revelations of a popish plot caused some of them to develop new suspicions about their leaders.[38]

The rumours that circulated around the northeast in early 1689 looked quite similar to those in the West Indies. In both cases, vague reports of political turmoil at home combined with specific fears of local officials and suspicious outsiders to cause popular panic. What was different, however, was the official reaction. First of all, Governor Andros and his deputies did all they could to suppress any rumours of the revolution in England, even imprisoning a man who distributed Orangist publications and spread news of the prince's victory around Boston. Dominion authorities were merely being cautious; they had no official word that the crown had changed hands, and they remembered that premature reports of the duke of Monmouth's victory had flooded the colonies in 1686, even months after the duke's ignominious defeat.[39]

In addition to suppressing unauthorized news, dominion leaders also dealt harshly with those who circulated rumours. When Newbury magistrate Caleb Moody told two justices of the peace about Joseph Bayley's 'paper', they charged him with 'publishing a Scandelous & Seditious Lybell' and threw him in jail. The justices immediately branded Caleb as a malcontent, probably because he was a brother to one of the Dominion's most bitter enemies, the Reverend Joshua Moodey of Boston. They did the same to the Sudbury residents who told local officials about the Indian testimony against the governor. Justice William Bond of Watertown asked the men 'what mony wee gave the indian to tell us such nuse', while the Boston judge, Benjamin Bullivant, complained that 'a parsell of felows had devissed a parsell of lys and had fathered them on a pore Indean'. The New England authorities made a fatal mistake: they viewed these rumours as so patently ridiculous that they did not even answer them. They did not realize that idle talk of a catholic conspiracy could motivate previously neutral colonists to join forces with local *élites* who had long resented the increase of royal authority.[40]

Boston teetered on the brink of political chaos through much of the early spring. The first signs of trouble appeared on the northern coast of Maine. In the middle of March Governor Andros, who had spent most

38 Affidavits concerning the agreement of Andros with the Indians, in *Documents Relative to the Colonial History of the State of New York*, ed. Edmund B. O'Callaghan and Berthold Fernow (15 vols, Albany, NY, 1853–87) [hereafter *NYCD*], III, 659; T.N.A., P.R.O., CO 5/1081/41.

39 *NYCD*, III, 660: Affidavit of Greveraet and Brewerton, 13 Dec. 1689; Mass. Arch., 35: 216: Deposition of John Winslow.

40 *DHSM*, V, 29: Deposition of Caleb Moody; *ibid.*, IV, 449: Depositions of Browne et al.; *ibid.*, IV, 446: Testimony of Graves et al. For inexplicable reasons, Caleb usually chose to spell his surname without the letter 'e', unlike his brother Joshua.

of the winter searching for Indian enemies with his troops, heard urgent reports of political strife in Boston. He sailed back to the capital on 15 March, and in his absence morale among the troops reached new depths. Sometime before 12 April 'Severall of the Souldiers' in John Floyd's Saco garrison 'in a Mutinous manner Left & deserted their post & Station' and began 'Marching towards Boston without the Officers Commands'. Andros learned of the desertion and ordered Floyd and other commanders to force the mutineers back into service. At the same time, the governor heard that Lieutenant John Puddington, the commander at Kennebunk, had 'Quitted & Discharged the Garrison & Souldiers' contrary to orders. A week before the insurrection, Andros knew that at least 100 angry mutineers had begun to march toward the capital.[41]

The governor's leading opponents also received word of the troops heading for Boston. According to Samuel Mather, a member of the prominent family that included Boston's leading preacher and agent in London Increase Mather, the 'gentlemen' of Boston feared that deserting troops from the 'Eastern War' would 'make a great Stir and produce a bloody Revolution', perhaps even killing the governor. The town's leading citizens met to consider such a possibility, and while they opposed revolt, they resolved that if 'the country people to the northward' descended on the city, 'some of the Gentlemen present would appear in the Head of what Action should be done; and a Declaration was prepared accordingly'. Thomas Danforth corroborated Mather's account, claiming that the 'ancient magistrates and elders' were 'compelled to assist with their presence and councells for the prevention of bloodshed, which had most certainly been the issue if prudent counsells had not been given to both parties'. The elite rebellion, in other words, was one of necessity rather than choice, not quite the 'Protestant putsch' that dominion officials and subsequent historians considered it to be.[42]

Matters came to a head several days before 18 April. The carpenter of the king's frigate in Boston Harbor, the *Rose*, deserted his post and joined the

41 *Edward Randolph: Including his Letters and Official Papers … 1676–1703*, ed. Robert N. Toppan and Alfred T.S. Goodrick (6 vols, Boston, MA, 1898–1909) [hereafter *Randolph Letters*], IV, 279: Edward Randolph to the Lords of Trade and Plantations, 29 May 1689; *The Andros Tracts: Being a Collection of Pamphlets and Official Papers Issued During the Period between the Overthrow of the Andros Government and the Establishment of the Second Charter of Massachusetts*, ed. W.H. Whitmore (3 vols, Boston, MA, 1868–74), III, 33: 'Account of forces raised agt Indians in 1688'; *DHSM*, VI, 474–5: Warrant for Assistance to Capt Jno Floyd on his March to Saco, 12 Apr. 1689.

42 *The Glorious Revolution in America*, ed. Michael G. Hall, Lawrence H. Leder and Michael G. Kammen (Chapel Hill, NC, 1964), pp. 39–40: Report of Samuel Mather; Massachusetts Historical Society, *Collections*, 4th ser., V (1861), 191: Thomas Danforth to Thomas Hinckley, 20 Apr. 1689; *Hutchinson Papers*, ed. Thomas Hutchinson (2 vols, Albany, NY, 1865), II, 310–1: Thomas Danforth to Increase Mather, 30 July 1689. For 'Protestant putsch', see Webb, *Lord Churchill's Coup*, p. 195.

'rebels' in town, claiming that Captain John George and other officers had made disparaging comments about William of Orange's victory in England. Some of the crew prayed for James's victory, and one man even expressed hope 'that it would Raine hell, fire, & Brimstone upon the Prince of Orange, London, & ovore all England for seven days'. Captain George, meanwhile, pledged that since 'King [James] was fled into france', the captain would 'carry his ship' there as well, supporting himself by raiding merchant vessels heading for Boston. Additionally, according to the carpenter, George and Andros conspired to escape from Boston in a blaze of glory. The governor 'intended to fire the Towne at one end', while the *Rose* fired on the other, after which the officers would 'goe away in the smoake, designeing for France'.[43]

The insurrection started early in the morning of 18 April. In the town's North End, Samuel Prince 'saw boys run along the streets with clubs in their hands, encouraging one another to fight'. Within minutes a crowd of over 1,000 people had gathered on both ends of the town. They formed themselves into militia companies and beat drums to call people to action. Around ten o'clock the crowd seized Captain John George. When he asked by what authority they took him, the men 'shewed their Swords, saying that was their Authority'. The newly-formed companies then confronted the few redcoats stationed at Boston's fort and castle, who despite orders, refused to fire on the colonists. By 2 p.m. townspeople from around the province had surrounded the fort. Witnesses estimated their numbers at 20 companies or over 5,000 men in arms. The throngs of angry colonists outnumbered the governor's troops many times over.[44]

The 'strange and sudden appearance' of so many subjects in arms surprised Governor Andros. Around noon several men approached the fort and desired an audience with the governor. They handed him a printed declaration explaining why the people had risen against him and demanded that Andros surrender both himself and the keys to the fort and castle 'in order to appease the People'. The governor initially refused, but when he ventured to the town house to negotiate with members of the newly self-appointed 'Council' they took him prisoner. Within a day the rebels obtained the surrender of both the castle and the fort, as their commanders

43 Mass. Arch., 107: 4: Information of the crew of the Rose Frigate, 29 Apr. 1689; *ibid.*, pp. 9–10: Information of the Rose Frigott Company, 1 May 1689; *Narratives of the Insurrections, 1675–1690*, ed. Charles McLean Andrews (New York, 1915), pp. 215–19: John George to Samuel Pepys, 12 June 1689; *Hutchinson Papers*, II, 313: Thomas Danforth to Increase Mather, 30 July 1689.

44 *Glorious Revolution in America*, ed. Hall, Leder and Kammen, p. 41: Samuel Prince to Thomas Hinckley, 22 Apr. 1689; T.N.A., P.R.O., CO 5/905/85; CO 5/855/2; Nathaniel Byfield, *An Account of the Late Revolution in New England* (1689), in *Glorious Revolution in America*, ed. Hall, Leder and Kammen, p. 47; 'Diary of Lawrence Hammond', MHS, *Proceedings*, 2nd ser., 7 (1891, 1892), 150.

recognized themselves to be hopelessly outnumbered. Miraculously, the revolution occurred without any reported casualties.[45]

The 'seed of Sedition' quickly travelled from Boston to outlying parts of the far-flung Dominion of New England. Reports of Boston's revolution alarmed residents of Suffolk County on Long Island, an English Congregational stronghold that had always looked to Boston rather than New York as its exemplar. The 'freeholders' of the county declared their readiness to defend their liberty and property 'from the Intented invasion of a foraign French design' and reflected on 'more than Turkish crueltyes' already acted by the French on English people in other parts of the world. In Westchester and Queens Counties as well as Suffolk, colonists turned out magistrates and officers who had served under the old dominion government, believing that these officers were unable or unwilling to defend their communities from attack.[46]

Rebellious Long Islanders declared the colony's security to be their first concern. In the town of Jamaica in Queens County, for example, residents worried that the fort in New York City was not strong enough to endure a French invasion. On 15 May the town's militia marched toward the city, 'exceedingly concerned and zealous for the safety of the Citty and fortt against any attack or invasion off the French'. Francis Nicholson, the dominion's lieutenant governor and leading official in New York, believed that enemies of the government incited the crowd in order 'to stirr up the Inhabitants of this City to sedition and Rebellion'. Still, he recognized that he had to take action to quiet his subjects, and worked to strengthen New York's fortifications. While not willing to go as far as Stede in endorsing the uncertain revolution in England, New York's embattled leader had begun to understand the delicacy of his position.[47]

In the meantime, the circulation of further rumours fed popular fears. Some reports questioned Lieutenant Governor Nicholson's protestantism. One colonist claimed to have seen Nicholson attend a catholic mass in England, while another complained that he neglected to destroy the popish 'Images' erected in the fort by his predecessor, the catholic Governor Thomas Dongan. Other rumours indicated that French or Indian war parties approached the colony, and that 'several Souldiers, of which there was a number of Papists', had escaped New England and now resided in New York's

[45] *NYCD*, III, 723: 'Sir Edmund Andros's Report of his Administration'; T.N.A., P.R.O., CO 5/905/85–7; *The Glorious Revolution in Massachusetts*, ed. Robert Earle Moody and Richard Clive Simmons (Boston, MA, 1988), p. 53.

[46] *NYCD*, III, 575: Nicholson and the Council of New York to the Board of Trade, 15 May 1689; *ibid*., p. 577: Declaration of the Freeholders of Suffolk county, 3 May 1689.

[47] *NYCD*, III, 575: Nicholson and Council to the Board of Trade, 15 May 1689; 'Documents Relating to the Administration of Leisler', *Collections of the New-York Historical Society*, I (1868), 260.

fort. The most potent rumour, according to an anti-revolutionary pamphlet, told of a 'horrible design' to murder the city's inhabitants on the first Sunday in June 'as they were worshipping of God in the Dutch Church within the Fort'. While authorities tried to suppress these reports, New York's Mayor Stephanus van Cortlandt claimed that the people were 'so possest with jealousyes and feares of being sold, betrayed, and I know not what, that it was almost impossible to do anything that would please them'.[48]

Fear flowered into open rebellion on the last day of May. On that day a Dutch militia captain named Hendrick Cuyler approached Francis Nicholson and asked to place a sentinel at Sally Point. The contents of their conversation are murky, as Cuyler claimed not to speak English, but apparently Nicholson became angry at the request. He had been deluged with demands from subordinates and wanted to make his authority clear. According to witnesses, the lieutenant governor berated Cuyler and threatened to 'Pistoll' another officer who accompanied him. In his anger, Nicholson made an unfortunate comment; he shouted that if the militia did not become more obedient, he would turn the fort's guns on New York and 'set the town a fire'. The comment played right into the hands of his nervous opponents, since many protestants believed that catholics had a penchant for arson.[49]

Nicholson's outburst travelled around the town. For the nervous militia men who already suspected foul play on the part of their leaders, this latest development proved that Nicholson was a 'pretended protestant' who would not defend the town from the papists who threatened it. As a result, the local militia took action. According to van Cortlandt, the fort filled with burghers, 'armed and inraged', who declared that they were 'sold, betrayed and to be murdered, [and] it was time to look for themselves'. Most of the militia commanders – including a German-born merchant and devout calvinist named Jacob Leisler, who eventually became the movement's de facto leader – placed themselves at the head of the trained bands and demanded the keys of the fort from Nicholson. The council met and decided

48 *Documentary History of the State of New York*, ed. Edmund B. O'Callaghan [hereafter *DHNY*] (3 vols, Albany, NY, 1849–51), II, 27, 28; T.N.A., P.R.O., CO 5/1081/11; *An Account of the Proceedings at New-York. 1689* (Boston, MA, 1689); *A Modest and Impartial Narrative …* (1690), in *Narratives*, ed. Andrews, p. 323; *NYCD*, III, 592; 'Documents Relating to Leisler', *NYHS Collections*, I, 284–5.

49 *NYCD*, III, 593; *DHNY*, II, 12–3. This incident marked the event known to historians as Leisler's Rebellion. Virtually every historian of colonial New York has attempted to interpret the event; the most influential for me have been Voorhees, "In Behalf of the True Protestants Religion"'; *ibid.*, 'The 'Fervent Zeale' of Jacob Leisler', *William and Mary Quarterly*, 3rd ser., LI (1994), 447–72; and John M. Murrin, 'The Menacing Shadow of Louis XIV and the Rage of Jacob Leisler: The Constitutional Ordeal of Seventeenth-Century New York', in *New York and the Union*, ed. Stephen L. Schechter and Richard B. Bernstein (Albany, NY, 1990), pp. 29–71.

that they had no choice but to surrender 'to prevent bloodshed'. New York's only substantial military body had turned against its government.[50]

In New York, as in Massachusetts and Barbados, power devolved to those who acted most decisively against the popish threat. An incident on Staten Island revealed how fear helped to shape politics. Around the time of the rebellion, authorities heard reports that 'the Papist' on Staten Island 'did threaten to cut the inhabitants throats & that the People had left their Plantations & were running in the woods'. The reports also claimed that the catholic in question – a Mr de la Prairie – stockpiled weapons at his house and that Thomas Dongan's brigantine sat off the coast 'fitted out with a considerable quantity of Guns & amonitions'. The papists awaited reinforcements from Boston to begin their design, which included burning the city of New York. The militia commander and Nicholson partisan Nicholas Bayard visited the island to investigate these reports, and found that the islanders 'were afraid to Lay in their beds for fear of the Papists'. Bayard belittled their fears, claiming that the island's catholics were too few in number to threaten protestants. After the rebellion, however, representatives of New York's new 'Committee of Safety' returned to Staten Island. They took depositions recording Bayard's misconduct, and confiscated arms from one 'known papist' on the island. These actions gave legitimacy to the new government by showing that they would provide protection against enemies of the community.[51]

By June the Dominion of New England, the great experiment in direct royal rule, had ceased to exist. Most of its former leaders were either in jail or had fled to England, chased out by a combination of opposition by local *élites* and popular rage. With the benefit of hindsight, it is easy to declare that the dominion failed because it offended the colonists' republican sensibilities, yet on examination the crisis in New England and New York appeared remarkably similar to the one in Barbados. There too, a Stuart appointee ruled in an arbitrary fashion, making many enemies among the planter *élite*. There too, rumours of a popish plot caused panic in the countryside. But Edwyn Stede survived, while Edmund Andros ended up in prison. The difference between the two men was less in political ideology or methods than in rhetoric: Stede cast himself as a defender of protestantism, while Andros would not. The easiest option would have been for Andros and Nicholson to turn against the region's catholics. The former New York governor Thomas Dongan was an obvious choice, and there were several catholics in inferior civil and military offices in the dominion who could have played the role that Montgomery did in Barbados, taking the fall so that the rest of the government could keep functioning. Instead, by down-

[50] *NYCD*, 3: 594: Van Cortlandt to Andros, 9 July 1689; 'Documents Relating to Leisler', *NYHS Collections*, I, 268, 288.

[51] *DHNY*, II, 29–30; T.N.A., P.R.O., CO 5/1081/65; CO 5/1081/46.

playing anti-catholic fears, Andros and Nicholson lost control, a lesson that future imperial governors would not forget.

III

The other major region in English America – the tobacco settlements on Chesapeake Bay – also experienced turmoil in 1689. If the West Indies represented one extreme and New England another, then the Chesapeake fell firmly in the middle. One of the region's administrations, in the royal colony of Virginia, managed to avoid trouble by responding to the panic much as Stede did in Barbados. The other one, in the proprietary colony of Maryland, refused to give credence to popular fears, and ended up falling to a rebellion very similar to those in Boston and New York. In some ways, the Maryland rebellion stands alone, as colonists there dismantled a proprietary regime rather than a royal colony, and Roman catholics controlled the government. Nonetheless, the rumours that brought about the crisis looked quite similar to those in other colonies, as did the behaviour of local officials.[52]

When word of a revolution at home began to circulate, Maryland's governors acted more suspiciously than their counterparts in neighbouring colonies. Unlike Andros, William Joseph, president of the Maryland Council, actually was catholic, like the absent proprietor, Lord Baltimore, and many other prominent men in the majority-protestant colony. These catholic officials suppressed news of William's victory and made several comments that indicated their support for James II. Jesuit priests publicly prayed for the success of the king's armies and spread rumours of James's victories over 'the rebells[,] as they tearmed the protestants'. Besides suspecting that their catholic overlords prayed for James's victory, Maryland protestants levelled specific charges against their leaders, charging that catholic officials contracted with Indians and the French to invade the colony and kill protestants.[53]

The first step in this plot was to confiscate the colonists' arms. On 19 January 1689, Maryland officials ordered inhabitants to deliver all weapons to their county sheriffs, who sent the arms to smiths to be 'amended fixed and made ready and fitt for service' before being returned to colonists. Colonial leaders claimed that they only aimed to put the colony in a better posture of defence in case of a Dutch invasion, but many colonists believed their leaders had other motives. By depriving people of their arms, Mary-

52 While there is relatively little scholarship on the rebellion in Maryland, it includes perhaps the best monograph on the period, Carr and Jordan, *Maryland's Revolution in Government*.

53 'Mariland's Grievances Wiy The[y] Have Taken Op Arms', January 1690, in *Glorious Revolution in America*, ed. Hall, Leder and Kammen, pp. 182–3.

land's leaders prepared the country for an Indian assault that would preserve the colony for King James.[54]

In March 1689 word spread around Charles County of a large force of Indians gathered at the head of the Patuxent river. This army, which some claimed to be larger than 10,000 men, allegedly consisted of Seneca Indians and local Nanticokes, aided by the French. For decades Marylanders had hated and feared the 'Senecas' – a name they applied indiscriminately to all members of the Iroquois Confederacy – who often conducted raids on the frontiers of Maryland and Virginia that targeted English livestock and occasionally English people. Even though Virginia's governor had recently travelled to Albany and signed a treaty with the Iroquois, many colonists still believed the Indians had bad intentions. To make matters worse, they also began to think that their own leaders, especially the catholic Lord Baltimore, commanded the Indian army that lurked on the colony's frontier.[55] Rumours implicated three Maryland officials in the plot. According to one colonist, the proprietary official Henry Darnall – like Sir Thomas Montgomery, a recent convert to catholicism – and two of his cohorts had approached some local Indians and hired them 'to fight for My Lord [Baltimore] against the Protestants'. Baltimore's administration had always maintained good relations with local natives, making it easy, his opponents believed, to enlist them in the popish army.[56]

These reports probably originated across the Potomac river in Stafford County, Virginia. In the middle of March residents of that county began to hear 'some discourse that was talked by the Indians'. The county court ordered Burr Harrison to examine the Indians in question, who related that Henry Darnall had contracted with Seneca Indians to 'kill the protestants'. They had to act quickly, Darnall claimed, so that their bloody work would be complete before word of William's victory arrived from England, at which time 'the protestants would kill all the papists and then all the Indians'. Harrison and his partner – a local clergyman named John Waugh – spread this Indian report around the region, not only to neighbouring Rappahannock County but to Maryland as well. As colonists learned of the popish plot against them, they scrambled to arms and declared their support

54 *Archives of Maryland*, ed. W.H. Browne et al. (Baltimore and Annapolis, MD, 1883–) [hereafter cited as *Arch. Md.*], VIII, 56, 67. Similar fears surfaced in Maryland in 1659 and 1681. See S.J. Michael Graham, 'Popish Plots: Protestant Fears in Early Colonial Maryland, 1676–89', *Catholic Historical Review*, LXXIX (1993), 197–216; and Stanwood, *The Empire Reformed*, pp. 57–66.

55 *Arch. Md.*, VIII, 93: John Addison to John West, 25 Mar. 1689, John Courts to Lawrence Washington, 26 Mar. 1689.

56 *Arch. Md.*, VIII, 224. See also *ibid.*, p. 71.

for William and Mary, opposing any magistrates who did not act to ensure public safety.[57]

Ordinary people placed authority in the hands of local leaders who would provide for defence. In Charles and Calvert counties colonists 'Assembled in Armes' under a militia officer named Henry Jowles, who informed officials in St Mary's of the widespread rumour 'That the Catholicks and Indians have plotted together to disturb [and] cutt off all the protestants in the province'. The people felt their leaders had the duty to protect them from enemies, and they believed that the confiscation of their arms by the central government undermined their ability to defend themselves. Jowles demanded that the sheriffs 'returne the Armes with powder and bulletts sufficient for the defence of the Countrey', and warned that 'until you doe that', the people 'will hold themselves betrayed by your hon[o]r to the Comon Enemy'. Moreover, Marylanders proved all too willing to look across colonial boundaries for assistance. When Darnall arrived in Charles County, he found that 'the people' were 'sending for the Virginians to come to their assistance'. Relations between Maryland and Virginia had never been tranquil, but the 'common enemy' inspired residents of both places to fashion an alliance.[58]

Officials in both colonies reacted to the panic in a very different way from their counterparts in the Dominion of New England. Instead of believing the rumours to be attacks from political rivals, they saw class motives at work. According to William Joseph and his deputies, certain 'ill minded persons' of 'the meanest quality' spread the rumours 'to affright then confuse and then to pillage and plunder the people Especially such as had anything to loose'. The Virginia secretary Nicholas Spencer, caretaker of a government whose executive had recently sailed for England, agreed, claiming that the rebels targeted their economic betters, 'good men who had any estate'. These attacks had little to do with politics, Spencer claimed, since 'to have an Estate [was] a Crime sufficient to have laid a man open to popular Rage, w[hi]ch would not be assuaged but by satiating their appetites with plunder'.[59] While these statements reflected the class biases held by elites in the Chesapeake and elsewhere, they indicated that leaders in Maryland and Virginia understood the power of rumour in a way that northern officials never did. They recognized that the opposition to their administration was a popular front, rather than a small interest group.

57 *Arch. Md.*, VIII, 77–8, 82, 84–6; CW, Blathwayt Papers, vol. 16, folder 5: Nicholas Spencer to William Blathwayt, 27 Apr. 1689; *Executive Journals of the Council of Colonial Virginia*, ed. H.R. McIlwaine (3 vols, Richmond, VA, 1925), I, 104–5.

58 *Arch. Md.*, VIII, 70–1, 72, 81. For a biographical sketch of Jowles, see Carr and Jordan, *Maryland's Revolution of Government*, pp. 266–8.

59 *Arch. Md.*, VIII, 79–80, 82; *Executive Journals of Virginia*, I, 105; CW, Blathwayt Papers, vol. 18, folder 3: Spencer to William Blathwayt, 10 June 1689.

Maryland officials attempted to provide public assurances that the rumours were not true. After learning of the panic, Joseph sent two of his deputies, William Digges and Henry Darnall, to investigate the alarms. In the company of Henry Jowles and another militia officer, Ninian Beale, they ranged the woods of Charles County and confirmed that no army of Senecas threatened the colony. They also collected depositions establishing the innocence of the proprietary officials accused of being parties in the plot. Darnall convinced Jowles and others to sign a declaration that the conspiracy was 'groundless and imaginary' and had been 'fomented by the Artifice of some ill minded persons'. In the most critical concession to popular opinion, Joseph ordered that confiscated weapons be returned to the counties. These actions seemed to calm people's fears.[60]

Virginia officials reacted in a similar fashion. They worked to discredit the plot, finding the Indian who disseminated the rumours and convincing him to recant his story. They also ordered the three men who spread the reports to appear before the General Court, which prohibited John Waugh from preaching 'Publickly or Privately', since he 'Stirs up the People in Stafford to Sedition by his Sermons'. Besides punishing these malcontents, officials also investigated the reports. They searched the home of Stafford County's most prominent catholic, George Brent, whom they confined at the house of a local magistrate. This public investigation showed the people that Brent had not hoarded weapons on his plantations and probably saved him from being plundered by a local mob, 'For the Stafford men were wholly intent to kill robb and burne what Capt Brent had.' According to Nicholas Spencer, by the end of March 'the fears and Jealousies of the people' in Stafford County had 'much abated'.[61]

The Virginia authorities took a final step to assuage popular fears. On 27 April, the colony became the first to declare publicly that William and Mary were the rightful monarchs of the English empire. As Secretary Spencer explained to royal officials, 'the difficulties of maintaining order would have remained insuperable' without proclaiming the new monarchs, since many people believed 'that there being no King in England, there was no Government here'. The Maryland authorities refused to follow suit, even though the colony's inhabitants were 'rageingly earnest for proclaimeing their present Majesties'. In Spencer's view, the reluctance of his neighbours to proclaim William and Mary risked a popular revolt that could 'unhinge the whole Constitution of that Government And dissolve the whole forme

60 *Arch. Md.*, VIII, 73, 77, 78–9, 86, 88–9, 91.

61 CW, Blathwayt Papers, vol. 18, folder 3: Spencer to Blathwayt, 10 June 1689; 'The Randolph Manuscript: Memoranda from Virginia Records, 1688–90', *Virginia Magazine of History and Biography*, XX (1912), 3–4, 10; *Arch. Md.*, VIII, 92, 93–4; *William Fitzhugh and his Chesapeake World, 1676–1701*, ed. Richard Beale Davis (Chapel Hill, NC, 1963), p. 250.

of it'. The secretary's prediction proved to be prescient. Of the four mainland colonies that experienced panics in the spring of 1689, only Virginia weathered the crisis.[62]

From March to July proprietary officials in Maryland maintained a precarious hold on their troubled province, but by mid-July popular fervour finally became more than proprietary officials could handle. New rumours circulated of Indians threatening the colony, and a group of armed men gathered in Charles County on the Potomac river, motivated by reports 'that the Papists had invited the Northern Indians to come down and cutt off the protestants and that their descent was to be about the latter end of August'. The leaders of the armed men were long-time opponents of Lord Baltimore, led by the long-time malcontent John Coode.[63]

Coode bore a striking resemblance to revolutionary leaders in other parts of North America. Like Jacob Leisler, for example, he combined religious zeal with military acumen. Ordained as a minister in the Church of England, Coode lacked the orthodox calvinist beliefs that defined his counterparts to the north, but he displayed a distaste for papists that rivalled anyone on the continent. Also like Leisler, he was a militia commander, and became politically active in order to save the colony from impending attack. Opponents of the rebel leaders in Maryland and New York described the two men in nearly identical terms. One of Baltimore's allies referred to Coode as 'our Masinella' – referring to Tomaso Aniello, the fishmonger who led a popular insurrection in Naples in 1649 and epitomized the dangerous consequences of allowing common people to rise to positions of leadership.[64]

In late July Coode's 'mob' set out from Charles County toward the provincial capital at St Mary's. The force intended to seize the colony's records – probably to search for evidence of popish plotting – and place local government into the hands of the militia. Baltimore's men showed no inclination to surrender to such a motley rabble. Henry Darnall and Nicholas Sewall tried to raise a party of men to meet the rebels, but while many militia officers joined their ranks, 'their men were possessed with the belief that Cood rose only to preserve the Country from the Indians and Papists and to proclaim the King and Queen'. Since they thought the rebels would 'do them noe harm', most men refused to march against them. The underlings of one militia officer, Richard Smith, told him that 'they were willing to march with him upon any other occasion, but not to fight for

62 'The Randolph Manuscript', p. 5; T.N.A., P.R.O., CO 5/1305/30–1; CW, Blathwayt Papers, vol. 18, folder 3: Spencer to Blathwayt, 10 June 1689.

63 *Arch. Md.*, VIII, 153.

64 *Arch. Md.*, VIII, 158. The best sketch of Coode's career is David W. Jordan, 'John Coode, Perennial Rebel', *Maryland Historical Magazine*, LXX (1975), 1–28. On the reference to Masaniello, used against Leisler as well as Coode, see Lovejoy, *Glorious Revolution in America*, pp. 296–311.

the papists against themselves'. When the rebels reached the state house, most of the men who defended it were 'not willing to fight'. The council president and his partisans retreated to Lord Baltimore's estate at Mattapany while the rebels occupied the capital. By convincing their neighbours that the ensuing political conflict was a religious matter, Coode and his allies neutralized their opposition.[65]

Baltimore's men hoped they could wait out the storm in the security of their lord's country estate. But once again, they underestimated the amount of rage that ordinary people possessed against a colonial government they believed to be conspiring against them. Coode's troops surrounded Mattapany House, and grew in size as reinforcements arrived from throughout the colony. According to Henry Darnall, the rebels circulated more rumours in order to set the people against the proprietor. While the militia camped out at Mattapany, for example, the ringleaders allegedly 'caused a man to come riding Post with a Letter wherein was contained that our neighbour Indians had cut up their Corn and were gone from their Towns, and that there was an Englishman found with his belly ript open'. Within days, Darnall and his men realized they had 'no hope left of quieting or repelling the People thus enraged', and they surrendered to Coode and the rebels on 1 August. The terms allowed all armed men in the garrison to return home, but pledged that 'noe papist in this Province' occupy 'any Office Military or Civil'. In a matter of days, the people of Maryland turned from power many of the men who had determined colonial policy since its founding.[66]

The circumstances in the Chesapeake could not be directly compared to the other regions of English America, since the rebellion dismantled a proprietary colony run by actual Roman catholics. It would have been difficult for catholic officials to stay in power in 1689 without renouncing their faith, and they did not have the option of diverting popular rage toward inferior officers. At the same time, however, the parallels are striking. The similarities in the composition of the rumours points both to a common worldview shared by protestants around the empire and a subterranean communication network that must have spread details of the plots by word of mouth from Barbados to New England to the Virginia frontier.

One final piece of evidence gives a sense of the depth of these intercolonial communication networks. Among the items sent to Whitehall as evidence against Sir Thomas Montgomery, Stede included a letter to the Barbadian official from a Capuchin monk in Virginia named Alexander Plunkett. The short letter, written in February 1689, claimed that Montgomery's 'endeavours for the propagation of the Holy Catholick Religion has spread itself

65 *Arch. Md.*, VIII, 148, 156.

66 *Arch. Md.*, VIII, 107–8, 119, 157.

farr & neare & extended itself to those parts of Virginia where now I am'.[67] The comment is tantalizing in that it gives a glimpse of a vast network of rumour and correspondence that is all but invisible to historians. Perhaps Plunkett heard from other catholics, travelling through Virginia in disguise, that an official in far off Barbados was doing good service for the church. Or maybe he overheard some of his protestant neighbours speaking about a diabolical plot against the empire, one that implicated a minor officer in a colony hundreds of miles away. Either way, it demonstrates that the colonial peripheries were not aloof from the political and religious intrigues that convulsed Europe in the last years of the seventeenth century.

IV

While most colonies avoided the dramatic upheavals that struck the Dominion of New England and Maryland, advocates of a stronger empire in North America could not have been pleased by the events of 1689. One disgruntled merchant declared in the wake of the rebellions, 'Now Each Tub stands upon his owne Bottome', meaning that 'each Colony or Government' looked out for its own affairs without considering the welfare of the mother country or its empire. Another colonist complained that 'Every man [is] a Governour', while a Rhode Islander asserted that 'wee are heare in Great confution & without any Government'. From one end of English America to another it was this uncertainty, more than anything else, that made government difficult. Even in Barbados, Lieutenant Governor Stede urged his overseers in London to send a thorough report of William and Mary's victory over James II, so he could be sure he had actually picked the right side.[68]

In spite of the fear and confusion, however, the implications of 1688–9 for the future of the empire were actually much more positive than they appeared. The lessons were obvious: in a colonial context, whether on the mainland or the islands, power belonged to those who provided protection from the local manifestation of the popish enemy, whether French, Irish, or Indian. While the particular aftermath of the revolution lies beyond the scope of this chapter, one brief biographical sketch can serve as an illustration. In 1690, less than a year after his disgraceful exit from New York, Francis Nicholson returned to America, this time as lieutenant governor of Virginia. He became immensely popular, mostly because he provided defence against Indians, also serving as an informal strategist of the English war effort against France. During the next decade Nicholson established himself as the exemplar of both anti-French militancy and tory anti-

67 T.N.A., P.R.O., CO 28/37/7.vii.
68 T.N.A., P.R.O., CO 5/855/29; CO 29/4/120.

catholicism, working with the former Scottish covenanter Samuel Vetch to conquer French Acadia. By 1710 Nicholson, the former suspected papist, was received in New England as a protestant hero. He may have lost his command in 1689, but in the end Nicholson, like other imperial officials, used the lessons of that fateful year to build an empire.[69]

[69] This sketch of Nicholson's later career has been constructed from my own reading in his correspondence in the Colonial Office Papers, as well as Stephen Saunders Webb, 'The Strange Career of Francis Nicholson', *William and Mary Quarterly*, 3rd ser., XXIII (1966), 513–48. For a fuller account, see Stanwood, *The Empire Reformed*, pp. 207–20.

9

The Revolution in Foreign Policy, 1688–1713[*]

TONY CLAYDON

Over recent decades, there has been much debate about the 'revolutionary' nature of 1688–9. Historians from every part of the discipline have argued whether William III's invasion was a turning point for the constitution; whether it transformed relations between British protestants or the three Stuart kingdoms; or whether it accelerated capitalist enterprise, social mobility or the emergence of the public sphere. In one area, however, the radical nature of 1688–9 seems clear. It was at this point that England ceased her occasional, incoherent and usually disastrous, interventions on the European continent, and instead came to lead a sustained military effort against a constant enemy. A country which had stayed out of most the great continental conflicts of the seventeenth century, and had fought only short and opportunistic wars against a variety of foes, began a hundred year struggle with France. This great contest saw active fighting in 1689–97, 1702–13, 1740–8, 1756–63, 1778–83, 1793–1802 and 1805–15 – and almost constant tension between these dates.[1]

This transformation went far deeper than foreign policy. The wars fought by England (and after 1707 by Great Britain) remodelled the country as an efficient fiscal-military state, and as a world power. Starting in the 1690s, the challenge of organizing and paying for prolonged conflict wrought considerable administrative, political and socio-economic change. Unprecedented levels of taxation were approved. Intrusive mechanisms such as the excise department, and land tax assessment, were developed to collect it. Funded public credit and the Bank of England became the central features of national finance. Bureaucracies expanded to manage large armed forces,

* I am grateful to Tim Harris, Stephen Taylor, Andrew Thompson, members of the Cambridge 'Restoration to Reform' seminar and members of the Society for Court Studies, for their comments on versions of this essay.

1 For remarks on the change, see J. Brewer, *The Sinews of Power* (London, 1990), part 1. By contrast, Jeremy Black has stressed the period of alliance between England and France, 1716–31 – see his *Natural and Necessary Enemies* (1986).

and these became major customers in the market for domestic goods. Huge proportions of the population (over five per cent of adult males as early as 1695) were drafted into the military.[2] Overseeing the whole effort, parliament took on new roles legitimating and scrutinizing government activity.[3] By the mid-eighteenth century, this mass mobilization of society for war was having an international reward. As the key member of anti-French alliances, Britain was soon recognized as a premier power. As she began to capture French colonies and establish bases in India, North America, the Mediterranean and Caribbean, she was set on the path to global dominance.

Given the far-reaching consequences of the shift in England's foreign relations in 1689, it is important to explain this transformation. One account is very simple. At the Glorious Revolution, the kingdom was seized by a man with a lifelong mission to contain the French ruler, Louis XIV. The key moment in William III's career had been France's invasion of the Netherlands in 1672. At that point, the young prince of Orange had come to dominate Dutch politics by promising to deliver his homeland from this crisis, and he worked to limit Bourbon power ever after. Personally insulted by Louis's annexation of his ancient family lands, and politically leading a nation threatened by France's eastward expansion, William led Dutch armies through to the 1678 peace of Nijmegan and then remained wary till the French attacked the Rhineland in 1688. From the prince's perspective, therefore, invading England was vital to contain France's threat. Only by neutralizing or displacing James II could William ensure the Stuart realm would fight on his side in his European struggle. It was therefore understandable that he took command of the navy and ordered English ships to attack the French even before he was declared king.[4] Once crowned he worked to bring England into the first Grand Alliance against Louis; he encouraged his subjects to keep fighting for the nine long years to 1697, and was setting them back on the course to war when he died in March 1702 (the actual declaration came in May).[5]

[2] By contrast, Michael Braddick has stressed that the foundations for a powerful state were laid in the interregnum and Restoration eras – see M.J. Braddick, *The Nerves of State* (Manchester, 1996); and his *State Formation in Early Modern England, 1550–1700* (Cambridge, 2000).

[3] See T. Claydon, *William III* (Harlow, 2002), pp. 143–55. Some historians have even claimed the war-driven advance of parliament was more significant than the 1689 settlement, or even the mid-century revolution – see J. Carter, 'The Revolution and the Constitution', in *Britain after the Glorious Revolution, 1689–1714*, ed. G. Holmes (1969), pp. 39–58; A. McInnes, 'When was the English Revolution?', *History*, LXVII (1982), 377–92.

[4] See his communications to Admiral Herbert in December 1688: *Correspondentie van Willem III en van Hans Willem Bentinck*, ed. N. Japikse (5 vols, The Hague, 1927–34), III, iii, 78–81.

[5] Claydon, *William III* provides a brief overview of William's career and priorities. The

William's personal and continental agenda thus accounted for the immediate re-orientation of English foreign policy. It could not, however, be a complete analysis of this revolution. It does not explain why England went on fighting France into the eighteenth century, and even in the 1690s it was clear warfare could not depend on the priorities of one man – even if that man were the king. Technically, the 1689 settlement had left the monarch in charge of foreign policy. Yet William was smart enough to realize that in the political uncertainties of a revolution he must secure wider support before taking his new realm into battle, and so initially he limited himself to presenting parliament with the details of Louis's aggression and waiting for the legislature itself to demand war.[6] Moreover, even though a conflict might start, it could not be sustained without popular approval. After the 1689 declaration of rights, there could be no money for the military without parliamentary votes, and as the record of Commons-transforming elections in the period proves, parliamentarians had to have at least one eye on their wider constituency.[7]

Perhaps more importantly, the English state could only work with broad consent. Even by the late Stuart era, England's systems for tax collection, for day-to-day administration, and for keeping public order, were heavily dependant on 'volunteer' officials drawn from a broad social stratum. People such as justices of the peace, members of town corporations or parish vestrymen, gave their time to administer their localities out of a sense of public duty and were essential to the smooth running of government. In 1639–40, and again in the summer of 1688, many from these classes of people withdrew their labour in protest at royal policy (at least in part objecting to attempts to build or mobilize armies) and regimes were crippled.[8] Acknowledging this, our account of the revolution in foreign policy must range well beyond William's personal goals. We must ask what convinced the key sections of society to agree with their monarchs that France was a pressing and continued threat, and so to pay for, to administer and to fight in such draining wars against her. We need to look at the vigorous print industry and the vibrant public sphere which have emerged as such

fullest English accounts are S.B. Baxter, *William III* (1966); and W. Troost, *William III: Stadhouder-King* (2005).

6 See the king's speech to parliament (18 Feb., 1689), *L.J.*, XIV, 128; and Claydon *William III*, pp. 143–4.

7 Parliament's power to stop a war had been evident even earlier, when the Commons crippled Charles II's final conflict with the Dutch; see J. Spurr, *England in the 1670s* (Oxford, 2000), pp. 33–58. The elections of 1708 and 1710 transformed the possibilities of forming administrations (whig and tory triumphs, respectively); the elections of 1690 and 1700 saw significant swings to the tories, those of 1695 and 1701 to the whigs. For the classic statement of the electorate's importance, see G. Holmes, *The Electorate and the National Will in the First Age of Party* (Lancaster, 1976).

8 See C. Russell, *The Fall of the British Monarchies, 1637–1642* (Oxford, 1991); P. Halliday, *Dismembering the Body Politic* (Cambridge, 1998), ch. 7.

characteristic features of this period in recent studies, and examine what arguments were being used to persuade the political nation to support military effort. To ensure the project is manageable, we should concentrate on the earliest conflicts. It was during the Nine Years War (1689–97) and the War of Spanish Succession (1702–13) that Britain made her most dramatic progress towards the sort of state which could become a world power.

Surprisingly, as Craig Rose observed in his history of England under William, the ideology of the late Stuart wars was not much studied before the mid-1990s. Rose himself placed much emphasis on religious understandings of the struggle with Louis, but in doing this he ran against the existing consensus.[9] For most earlier historians, English willingness to fight was based on calculations of national interest, conceived as avoiding one-power hegemony on the continent. Whilst disgust at French popery played some role, France was seen mainly as a geo-political menace. According to this standard account, people fought because they recognized that Louis's steady expansion on his eastern borders, his threat to absorb Flanders, and his bullying of the Netherlands and Spain, endangered their own independence and livelihood. The only way to secure these was to follow their monarchs into an alliance with all who opposed France. This would restore a balance in Europe, it would give the island realms autonomy from developments on the continent, and it would free them for colonial and commercial expansion overseas.[10]

This explanation of the turn to war in 1688–9 is plausible, and is in fact supported by much of the evidence we might use to test it. If we examine the polemic urging support for war (material which includes the official declarations which initiated conflict; the royal speeches which asked for money from parliament; the sermons for the fast days called to ask for God's blessings on the troops; and the myriad pamphlets, periodical articles and patriotic poems which cheer-led the military effort), all stressed that the French had become too strong and aggressive. In a phrase which became popular in Anne's reign, and was in fact used by the queen as she declared war, Louis had fatally upset the 'balance of power'.[11] In this situation, Anne's subjects

9 C. Rose, *England in the 1690s* (Oxford, 1999), pp. 106, 107–16.

10 For works broadly endorsing this analysis, see G. C. Gibbs, 'The Revolution in Foreign Policy', in *Britain after the Glorious Revolution*, ed. Holmes, pp. 59–79; J. Black, *A System of Ambition?* (Harlow 1991), esp. pp. 28–9, 138; G. Holmes, *The Making of a Great Power, 1660–1722* (Harlow, 1993), pp. 229–31; R. D. McJimsey, 'A Country Divided? English Politics and the Nine Years War', *Albion*, XXIII (1991), 61–74.

11 See *Her Majesties Declaration of War against France and* Spain (1702). The queen talked of the balance in later royal speeches – see *The Parliamentary History of England*, ed. W. Cobbett (36 vols, 1806–20), VI, 451, 543; parliament used it in its 1708 resolution to continue the war – *ibid.*, 609; it was a commonplace in the pamphlet literature of the day – for one example, see its frequent use in *A Few Words upon the Examiner's Scandalous Piece* (1711); and one late attack on Louis even took it as its title: *The Ballance of Power: or a Comparison of the Strength of the Emperor and the French King* (1711). The phrase had

must join with other states to prevent him over-running the continent. Alongside the concept of balance, writers used the discourse of 'universal monarchy', which has been analysed by Steven Pincus. In this rhetoric, a universal monarch was a ruler who would make his writ run everywhere and would destroy the independence of all other nations. Under Elizabeth I, the Habsburgs had been accused of aspiring to this position; in the mid-seventeenth century the Dutch had been cast in the role (and this had led to three Anglo-Dutch wars); but after 1672 – when Louis's near total triumph over the Netherlands had made everyone reassess – the French became the best candidates.[12] In the war propaganda of William and of Anne's reigns, Louis was described as a universal monarch over and over again. Unless he was contained by a balancing coalition, a plethora of writers warned, he would come to dominate the world.[13]

The public, therefore, were urged to fight the French because Louis's continental dominance would threaten their country's interests and independence. Yet although this begins to tell us *how* the people were persuaded, it does not really tell us *why*. The problem is that this most obvious explanation is less convincing than first appears. It would be easy to argue that France was cast as a worrying hegemonist simply because she was the most powerful and expansionist nation in Europe. Anyone viewing geopolitics in the late-Stuart era, we could assume, would have instantly recognized the danger. Yet this was questionable. For all Louis's aggression, there were other powers that could be charged with trying to dominate Europe, and sometimes actually were. Although the France was the foreign power most commonly described as a potential universal monarch, not everyone presented it in this way at all times. The problem in explaining England's commitment to war is, therefore, understanding why fear of the French was more consistent than concerns about other nations and ultimately displaced

been used in the seventeenth century – but had perhaps been popularized by Charles Davenant's influential analysis, *Essays upon 1. The Ballance of Power etc* (1701).

12 For these shifts, see S. Pincus, *Protestantism and Patriotism* (Cambridge, 1996); and his 'From Butterboxes to Wooden Shoes: The Shift in English Popular Sentiment from Anti-Dutch to Anti-French in the 1670s', *H.J.*, XXXVIII (1995), 333–61.

13 For a summary of such material from William's war see S. Pincus, 'To Protect English Liberties: The English Nationalist Revolution of 1688', in *Protestantism and National Identity*, ed. T. Claydon and I. McBride (Cambridge, 1998), pp. 75–104, especially 95–102 – and for specific examples, see *A View of the True Interest of the Several States of Europe since the Accession of their Present Majesties* (1689), p. 45; *Nero Gallicanus: or the True Portraiture of Lewis XIV* (1690), p. 2. For a small – but nicely spread – selection from Anne's reign, see *The Dangers of Europe from the Growing Power of France* (1702), p. 2; J. Piggot, *A Sermon Preach'd on the 7th of September 1704, Being the Thanksgiving Day for … Blenheim* (1704), p. 33; [J. Addison], *The State of the War* (1708), p. 2; *The French King's Thanks to the Tories of Great Britain* (1710), p. 2; *A Full Answer to the Conduct of the Allies* (1712), p. 93.

them in the key sections of public opinion. Louis's unique strength and his unparalleled ambition were not always uncontested facts.

One power which could still be viewed as a danger was the United Provinces of the Netherlands. This might at first seem surprising, since historians have traditionally seen the Dutch in decline in the later seventeenth century. As Pincus has argued, it became harder to see them as universal monarchs after the near catastrophe of 1672, when the Dutch had saved themselves from the French invasion (undertaken in league with Charles II of England) only by breaching the dykes to flood their fields and by retreating to a small remnant of their territory in Holland and Zeeland.[14] Yet by Pincus's own admission, no one had ever thought the Dutch would do well in the kind of war fought in 1672. Their threat had come, not from the land armies needed to withstand the French, but from a dominance of world trade. This would allow the Provinces to strangle their rivals' economies, and to buy the more immediate military support they needed.[15] What happened after the French invasion confirmed this danger. In 1672, the Dutch allied with the Habsburg powers, Spain and Austria. In the years which followed they paid for these nation's campaigns; and as early as 1673 were joining with them to strike deep into the territories of Louis's allies. By the mid-1670s they had forced French troops off their land and Charles II out of the war, and made it clear they were still a contending power on the European stage. Over the next decades, their influence may actually have reached its apogee. In 1688 they provided the ships and men for William III's invasion of England and so proved capable of altering the regime of an extremely powerful neighbour, and of moulding this formerly independent realm to their anti-French policy.[16] From 1689 to 1697, and from 1702 to 1713, they were merely one element of a great European confederacy, yet they persuaded it to spend most of its effort protecting *them*. Huge armies of Spaniards, Britons, Germans and Austrians blocked French invasion of the Netherlands through Flanders.[17]

For those still hostile to the Dutch, this record was more than enough material for denigration. From as early as the closing months of 1688, Jacobites cautioned that William's invasion, and the war against France which

14 Pincus, 'From Butterboxes to Wooden Shoes', pp. 354–5. The fullest account of the war in English is in the closing chapters of H.H. Rowen, *John de Witt* (Princeton, NJ, 1978).

15 Pincus, *Protestantism and Patriotism*, pp. 256–68.

16 The importance of the Dutch in 1688/9 is stressed in J.I. Israel, 'The Dutch Role in the Glorious Revolution', in *The Anglo-Dutch Moment*, ed. J.I. Israel (Cambridge, 1991), pp. 105–62.

17 There is a vigorous debate in Dutch historiography about the timing of Dutch decline (I am grateful to David Onnekink for guiding me through this). The possibility that the Netherlands may have remained vigorous into the eighteenth century has begun to filter into English textbooks – see J.L. Price, *Dutch Society, 1588–1713* (Harlow, 2000), p. 243; J.I. Israel, *The Dutch Republic* (Oxford, 1995), p. 998.

would stem from it, were devices to increase the Netherlands' wealth and influence, and so secure the global dominance which the United Provinces had so long desired. Even before William arrived in London, pamphlets supporting King James warned that the prince of Orange had come to hobble English resistance to Dutch hegemony.[18] Through the 1689–97 conflict, an underground press continued this charge, citing heavy loss of English men, trade and coin as evidence that Netherlanders were bleeding the only nation who might stand up to them.[19] Sometimes Jacobite suspicion spilled over into more loyal channels. Particularly in the early 1690s, when little progress was being made on the battlefield, 'country' pamphleteers and backbench M.P.s wondered whether Dutch counsels were behind mismanagement of the war.[20] Though this rarely led to outright questioning of anti-French policy, it probably fed the war-weariness that would lead parliament to disband William's army when peace was secured, and so to reject the king's insistence that Louis was still a pressing threat.[21] There was even more sustained and open criticism of the Netherlands in the last years of Queen Anne's reign. By this stage, many people had begun to wonder whether prolonged conflict to protect the Dutch was in their interests. Most notoriously Jonathan Swift, in his first pamphleteering triumph, accused Hollanders of grabbing power at everyone else's expense. His *Conduct of the Allies* (1711) argued the Dutch had tricked Britain into bearing most of the cost of the fighting against Louis, and so of weakening both their French enemies and their gullible allies.[22] A host of other publications joined this chorus as Swift's periodical *The Examiner* accused the Dutch of arrogant interference in British politics, and inspired other tracts and parliamentary addresses.[23] Authors denounced the benefits Holland had gained from the

18 For example, *The Dutch Design Anatomized, or a Discovery of the Wickedness and Unjustice of the Intended Invasion* (1688) esp. pp. 7–8; *The Prince of Orange his Declaration … and Some Modest Remarks on it* (1688), esp. p. 17; [N. Johnston], *The Dear Bargain* [1688].

19 For example, *Min Heer T. van C's Answer … Representing the True Interest of Holland* [1690]; *The Sad Estate of the Kingdom* [1690]; *A Letter to a Member of the Committee of Grievances* (1690); *The Price of the Abdication* [1693]; *The People of England's Grievances to be Inquired into* [1693]; [W. Anderton], *Remarks upon the Present Confederacy* (1693).

20 See the speeches recorded in *The Parliamentary Diary of Narcissus Luttrell, 1691–1693*, ed. H. Horwitz (Oxford, 1972), pp. 216, 267, 288–90, 304 (fears that money was leaving the country, and the Dutch were not contributing much to their own defence); 242–4 (fear of Dutch counsels swaying the king); 253–7 (complaints that English soldiers were sacrificed cheaply when placed under Dutch command).

21 For the link between Commons pressure to disband in 1697, and earlier concern about the Dutch priorities of the force, see John Childs, *The British Army of William III, 1689–1702* (Manchester, 1987), ch. 8.

22 [J. Swift], *The Conduct of the Allies and of the Late Ministry* (Edinburgh, 1711), esp. pp. 7–8, 17–18.

23 *The Examiner: or Remarks on Papers and Occurrences*, I, 5 (31 Aug. 1710).

1709 Barrier Treaty (Britain had agreed to secure a string of fortresses and trading rights for the Netherlands in Flanders), and even hinted at war to reverse Dutch progress.[24] Taken together, this rhetoric demonstrates that old anxieties had not died. The lowlanders, it was feared, might still use commercial strength and political guile to trap all Europe in their web.

If the old Dutch enemy might plausibly be constructed as a threat to the European balance of power, the even older Habsburg foe might be as well. Again, historians have tended to assume this force had declined by 1688. Under Charles V in the early sixteenth century, the Habsburg lands had been united, rich and strong: but since his abdication, their potency seemed to have dissipated. In 1555 the Habsburg empire had been split between Spanish and Austrian branches, and neither had subsequently prospered. In the seventeenth century Spain had fallen into economic decline and lost her Dutch provinces to revolt, whilst Austria's ultimate failure to dominate Germany in the Thirty Years War, and the threats to her eastern border, had also ruled her out as a potential universal monarch. Yet whilst many English commentators *did* remark on Habsburg decline in the Stuart era, this was neither the only, nor the only possible, interpretation.[25] Although the two branches of the family had been divided, they still allied in almost every international contest, and together they still packed a powerful punch. They were, for example, known to be essential in any confederacy to balance France. They provided the vast land armies which the 'maritime' powers (Britain and the Netherlands) lacked, and so were needed for any serious continental operation. They had also both extended their territories since Charles V's day (Spain in the Pacific, Austria in the Danube basin): if these realms ever reunited they would constitute a global empire on which the sun would not set.

Actual concern about this outcome was muted for most of William's reign, since the Habsburgs were allies against France. Yet after 1697 the real possibility of Habsburg reunion was raised – and alarm became palpable. The reason was the parlous state of Carlos II's health. This king of Spain had no direct heirs, so when he died there was a chance his Iberian, Flemish, Italian

24 For examples, [J. Swift], *A Letter to the Examiner* (1711); [J. Swift], *Some Remarks on the Barrier Treaty* (1712); *The Queen, the Present Ministry, Lewis XIV and Philip V Unanswerably Vindicated* (1712), esp. p. 11; *The Miserable Case of Poor England Fairly Stated* (Amsterdam, 1712). For addresses see *Parliamentary History*, ed. Cobbett, VI, 1093, 1095–1106.

25 From at least the late 1660s, pamphleteers had explained France had taken over from Spain as the potential universal monarch – see, for example, *A Free Conference Touching the Present State of England* (1688), esp. pp. 8–9. In 1711–13, whigs who upheld Austrian claims to Spain argued it was safe to reunite the Habsburg lands as they had been greatly weakened – see for example, *A Caveat to the Treaties, or the Modern Schemes of Partition Examin'd* (1711), pp. 47–51 (this explicitly denied any comparison with Charles V's realm); *A Vindication of the Present M_____y from the Chorus Rais'd against them* (1711), pp. 32–8.

and American territories would go to his Habsburg relatives in Austria and fatally upset the balance of power. William coped with this possibility by negotiating a partition of the Spanish realm with Louis. Under the deal, France would annex most of the lands in Italy on Carlos's death, but the rest of Spain's empire would go to a junior branch of the Austrian Habsburgs in the hope that they would never unite with the main dynasty's lands. In 1700, concern about continental dominance swung back to France, since Louis reneged on the partition treaty and accepted Carlos's will. This document left *all* of the deceased king's lands to the French ruler's cadet grandson, so in the War of Spanish Succession a confederacy including the British, Dutch and Austrians fought France to block this inheritance.[26] This did not, however, end concern about Habsburg hegemony. In 1711 the Emperor Joseph I died. This made the confederacy's candidate for the Spanish throne (Archduke Charles Habsburg) direct heir for the Austrian lands as well, and revived the possibility of a Europe-embracing empire. In the light of this development, there was rapid reconsideration in London. Soon, Queen Anne's ministers were exploring a settlement which might leave Louis's grandson in charge in Madrid (albeit with some of his empire shaved away), and would thus limit Habsburg power.[27]

As might be expected, this diplomacy received close comment in the press. Especially in the aftermath of the partition treaty, and again after Joseph's death, concern about Louis's strength could be mixed by worries about the Habsburgs. In the earlier of these periods, anxiety crossed the political spectrum, though it was fed by rather different assumptions at either pole. Until Louis broke the terms of the 1697 peace by re-recognizing James II's claim to the English throne, many tories had been reluctant to return to war. This was primarily out of horror at the domestic changes conflict had wrought, but there was at least some space for criticism of Austria as a dangerous and unsavoury power whom England should not fight to advance.[28] Whigs, by contrast, urged war to punish Louis for breaking the partition treaty. However, since this treaty had extended France's territories as part of its plan to prevent the whole Spanish empire falling into either Bourbon or Habsburg hands, they were forced to defend it as a barrier against Austrian as much as French dominance. Louis, they contended, had scuppered a deal which acknowledged Spain's whole realm would be as lethal in Habsburg as in his own hands, and which had offered the only chance of peace. In fact, hopes of avoiding war had been slim. Neither the Spaniards

26 There were actually two partition treaties (1698 and 1700) since the heir to Spain named in the first one died. D. Ogg, *England in the Reign of James II and William III* (Oxford, 1955), ch. 15, still provides one of the clearest expositions of this dizzying diplomacy.

27 For a concise, clear account, with suggestions for further reading, see J. Hoppit, *Land of Liberty?* (Oxford, 2000), pp. 120–3.

28 For example, *An Argument against War* (1701), p. 10.

nor the Austrians had agreed to partition, and would have fought to prevent it. Logically, therefore, whigs who defended the treaty were accepting that England might have been forced to join Louis to impose it, and had only avoided war against the Habsburgs when the French reneged on the whole agreement.[29] For such whigs there were conceivable circumstances in which the danger of Spanish or Austrian ambition might overbalance that from France, and would dictate a quite different pattern of alliances.[30]

Towards the end of Anne's reign, anti-Habsburg sentiment was more partisan; it was also more vigorous and sustained. War-weary tories, who suspected the conflict was being prolonged to enrich their whig enemies, seized on the death of Emperor Joseph as a change of circumstance which could justify peace. They urged that a quick settlement might leave the French in charge in Madrid, since if Britain stuck to her original war aims she could create a dangerous Habsburg *imperium*.[31] Some of the finest, and subsequently the most famous, writers of the day were employed in this cause. Jonathan Swift's *Conduct of the Allies* directed most criticism at the Dutch, but also took side swipes at the Austrians. It warned that a union of Spain and Austria was as dangerous as one between Spain and France, and accused the Empire of securing its hold in Hungary instead of using its troops for the wider allied cause.[32] More surprisingly, Daniel Defoe took up the theme. Although whiggish by inclination, he was in the pay of Robert Harley (the ex-whig leader of the tory administration from 1710), and upheld the minister's policy of seeking an early peace without Spain going to Austria. In his thrice weekly *Review*, and a steady stream of pamphlets, Defoe warned about a resurgence of Habsburg power.[33] As he explained in the *Review* issues for autumn 1711 – the ones announcing the periodical's conversion to a peace policy – the war had been fought to avoid any 'exorbitance' of power in one nation's hands. When Britain had found this excess

29 For pamphlets defending the partition treaty, see [D. Defoe], *The Two Great Questions Considered* (1700) – this urged Louis to return to the principle of partition, and join a strong Anglo-Dutch alliance to enforce it; *The Partition Examin'd and its Rejection by the French King Fully Stated* (1701); *Two Letters to a Friend Concerning the Partition Treaty* (1702), esp. p. 10.

30 In fact, after the 1713 peace treaty had partitioned Spain's realm, France and a whig-governed Britain *did* ally to enforce it. From 1718–20 they co-operated against Spain when she tried to regain her lost Italian possessions. In 1725, the Anglo-French alliance was renewed in the face of a treaty between Spain and Austria: whigs defended this well into the 1730s – see, for example, *A Series of Wisdom and Policy* (1735).

31 For examples of pamphlets, see *The Ballance of Europe* (1711); *Queries A-Propos, about the Review's Question* (1712).

32 [Swift], *Conduct of the Allies*, pp. 30, 46.

33 For the pamphlets, see [D. Defoe], *Reasons Why this Nation Ought to Put a Speedy End to this Expensive War* (1711); [D. Defoe], *An Essay at a Plain Exposition of that Difficult Phrase, a Good Peace* (1711); [D. Defoe], *The Felonious Treaty* (1711); [D. Defoe], *Imperial Ingratitude* (1712).

in France, she had been right to fight Louis, but if 'we find it in *Germany* or *Spain*, in the House of *Austria*... we must fight with it there'.[34] Later issues became quite hysterical about the Habsburgs. In the sixteenth century, Defoe reminded his readers, the Emperor Charles V had nearly become the 'Universal Monarch of Europe'.[35] Britain must now counter the continuing threat from his family: if she allowed Austria and Spain to unite, subsequent generations would 'Curse their Fathers who Erected a Power in Europe, which all their Strengths and Blood will not put down'.[36]

A further non-French candidate for continental tyranny was even older than the Dutch or the Austrians. Since the late middle ages, western Europe had been threatened by the Ottoman Turks. This Islamic force had captured Constantinople in 1453, and had expanded through the Balkans and Mediterranean under Sultan Suleiman the Magnificent in the sixteenth century. Philip II of Spain's victory at Lepanto (1571) had stalled expansion for a while, but soon the Turks were on the move again. From the mid-1640s they began a war with Venice, which expunged that republic's influence east of the Adriatic. After capturing Crete in 1669, they turned north and advanced along the Black Sea coast, before turning their attention to Hungary. In 1683 they launched their most daring raid. Taking advantage of internal disputes in the Austrian empire, they marched a huge army from Constantinople and up the Danube to Vienna. Habsburg resistance crumbled, and the imperial court retreated leaving only 12,000 troops to hold the capital. It was besieged for two months before a united force of Germans, Austrians and Poles could rescue it.[37]

Panic about the Turkish threat spread across Europe, and reached England. The Ottomans' advance had been followed through the 1660s and 1670s in London, and dire warnings were posted about the cruel rule that might soon engulf the continent.[38] In 1683, coverage became fevered. Even though the siege of Vienna was half a continent away, printers informed the English about it as it unfolded, and made it clear that if this 'bulwark' fell there was nothing to stop the Ottomans sweeping into the heart of Germany.[39] If readers were not chilled by prose, maps and prospects of the Austrian capitol illustrated the danger pictorially. The Turks, these representations demonstrated, were literally at the gates, and their alien clothes and visages

34 [D. Defoe], *A Review of the State of the British Nation*, VIII, 87 (13 Oct. 1711).

35 *Ibid.*, VIII, 88 (16 Oct. 1711).

36 *Ibid.*, VIII, 10 (13 Nov. 1711).

37 H. Holborn, *A History of Modern Germany, 1648–1840* (1965), pp. 83–7 is as clear as later works, and absolves Louis from real blame for the Turks' incursion.

38 For early concern, see H. Marsh, *A New Survey of the Turkish Empire* (1663); *Europea Modernea Speculum* (1665).

39 Works produced before the siege was raised included *A Particular Account of the Sudden and Unexpected Siege of Vienna* (1683); and *A True Copy of a Letter from Count Starenbergh to the Duke of Lorraine, Concerning the Present Condition of Vienna* (1683).

proved how strange and humiliating rule by the Ottomans would be.[40] It is true that the height of the danger was brief. The Turks were driven from Vienna, and over the next two decades they were pushed back further. By the 1699 peace of Karlowitz, the Habsburgs had secured control of Hungary and Transylvania and were consolidating their positions towards Belgrade. Yet the struggle was hard and sense of danger remained – facts made clear in English relief at each christian victory. Some triumphs were greeted by formal thanksgivings; all engendered histories, pamphlets and news reports celebrating progress.[41] As late as 1695, one writer could still stress containing the Ottomans as a crucial part of any general peace settlement in Europe, and suggested France might be persuaded to redirect its forces to this task in the east.[42] At the same time, fear of the Turk was manifest in attacks on Louis XIV. The French king was accused of aiding Turkish advance as a distraction to his German rivals and pamphlets which took this line emphasized the scale of the betrayal. Europe had been sold to a force which could crush its liberties and sweep away its civilization.[43]

France, then, was very often understood as the candidate for European hegemony which England, and then Britain, must oppose. But she was not the only possible candidate, and certain groups, and at times wide swathes of opinion, could easily construct the Dutch, the Habsburgs or the Turks, as the main danger. Given this, it is not enough to describe foreign policy swinging against Louis simply because he was unquestionably the most threatening ruler. We have to understand why he was understood as this threat: why – consistently over time, and in the mainstream of significant public opinion – his power was thought more pernicious and destabilizing than that of his several continental rivals. To explain this, we must re-examine the polemic urging people to war. When we do this we discover that France was denounced not only as a challenge to the balance of power. She also imper-

40 *A True and Exact Description of the City of Vienna, Together with the Encampment of the Turks* (1683); *A Description of Vienna in its Ancient and Present State, with an Exact and Compleat Account of the Siege Thereof* (1683).

41 *A True and Exact Relation of the Raising of the Siege of Vienna* (1683); *A Full and True Account of the Great Battle Fought … before the City of Presburg* (1683); *Predictions of the Sudden and Total Collapse of the Turkish Empire* (1684); J. Shirley, *The History of the Wars of Hungary* (1685); *A Historical Description of the Glorious Conquest of the City of Buda* (1686), p. 68; *A Form of Prayer and Thanksgiving … for the Prosperity of Christian Arms … to be Used 12 September* (1686); J. Richards, *A Journal of the Siege and Taking of Buda* (1687). For stress on the tough struggle after 1683, see M. Hochedlinger, *Austria's Wars of Emergence, 1683–1797* (2003).

42 T. Houghton, *Europe's Glory* (1695).

43 For example, *Mars Christianissimus … or an Apology for the Most Christian King's Taking up Arms against the Christians* (1684), esp. pp. 63–7; *The History of the Late War with the Turk … with an Account of the Underhand Dealings of France in that Affair* (1684); *The Detestable Designs of France Expos'd* (1689), esp. p. 23; *The Intreigues of the French King at Constantinople* (1689).

illed international spiritual entities to which it was assumed the English and British belonged, and it was to defend these that the country must fight.

The first and most obvious of these wider communities was European protestantism. In the sixteenth century, England had emerged as the most populous and powerful of the nations which had embraced the reformation. In consequence, many of her subjects had come to feel she had a duty to succour protestants across the continent, and this responsibility was transferred to the new nation of Britain in 1707. From the moment Louis took power in France, his actions had been a call to this duty. Domestically, he had ramped up the pressure on his own calvinist minority. The French reformed church had been granted wide toleration under the 1598 edict of Nantes, but Louis soon set about limiting this. He billeted troops on protestant households; he erected legal barriers to protestant education, employment and inheritance; and in 1685 he dealt the final blow with the revocation of the Nantes edict. From that moment the calvinists – who were forbidden to flee – were to convert to catholicism or suffer terrible persecution. Louis's record abroad was no better since his eastward expansion was accompanied by suppression of the reformed faith. He annexed protestant cities in Orange and Strasbourg; he encouraged allies such as the duke of Savoy to persecute their own protestant communities; and his invasions of foreign lands (such as that of the Netherlands in 1672, of the Rhineland in 1688) were accompanied by the humiliation of reformed christians.[44]

In British polemic such treatment of protestants was reason enough to go to war. Many English pamphlets presented William's war as a crusade to rescue the European reformation, whilst a series of monthly fast days, with accompanying sermons and liturgies, set the conflict in a providential context and portrayed it as God's protestant cause.[45] Such rhetoric continued under Queen Anne. As in the 1690s, protestant polemic was handicapped by England's alliances with catholic Spain and Austria. But at least Rome had now lined up squarely with France to add credibility to the popish threat (Innocent XI, pontiff 1676–89, had fallen out with Louis and it had taken his successors a decade to restore relations) and, as in the earlier conflict, attention could be distracted from catholic friends by stressing Louis's unique cruelty.[46] Thus the programme of fast days was nearly as intense under Anne as it had been under William. It still included prayers

44 Clear summaries of Louis' religious policies can be found in G. Treasure, *Louis XIV* (2001), ch. 9; and *The Reign of Louis XIV*, ed. P. Sonnino (1990), ch. 10.

45 T. Claydon, *William III and the Godly Revolution* (Cambridge, 1996), pp. 100–10, 134–47; Claydon, *William III*, pp. 134–42.

46 Whilst early Williamite propaganda had highlighted the papacy's disgust at Louis, claiming it showed how vile the French king was – note, for instance, *The Spirit of France and the Politick Maxims of Lewis XIV* (1689), p. 18 – under Queen Anne the pope was firmly back in his anti-christian role, serving as a spiritual side-kick to Louis – see, for example, *The Dangers of Europe from the Growing Power of France* (1702), p. 7. J.N.D.

for the welfare of the foreign reformed churches and preaching that worried about protestants across the continent.[47] Meanwhile, the greater number of military victories in the new reign gave more opportunities for national thanksgivings. On these solemnities, congregations were urged to celebrate but were also told that the queen's forces were fighting a tight struggle against the popish Antichrist.[48] Meanwhile pamphlets expressed horror at the retreat of the European reformation. Authors argued war against Louis was the only way to reverse this decline: one effort in 1702 suggested that 'England and the whole *Protestant* Interest are now at a Crisis' and urged all to unite against the French king who menaced them.[49]

Quite apart from France's sins against protestantism, she also offended christianity as a whole. Through the late Stuart period, the British retained a strong sense of 'Christendom' as in important international entity. They employed the word frequently in public discourse, and analysis of its use suggests it was far more than a rhetorical shorthand for 'Europe'. For people of the day, Christendom was a meaningful spiritual body. It transcended confessional divisions between protestants and catholics (the position of the orthodox in the east was rather more hazy because the English knew so little about them), and it demanded that all christians defend their united community when it faced external attack. Christendom also set moral values to which all its members should aspire. It dictated, for instance, that one deal honestly with co-religionists, and show them charity and mercy. A number of scholars have begun to explore these meanings in seventeenth-century writings, but here much of their purchase should be clear from accusations that Louis was betraying this shared European identity.[50]

Kelly, *The Oxford Dictionary of Popes* (Oxford, 1985), pp. 287–92 gives a clear account of the various pontiffs' attitudes.

47 Note, for instance, *A Form of Prayer to be Used on Wednesday the Tenth Day of June, Being the Fast Day* (1702); *A Form of Prayer to be Used ... Wednesday the Fourth Day of April ... being the Fast Day* (1705); J. Harris, *A Sermon Preach'd in the Parish Church of St Mary Magdalen ... Wednesday the Twenty Sixth of May ... Being the Fast Day* (1703), especially pp. 8–10; R. Chapman, *The Necessity of Repentance Asserted* (1703), especially pp. 16–17.

48 For example, the very large number of sermons published as part of the thanksgiving for Marlborough's victory at Blenheim in 1704. Among the most 'protestant' of these were: A. Archer, *A Sermon Preached in the Chappel at Tunbridge Wells, September 7* (1704); E. Fowler, *A Sermon Preach'd at the Chappel at Guild-Hall upon Thursday the 7th September* (1704); J. Gaunt, *Deborah and Barak* (1704); N. Hough, *Success, When the Signs of Divine Favour* (1704); White Kennett, *A Sermon Preached in the Church of St Botolph Aldgate ... on September VII* (1704).

49 *Directions to the Electors of the Ensuing Parliament* (1702), pp.19–20. For examples of later pamphlets blackening Louis with his popish bigotry, see *The Life and Bloody History of Louis XIV* (1709); *A Caveat to the Treaties* (1711), esp. p. 59; [F. Hare], *The Management of the War* (1711).

50 Rose, *England in the 1690s*, pp. 112–15; T. Claydon, *Europe and the Making of England, 1660–1760* (Cambridge, 2007).

The clearest charge against France was of abetting the infidel Turk. As we have mentioned, polemicists indicted Louis for doing so, and his actions certainly provided fuel for their flames. In the late 1670s and early 1680s, France had provided support for Hungarian rebels against the Austrian emperor. Louis had hoped this would distract the Habsburgs from defending western Germany – but when the Hungarians allied with the Ottomans during the invasion of 1683, the French king appeared to have encouraged the anti-christian deluge. Louis compounded the problem with close diplomatic contact with the Turks, and by his apparent indifference to the plight of the beleaguered Habsburgs. He sent no help in 1683 (though a very wide alliance of Venetians, Poles and both protestant and catholic Germans came together to relieve Vienna) and he was said to have banned French celebration of Austrian victories.[51] As a result, Louis could be presented as an enemy of Christendom. In numerous pamphlets, the French king was labelled a 'most Christian Turk' and portrayed as an apostate in the midst of christian lands.[52] As even the 1689 Commons declaration against Louis stressed, he had threatened the faith from within just as it faced its most serious test in the east.[53]

Beyond this Ottoman entanglement, Louis was attacked for betraying the ideals which held Christendom together. Partly this was standard war propaganda. The French were accused of needless aggression and cruelty which resulted in merciless slaughter of fellow christians. Within this rhetoric, it was stressed that catholics as well as protestants suffered. Louis thus proved himself the scourge of all God's followers.[54] More particularly, and more interestingly, the French king was accused of systematic breaches of his promises. The charge was so common there is little point citing particular instances: very few propagandists left the theme alone. At a literal level, this breach of faith meant he had broken treaties. His word could not be relied upon, and people should expect to be betrayed if they entered into any contract with him. The label for this perfidy, however, was significant. Louis, it was stressed, had broken *faith*. Writers insisted he had not only deceived individuals, but had abused the ties of charity, trust and interdependence which prevented christians degenerating into a heathen mass of selfish individuals.

51 For more details, see Treasure, *Louis XIV*, pp. 208–21; Louis's ban on pro-Christian festivities was noted by contemporary pamphleteers; see *Spirit of France*, p. 20.

52 T. Claydon, 'Protestantism, Universal Monarchy, and Christendom in William's War Propaganda, 1689–1697', in *William III*, ed. Esther Mijers and David Onnekink (2006). The quote comes from the title of *The Most Christian Turk: or a View of the Life and Bloody Reign of Lewis XIV* (1690).

53 *An Address upon the French War, and Read in the House of Commons, April 19th, 1689* (1689), p. 2.

54 Witness the splendidly titled *The Present King of France Demonstrated an Enemy to Catholick as well as Protestant Religion* (1689).

The evidence for Louis's betrayal was depressingly impressive. The French monarch always had explanations for his behaviour – some of them good ones – but he had nevertheless broken a substantial number of agreements. When marrying a daughter of the Spanish king in 1659, he had renounced all claims to Spanish territory. Yet when he failed to secure the full dowry for his bride, he declared this nullified the agreement, and invaded Brabant in the Spanish Netherlands. English and Dutch pressure persuaded Louis to accept only minor territorial gains at the 1668 Treaty of Aix-la-Chapelle, but this proved no lasting settlement, since the French continued to put pressure on Flanders in contravention of its terms. In 1666, England had suffered France's perfidy. Diplomats from London had been sure they were close to securing Louis's alliance in their war with the Dutch: but they could only watch in horror as he came out on the side of the Netherlands and attacked the English fleet without warning. In the 1670s and 1680s, the Dutch in turn became victims. They had thought they were on good terms with Louis immediately before he attacked them in 1672; and then they found that neither the Treaty of Nijmegan in 1678, nor a 1684 truce would restrain his eastward expansion as he had promised. Most infamously, Louis shattered the partition treaty in 1700. As we have seen, he tore up his agreement with William, and accepted Carlos II's will, without sign of shame or regret. At the same time he went back on his undertaking at the 1697 peace of Ryswick to recognize the 1689 revolution, and re-commenced his support for the exiled Stuarts. Given this record, it was not surprising that nearly every anti-French pamphlet accused the Louis of insincerity and some did little more than list his broken promises.[55]

Such a perfidious litany was bad enough, but many contemporaries thought the French king posed a terrifying threat to the christian faith itself. For them, Christendom was as much injured by each broken treaty as the individual aggrieved parties. The 1689 declaration of war put the case officially. In this document, William and Mary called Louis 'the common Enemy of the Christian world', whose worst crime had been the 'manifest Violation of Treaties'.[56] The logic behind such charges was often tacit: but in places it was spelled out, and it was in any case pretty obvious to anyone who thought of christians' duties to one another. Christ had urged his followers to live in peace and charity. This was clearly impossible unless people trusted one another, so to break one's word was to disrupt the community that Jesus had attempted to found. In international relations, this principle was enshrined by treaties, and in most of the war propaganda elucidation of this simple religious point substituted for any extended analysis of international law. States made solemn and public agreements (which were frequently sworn

[55] For example, *A General Collection of Treatys, Declarations of War, Manifestos and Other Publick Papers* (1710); *A Clear View of the French King's Bona Fide* (1711); *The Friendship of King Lewis Always Fatal* (1712).

[56] *Their Majesties Declaration against the French King, 7 May, 1689* (1689).

before God) to remind them of the seriousness of what they were undertaking: to breach such a pact was to tear at Christendom. If nations were not bound by treaties, anarchy would destroy the christian community – so in this worldview keeping faith could be equated with keeping *the* faith.[57] One pamphlet to make this absolutely clear was the 1702 production *Anguis in Herba*. The author of this work explained that a man as ambitious as Louis could not keep treaties because they stood in the way of his ambition. He could therefore 'have no Faith', nor 'be of any Religion', because both his ends and means were unjust. Without christian restraint his rule would be a simple record of 'Treasons, Rebellions, Wars, Blood, Desolation and Oppressions, with all those trains of Ruin and Misery that attend them'.[58]

France, then, was interpreted as a moral and religious danger, as well as a threat to the national interest. It was, we could argue, these spiritual evils that hardened hearts more thoroughly against her than other powers. Yet even if this is true, we need to probe still deeper and ask why she was so roundly denounced in these terms. Although Louis's policies contain much of the answer (he did persecute protestants, break treaties, and at least appear to help the Turk), we must remain rather cautious in our interpretation. One could construct the French as evil enemies to true religion, but again it was possible to indict other nations of very similar crimes.

The Habsburgs, for example, could easily be portrayed as popish bigots. Even leaving aside the excesses of Spain's inquisition, the British knew that the Austrians had taken a harsh stance against protestantism. They had tried to root out the faith in their territories in the early seventeenth century; they had led the catholic forces in the Thirty Years War; and they seemed intent on mopping-up operations (which involved persecutions in Silesia, Hungary and Salzburg) right through into the eighteenth century. Many writings, particularly Defoe's *Review* for 1711–12, lost no time in pointing all this out – and the theme became steadily more prominent as Louis's successful persecutions ended confessional tensions in his lands and moved attention to central Europe.[59] Similarly, Netherlanders could be seen as christian apostates. This view has emerged in the mid-century wars, when the Dutch had been accused of caring more about money and power than

57 This philosophy had been explained before 1689 in such works as [F. de Lisola], *The Buckler of State and Justice* (1667), preface, also pp. 273–4. This was a translated work by an Austrian diplomat, but was published with the support of the English ministry and became a popular success. From the same propaganda campaign, see *A Free Conference Touching the Present State of England* (1668), p. 60.

58 *Anguis in Herba: Or the Fatal Consequences of a Treaty with France* (1702), pp. 4–5. For similar analysis, see *Nero Gallicanus: or a True Portraiture of Lewis XIV* (1690), pp. 63–5; *Reflections upon the Conditions of Peace Offer'd by France* (1694), pp. 6–7.

59 For example, [Defoe], *Review*, VIII, 99 (10 Nov. 1711); VIII, 101 (15 Nov. 1711); VIII, 104 (22 Nov. 1711). I am grateful to Andrew Thompson for the point about shifting attention in accounts of persecution.

the true faith. In pursuit of their goals, it had been alleged, they would break contracts with christians, they would treat people with barbaric cruelty, and they would deny their faith if it brought advantage with Oriental or African potentates.[60] In the late Stuart era, these charges were revived, and in particular, the memory of Amboyna was kept alive.[61] In 1623, the Dutch garrison of this Indonesian town had tortured and killed most of the English residents. A standard example of faithless cruelty in the mid-century polemic, the events at Amboyna were rehearsed repeatedly in late Stuart material.[62] Finally and most obviously, the Turks were religious enemies. The spread of this Muslim power threatened to extinguish christian civilization itself – or at least spelt suffering for christian communities caught in its tide – and the tracts which warned of the Ottoman danger built their case on these fears.

In English and British polemic, therefore, France was no more uniquely anti-protestant or anti-christian than she had been the sole candidate for universal monarchy. Yet, arguably, there *was* a difference between the French and other powers. Alone among European states, France's behaviour under Louis made her susceptible to *all* the charges at once. Not only was she powerful, aggressive and expansionist – but she wanted to crush the reformation, and was willing to betray Christendom, to boot. By contrast, the actions or position of other powers prevented such an across-the-slate indictment. Each had real mitigating features which made it difficult to condemn them comprehensively, and led to a more equivocal attitude among the English.

The Dutch, most obviously, were fellow protestants. However un-christian their policies might sometimes seem, they had been the other great champion of the reformation, and any attempt to blacken them stumbled on this confessional solidarity. During the Anglo-Dutch wars of the mid-seventeenth century, there had been a substantial body of opinion in England that questioned attacking a fellow protestant power. It had caused unease during the first two conflicts, and when mobilized by effective Dutch propaganda after 1672, it ended the third war.[63] After 1688, awareness that

60 For a flavour, see C. Molloy, *Holland's Ingratitude: or a Serious Expostulation with the Dutch* (1666); H. Stubbe, *A Justification of the Present War against the United Netherlands* (1672).

61 For example, *England's Crisis: or the World Well Mended* [1689]; *The Ballance Adjusted: Or the Interest of Church and State Weighed* [1689]; *A Letter to the Examiner, Concerning the Barrier Treaty* (1713), p. 13.

62 For example, [C. Leslie], *Delenda Carthago: or the True Interest of England in Relation to France and Holland* (1695), p. 3; *The D ---- Deputies. A Satyr* (1705) – this claimed not to want to raise old issues, but of course did so in the very denial. John Dryden's play *Amboyna, a Tragedy* (1673), which was written in the middle of the last Anglo-Dutch war, was reprinted in 1691.

63 The classic study of Dutch propaganda in 1672–4 is K. H. D.Haley, *William III and the English Opposition, 1672–4* (Oxford, 1953). Pamphlets which appealed to protestant solidarity included: [S. Bethel], *The Present Interest of England Stated* (1671); [R. McWard],

the whole European reformation was in danger from Louis again limited expressions of hostility. For example, in the 1690s, parliamentary speeches critical of the Netherlands were swiftly answered with assertions that only an Anglo-Dutch alliance could save the true faith; whilst pamphlet literature celebrated William's efforts to unite and defend the European reformation.[64] Similarly, in the last years of Queen Anne's reign, criticism of the Netherlands was muted, or soon rebuffed. For instance, even after Defoe was convinced the war had gone on too long and that the Austrians had become a threat, he still tried to cool anti-Dutch hysteria. He criticized Swift for attacks on Holland, despite the fact that the two writers were working for the same ministry; and he insisted that the premier protestant powers of Europe – Britain and the Netherlands – must stand together to defend their faith.[65]

If the Dutch could cite their protestantism against charges they were anti-christian, the situation for the Habsburgs was the exact reverse. They might be persecuting papists, but their role as a bulwark against Islam, and the repeated punishment of their good faith by an untrustworthy France, meant it was difficult to suggest they undermined Christendom. In the pamphlet literature the Habsburgs were lauded for their efforts in their war with the Turks. They had brought together the alliance which drove the Ottomans from Vienna in 1683, and they continued to risk the lives of their troops as they secured Europe's borders against the Muslim threat.[66] Similarly, the Habsburgs were seen as the principal victims of French perfidy. They had entered into the 1659 marriage alliance with Louis in good faith, but were left appealing to all christian nations as France began to encroach on their Flemish territories. Later, the Habsburgs may not have agreed to the partition treaty, but they were certainly the principal losers when the French broke it. Louis tried to deny the family its rights in Spain, and in huge tracts of America, Italy and the Netherlands: if theft and betrayal on this scale were not punished, then the public faith of agreements (and the christian community nations it supported) would have little meaning. As one writer put it, agreeing to French control of Madrid would mean sharing

The English Ballance (1672); [P. du Moulin], *England's Appeal from the Private Cabal at Whitehall* (1672) – this one of the first products of William III's impressive propaganda machine.

64 For example, *The Happy Union of England and Holland* (1689), and Sir Charles Sedley's speech identifying Holland as a bulwark against popery, 5 Dec. 1695 – *Parliamentary History*, V, 795.

65 [D. Defoe], *An Enquiry into the Danger and Consequences of a War with the Dutch* (1712); [D. Defoe], *A Defence of the Allies and the Late Ministry* (1712), esp. pp. 8, 16–17; [Defoe], *Felonious Treaty*, pp. 43–5; [Defoe], *Review*, VIII, 105 (24 Nov. 1711). Andrew Thompson has shown that an Anglo-Dutch alliance formed the core of a 'protestant interest' in conceptions of foreign policy under George I and George II: *Britain, Hanover and the Protestant Interest, 1688–1756* (Woodbridge, 2006).

66 All the pamphlets quoted in note 40 above treated the emperor as a christian hero.

Louis's guilt for the 'Perjury, Usurpation and Blood he has shed'. Making them accomplices through their sins of omission, it would turn the British into 'Criminals before God'.[67]

Of course the remaining potential hegemonist came much closer to the totality of evil. The Turks, as an Islamic power, threatened all forms of christian religion as they expanded their earthly dominion. As we have seen, their barbarous hostility to the cross was central to their image in British eyes. Yet for all this, aspects of their position and behaviour made it difficult to condemn them completely. Even though people still feared the Turk after 1689 (and the Book of Common Prayer retained its supplications against them), the enemy was in steady retreat after the siege of Vienna so it was hard to construct it as an immediate danger. Moreover, the Ottomans' record towards the true faith was not as bad as one might have supposed. Though Muslims might carry those who actively fought them into slavery, writers noted that christians could live peaceably within the Turkish empire. To back this impression, the Sultan's supposed declaration of war on Austria in 1683 was published in English. Whilst this certainly stressed that the Sublime Porte was the 'destroyer of all Christendom', it also promised it would be the 'Patron and Protector of all Christians that will submit', and that those who surrendered would enjoy a 'free exercise of their Religion' as well as keeping their lands.[68] Other writers could not resist contrasting this to Louis's intolerance. They suggested the Turks would be astonished at French destruction of christians (they themselves would be have afraid and ashamed to attempt it), and they implied that life under an Ottoman tyrant might be better than under Louis.[69] A strange sympathy for the Sultan also arose from the belief that the French were playing a double game in the Balkans. Louis had, writers argued, encouraged the Turk against Vienna. Yet he had also hoped the Austrians would reach such a point of despair that they would appeal for his help and so allow him to march across Germany

67 *Caveat to the Treaties*, p. 75. Preachers and propagandists had argued this line through the 1702–13 war; but it became the particular preserve of whigs after 1711, who argued that Britain herself would be guilty of perfidy if she agreed to peace while the French retained Spain. See for example, *Remarks upon the Present Negotiations of Peace* (1711); *The Allies and the Late Ministry Defended* (1711), p. 35; *Armageddon: Or the Necessity of Carrying on the War* (1711), pp. 13, 19.

68 *A Defiance and Indiction of War sent by the Sultan Mahomet IV to Leopold Emperor of Germany* (1683). The Ottomans did not, in fact, declare war on christian countries as they perceived a perpetual and underlying state of conflict which did not need to be re-announced each time it actually flared. Instead, declarations were produced in Austria to rally the populace against the Turks. I am grateful to Pärtel Piirimäe for clarifying this. In these documents, the clauses promising amnesty for surrendering christians certainly reflected Turkish practice, but may also have been intended to encourage disgust at those who took this easy option or (in 1683) to provide grist for attacks on French intolerance.

69 *Detestable Designs of France*, p. 28; *The Emperor's Letter to James II* (1689); *The Secret Intreagues of the French King's Ministers at the Courts of Several Princes* (1691), pp. 56–7.

to the battlefield. If this had happened, Louis would have ended his alliance with the Sultan, and left the Turks as duped as everyone else.[70] Taking all this together, some were prepared to elevate the Ottomans well above the French in the moral pecking order. At Constantinople, one writer maintained, one might find 'more humanity and good faith' than at Versailles.[71]

In the suggestions presented above, we see the complex interplay of the solid facts about nations' behaviour, and the possibilities of constructing images of them. To begin, we argued that images were quite flexible. Many nations could be presented as the potential universal monarch, even from the same facts about the international situation. Similarly, different states might be portrayed as the true enemy of the protestant reformation, or of Christendom. Yet we are now suggesting there were limits to this rhetorical fluidity. Real facts about nations (the protestantism of the Dutch; the Habsburgs' long struggle with the Turk and their deception by Louis; the Turks' willingness to tolerate christians) prevented certain charges being made against them. This left France as only power with no defence in the discourses – universal monarchy, protestant solidarity and the protection of Christendom – which were being used. We are claiming that this is why France's threat seemed so pressing. Louis's policies went to the heart of *all* English and British concerns: and especially to that vital sense of duty to foreign protestants and to the community of christians. It was this that made it easier to sustain public support for hostility to his kingdom than any other.[72]

Of course, given the complexity of interplay between fact and image, we should have robust doubts about such reasoning. We must, for example, worry how solid our supposed 'facts' actually were. Were the Dutch really champions of the reformation, or had their self-interest merely happened to place them in opposition to catholic powers and so allowed them to be presented as protestant heroes? Were the Habsburgs really injured victims of French perfidy, or had their foreign policy merely been spectacularly incompetent? Were the tolerant and honourable strands in Turkish policy real, or had they been invented by commentators to blacken the France in comparison with an obviously un-christian power? Questions of this order bedevil any attempt to explain why one nation should be selected as another's enemy. As disturbingly, we must acknowledge that the true roots of France's demonization might not have been expressed in the polemic against her. It is quite possible that Louis was hated for reasons other than the ones we have been exploring, but that people already convinced the

70 *Reflexions upon the Conditions*, p. 4.

71 *The True Interests of the Princes of Europe* (1689), p. 34.

72 For slightly fuller reflection on image and fact in the formation of attitudes to foreign countries, see T. Claydon, 'Holland, Hanover, and the Fluidity of Facts', in *Britain and Germany Compared*, ed. Joseph Canning and Hermann Wellenreuther (Göttingen, 2001), pp. 85–98.

French monarch must be stopped reached for a combination of discourses that would uniquely condemn him.

For example, anti-Jacobitism certainly played a role. Although this sentiment did not feature as prominently as one might expect in the anti-French material, the fact that Louis had given refuge to the deposed and generally hated Stuarts, and aimed to restore them to the British thrones, must have weighed on minds.[73] Again, France may have been singled out simply because she was so geographically close. It is true the Dutch were also nearby, as were the Habsburgs if one remembered their territories in the Spanish Netherlands. It is also true that contemporary understanding of geopolitics did not require proximity for nations to be a threat. World domination was seen as resting on control of extra-European empires and trade, so Spain and Holland were seen as dangerous for their dominions in America and the East Indies rather than for their forces in Europe.[74] Yet despite all this, France's position immediately across the Channel must have magnified her apparent peril. Invasions of the isles from French ports would have been relatively easy given the short distances involved, and indeed Louis planned or effected amphibious operations in 1689–91 (helping Irish catholic forces); 1692 and 1696 (preparing to co-ordinate with English Jacobite risings) and 1708 (the old Pretender's attempt to reach London through Scotland). Finally, as Rose suggests, ancient rivalries may have been important. Though England had clashed with many other powers over the centuries – and had actually allied with the French from time to time – she nursed a traditional enmity with her Gallic neighbour which dated to the Hundred Years War. Though rarely the chief theme of polemic in the late Stuart era, this may have been poisoning pens against Louis: struggle against Turks, Dutch and Habsburgs did not have quite the same pedigree.[75]

With these doubts and alternative explanations, the 1689 revolution in foreign policy looks far more complex, perhaps even more mysterious,

[73] Louis's support for the Stuarts was used in polemic – but surprisingly rarely as the key justification for war. Instead, it either illustrated his perfidy (he never kept promises not to aid the Stuarts) – see for example ,*The French King's Promise to the Pretender* (1712); or would be the means of his imposing his persecution on the British realms – see for example, *Present French King*, preface, p. 5. Henry Sacheverell's sermon, *A Defence of Her Majesty's Title to the Crown and a Justification for her Entering into a War* (1702), provided an anti-Jacobite apologia for conflict, but only as the second reason for force, after Louis's poor faith. Against all this, one has to acknowledge enthusiasm for a return to war at the end of William's reign was muted until Louis recognized James II's son as his successor to the British thrones.

[74] In the mid-century wars, the Dutch had been accused of starting their hegemony in the Indian and Pacific Oceans – for example, J. Darrell, *A True and Compendious Narration* (1665), esp. p. 35. Under Anne, Spain was seen as a valuable prize for its American as much as European possessions – for example, [Defoe], *Two Great Questions*, p. 35; [Addison], *The State of War*, p. 9.

[75] Rose, *England in the 1690s*, p. 116.

than it first appeared. There does not seem to be a simple explanation for the horror of Louis which gripped people in the late Stuart era. Amid the uncertainly, though, two conclusions do shine out. First, we cannot explain English or British attitudes after 1689 solely in terms of France's potential hegemony. France was not the only conceivable candidate for universal monarchy, and she was not condemned for this ambition alone. Second, whether rooted in reality, or merely in rhetoric, international protestantism and Christendom remained vital to the articulation of England and Britain's role in the world. These nations cared (or, as importantly, said they cared) about the survival of the European reformation, and about the protection of a continental community of christians.[76] They defended their external initiatives with reference to these concerns, and so became a great power breathing the spirit of crusade.

76 For further exploration of these themes over a wider set of issues and time frame, see Claydon, *Europe and the Making of England*.

10

Political Conflict and the Memory of the Revolution in England 1689–c.1750

GABRIEL GLICKMAN

In 1735, a purported Persian fable entered the London printing press. The 'Tale of the Troglodytes' claimed to capture the descent of a community into moral and political corruption, offering the sobering example of how a people might become 'wickeder and more miserable in a State of Government, than they were left in a State of Nature'. Its narrative rested on a country delivered from conflict by a warrior prince, whose leaders proceeded, in a fatal slide into 'innocence', to raise him to their throne 'without prescribing any bounds to his authority'. They had left themselves unshielded against the corruptible tendencies inherent in human politics, deluded that 'when Virtue was on the Throne, the most absolute Government was the best', and therefore disarmed when ambition and insecurity propelled their new sovereign into arbitrary rule. 'From this single root sprung up a thousand Mischiefs; Pride, Envy, Avarice, Discontent, Deceit and Violence', as the king exploited the legislative machinery to create divisions between his subjects, with fratricidal conflicts eroding the civic spirit, and a tangled matrix of debts, bad laws and social ills displacing 'ancient Customs', overthrowing the 'dictates of natural justice' and destroying 'the natural Obligations to Virtue … by the foreign Influence of human Authority'. Such was the condition of any people 'when they had quitted their own Nature, and so bewildered were they in the Labyrinth of their own laying out'.[1]

One chapter in a political commentary thinly veiled under the guise of *Persian Letters*, the 'Tale of the Troglodytes' fell within a corpus of imaginative literature that dramatized anxieties still felt within the British Isles half a century after the Glorious Revolution. Its author, the whig opposition leader George Lyttelton, would conventionally have been viewed as a natural supporter of the revolutionary legacy.[2] Yet his fears pinpointed

1 *Letters from a Persian in England to his Friend at Ispahan* (1735), pp. 43, 46–7, 50.

2 *Memoirs and Correspondence of George, Lord Lyttelton*, ed. Robert Phillimore (2 vols, London, 1845).

a strain within the political nation that remained gripped by uncertainty over the moral and political resilience of the settlement forged after the overthrow of James II. In the year that Lyttelton's work was published, one Jacobite claimed that 'Some to this day talk with a lively sense of their great deliverance from danger by the Revolution, as if it had happened the other day, and was no more fixt.'[3] Scarcely more confident, the earl of Marchmont, like Lyttelton, a patriot whig, addressed the 'Electors of Great Britain' in 1740 to predict 'A Crisis of Time … now approaching', in which 'you are to consider whether the Ends of that Revolution have been arriv'd at and preserv'd, or whether they have not been … cunningly and basely frustrated and eluded'.[4] When conflicting ideas still abounded as to the meaning, purpose and permanence of the Glorious Revolution, the state of the political nation appeared, at least to a wide stripe of public opinion, to have become distinctly fragile.

This essay will explore the conflicts aroused in British politics by the events of 1688–9, examining the debates that reconstructed and reappraised the events of the revolution, and tracing the emerging lines of criticism and disaffection. Recent work by Steve Pincus and Tim Harris has reinforced the point that the public domain was disturbed for a generation after 1689 by contention focused on the shape of church and constitution, on relations between the three kingdoms, and on clashing conceptions of political economy.[5] This essay will look at how these divisions were rooted in conflicting interpretations of the events of 1688: how far the fall of James II could be located within the political and governmental conventions of the realm, and what precedents it set for the future. The legacy of an event that was examined in over 2,000 tracts and treatises within 12 months still seemed less than lucid, 50 years after contemporaries had perceived 'one of the strangest catastrophes there is in any history' and saw 'so many visible and apparent accidents any one whereof had they not happened the whole design must certainly have miscarried'.[6] The uncertainties voiced within the Convention parliament after 1689 cast a long shadow over later public discourse, when no new 'rulebook' for the constitution had emerged, when William and Mary left the basic grounds of their right to the throne unaddressed and the revolution could still be imagined by turns as a triumph of providence, a moment of radical popular election, a legitimate conquest or a violent usurpation. The many meanings invested

3 Lancashire County R.O., RCWB/5, pp. 507–8.

4 Hugh, Second Earl of Marchmont, *A Serious Exhortation to the Electors of Great Britain* (1740), p. 9.

5 Tim Harris, *Revolution: The Great Crisis of the British Monarchy* (2006), pp. 477–517; Steve Pincus, *1688: The First Modern Revolution* (New Haven, CT, 2009), pp. 437–86.

6 *The Anglo-Dutch Moment*, ed. Jonathan I. Israel (Cambridge, 1991), p. 6; W.A. Speck, *Reluctant Revolutionaries: Englishmen and the Revolution of 1688* (Oxford, 1988), p. 71; *Bishop Burnet's History of His Own Time* (1850), p. 398.

in the revolution were infused into debates over the wars with France, splits within the Church of England, the growth of a centralizing state apparatus across the British Isles, and the transference of a protestant succession to the house of Hanover. Many of the same critiques of the Revolution first raised in the parliaments of William III continued to haunt political debate into the reigns of Anne and the first two Georges. All of these uncertainties were played out in a market for political literature unleashed by the lapsing Licensing Act in 1695, and brought home in 12 general elections between 1689 and 1715.

In recent decades, historians have challenged the old conception of an eighteenth-century 'age of stability' arising naturally from the revolution settlement. More controversial works have highlighted the persistence of Jacobite sympathy, rediscovering the campaign to restore the exiled Stuarts as a more capacious and appealing movement of conspiracy, diplomacy and political expression.[7] For Jacobites, the deposition of James II violated ancient laws, if not sacred hierarchies; by contrast, radical voices viewed at best a catastrophic missed opportunity, at worst a betrayal that left the British Isles in thrall to a line of new oligarchs. Defeated in 1689, these 'legitimist' and 'Commonwealth' arguments were kept alive by contention raised over the actions of successive post-revolution governments. Remarkably, the different streams of opposition began to converge towards a common language of protest against the new state forged by William and his ministers, with its unprecedented levels of taxation and mobilisation, and alleged infringements on the liberty of the subject. Repeatedly, those who rejected the overthrow of the king in 1688 were given a lease of life by the disillusioned advocates of a revolution more far-reaching than that eventually achieved. When George Lyttelton penned his *Persian Letters*, the patriot opposition in parliament and the press had integrated forms of tory, radical and even Jacobite rhetoric into the diagnosis of a dangerous malaise in politics, society and public morals, seen to derive from certain conditions inherent in the settlement of 1689. The case against the new political order called upon mythic conceptions of England's gothic freedoms, invoked the struggles of the Roman Republic, and assimilated touches of cosmopolitan and utopian thought. This essay will show how its expression gave a political salience to the events of the revolution that long outlasted the lives of its main actors.

7 See especially *The Jacobite Challenge*, ed. Eveline Cruickshanks and Jeremy Black (Edinburgh, 1989); Paul Monod, *Jacobitism and the English People* (Cambridge, 1989); Howard Erskine-Hill, 'Literature and the Jacobite Cause: Was there a Rhetoric of Jacobitism?', in *Ideology and Conspiracy: Aspects of Jacobitism, 1689–1759*, ed. Eveline Cruickshanks (1981), pp. 49–69.

I

The original critique of the revolution was forged out of the discarded fragments of alternative settlement proposals defeated in the Convention Parliament of 1689. Here, the main impetus for dissent came from those who protested outright against the switching of the crown. 'I can take God to witness that I had not thought when I engaged upon it … that the Prince of Orange's landing would end in deposing the king', the tory M.P. Peregrine Osborne was to insist, and his claim could find ready support on the tory benches from those who denied that the corollary to opposing the policies of James II was to deprive him of his throne.[8] Even Sir Edward Seymour, no admirer of the fallen king, suggested that William's taking of the crown had violated his original declaration to the English people, submitted the previous October, and this sentiment informed successive attempts within the house of lords especially to prevent the coronation of a new king, whether by calling back James II, installing a regency or even crowning the Princess Mary alone.[9] 'I look upon today's work to be the ruin of monarchy in England', announced the earl of Thanet, after these plans had finally fallen away on 6 February, 'for we have made the Crown elective.'[10] Faced with the reality of the joint coronation, Thanet and most of his coevals kept their opposition muted. But a more trenchant high tory camp would soon start to resuscitate these concerns, aiming to unearth the deeper moral and spiritual wounds they saw brought about by the expulsion of England's legitimate sovereign.

Murmurings of discontent from the old supporters of Stuart monarchy did not translate inevitably into Jacobitism. However, the issue of the contested throne was brought repeatedly into public discourse by disputes raised over the state oaths to William and Mary, accompanied by successive government attempts to make public officeholders renounce the deposed royal line. The most dramatic manifestation of discontent was the 'Non-juring schism' within the Church of England after seven bishops and 400 lesser clergymen chose to abandon their posts rather than abjure their oaths to James II: their credibility was symbolized when their number included five of the seven ecclesiastics who had previously entered the Tower rather than endorse the pro-catholic agenda of the deposed king. In Scotland, the disruption

[8] Robert Beddard, *The Revolutions of 1688* (Oxford, 1991), p. 110.

[9] *The Autobiography of Sir John Bramston*, ed. Lord Braybrooke, Camden Soc, 1st ser., XXXII (1845), 338; *The Correspondence of Henry Hyde, Earl of Clarendon, and of his Brother Laurence Hyde, Earl of Rochester, with the Diary of Lord Clarendon from 1687 to 1690*, ed. Samuel W. Singer (2 vols, 1828), II, 238; Lois Schwoerer, 'A Journall of the Convention at Westminster begun the 22 of January 1688/9', *Bulletin of the Institute of Historical Research*, XLIX (1976), 242–63.

[10] *The Parliamentary History of England*, ed. William Cobbett (36 vols, 1806–20), V, 92; Harris, *Revolution*, pp. 320–8.

was amplified by a purge of episcopalian ministers from their parishes, with a presbyterian church order rebuilt upon the ruins of the old Restoration Kirk. 'The Church is widow'd, destitute the state... Our Israel is deprived of her defence', lamented one hymn to the secessionist bishops, and for many sympathizers outside their fold, the actions of the non-jurors served to create a powerful moral case against the governing powers.[11] In 1692, their example emboldened tory M.P.s to defeat the Abjuration Bill against the house of Stuart; four years later, 100 of their number declined to vote for the new oath of association to William III and in 1701, even the resolutely non-Jacobite earl of Nottingham refused to recognize that William, as a conquering 'king by descent', could be considered the 'rightful and lawful' holder of the crown.[12] With James II swift to release a document from exile denying that he had abandoned his throne, with a 'shadow court' establishing itself on the outskirts of Paris and armed forces mustering for the Stuarts in Scotland and Ireland, the rhetoric of the non-jurors began to crystallize into a larger literature of Jacobitism.[13]

The fact that the royal succession was deemed unstable enough to require ratification on five further occasions before 1716 showed that Britain, like Spain, and, subsequently, Poland and Austria, had become subject to the threat of a dynastic contest, with all its domestic and international ramifications.[14] Early Jacobite political argument was hewn to suit the temper of a time of military conflict, brimming with scriptural appeals towards the restoration of the rightful king and prophetic lamentations for the 'long train of famine, want, war and destruction' set to engulf a sinful land.[15] 'Farewell the Fortune of England', declaimed the clergyman Thomas Wagstaffe, evoking images of sickening corn, withering flowers and virtuous patriots cast out, hunted into the wilderness: 'I know not what heavier or more dreadful Judgment can befal us, than for Englishmen to become their own Executioners.'[16] Allegiance to James II remained, for John Kettlewell, 'the doctrine of the Cross': the claims of the prince of Orange offered only the temptations and compulsions of a fallen world, 'the rude Batteries of Noise and Violence ...

11 *A Pindaric Ode Sacred to the Memory of the Most Reverend Father in God, Dr William Sancroft* (1694).

12 *The Parliamentary Diary of Narcissus Luttrell 1691–1693*, ed. Henry Horwitz (Oxford, 1972), pp. 314–19; *Parliamentary History*, V, 992; J.E. Thorold Rogers, *A Complete Collection of the Protests of the Lords* (3 vols, Oxford, 1875), I, 161; Henry Horwitz, *Revolution Politicks: the Career of Daniel Finch, Second Earl of Nottingham 1647–1730* (Cambridge, 1968); *Correspondence of Clarendon*, II, 278–319.

13 James II, *By the King: A Proclamation ... To all our Loving, Subjects, Greetings* (Dublin, 1689); Paul Hopkins, *Glencoe and the End of the Highland War* (Edinburgh, 1986); J.G. Simms, *Jacobite Ireland* (1969).

14 Daniel Szechi, *The Jacobites: Britain and Europe 1688–1788* (Edinburgh, 1986).

15 Nathaniel Johnston, *The Dear Bargain, or a True Representation of the State of the English Nation under the Dutch* (1690), p. 8.

16 Thomas Wagstaffe, *An Appeal to all True Englishmen* (1699), pp. 6–7.

the Wanton Sport or Malicious Strokes of Profane Wits' who would work to 'carnalize and corrupt the Spirits of Men'.[17] The notion that men could live safely outside the shield of a legitimate, hereditary monarchic order was denounced as a fallacy that would drive the nation into 'Mr Hobbs's state of war', and deliver the realm up to 'the rabble': a 'thousand new tyrants' who would impose the reality of arbitrary government with all its 'Injustice and Inhumanity' upon English subjects.[18] James II could be understood, like his father Charles I, as a paragon of nobility and self-sacrifice, with his loyal followers raised, in the judgment of another non-juror, Samuel Grascombe, to the status of 'God's People' – though 'some of us should be cut off; yet the fall of those may prove the rise of more, for Martyrs' blood is rich and fruitful'.[19] The whigs were duly represented as a new generation of regicides, with William, rendered, in the words of the Jacobite soldier Robert Charnock, 'a wolf or wild beast' who had 'corrupted and debauched the King's sworn subjects' to pull apart 'all the ties of Nature and Consanguinity'.[20] Charnock's fulmination, delivered in 1696 to justify a failed assassination plot against the reigning monarch, stood at the violent limits of a Jacobite challenge that turned fears of invasions and conspiracies into a recurrent motif of the reign of William III.[21]

While the initial Jacobite case against the revolution remained based upon the sanctity of the hereditary royal line, later expositions of the cause sought to find an alternative to the stern anathemas of the non-juring clergymen. By 1692, the exiled court was seeking to overthrow the Stuart reputation for 'popery and arbitrary government' with new manifestos reaffirming the privileges of parliament and the protestant religion, tempered only by a promise of liberty of conscience extended to recusants and dissenters in the event of a Jacobite restoration.[22] A genre of popular balladry recaptured James II's son and grandson through the festive motifs of older cavalier poetry, celebrating the exiled 'royal roses' whose return would strike spring-like redemption into a barren and oppressed land.[23] Outside the private clubs, codes and cabals of loyal gentlemen, the exiled Stuarts benefited

[17] John Kettlewell, *Christianity, A Doctrine of the Cross* (1691), pp. 2, 9–10.

[18] *The Debate at Large between the House of Lords and House of Commons ... 1688* (1695), p. 61; John Kettlewell, *The Duty of Allegiance Settled upon its True Grounds* (1689), pp. 44–5; *idem*, *Christianity*, p. 99.

[19] Samuel Grascombe, *Resolution of a Case of Conscience* (1689), p. 8; Kettlewell, *Duty of Allegiance*, p. 89; Laura Lunger Knoppers, 'Charles I as Jacobite Icon', in *The Royal Image: Representations of Charles I*, ed. Thomas N. Corns (Cambridge, 1997), pp. 263–87.

[20] *State Trials*, ed. T.B. Howell (23 vols, London, 1809–26), XII, 1462–4.

[21] Paul A. Hopkins, 'Sham Plots and Real Plots in the 1690s', in *Ideology and Conspiracy*, ed. Cruickshanks, pp. 89–110; Jane Garrett, *The Triumphs of Providence* (Cambridge, 1984).

[22] James II, *His Majesty's Gracious Declaration to His Loving Subjects* (1693); Daniel Szechi, 'The Jacobite Revolution Settlement 1689–96', *E.H.R.*, CVIII (1993), 611–28.

[23] Monod, *Jacobitism and the English People*, pp. 45–69.

from external circumstances – the fluctuations in great power politics that brought periods of diplomatic sympathy from the French, Spanish, Russian and Swedish courts, and the attachment of the Jacobite cause to a febrile brew of Scottish national grievances raised after the passing of the Act of Union.[24] Across the Irish Sea, the legacy of three years of armed conflict between James and William was to create a cauldron of Jacobite sympathy, fatally deepening the divide between catholic and protestant, and offering a potential landing base for any foreign invasion.[25] In England, however, the main intellectual material for Jacobitism was created out of anxieties undimmed within a section of the tory party after 1689: resentments falling not merely on the way in which the crown had been resettled, but on the political consequences that followed the accession of William III.

As early as 1689, the earl of Sunderland had warned William III that while it remained 'very true that the tories were better friends to monarchy than the whigs', the new king 'was to consider that he was not their monarch'.[26] While they might accept him, grudgingly, as a de facto king enthroned by right of conquest, or as the only man who could be found to fill a vacant throne, the lingering tory doubts over William's legitimacy were compounded by a series of unwelcome political developments within the course of the reign. Most immediate to party concerns was the fear that William leant his natural bias to their political opponents, a belief that appeared far from misplaced as the 'junto' of whig ministers consolidated their grip on government after 1694. A deeper ideological anxiety was fixed upon the welfare of the Church of England, left in the hands of a calvinist monarch, and, later, faced with the prospect of succession by the lutheran house of Hanover. While the non-juring schism inflicted a lasting dent in the collective morale, the anglican sacraments appeared subject to further violation after 1689, when the new Toleration Act broke the principle of religious 'unity through uniformity' and granted legal recognition to protestant non-communicants. The phenomenon of 'occasional conformity' ushered a wave of practising dissenters into public office, their elevation made possible with only minimal observance of anglican rites. Worse, in the eyes of high tory commentators, the whole process appeared to be aided and abetted by the new generation of whig-inclined ecclesiastics occupying the bishops' bench: figures such as John Tillotson, Thomas Tenison and Gilbert Burnet whose erastian, more comprehensively protestant conception of the English Church appeared to legitimize moves to enlarge the powers of the state and expand the rights of dissenters at the expense of the anglican

24 Daniel Szechi, *1715: The Great Jacobite Rebellion* (New Haven, CT, 2006), pp. 30–51.

25 Eamonn O'Ciardha, '*A Fatal Attachment*': *Ireland and the Jacobite Cause 1688–1788* (Cambridge, 2002).

26 Burnet, *History*, IV, 5.

clergy.[27] The conception of a 'Church in Danger' proved as potent a weapon in the hands of lay politicians as disgruntled parsons. Amid this mood of disaffection, the rumour of treasonable tory sentiments refused to expire: exaggerated for their own purposes by the whig leadership, but gaining substance from repeated exposures of Jacobite sympathies within the ranks of the parliamentary opposition. The defection of the earl of Middleton to the exiled court in 1693, followed four years later by the execution of the M.P. Sir John Fenwick on grounds of high treason, served to taint the tory party with the reputation of being glued to the Jacobite interest 'as clay at the feet of Nebuchadnezzar's image', in the words of one M.P.[28] The reports of a smattering of dissident tories paying homage to James II in St Germain in 1699 sealed an image that proved extremely difficult to dislodge.[29] If the tories remained theoretically wedded to the principle of non-resistance to kings, elements within their ranks appeared highly uncertain over precisely which monarch not to resist.

Yet, in spite of these whispers of sedition, it was not for the benefit of the exiled princes, but in the service of Queen Anne that a high tory challenge to the tenets of the revolution gained fullest expression. The younger daughter of James II possessed scarcely greater legitimacy under principles of a strict lineal succession than her regal predecessors. But when a Stuart monarch could seemingly be taught, once again, to rule within the anglican mould of Charles I and Charles II, tory statesmen sensed a chance to reinvigorate a vision of church, state and society that threatened to bury the memory of the revolution, and certainly refuted the idea that the event had established any kind of new political order. The tory revival was unleashed in a 'rage of party', extending from Westminster into the borough and county corporations and the lower house of the anglican convocation, which provided the base for a bid to reclaim the lost authority of the Church of England. Tory domination of the parliaments of 1710 and 1713 was assisted by the rise of a talented generation of political leaders, congregating around the personality of Henry St John, Viscount Bolingbroke.[30] The party's preachers and pamphleteers used electoral campaigns to raise 'the bloody flag and banner of defiance' and attack whiggish principles drawn out of the revolution as

27 G.V. Bennett, *The Tory Crisis in Church and State, 1688–1730* (Oxford, 1975). For the whig predilections that entered into elements of the Williamite church, see Mark Goldie, 'John Locke, Jonas Proast and Religious Toleration', in *The Church of England, c. 1689–1833*, ed. John Walsh, Stephen Taylor and Colin Haydon (Cambridge, 1993), pp. 144, 152, 157, 165.

28 H.M.C., *Kenyon*, p. 375.

29 Duke of Manchester, *Court and Society from Elizabeth to Anne, Edited from the Papers at Kimbolton* (2 vols, London, 1864), II, 113–20.

30 Henry Horwitz, 'Party in a Civic Context: London from the Exclusion Crisis to the Fall of Walpole', in *Britain in the First Age of Party 1680–1750*, ed. Clyve Jones (1987), pp. 181–8; W.A. Speck, *Tory and Whig: the Struggle in the Constituencies* (1970), pp. 5, 65.

a perversion of 'the Ancient and Eternal Truths of the Bible' serving only 'to fire the Spirits of the Mob ... to the overturning of all Religion and Government'.[31] To Mary Astell, 'no revolution (except by foreign conquest) can be compassed ... but upon those principles by which the Martyr lost his head'; the fact that the fall of James II was still being celebrated in certain quarters confirmed the terrifying reality that England remained home to 'a Party, and that a restless and busie one, who act by those very Principles that brought the Royal Martyr to the Block'.[32] The spirit of this 'Plotter in masquerade', as it appeared to Charles Leslie, resided chiefly among the protestant dissenters, the apparent heirs to England's puritan 'Phanatics', but the finger was pointed no less at higher political circles. The rise after 1689 of successive whig 'juntos' over the power of the crown was seen to pose a far greater threat to 'the Queen's White Neck' than any Jacobite pretender.[33] The tory challenge to 'revolution principles' left politics in the reign of Anne streaked with fearful memories seeping out of events of the previous half-century. Moreover, after the queen failed to produce a living heir, their arguments possessed more than merely theoretical significance. When Bolingbroke and his circle withdrew the country from the war with France, and showed themselves open to flirtation with the exiled court of 'James III', it was not just the most strident whigs who feared that the legacy of 1688 was set to be dismembered.[34]

The problem for the tories was that their resurgence ran up against one insuperable obstacle – the attempt to change the political and ideological landscape was confined to the lifetime of an ageing queen with no children to succeed her. Short of moving into explicit Jacobitism, the party possessed no obvious route to creating substantial political change, and in his refusal to renounce a tolerant but steadfast catholic faith, the 'Pretender' James Edward Stuart preserved the single greatest barrier to an overthrow of the 1689 settlement. The tories succeeded instead only in estranging themselves from George I without doing enough to rock his claims to the throne, and after 1714 the party as a whole was set to suffer from the evidence of sedition within its ranks. The swathe of arrests that followed the 1715 Jacobite rising and the 'Atterbury Plot' of 1722 left their legacy in the proscription of a generation of tories from public office.[35] The high tory intellectual challenge

31 *An Old Story Everyone Knows* (1711), pp. 28–9; Charles Leslie, *The Nature and Mischief of Prejudice and Partiality* (1703), p. 31; John Kenyon, *Revolution Principles: The Politics of Party, 1689–1720* (1977), pp. 102–45.

32 Mary Astell, *An Impartial Enquiry into the Causes of Rebellion and Civil War* (1704), pp. 16–17, 57.

33 Leslie, *Nature and Mischief*, p. 31; Astell, *Impartial Enquiry*, pp. 23, 25–8.

34 Daniel Szechi, *Jacobitism and Tory Politics* (Edinburgh, 1984).

35 The extent of Jacobite sympathy within the Tory party is debated in Eveline Cruickshanks, *Political Untouchables: The Tories and the '45* (1979) and Linda Colley, *In Defiance of Oligarchy: The Tory Party 1716–60* (Cambridge, 1982). For the 1715

had not been driven from the scene. Attacks upon the revolution remained lodged, with thinly-veiled Jacobite asides, in the scholarship of high church divines such as Thomas Carte, William King and Thomas Salmon, their works reasserting that 'Regicides are Regicides, though acting under the Title of a High Court of Justice; and Usurpers will be Usurpers, though sitting in St. Stephen's Chapel, and calling themselves Representatives of the good People of England'.[36] However, for all their periodic vehemence, most tory Jacobite sympathizers did not seek to stand outside the pale of English society. Desperate martyrs represented more the exception than the rule, when the cause would conventionally be found in the private realms of figures like Edward Gibbon, father of the historian: his household pervaded with non-juring pious literature, but his professional and commercial allegiances anchoring him within the new political world, as a contractor for the armies of William III.[37] The political and social connections of tory parliamentarians similarly earthed them within the status quo. For the M.P. Sir John Hynde Cotton, the leader of the party on the eve of the 1745 rising, correspondence with Jacobite agents represented only one of three political options, when he experimented with support for Frederick, prince of Wales, and even entered government as part of Henry Pelham's short-lived cross-party coalition.[38] His backbench following appeared scarcely more decisive.

Tory Jacobitism could all-too-readily appear, in the verdict of one disenchanted critic, as no more than chimerical faith in a 'mighty charm... that will dispel at once the follies and wickednesses of men' in 'hope (and perhaps some poet will tell us how) that the golden age will be restored'.[39] However, political dissent against the revolution was kept alive less by the intrinsic appeal of the Stuarts than larger sources of opposition and disaffection, lingering within sections of the political nation beyond the lifetime of William III. It was not merely the high tory contingent in English politics that proved receptive to an argument levelled at successive post-revolution governments, by authors attacking stances associated very closely with the reigning monarchs, and targeting certain ills seen to derive directly from the proceedings of the 1689 Convention parliament.

rebellion, see Szechi, *1715*. For Jacobite activity in 1722, see Eveline Cruickshanks and Howard Erskine-Hill, *The Atterbury Plot* (Basingstoke, 2004).

36 Thomas Salmon, *A Review of the History of England* (2 vols, London, 1724), II, 20, 28, 32–3; H.M.C., *Egmont Diary*, III, 312; *The Orrery Papers*, ed. Countess of Cork and Orrery (2 vols, 1903), II, 32–3, David C. Douglas, *English Scholars* (1939), pp. 1–10, 60, 91–4.

37 *The Autobiographies of Edward Gibbon*, ed. J. Murray (1896), p. 10.

38 Gabriel Glickman, 'The Career of Sir John Hynde Cotton (1686–1752)' *H.J.*, XLVI (2003), 817–41.

39 Edward Bentham, *A Letter to a Fellow of a College* (1749), p. 34.

II

Contrary to tory claims, that cohort within the whig party that looked to reclaim the 'good old cause' of puritan radicalism was far from satisfied with the outcome of the Glorious Revolution. It was the most potent indication of the polarizing tendencies in English politics that the legacy of 1688 was, within a year, being attacked just as vociferously from the vantage point of 'republicans' and 'Commonwealthsmen' as it was in the sermons of high churchmen. Radical complaints emanated from the perception of a lost moment of opportunity. Throughout 1689, pamphlet voices suppressed within the previous decade of Stuart rule had urged the Convention parliament to seize the chance 'to obtain, which we can never recover again, if it be lost ... the Delivery of the People from Slavery'.[40] From this perspective, the deposition of James II affirmed the essential truth that English government, sanctioned by tradition and civil prudence, rested on forms of popular consent, that the fragile remnant of an ancient political 'contract' remained the source of sovereignty, even if it had been all but buried beneath centuries of despotism. The commonwealthsmen spoke in anticipation of success. Parliamentarians close to the whig mainstream – John Somers and John Maynard – appeared to endorse contractualist ideas in their addresses to the house, similar sentiments appeared from the lords Mordaunt, Delamare, Macclesfield, Wharton and an ageing generation of radicals, including John Hampden and the former Leveller John Wildman saw their re-election to the Commons as a cue to re-enter the lists for the lost constitution of the English nation.[41]

The radical construction of events behind the Glorious Revolution was articulated in a furious burst of pamphleteering in January 1689 and a petition of 15,000 signatures presented to parliament by the City whigs.[42] James, according to the republican author John Humfrey, had violated the 'original agreement of the people', formed before the Norman Conquest out of a 'company' of families' for the needs of 'mutual defence'.[43] The recovery of the rights of parliament was not therefore in itself the end of the revolution, merely a means to the reconstruction of a 'free state', in which 'a parliament makes laws for the administration, but 'the people as a community make laws for the constitution'. While he acknowledged the necessity

40 John Humfrey, *Good Advice before it be Too Late* (1689), p. 23.

41 Mark Goldie, 'The Roots of True Whiggism, 1689–1694', *History of Political Thought*, I (1980), 195–236.

42 Gary S. De Krey, 'Political Radicalism in London after the Glorious Revolution', *Journal of Modern History*, LV (1983); Gary S. De Krey, *A Fractured Society: The Politics of London in the First Age of Party 1688–1715* (Oxford, 1985).

43 Humfrey, *Good Advice*, p. 20. See also William Atwood, *The Fundamental Constitution of the English Government* (1690), pp. 2–5.

of fixing first a protestant condition on the throne, Humfrey believed that the parliamentarians would commit a far graver crime to posterity 'if, after the Danger we have been in, of Arbitrary Domination and Popery, by the King's raising Arms, and putting Judges in and out at his pleasure, they do not take more care of the Supream Power, to lay it and its Rights better together'.[44] Without this step, as another radical commentator was later to reflect, England would owe its salvation merely to 'a foreign force' – a Dutch prince and his army of mercenaries – 'and how dangerous a remedy that is, the histories of all ages can witness'.[45] From this diagnosis, the commonwealthsmen unfurled their solutions: a grand committee of the Lords and Commons to set the constitution on a new footing, a wide-ranging declaration of rights laid down as the foundation of all sovereign authority, and a new king visibly elected by popular will.[46]

Resurgent 'commonwealthsmen' impressed upon William III that a mere exchange of the throne, without underpinning changes to the constitution, would render him no more secure against the caprices of political fortune than the past claimants and combatants of York and Lancaster. Moderate whigs who pressed for a limited, dynastic change may have offered a short-term heightening of the king's power, but their loyalty could not be deemed safe. With no more than a choice between two rival princes at stake, it was argued, 'the least puff of wind ... would blow up that Fire covered with deceitful Ashes' and venal statesmen would return to their old Stuart allegiance.[47] Commonwealthsmen asserted that William would only find security in the creation of a new political apparatus, which tied his claims firmly to the matter of the people's rights and liberties. The king did not agree. The mayor of London registered the complaint from court against 'divers Persons... [who] in a tumultuous and disorderly manner, have lately disturbed the present Convention, upon pretence of Petitioning'. City aldermen were instructed to restrain 'every inhabitant within your ward' from bringing any such disruptive protests within reach of the parliament.[48]

Inside the convention, radical hopes collided with a different set of 'revolution principles', engendered by William's need to win acceptance from more pragmatic tories who might acknowledge the claims of the king, but could never concede vital ideological ground by recognizing any element of 'election' behind the overthrow of James II. To inhibit the threat of a Jacobite reaction, contain the damage of the non-juring schism, and pave the way for the passage of the tory leaders Nottingham, Camarthen and Godolphin into the new government, William's leading whig supporters had to find the words to undermine the 'revolutionary' character of 1688, agree

44 *Ibid.*, pp. 24–5.

45 *The Political Works of Andrew Fletcher* (1737), p. 27.

46 *Now is the Time: A Scheme for a Commonwealth* (1689).

47 Atwood, *Fundamental Constitution*, p. xii.

48 *By the Mayor, to the Aldermen* (1689).

with Sir George Treby that 'we found the throne vacant, we did not make it so' and link their right instead, with Gilbert Burnet, to the 'prodigies and miracles of Providence, that have attended our deliverance'.[49] To serve the needs of consensus, it was safer to see William as a protestant monarch borne in by the will of God, or even as a conquering warrior prince than an elective tribune of the nation. Correspondingly, the architects of the declaration of rights may have claimed to voice the 'true, ancient and indubitable rights of the people', but their document was not embedded as any form of condition for William III; it offered no new liberties to English subjects, and no justification for the removal of a tyrant. Its fragile status was compounded by the eventual disappearance of drafted provisions for the independence of judges, the restoration of rights to borough corporations and an injunction against 'the too long continuance of the same parliament'.[50] Such changes moved with the grain of opinion, as the Convention parliament turned towards compromise. The revolution could not be at once a conquest *and* an assertion of lost constitutional rights.

The turn in 1689 towards interpreting the 'abdication' of James II as physical flight creating a royal 'vacancy' rather than a popular deposition carried shattering implications for the radicals. While their erstwhile allies – Charles Montagu, Lord Somers, John Trenchard – entered the administration, an electoral rout in 1690 saw 46 commonwealthsmen losing their seats, compelled, in the later reflection of one supporter, to watch their 'golden dreams' degenerate towards a settlement that became 'the true Spring and Fountain [of] … that bare-fac'd and openly avow'd Corruption, which, like a universal Leprosy has so notoriously infected and overspread both our Court and Parliament'.[51] The failure of the republican moment in 1689 drove a wedge between the whig leadership and its old radical wing, and left a voice of protest and dissent giving vent through the city councils and the pamphlet press to its claim that the Convention Parliament had replanted 'the slavish non-resisting doctrine', turning the coronation of William III into a degenerate counter-revolution.[52] It was therefore not just anguished high tories who refused to grant the settlement its full seal of constitutional approval: the votes against the bills of abjuration, the 1696 Oath of Association and the attainder against the Jacobite Sir John Fenwick drew support from the tattered remnant of commonwealthsmen still in parliament. John Toland, the avant-garde deist, polemical historian and pamphleteer,

49 Anchitel Grey, *Debates of the House of Commons 1667–1694* (10 vols, 1763), IX, 15; Kenyon , *Revolution Principles*, p. 24. See also Edward Stillingfleet, *The Unreasonableness of a New Separation* (1689).

50 Lois Schowerer, *The Declaration of Rights of 1689* (Baltimore, MD, 1981), pp. 299–300.

51 John Toland, *The Danger of Mercenary Parliaments* (1698), p. 3.

52 Atwood, *Fundamental Constitution*, p. ii; *Plain English* (1690), pp. 1–4; Blair Worden, 'The Revolution of 1688–89 and the English Republican Tradition', in *Anglo-Dutch Moment*, ed. Israel, pp. 241–77.

raised his own 'bloody flag' to invoke 'martyrs of the Commonwealth' from Edmund Ludlow to Algernon Sidney and republished canonical texts of John Milton and James Harrington to locate himself within a lineage traced back to Thomas More and Titus Livy, of men who had tried to restore virtue to governance, through the 'Liberty of writing freely, fully and impartially'. The last hopes of the Revolution, he insisted, could only be salvaged by a campaign to rearm, re-empower and re-educate the citizens of the three kingdoms, through 'a Government of Laws enacted for the common Good of all the People, not without their own Consent or Approbation': otherwise, the eternal cycles of history, gleaned from classical and Renaissance writings, presaged a return to an even darker form of tyranny.[53]

III

Although radical renderings of 1688 lingered in popular, extra-parliamentary discourse, the 'good old cause' could all-too-easily become as quixotic as lamentations on the theme of Stuart 'Divine Right'.[54] Certainly, there was a forlorn tone to Robert Molesworth's 1711 reproduction of the republican huguenot text *Franco-Gallia* – the preface invoked a lost ideal of 'true whiggery' with calls for universal religious toleration, annual parliaments and a foreign policy fashioned to bring 'Civil and Religious Liberty' to 'Fellow-Citizens of the World'.[55] However, the case against the revolution – whether Jacobite or republican – was not static, and, far from dwelling solely upon imperfections in the settlement, both genres of opposition literature were galvanized by the transformations of the following decade. A strong case can be made that the truly radical and divisive revolution in England proceeded not in the compromising political climate of 1689, but in the transformation of domestic and foreign policy emerging across the subsequent decade, as William and his ministers began to reshape the character and ambitions of the English government apparatus. Cast into the storm of a major international war that obliged the king to spend almost 40 per cent of his reign on foreign shores, the revolutionary legacy in the three kingdoms seemed repeatedly threatened by crisis. British forces crashed to defeat at Mons, Namur and Steenkirk in 1692, in encounters that left one third of

[53] John Toland, *The Life of John Milton Containing, Besides the History of his Works, Several Extraordinary Characters of Men and Books, Sects, Parties and Opinions*, (1699) p. viii; *idem*, *The Oceana of James Harrington and his Other Works* (1700); Blair Worden, 'Whig History and Puritan Politics: The *Memoirs of Edmund Ludlow* Revisited', *Historical Research*, LXXV (2002).

[54] Kathleen Wilson, 'Inventing Revolution: 1688 and Eighteenth-Century Popular Politics', *Journal of British Studies*, XXVIII (1989), 349–86.

[55] *Franco-Gallia, or, An Account of the Ancient Free State of France, and Most Other Parts of Europe* (1711), pp. xi–xiii, xv, xxi, xxxi.

the Williamite forces slaughtered or maimed. In June 1693, the destruction of 92 merchant vessels by a French fleet at Smyrna brought the loss of a cargo worth over £1 million.[56] In this context, the needs of self-preservation alone began to push William's ministry towards the forging of a state explicitly the purpose of European military interventions, a modernized revenue-raising infrastructure, and a government that would prove more 'absolute' and far-reaching in the lives of its subjects than any previous Stuart executive. The number of men employed at the expense of the taxpayer was set to rise three-fold between 1688 and 1714, with not all of them entering of their own volition – the proportion of impressed soldiers exceeded that of volunteers among the new recruits by six to one in 1709.[57] A new land tax, together with rising duties on commercial goods, helped to meet the costs; scarcely less alarming to William's critics was a funded national debt that, in tandem with the new national bank, planted financial speculation at the heart of government and society. Soon, the old assaults upon the 1689 settlement – tory, Jacobite and radical – would start to reappear, in a shared conviction that dangerous innovations had crept into the heart of politics, that 'we have walked without Guides, amidst dark and dangerous Precipices ... and we have been imposed upon by the cunning and artificial Disguises of self-designing and ambitious Men'.[58]

The changes proceeding within the British Isles brought together a coalition of the disaffected, in and outside parliament. Historians have divided over whether opposition ideologies were informed more strongly by the ancient tenets of renaissance civic humanism or an emerging discourse of political economy, but within three years of William's reign a cacophony of voices began to diagnose certain ills glimpsed in the social, political and commercial condition of the kingdom, and linked these maladies back in 'a chain of Errors' to the revolution settlement itself.[59] In 1692, William was forced to veto opposition bills that would have removed his ability to dismiss judges and imposed closer regulation on the conduct of treason trials; two years later an especially riotous session compelled him to accept a bill for triennial parliaments. Committees of the Lords and Commons turned aggressive scrutiny on a state they saw riddled with corruption and nepotism, attacking the presence of Dutch placemen and military officers in parliament and the public companies, heightening the assaults on William's authority in 1697 with the clamour to cut back the standing army to its

56 Geoffrey Holmes, *The Making of a Great Power* (1993), pp. 92–100.

57 David Ormrod, *The Rise of Commercial Empires* (Cambridge, 2003).

58 James Montgomerie, *Great Britain's Just Complaint for her Late Measures* (1696), p. 2.

59 For conflicting views of the main influences active on opposition ideology, see Pincus, *1688*, pp. 367–9, 396–9 and J.G.A. Pocock, 'Early Modern Capitalism: The Augustan Perception', in *Feudalism, Capitalism and Beyond*, ed. Eugene Kamenke and R.S. Neale (1975), pp. 68–71.

1680 level, if not abolish it entirely.[60] At the zenith of the crisis, the king even contemplated returning to the United Provinces, drafting an abdication speech in readiness.[61] The eventual Act of Settlement of March 1701 brought William's opponents together in a final stand against 'Ministerial Despotism', establishing that the monarch must rule as an anglican, that he or she could leave the realm only with parliamentary consent, and that no foreigners could become privy counsellors, parliamentarians or office-holders. There was little in the king's mood on his deathbed in 1702 to suggest that he had revised a verdict originally reached in despair at the truculence of the Convention Parliament: 'I am not made for this people, nor they for me.'[62]

The political opposition to William III was centred on the actions of a new so-called 'Country party' in the Westminster parliament. Though the movement was bound together more by a loosely shared set of anxieties than a formal party organization, its development cast a mirror over unexpected shifts in English politics. The doctrines of the 'country' – frugal, militantly patriotic, hostile to the metropolitan and Europeanizing influences of the royal court – had developed among opponents of the house of Stuart in the reign of Charles II. But by 1693, with the majority of the whigs becoming absorbed into governing circles, the remaining dissident tendency, fronted by Robert Harley, was finding a greater hearing among the ranks of the disquieted tories. The opponents of William III may have been accused, by the minister Charles Montague, of designing to replace royal power with 'a Senate of Venice', but increasingly their campaigns incorporated fewer republicans and more suspected Jacobites.[63] The political transformation of the country opposition would be paralleled in the Edinburgh parliament a decade later, where the party voicing Scottish political, commercial and religious rights against English domination emerged originally from a disaffected whig-Presbyterian tendency – from Andrew Fletcher of Saltoun to the 2nd Lord Belhaven – but became increasingly associated with agitation for the house of Stuart.[64] The challenge to the legacy of the Glorious Revolution developed most overtly in a press campaign that ushered 'old whig' arguments into union with the political interests of the tory party.

[60] Dennis Rubini, *Court and Country 1688–1702* (1968), pp. 46, 72–81; Lois Schwoerer, *No Standing Armies!* (Baltimore, MD, 1954); Henry Horwitz, *Parliament, Policy and Politics in the Reign of William III* (Manchester, 1977).

[61] Lois Schwoerer, 'The Role of William III in the Standing Army Controversy, 1697–99', *J.B.S.*, V (1966), 74–94.

[62] Stephen Baxter, *William III* (1966), p. 255.

[63] Grey, *Debates*, x, 370; Luttrell, *Parliamentary Diary*, pp. 390–416; Paul Monod, 'Jacobitism and Country Politics in the Reign of William III', *H.J.*, XXX (1987), 289–310.

[64] Fletcher, *Political Writings*, p. 132; *Letters of George Lockhart of Carnwath, 1698–1732*, ed. Daniel Szechi, Scottish History Society, 5th ser., 2 (1989).

By 1693, political philippics taken from the radicals of 1689 were being voiced by the non-jurors Charles Leslie and Nathaniel Johnston and the tory barrister Bartholomew Shower, to highlight the moral failings of the new state. The trend was taken to its paradoxical extreme when a small but talented minority of disenchanted radicals, drawn from that section of dissent and whiggery that had previously embraced the toleration policies of James II, began to cultivate the statesmen of the exiled Jacobite court. At the limits of the country movement, the authors Charlwood Lawton, Sir James Montgomery and Robert Ferguson suggested that the regeneration of the commonwealth could only proceed by a complete overthrow of England's newly-founded 'Dutch tyranny'.[65]

Throughout the reign of William III, the country press aimed to 'delineate the Scars, and Wounds the Bloodsheds, and Distresses' inflicted upon the three kingdoms, voicing a darker, alternative vision of a revolution blown off course by ministers working to 'trample upon the Laws & Liberties of the People'.[66] The authors spoke of Jacobite suspects imprisoned without charge; they gave lurid exposure to accounts of judicial torture, the use of perjured informers hatching designs on English catholic estates, and the massacre perpetrated on the clansmen at Glencoe to dramatize their narrative of a government twisting popular alarm over plots, wars and a disputed throne to its own self-serving ends.[67] Swelling taxes, press-ganged standing armies and reports of judges sidelined for political non-compliance formed the key ingredients of John Toland's claim that the *fear* of a catholic prince descending from abroad was being exploited to construct a state far closer in reality to the militant absolutism found on the continent than anything hitherto attempted by the 'popish' house of Stuart: 'It is very strange that King James … should thus be made their publick Bugbear to frighten us out of our Senses like Children … must be made the instrument of our Slavery by those very Persons who pretended their greatest merit to consist in delivering us from him.'[68] To Robert Ferguson, Tacitean depictions of imperial tyranny could be fused together with the nightmares of contemporary foreign dominions to present the best guide to the political changes proceeding after the revolution, when England's new rulers established in 'the smooth Whitehall and Kensington language', a 'Court of Inquisition', acting against Jacobites and commonwealthsmen alike 'with no less

[65] Most recently considered in Mark Goldie and Clare Jackson, 'Williamite Tyranny and the Whig Jacobites', in *Redefining William III*, ed. Esther Mijers and David Onnekink (Aldershot, 2007), pp. 177–200.

[66] Charlwood Lawton, *The Jacobite Principles Vindicated* (1693), p. 25; Bodl., MS Rawl. D, 1079, fos 97–8.

[67] Bartholomew Shower, *Reasons for a New Bill of Rights* (1692), p. 20; Robert Ferguson, *A Letter to the Right Honourable, my Lord Chief Justice Holt* (1694), p. 6.

[68] John Toland, *Mercenary Parliaments*, p. 6.

Rigour and Unmercifulness than the great Body of Inquisitors at Rome and Madrid... on the Motive of what they stile Heresie'.[69]

England's ills had, it was believed, arisen through an insidious change in the method of absolutism, from the sidelining of parliament to its *corruption*, unbalancing the constitution by enlarging the influence of the court and the ministers over the chamber. Now, 'the multitude of Officers and Pensioners that corrupt all the debates of our Senate House', purchasing borough corporations to prevent the election of freethinking opponents, had left the eyes of the representatives so 'blinded with the dust of Gold, and their Tongues lock'd up with Silver Keys, they durst not cry our for the rescue of their Country', as Toland lamented.[70] This condition followed inexorably from the original error of inviting 'a Foreign Prince to do our own proper work, instead of ... rescuing ourselves our Liberties', as Charlwood Lawton had it, and if William could be sarcastically applauded for acting as a true 'Dutch patriot', his new subjects could now 'aspire no higher' than any other 'Conquered People': compelled 'to eat the Bread of Tribulation and Affliction with Patience'.[71] The toll was levied most unsparingly by the new continental burdens brought upon the nation after 1689. For Montgomery, the original strike against the overweening power of France might be supported, but the country had since been caught with no voice inside a contest ebbing and flowing between vast armies, 'pouring out' English blood 'yet more plentifully' on foreign fields, to feed the vainglory of warrior-princes.[72] While defences of Williamite foreign policy melded old conceptions of 'the protestant interest' with new commitments to 'the balance of Europe' and 'the law of nations', country dissidents meditated on the decline of empires by military exhaustion, and the incompatibility of conflict with successful commerce.[73] The apparent hypocrisy behind the 'protestant' revolution was extrapolated from a war that appeared to bring down France only to raise up even more potent villains of the English imagination – William's catholic allies the emperor and the king of Spain, whose interests had supplied an estimated '4,000 papists' into the Orangist armies, and whose actions were applauded in the Holy See.[74] 'It is pleasant enough

69 Robert Ferguson, *A Brief Account of Some of the Late Incroachments and Depredations of the Dutch* (1695), p. 66; Robert Ferguson, *A Letter to Mr Secretary Trenchard* (1694), pp. 6, 12.

70 [Charlwood Lawton], *A Reply to the Answer Doctor Welwood has Made* (1694), pp. 25, 26; Toland, *Danger of Mercenary Parliaments*, p. 3.

71 Montgomerie, *Just Complaint*, pp. 23–6; Charlwood Lawton, *A French Conquest Neither Practicable Nor Desirable* (1693). pp. 13–14.

72 Lawton, *French Conquest*, p. 22; *Reply to Welwood*, p. 9.

73 *A View of the True Interest of the Several States of Europe* (1689); Andrew Fletcher, *Discourse Concerning the Affairs of Spain* (1698); Charles Davenant, *Essay upon Universal Monarchy* (1701); Tony Claydon, *Europe and the Making of England 1660–1760* (Cambridge, 2007), pp. 170–3.

74 *Memoirs of Sir John Reresby*, ed. Andrew Browning (Glasgow, 1936), p. 553.

to imagine that the Pope, the Fathers of the Spanish Inquisition, and the Authors of the Hungarian and Piedmontese Persecutions ... should be so concerned to establish the protestant Belief amongst us', was Montgomery's waspish verdict.[75] By 1695, in an example of the agility and effrontery of country rhetoric – William's revolution would be labelled by Jacobite and radical authors as the only 'Popish Plot' ever to succeed in English history.[76]

IV

To salvage any hope that the revolution might be made meaningful, country writers insisted that bills and declarations pronouncing 'the lofty and agreeable sound of *Religion, Liberty and Property*' could signify nothing without the restoration of an Englishman's inner virtue.[77] Turning to Gothic and Florentine myth, the heroic narratives of ancient Athens and the precedents of republican Rome, they re-imagined the English as civic personalities, extracting a legend of the 'ancient constitution' to argue that 'whoever looks into our Antiquities will find the footsteps of our Liberties are ancient as our Being'.[78] Lawton imported a puritan's moral rigour into his crusade for further 'political reformation'. Venetian secret ballots, prohibitions of alcohol and a clampdown on bribery and electoral rioting would return 'Heroical Vertue' to the legislature – an M.P. must 'believe that it is a pleasurable and noble employment even to sacrifice himself and all private Considerations for his Country' and corporations should store up funds so that the virtuous poor might gain a share in these duties.[79] Modern political economies pushed country or tory authors towards new schemes for the defence of the landed interest, which they saw in danger of displacement by the advocates of city finance or manufacturing.[80] Attachment to the maxims of the ancient world roused them seek the moral reawakening of English freeholders 'out of the supine stupidity and ignorance of their own good into which they seem to be sunk, and which is both the cause and effect of Tyranny'.[81] In imitation of the Dutch Republic, Lawton demanded the elevation of 'a Seaman, a Souldier, a Merchant, a Civilian, a Common Lawyer

75 Montgomerie, *Just Complaint*, pp. 17, 31, 36; William Anderton, *Remarks upon the Present Confederacy* (1692).

76 Robert Ferguson, *Whether the Preserving the Protestant Religion was the Motive* (1695); Bevil Higgons, *A Short View of the English History ... to the Revolution, 1688* (1723), p. 96; Bodl., MS Rawl. D. 178.

77 Montgomerie, *Just Complaint*, p. 3.

78 Charlwood Lawton, *Some Reasons for Annual Parliaments* (1693), pp. 1, 6; *idem*, *Jacobite Principles*, pp. 18–25.

79 [Lawton], *An Honest Commoner's Speech* (1694), p. 9; Lawton, *Annual Parliaments*, p. 8.

80 Pincus, *1688*, pp. 394–6.

81 *Ibid.*; *Annual Parliaments*, p. 10.

and some Country Gentlemen' to every governing council across the land. He sought changes to the franchise and distribution of parliamentary seats to reflect property-holding among the 'middling sort', with free elections extended to cover the appointment of county sheriffs, the boards of customs and excise and even the clergy.[82] Country writers demanded the dissolution of the standing army and 'the arming and training of all the freeholders of England, as it is our undoubted ancient Constitution, and consequently our Right'.[83] Finally, for Lawton and Toland, national renaissance would extend to foreign affairs, with the recovery of a 'blue water' policy focused on the Atlantic and the colonies over the ties of the continent. Proper political concentration on an 'empire of the seas', forged to spread 'all the productions of Art and Nature' across the globe, would elevate London as 'a New Rome in the West' and raise Britain to her destiny as 'Soverain Mistress of the Universe': an 'umpire' and 'arbitrator' rather than an actor in the wars of clashing continental tyrants.[84]

Set against this high moral and political standard, some country campaigners were beginning to question certain assumptions implicit in the essential reading of the revolution, to the extent of reappraising whether the downfall of James II had been inevitably beneficial for the constitution. As he made his embrace of the Jacobite cause, Charlwood Lawton declared his conviction that the fatal errors of the settlement arose from a chain of historic whig misjudgments, beginning with the Bill of Exclusion in 1680, in which 'hatred to the Duke of York' had aroused a 'Quarrel' that was 'more Personal than National', allowing animus against an individual Stuart prince to exceed the greater question of the country's liberties.[85] Like the catholic extremists who had sought to bring down Henri IV of France, Englishmen had chosen 'to make a Prince's Religion a Crime', concentrating in this case on James's catholicism rather than the true causes of tyranny, which lay rather in the 'visible Marks of worldly Ambition, Self-interest and corrupted Designs and Artifices'.[86] In seeking deliverance from the protestant credentials of the prince of Orange, they had forgotten that it was 'the Constitution of our Government' rather than 'the Religion of our Kings' that offered the bulwark of freedom. Nothing symbolized the tragedy better for Montgomery than the fact that the same 'Ministers, the Darlings, the Favourites' behind 'the most arbitrary and grievous Proceedings, which were complained of during the Reigns of the last two Monarchs' remained seated

[82] *Honest Commoner's Speech*, p. 6; Wildman, *Some Remarks upon Government* (January 1689).

[83] *Franco-Gallia*, ed. Molesworth, p. xxvi.

[84] Lawton, *French Conquest*, preface, pp. 18, 22; Toland, *Mercenary Parlimants*, pp. 36–40.

[85] Charlwood Lawton, *Better Late than Never* (1690), pp. 1–3.

[86] *Ibid.*, p. 3. See also Fergson, *Letter to Trenchard*, p. 2; Montgomerie, *Just Complaint*, p. 47.

in the highest royal counsels – most explicitly the 'court tories' incorporated as the 1689 settlement moved towards compromise.[87] Now, as Lawton put it, the paradoxes underpinning English politics – 'To be roaring at Popery with Popish Confederates; and against Arbitrary Government with [the lords] Camarthen and Nottingham' – became the perfect epitome of a realm accepting levels of oppression from a usurper that she never would from a legitimate prince, to the daily mockery of 'that paltry Bill of Rights'.[88]

The language of 'country' literature in the 1690s created an intellectual environment in which the ultimate rejection of the revolution settlement – the Jacobite cause – could coexist with other manifestos along a continuous spectrum of opposition.[89] Lawton and Montgomery's 'whig Jacobitism' certainly sat incongruously with legitimist and non-juring renderings of the Stuart cause. There was the scent of chicanery, irresistible to pro-government authors, in the sight of an old radical haunt, the King's Head Tavern, Fleet Street, becoming a centre of Jacobite liaisons, or a tory author such as Bartholomew Shower, proposing remedies – a new bill of rights and annual parliaments – that would have been vilified by his party ten years earlier.[90] However, Lawton, Ferguson and Montgomery aimed to persuade James II to embrace political liberty as the condition for recovering his throne, and create a case reconnecting 'the broken Chain of the Lineal Succession' within 'the Old and Natural Frame of our Government'.[91] The rhetoric of the 'country' duly informed a series of new Stuart manifestos, and Lawton had received sufficient encouragement from St Germain by 1693 to deliver an appeal that subverted the conventional boundaries of political opinion: 'Awaken out of your Dreams, Get rid of your Phantams; Consider as Men, Act as Lovers of your Country; Rescue your Rights, Restore your King.'[92] If it did not succeed in establishing a serious alternative to the 1689 settlement, the effect of the polemical opposition literature emerging in the reign of William III was to dramatize ideological struggles over monarchy, constitution, church and foreign policy for an audience outside parliament, and fill the mental landscape of English politics and electioneering with images of rebellions, conspiracies and betrayals.[93] Surveying 'the temper of the nation' on the death of William III in March 1702, Gilbert Burnet gave

87 Lawton, *Better Late than Never*, p. 1.

88 Lawton, *Some Paradoxes* (1690); *Letter to Welwood*, p. 27.

89 Lawton, *Jacobite Principles*, p. 9.

90 *Original Papers: Containing the Secret History of Great Britain*, ed. James MacPherson (2 vols, London, 1776), I, 391; Shower, *Some Reasons*, pp. 1–6.

91 Browne MSS 93: Lawton to James II, 13 July 1691; [Ferguson] *Whether the Parliament be not in Law Dissolved by the Death of the Princess of Orange* (1695), p. 11; Lawton, *French Conquest* , p. 24; Montgomery, *Just Complaint*, p. 12.

92 Lawton, *French Conquest*, p. 24.

93 Mark Knights, *Representation and Misrepresentation in Later Stuart Britain* (Oxford, 2005), pp. 272–334.

vent to a mood of whig despondency towards the heat and partisanship exuding from the body politic. The nation had become 'more than half a Commonwealth', he believed, a trend that owed not merely to the rising authority and visibility of the triennial parliaments, but to the development of local party powerbases that 'kept up a standing faction in every County and Town of England'. Yet, for Burnet, 'tho' we were insensibly falling into a Democracy, we had not learnt the virtues, that are necessary for that sort of Government'. Instead, 'Luxury, Vanity and Ambition increased daily, and our animosities were come to a great height, and gave us dismal apprehensions'.[94] A larger, more active and ideologically-conscious public sphere was, he suggested, neither envisaged within the architecture of the 1689 settlement, nor welcomed by the architects themselves.

V

By the death of William III, attitudes towards the revolution settlement were beginning to drive larger shifts and realignments in English politics. As defenders of the revolution settlement, the whig leadership had been slowly pushed away from their 'commonwealth' inheritance, attaching themselves to the conception of a king-in-parliament monarchy that left considerable scope for advancing the political interests of the court. By the latter half of the king's reign, Williamite governments had become more confident in declaring the legal, more than de facto claims of the man who held the throne, defining a new political orthodoxy centred on the struggle for English, European and protestant liberties against the power of France, and extracting loyalty from British subjects more assertively through the oath of association that followed the exposure of the 1696 assassination plot.[95] Pro-government pamphlets railed against the 'unnatural' alliance of 'Old Jacobites, Republicans … Seditious Clubbers and Writers who are continually undermining Royal Authority, Reviling the Publick Ministry and Raising Causeless Jealousies and Suspicions'.[96] They sought to salvage the reputation of William III as a prince who has 'wrought such a Deliverance for the Nation as ought never to be forgotten, and can *never* be sufficiently Requited', and to educate his successors in virtues drawn out of the 1689 settlement. Though the Association had yielded a purported 450,000 signatures, whigs feared for the cultural and intellectual fruits of the Revolution, and were increasingly convinced that the tory resurgence under Anne left

[94] Gilbert Burnet, *History of My Own Time* (5 vols, Oxford, 1816 edn), III, 342.

[95] For the language of Williamite loyalty, see Joseph Addison, *A Poem to His Majesty* (1696); Sir Richard Blackmore, *A True and Impartial History of the Conspiracy against the Person and Government of King William III* (1723). For the oath of association, see Pincus, *1688*, pp. 464–9 and Knights, *Representation*, pp. 154–8.

[96] *Cursory Remarks upon Some Late Disloyal Proceedings* (1699), p. 1.

the claims of the house of Hanover hanging on a thread.[97] To the duke of Devonshire, the opposition had reduced the parliament from its 'consecrated fame' as a shield of liberty, to a house of faction, stirring 'imaginary Fears' and misusing the language of virtue to raise a persecuting high church spirit.[98] The same whig anxieties ran through the reigns of the early Hanoverian king. In 1720, Bernard Mandeville urged recalcitrant Englishmen to cease questing after 'an Eutopia', Jacobite or republican, that in all Human probability will never be brought about, and of which the very attempt… cannot cost less, if made with any Vigor or Resolution, than the ruin of at least half the Nation'.[99] Thirty years later, Horace Walpole believed that the obstreperous conduct of the opposition throughout successive reigns confirmed that the revolution settlement was a precarious monument, 'built upon whig principles, and alone supported by whig zeal'.[100]

The rediscovery of old country ideas in the Hanoverian parliaments after 1714 developed out of a brittle alliance of frustrated patriotic visions and dissident factions. The campaign against the new whig ascendancy could incorporate tory authors such as Alexander Pope and Jonathan Swift, alongside the 'independent whigs' John Trenchard and Thomas Gordon, held together by the shifting alliances of opposition circles in the chamber.[101] There was less continuity between the opposition manifestos of the 1690s and the reign of George II than the purest ideologues liked to claim. Developed by the circle of Viscount Bolingbroke, the new country party lacked the explicit radicalism of the 1690s, with a gulf especially gaping between the anticlerical sensibilities of whig dissidents like George Lyttelton and tory members who sought to preserve the high church platform developed under Queen Anne.[102] The opposition had also turned from a peace to a war party, agitating against threats to the marine empire posed by French and Spanish power.[103] However, the country campaign exposed the chasm between clashing concepts of moral philosophy and political economy seen to derive from conflicted readings of the revolution itself. Government supporters looked optimistically upon the commercial society empowering London's financial revolution, with its lotteries, funded debt and increas-

97 Pincus, *1688*, p. 464.

98 *An Allusion to the Bishop of Cambray's Telemachus* (1706), pp. 4–5.

99 Bernard Mandeville, *Free Thoughts on Religion, Church and National Happiness* (1720), pp. xiii, 334, 354–5.

100 [Horace Walpole], *A Memorial of Several Noblemen and Gentlemen of the First Rank and Fortune* (1753).

101 Isaac Kramnick, *Bolingbroke and his Circle* (Washington, 1968); Quentin Skinner, 'The Principles and Practice of Opposition: the Case of Bolingbroke and Walpole', in *Historical Perspectives*, ed. Neil McKendrick (1974), pp. 93–128.

102 James J. Sack, *From Jacobite to Conservative* (Cambridge, 1993), pp. 188–98; *Letters from a Persian*, pp. 57, 69, 99.

103 Marchmont, *Exhortation*, pp. 44–5; Brendan Simms, *Three Victories and a Defeat: The Rise and Fall of the First British Empire, 1714–1783* (2007), pp. 204–306.

ingly sophisticated banking system – Joseph Addison saw the new system of public credit as the Virgin Queen who presided over rising British power, making possible the series of military interventions carried through in the name of European liberty.[104] The search for a language of restraint and 'politeness' to guard against return to the dark partisanship of England's past stimulated Mandeville's view that 'To expect Ministries without faults, and Courts without Vices is grossly betraying our ignorance of human Affairs… There is Happiness in knowing the narrow bounds of temporal Felicity, and the surest way to Content is to moderate our Desires.'[105] Country authors by contrast began to interrogate the social and cultural consequences flowing from the revolution, to explore the deeper debilitation effected in a kingdom through a state of ministerial 'corruption'.

Opposition treatises brought an augustinian view of the fallibility of political life into contact with a civic humanist anatomy of the process by which civil virtue fell into decay. Where Addison and Mandeville envisaged a benign expansion of English freedom and capability under the protective shelter of the expanding state, Bolingbroke believed that 'liberty must always be in some degree of danger under every government', when 'the measures of faction' all-too-easily overcame a common love of the *patria*.[106] Where whig champions celebrated politeness and moderation, the authors of *Cato's Letters* saw England drifting towards a state of effeminacy reminiscent of the last days of Rome, when a cosseted citizenry failed to renovate the masculine spirit of the republic.[107] Where the 'court' heralded rising national wealth, the 'Country' perceived the snares of 'luxury', turning back to the Spartan credo voiced by Charlwood Lawton that 'Virtue and Liberty are a Nobler Happiness than excessive Riches, pompous Buildings, and all the other Glories that a People can possess'.[108] Calls for moral revival, nurtured alike by tory anglicans and low church reformers of 'manners', could be framed to meet the crisis of English liberties because, as George Lyttelton's Persian traveller asserted, the surest way for a ministry to entrench despotic power was to 'Fix it on the Vices of Mankind: Set up private Interest against the public; apply to the Wants and Vanities of Particulars'.[109] Thomas Gordon claimed vindication from Puritan critics of the court of Charles II for his

104 *The Spectator*, ed. D.F. Bond (5 vols, Oxford, 1965), I, 15; Istvan Hont, 'The Early Enlightenment Debate on Commerce and Luxury', in *The Cambridge History of Eighteenth-Century Political Thought*, ed. Mark Goldie and Robert Wokler (Cambridge, 2006), pp. 379–418.

105 Mandeville, *Free Thoughts*, p. 355; Nicholas Phillipson, 'Politics and Politeness in the Reign of Anne and the Early Hanoverians', in *The Varieties of British Political Thought, 1500–1800*, ed. J.G.A. Pocock (Cambridge, 1993), pp. 211–45.

106 [Bolingbroke], *Remarks on the History of England* (1749), p. 15.

107 *Ibid*., p. 21; John Trenchard and Thomas Gordon, *Essays on Liberty, Civil and Religious, and Other Important Subjects*, ed. Ronald Hamowy (2 vols, Indianapolis, IN, 1995).

108 Lawton, *Jacobite Principles*, p. 25.

109 *Persian Letters*, pp. 77–8.

assault upon endemic drunkenness, sexual immorality, foreign fashions and public debauchery at the London opera-houses as a 'Danger to Virtue, Danger to Christianity', 'making Traffick of one's Country' and hastening the enslavement of its people.[110] From across the confessional divide, Alexander Pope celebrated the charity, privacy and prayers of the recusant gentry households, as a corrective to the license all too vividly etched upon the face of the metropolis.[111]

From this perspective, country polemics fixed especially upon the developing financial institutions – 'creatures of the Revolution', in the words of the high churchman Thomas Carte, which according to Lyttelton had exposed the 'two things in Nature most repugnant and inconsistent with each other ... the Love of Liberty and the Love of Money'.[112] With the national debt swirling upwards to £50 million, the stock market was seen to have planted a 'Tree of Corruption', whose fruit bore the names 'Bond Contract', 'South Sea', 'East India' and 'Credit'. Thomas Gordon turned from a biblical to a pagan imagery to capture credit not as Addison's Virgin Queen, but a flighty, insubstantial spirit, putting a kingdom in thrall to Machiavelli's goddess of Fortune; the *Persian Letters* dubbed the masters of the public companies 'magicians' for their seeming ability to raise and destroy trades as they pleased.[113] The collapse of the South Sea Company in 1722 appeared to crystallize the different facets of national decline, exposing the nexus of government bribery that had raised a flawed investment scheme, unchecked by the 'septennial' whig parliament in place since 1715.[114] Country broadsides lambasted the state of debt, dependence and over-taxation that had engulfed the English squirearchy: almost 30 years after the crash, the tory M.P. Charles Gray blamed a fiscal system distorted by William of Orange to 'favour the interests of Holland' for draining English civic virtue by 'beggaring all the ancient gentry of the kingdom'.[115] Country polemics saw the only chance of renaissance in the replacement of the standing army by county militias, and a restoration of the ancient rights of borough corporations, to ensure that 'the property and interest and power of the kingdom' returned to those with a stake in the land. When the new finances had structured the British state on foundations of bad credit, political dishonour and false virtue, the radical Robert Molesworth could

110 Thomas Gordon, *The Character of an Independent Whig* (1719), pp. 22–4.

111 Alexander Pope, *Correspondence*, ed. G.E. Sherburn (5 vols, Oxford, 1956), I, 457; Howard Erskine-Hill, *The Social Milieu of Alexander Pope* (1975), pp. 42–68.

112 *Persian Letters*, p. 77; Windsor Castle, Stuart Papers, Box 1/299.

113 Gordon, *Independent Whig*, pp. 14–20; Thomas Gordon, *An Essay on the Practice of Stockjobbing* (1724), pp. 17–25; *Persian Letters*, p. 180; Kramnick, *Politics of Nostalgia*, p. 23.

114 Thomas Gordon, A *Complete History of the Septennial Parliament* (1722).

115 B.L., Add. MS 47012, A, fos 34–5; B.L., Add. MS 47092, p. 119; J.G.A. Pocock, *The Machiavellian Moment* (Princeton, NJ, 1975), pp. 452–70.

unite with the tory Jacobite Francis Atterbury to see the 'political blood of the kingdom' stored in the landed estates, whose holders brought together the Aristotelian model of the uncorrupted citizen with the Teutonic ideal of the sword in the hands of the independent freeholder.[116]

The gloom, satire and elegiac pessimism of country politics was therefore enlivened by the inheritance of a civic tradition that perceived the purpose of politics as the restoration of 'gothic ruins' 'to their 'ancient Glory and Splendour'.[117] 'Patriot' writers surveyed the parallel genre of imaginative literature that had satirized the absolutist tendencies of Bourbon monarchs in France, circulating Montesquieu's own *Persian Letters*, Fenelon's *Telemachus* and the utopian *Travels of Cyrus* by the radical, Masonic Jacobite, Andrew Ramsay through the ranks of the opposition.[118] Thomas Gordon drew upon Fenelon's christian-agrarian ideal, comparing 'a Rich and Populous City, abounding with a great Number of useless Artizans, and a barren uncultivated Country around it, to a Person that has a head of extraordinary Bulk, and prodigious Size, and all his other Parts extremely consum'd, and almost wasted to be a Skeleton'.[119] Charles Gray shared the vision of a 'patriot scheme', elevating human industry over the 'imaginary wealth' of public credit, while liberating trade and commerce, reforming the poor laws, and improving 'the natural Products of the Earth, in cultivating useful Arts and Sciences, and advancing Solid Learning and universal Knowledge'.[120] However, to Marchmont, these dreams could never be fulfilled without the overthrow of a government that has 'enslaved you with Excises, who pillage you with Taxes, who harass you with Soldiers'. Britons needed to send waves of liberty through a 'corrupt and adulating Senate', whose factions had so 'oppressed' each other by turns, that 'the prevailing Side has constantly fortified itself, by throwing Power into the hands of the Crown', leaving 230 M.P.s in some form of court 'employment' by 1740.[121] The revitalized country movement was therefore haunted by the shadow of the earlier moment, after the fall of James II, when, in the words of the pamphleteer James Ralph, 'such an opportunity was lost of resettling our old constitution as England is not like to have again'.[122] While his flirtation with Jacobitism

116 Molesworth, *Franco-Gallia*, p. xix; Francis Atterbury, 'English Advice to the Freeholders of England', 1714, in *A Collection of Scarce and Valuable Tracts*, ed. Walter Scott (13 vols, 1809–15), XIII, 541. See also Fletcher, *A Discourse of Government Concerning Militias and Standing Armies* (1697).

117 Marchmont, *Exhortation*, pp. 57, 60.

118 Gabriel Glickman, 'Andrew Michael Ramsay (1686–1743), the Jacobite Court and the English Catholic Enlightenment', *Eighteenth-Century Thought*, III (2007), 293–329; Lionel Rothkrug, *Opposition to Louis XIV* (Princeton, NJ, 1965), pp. 284–5.

119 Gordon, *Practice of Stock-Jobbing*, p. 16.

120 *Ibid.*, p. 10; Charles Gray, *Considerations on Several Proposals Lately Made for the Better Maintenance of the Poor* (1751); B.L., Add. MS 47012, A, fos 34–5.

121 Marchmont, *Exhortation*, pp. 11, 30, 48.

122 James Ralph, *The History of England* (2 vols, 1744), II, 5.

had ended in disillusionment by 1717, Viscount Bolingbroke continued nonetheless to view 'the political principles which had generally prevailed in our government from the revolution of 1688 to be destructive of our true interest'.[123]

VI

Mirroring the larger divides within the parliamentary opposition, Hanoverian country journals were not entirely at one in their attitudes towards the events of 1688–9. While Ralph's *Remembrancer* recalled the language of the original broadsides against the Convention parliament, one contributor to *The Craftsman* still hailed a revolution 'undertaken, carry'd on, completed on principles of civil and religious liberty': the point of corruption came later, under the governance of Sir Robert Walpole.[124] However, their arguments preserved aspects of the original radical and Jacobite challenges to the revolution, even as both causes threatened to expire. In the gardens of Stowe, the statues to Milton and Locke allowed the patriot magnate Lord Cobham to place himself within an heroic republican lineage. Conversely, Jacobite writers saw the Septennial Act as the fountain of another corrupted and tyrannical 'Long Parliament'. Marchmont lamented that, like another foreign monarch, William III, in the 1690s, the house of Hanover 'every Day more and more estranges the good Will and Fidelity of their Subjects'.[125] Bolingbroke acknowledged ruefully that 'every Jacobite in England' used the resources of 'old whig' argument and 'sinks his master's divine right in the popular topics of debts, taxes, and corruption'.[126] But rhetorical exchanges moved in both directions. In evoking images of rape, conquest, slavery and usurpation, county pamphlets snatched the emotive language of Jacobite treatises: simply substituting the terms 'parricide' against the country and 'Suicide in regard to yourselves' in place of old Stuart lamentations on the sin of 'regicide'.[127] Bolingbroke and Lyttelton yearned for a valorising 'Patriot King' to purge the realm of 'evil counsellors' and corrupted parliamentar-

123 Bolingbroke, *A Letter to Sir William Wyndham* (1717), p. 20.

124 *The Craftsman*, 12 Oct. 1745.

125 G. Clarke, 'Grecian Taste and Gothic Virtue: Lord Cobham's Gardening Programme and its Iconography', *Apollo*, 97 (1973), 566–71; *Revolution Politicks: Being a Compleat Collection of all the Reports, Lyes and Stories, which were the Fore-Runners of the Great Revolution in 1688* (1733); Marchmont, *Exhortation*, p. 20.

126 [Bolingbroke], *Remarks*, p. 35; Thomas Gordon, *A Short View of the Conspiracy* (1723), p. 9. See Paul Chapman, 'Jacobite Political Argument in England, 1714–1766', University of Cambridge Ph.D., 1983, for indications of the 'contractualist' and radical case made by Jacobite authors.

127 Marchmont, *Exhortation*, pp. 49–51; Howard Erskine-Hill, 'Literature and the Jacobite Cause: Was there a Rhetoric of Jacobitism?' in *Ideology and Conspiracy*, ed. Cruickshanks, pp. 49–69.

ians: their inspiration was the Elizabethan myth, and their hopes came to rest on Frederick, prince of Wales, the estranged son of George II, but their words informed the self-representation of the 'Young Pretender', Charles Edward Stuart.[128] The lament that legitimate royal power had simply been surrendered to a cabal of over-mighty ministers brushed against the oldest Jacobite critique of the Glorious Revolution.[129]

Jacobites and radicals may have diverged in their interpretations of the fall of James II, but they shared a belief that many maladies of the post-revolution state could be located in the original errors of the 1689 settlement: whether for betraying the original cause of freedom, for not proceeding far enough, or simply for installing a new form of despotism. Both movements combined to issue an alternative idea of social and political virtue, which challenged the perception that the revolution, the whig governments and a line of foreign monarchs represented suitable guardians of English civil liberty. Henry Fielding mocked the absurdity of a 'Jacobite-Republican' opportunist in his *Dialogue between an Honest Gentleman of London and an Honest Alderman of the Country Party* (1747), but the reality was embodied by the Westminster radical David Morgan, whose calls for annual parliaments and revived national militias ended after he was put to death following service for the Young Pretender in 1746.[130] The same unlikely convergence echoed through popular culture, in folk memories of Jacobite activity among the smugglers, highwaymen and poachers who defied new forest laws, taxes and enclosures: an image anticipated when John Gay made the chivalric brigand MacHeath an exemplar of lost virtue through the score of the *Beggar's Opera*.[131] While most Jacobite families made their return to loyalist politics under the reign of a tory prince, George III, the heralds of a later radical tradition – Wilkesite and Foxite – drew their rhetoric from a richly varied pedigree of dissident protest.[132]

At its lowest ebb, the tradition of dissent against the revolution settlement assembled a gallery of lost leaders, thwarted moments and defeated manifestos. While Jacobitism faded into a waning cultural memory, the 'commonwealth' vision was ultimately displaced onto another continent, as its followers looked to the American colonies to rebuild the politics of civic

128 H.T. Dickinson, 'Bolingbroke: *The Idea of a Patriot King*', *History Today*, XX (1970), 13–19; *An Authentic Account of the Conduct of the Young Chevalier* (1749); Szechi, *The Jacobites*, pp. 150–1.

129 *Persian Letters*, pp. 244–6, 275–7; Christine Gerrard, *The Patriot Opposition to Walpole* (Oxford, 1994), pp. 151, 163.

130 David Morgan, *The Country Bard: Or, the Modern Courtiers* (1739), p. 21; C.J., XXVI, 32; Erskine-Hill, 'Literature and the Jacobite Cause', p. 68.

131 Monod, *Jacobitism*, pp. 111–19; Kramnick, *Politics of Nostalgia*, pp. 223–30.

132 For tory or Jacobite associations with radical politics, see Nicholas Rogers, *Whigs and Cities* (Oxford, 1989), p. 81 and Linda Colley, 'Eighteenth-Century English Radicalism before Wilkes', *Transactions of the Royal Historical Society*, 5th ser., XXXI (1981), 1–20.

virtue through independent protestant churches, representative assemblies and a defence of the arms-bearing landed freeholder.[133] But the competing challenges to the Glorious Revolution and its legacy nonetheless shaped the debates of the public realm just as vigorously as the arguments offered in its defence. Indeed, the discourse of the opposition ironically gave the events of 1688 a centrality in English political culture that far exceeded the status of the earlier civil war. Together, radical and Jacobite traditions guaranteed the endurance late into the eighteenth-century of an old notion that to be a patriot entailed critical scrutiny as much as strict allegiance to the governing power of state.

133 Pocock, *Machiavellian Moment*, pp. 506–52.

11

Afterword: State Formation, Political Stability and the Revolution of 1688

STEPHEN TAYLOR

On the eve of the Seven Years' War in 1756 Britain was a very different state and nation compared with a century earlier. The British *state* itself had been created in 1707 by the Union between England and Scotland. A constitutional monarchy had been firmly established, in which parliament met for several months every year, and the focus of political power had shifted from Whitehall to Westminster. Both the Test Act of 1673 and the Toleration Act of 1689 had come to be regarded as almost as fundamental parts of the constitution as the Bill of Rights, the one guaranteeing the privileges of the Church of England and the other the rights of protestant dissenters, and creating, in effect, a de facto religious pluralism, which went far beyond the indulgence envisaged in 1689. Eighteenth-century Britain was also a remarkably successful military state. For almost half of the period between 1689 and 1756 it had been at war, mainly with France, an experience which had transformed it into a great European power and had necessitated the creation of a permanent naval and military establishment that was not only unprecedented in its scale but also gave government a novel peacetime coercive power. Britain's newfound status as a 'great power' was underpinned by fiscal and economic developments. War was funded by the ability of the government to raise enormous sums of money through taxation and borrowing, to manage its finances effectively through an expanded bureaucracy, and to keep on raising money as war was followed by war. In large part, this was made possible by the 'imperial dividend', as both government and nation began to benefit from the emergence of Britain as the great entrepôt of European and world trade. There was, of course, something deeply paradoxical about these developments, as it is difficult to imagine anyone alive in the Restoration period who would have welcomed them all.

The contributors to this volume are all agreed that the revolution of 1688 was a crucial moment in the transformation of British politics. This view was once unfashionable – the dominant accounts of the revolution in the second half of the twentieth century by J.R. Jones and J.R. Western played down the significance of 1688, in often conscious reaction against the triumphalist account of English exceptionalism offered by G.M. Trevelyan.[1] Dissenting voices, such as Lois Schwoerer, however, have recently been joined by the new overviews of Tim Harris and Steve Pincus which, from very different perspectives and in very different ways, reassert the revolutionary nature of 1688.[2] This volume has also been premised on the notion that the importance of 1688 needed to be understood in a much broader geographical context – British, European and Atlantic. In this 'Afterword', I want to develop further the argument that 1688 was a revolutionary moment in British history, but I shall begin by adopting an anglocentric perspective that has been largely eschewed in this volume hitherto. More specifically, I shall focus on the transformation in English political culture that occurred between the late seventeenth and early eighteenth century.

I

There is no denying the value of British, Atlantic and European perspectives on the history of the late seventeenth and early eighteenth centuries, but in many respects the English experience was different and distinctive. English politics and political society cannot easily be slotted into models of an *ancien régime*, derived primarily from the French example.[3] By the 1750s – arguably, indeed, by the 1730s – English political culture had been transformed in ways that encouraged foreign visitors as well as domestic commentators to write in terms that stressed, if not English exceptionalism, then, to borrow a phrase from E.P. Thompson, 'the peculiarities of the English'. Seventeenth-century England had witnessed not merely the turmoil of mid-century, culminating in regicide, military rule and a proliferation of religious sects that led otherwise sane observers to draw the frightening image of London becoming 'another Munster', but then continued instability through the Restoration.[4] Amid countless plots, conspiracies and

[1] J.R. Jones, *The Revolution of 1688 in England* (1972); J.R. Western, *Monarchy and Revolution: The English State in the 1680s* (1972); G.M. Trevelyan, *The English Revolution 1688–1689* (1938). See also, *Britain after the Glorious Revolution 1689–1714*, ed. Geoffrey Holmes (1969).

[2] Lois G. Schwoerer, *The Declaration of Rights, 1689* (Baltimore, MD, 1981); Tim Harris, *Revolution: The Great Crisis of the British Monarchy, 1685–1720* (2006); Steve Pincus, *1688: The First Modern Revolution* (New Haven, CT, 2009). The fiercest debates are, indeed, now ones that are being conducted within this new consensus. See e.g. Scott Sowerby, 'Pantomime History', *Parliamentary History*, XXX (2011), 236–58.

[3] Cf. J.C.D. Clark, *English Society 1688–1832: Ideology, Social Structure and Political Practice during the Ancien Regime* (Cambridge, 1985).

[4] William Prynne, *A True and Perfect Narrative of What was Done, Spoken by and between Mr Prynne, the Old and Newly Forcibly late Secluded Members, the Army Officers, and those Now Sitting, both in the Commons Lobby, House, and Elsewhere* (1659), pp. 58–9. A powerful interpretation of the continuities of seventeenth-century English history

rumours of rebellion, one of the king's chief ministers was forced into exile by impeachment for high treason and another spent over five years in the Tower on similar charges, two leading members of the nobility were executed for plotting a *coup d'état*, the bastard son of Charles II was executed for claiming the crown and leading a rebellion against his uncle, and, finally, in 1688, rival armies marched across the country for the second time in living memory before the reigning monarch was forced to flee by a combination of domestic revolt and foreign invasion. By the death of George I in 1727, the situation was very different. Eighteenth-century England witnessed no civil war and no major rebellions – in English terms the Jacobite rebellion of 1715 was a minor affair in the north, while the '45 was the invasion of the north of England by a Scottish army. The last impeachment of the monarch's first minister took place in 1715 and, significantly, that trial followed his fall from office rather than being part of the process. There were no major plots or conspiracies against the king or his ministers after 1721. Arguably the most notable trial of a member of the English *élite* was the court martial of Admiral Byng in 1757 for insufficient zeal in defence of the state rather than opposition to it. More intangibly, for all the period's reputation for 'corruption', it is inconceivable that members of the parliamentary opposition should have been in receipt of pensions from a foreign monarch or, indeed, that a foreign monarch could have hoped to exercise influence over the conduct of British policy in that way.[5]

This transformation of English political culture has not passed unnoticed. In an analysis that exerted a huge influence over historical scholarship for the best part of a generation, J.H. Plumb described it as 'the growth of political stability'.[6] Plumb, however, located the achievement of stability firmly in the early eighteenth century, in the ascendancy of Robert Walpole and in the establishment of single-party government. In his account the revolution of 1688 was another episode in the political instability of the seventeenth century, with the reigns of William and Anne witnessing the playing out of tensions that had often been exacerbated and sometimes caused by the revolution. And it is easy to see why the years from 1689 to 1715 may appear to have been a continuation of the turmoil of the seventeenth century. The issue of the succession to the crown, never far from the surface of English politics over the previous 200 years, remained at the centre of debate. Any lingering hopes that William and Mary might produce a protestant heir died with the queen in 1694, while the death seven years later of the duke of Gloucester, the only one of Anne's children to survive infancy, ended any prospect of the succession of a line of protestant, Stuart heirs. By the provisions of the Bill of Rights of 1689 the crown was to descend to the next

is provided by Jonathan Scott, *England's Troubles: Seventeenth-Century English Political Instability in European Context* (Cambridge, 2000).

5 David Ogg, *England in the Reign of Charles II* (Oxford, 1954), p. 551.

6 J.H. Plumb, *The Growth of Political Stability in England 1675–1725* (1967).

protestant heir (at that time the electress of Hanover), but the succession was contested by the existence of a Jacobite pretender who had a better hereditary claim to the throne, one supported, moreover, by the might of Louis XIV's France. The contacts maintained with the Jacobite court in exile at St Germain by a number of leading politicians, including some of William's own ministers and architects of the revolution such as the earl of Marlborough and Admiral Russell, may only have been an insurance policy. But they argue powerfully for contemporaries' sense of the precariousness of the protestant succession and a continuing uncertainty and instability in English politics, as does the fact that William and his ministers felt obliged to pass the Act of Settlement to clarify and confirm the provisions of the Bill of Rights.

At the same time, England was experiencing massive structural dislocation. The revolution had plunged the country into a major continental war against France, which continued, with a brief respite between 1697 and 1701, until 1713. This was the first time since the reign of Elizabeth that England had fought a prolonged foreign war, and the strain on society, as well as on the state's financial and administrative structures, was immense. An army, which had numbered little more than 15,000 at the beginning of 1685, had increased to 70,000 men by 1690 and averaged around 90,000 throughout the war of the Spanish succession.[7] This may have been small by comparison with the armies of France, but, particularly when combined with the expansion of the navy and the enormous resources required to keep it at sea, it necessitated a militarization of English society unseen since the 1650s. The cost of the war was enormous – government expenditure between 1689 and 1697 totalled nearly £50m, and nearly £100m was spent during the war of the Spanish succession.[8] By the time of the treaty of Utrecht in 1713 the British state had developed a complex, but highly successful method of financing war through a combination of long-term loans and taxation. But the birth-pangs of the financial revolution were acute, prompting a recoinage in 1696, a series of financial crises through the 1690s as many taxes failed to generate enough revenue to repay the loans charged against them, and the major innovation of the land tax.[9] Even so, a year after end of the war of the Spanish succession, government debt stood

[7] The *English* army numbered less than 9,000 at the beginning of James II's reign. John Childs, *The Army, James II and the Glorious Revolution* (Manchester, 1980), pp. 1–2; John Brewer, *The Sinews of Power: War, Money and the English State* (1989), p. 30.

[8] Brewer, *Sinews of Power*, p. 40.

[9] On the transformation of government finance in the 1690s, see P.G.M. Dickson, *The Financial Revolution in England: A Study in the Development of Public Credit 1688–1756* (1967); Brewer, *Sinews of Power*, ch. 4. Anne Murphy highlights the dependence of state finance on the development of sophisticated financial markets in London, and particularly the emergence of a secondary market in the national debt: *The Origins of English Financial Markets. Investment and Speculation before the South Sea Bubble* (Cambridge, 2009).

at some £40m, a sum which many believed threatened imminent national bankruptcy.[10] Inevitably this generated discontent, with the new 'monied' interest based in the City of London, which appeared to have profited from the war, and the massive expansion of government bureaucracy attracting particular hostility.[11]

For many historians, however, the most powerful testimony to the continuing political instability of England at the end of the seventeenth century is the depth and intensity of party strife. Few would deny that the post-revolutionary decades witnessed some of the most virulent controversy of what has been described as 'the first age of party', but it is much less obvious why what was in many respects a novel structure of politics should be regarded as evidence of the continuation of seventeenth-century instability. The portrayal of the conflict between whigs and tories as destabilizing enabled Plumb to identify the emergence of one-party government under the whigs in the late 1710s and 1720s as a key factor in the achievement of stability. But this argument is counter-intuitive: why should the exclusion of a significant section of the nation's political elite from the possibility of power be stabilizing?[12] Indeed, as a number of historians have demonstrated, tory proscription after 1715 fuelled not only widespread discontent with a corrupt whig oligarchy but also, on occasions, a virulent popular anti-Hanoverianism.[13]

Moreover, if we turn our attention to other aspects of the political structures of the post-revolutionary decades, we begin to get a sense of how much things had changed and, in particular, of the emergence of 'a sense of common identity' among the English political elite.[14] There is, of course, no doubt that war and finance were sources of division in post-revolutionary politics or that both played their part in the conflicts between whigs and tories.[15] Escalating government expenditure and the expansion of the state bureaucracy contributed largely to the formation of the 'new country party' during William's reign, to attempts to rein in government extravagance and

10 Dickson, *Financial Revolution*, p. 80.

11 Geoffrey Holmes, *British Politics in the Age of Anne* (rev. edn, 1987), pp. xlv–xli and ch. 5.

12 A point well made by Linda Colley, *In Defiance of Oligarchy: The Tory Party 1714–60* (Cambridge, 1982), p. 6.

13 Colley, *In Defiance of Oligarchy*, esp. ch. 2; Nicholas Rogers, *Crowds, Culture and Politics in Georgian Britain* (Oxford, 1998), pp. 21–57; Paul Monod, *Jacobitism and the English People, 1688–1788* (Cambridge, 1989). Eveline Cruickshanks's claim that it turned 'the Tory party into a Jacobite one', driving it into active allegiance to the exiled descendants of James II is unconvincing. E. Cruickshanks, *Political Untouchables. The Tory Party and the '45* (1979), p. 6.

14 The phrase is Plumb's and it is one of the three factors that he identifies as crucial in the achievement of political stability. *Growth of Political Stability*, p. xviii.

15 Tim Harris, *Politics under the Later Stuarts: Party Conflict in a Divided Society, 1660–1715* (1993), chs 6–7; Holmes, *Age of Anne*.

to efforts to control the power of the executive. With the coming of peace in 1697, attention focused on the standing army, which was denounced both as an unnecessary extravagance and as a threat to liberty. In Anne's reign there were regular tory attacks on the financial institutions of the whig 'establishment', especially the Bank of England, which appeared to be growing rich on the profits of war. The war itself was equally a source of division, as differences opened up between whigs and tories over questions of strategy – whigs tended to advocate a continental strategy, while tories inclined to one based on maritime and colonial operations. By 1708 these divisions were exacerbated by conflicting views on how, and on what terms, to make peace, issues which increasingly dominated political debate until the conclusion of the treaty of Utrecht in 1713. Despite the experience of the next 50 years, when Britain was engaged in two more major European wars, debt continued to spiral and the issue of the country's relationship with Hanover came to dominate debates on foreign policy, it would be difficult to make a case that the conduct and financing of war provoked such bitter divisions until the state was engaged in a conflict with its own colonists in North America in the late 1770s and early 1780s.[16]

More striking than these divisions, however, is the level of agreement about both the war and its financing during the post-revolutionary decades. There is little evidence of outright opposition to the war against France until 1709–10, when the tories began to present themselves to the electorate as the 'peace party'.[17] By this time two things were becoming clear: that the power of Louis XIV's France had been curbed, but that the objective of 'liberating' Spain from the rule of Philip V and placing the Habsburg Archduke Charles on the throne was militarily unattainable. The following year that objective also became politically undesirable, when Charles succeeded to the imperial crown on the death of the emperor: the recreation of the empire of Charles V was no more attractive to the tories than the rule of Spain by the grandson of Louis XIV. Prior to this, through both the Nine Years War and the war of the Spanish succession, very few voices could be found dissenting from the proposition that the war against France – and in defence of the revolution of 1688 – was necessary. Even more remarkable than this consensus was the willingness of the English *élite* to finance the war effort. The government, like all early modern governments, borrowed heavily. There were two keys to the financial revolution and thus to the financing of England's war effort: the development of a system of long-term loans guaranteed by the state and, as John Brewer has pointed out, the creation of a tax system that provided 'the government with a substantial and

16 Bob Harris, *Politics and the Nation: Britain in the Mid-Eighteenth Century* (Oxford, 2002), ch. 1; Stephen Conway, *War, State, and Society in Mid-Eighteenth-Century Britain and Ireland* (Oxford, 2006), ch. 6; *idem*, *The British Isles and the War of American Independence* (Oxford, 2000), ch. 4.

17 Holmes, *British Politics*, pp. 75–6.

regular income'.[18] During the Nine Years' War average annual tax revenue was more than double what it had been through the Restoration.[19] By the end of the war of the Spanish succession over nine per cent of national income was being appropriated by the state in tax.[20] Significantly, moreover, the English *élite* demonstrated an unprecedented willingness to tax themselves. The most important single source of government revenue through the post-revolutionary decades was the land tax, first introduced in 1692, which accounted for 42 per cent of all tax revenues during the Nine Years' War. During the wars of the eighteenth century the balanced shifted markedly towards more regressive forms of indirect taxation. But in the 1690s and even in the 1700s, while the landed classes regularly complained about the burden of the land tax, they continued to vote, pay and, indeed, collect it throughout the years of the war.[21]

The full significance of this consensus only becomes apparent when viewed in a longer chronological perspective. Throughout the seventeenth century one of the biggest problems for all Stuart monarchs, and one of the most significant causes of tension between them and their parliaments, was finance. Parliament repeatedly demonstrated its reluctance even to vote the money necessary to administer the country. In James I's reign, as Conrad Russell has noted, the House of Commons refused to recognize that parliamentary taxation was necessarily part of the regular income of the crown.[22] Extraordinary revenue, to wage war, remained a running sore into the Restoration. Just as Charles I repeatedly found his foreign policy undermined by parliament's parsimony, so the hostility of many M.P.s to the third Dutch war and the refusal of parliament to provide further subsidies to finance England's continued participation in it in late 1673 played a major part in forcing Charles II out of the conflict.[23] It might be argued that the 1680s witnessed a significant improvement in the monarchy's position, as increasing customs revenues gave the king greater independence of parliament and allowed James II to increase his army to over 30,000 men.[24] But

18 Brewer, *Sinews of Power*, p. 89.

19 *Ibid.*; C.D. Chandaman, *The English Public Revenue 1660–1688* (Oxford, 1975), p. 333.

20 Patrick O'Brien, 'The Political Economy of English Taxation, 1660–1815', *Economic History Review*, XLI (1988), 1–32.

21 Brewer, *Sinews of Power*, p. 95. The land tax was not collected by a professional bureaucracy, but instead by the gentry themselves acting as collectors and receivers. This arrangement may have been motivated by the desire to limit the expansion of the state bureaucracy, but it also testifies to the fundamental acceptance of the tax by English landed society.

22 Russell, *King James VI and I and his English Parliaments* (Oxford, 2011), pp. 76–7.

23 John Spurr, *England in the 1670s: 'This Masquerading Age'* (Oxford, 2000), pp. 47–57.

24 But the army had been rapidly expanded in the summer of 1688 and it is likely that a number of regiments were not ready for action at the time of William's invasion. Childs, *The Army, James II*, ch. 1.

the country was at peace, and James could still not have financed any military adventures without additional support from parliament.

The quarter-century after 1689 was, therefore, characterized by a very different set of attitudes from the previous 90 years. Not only were the post-revolutionary decades dominated by England's participation in a major European conflict, but they also witnessed a united, if occasionally reluctant, political elite giving concrete support to the crown's foreign policy by contributing unprecedented sums to finance the conduct of the war. The military mobilization of the 1640s and 1650s had taken place in the very different circumstances of civil war and its aftermath.[25] Despite the arguments and debates over war aims and strategy and about the ways of raising money, and despite widespread suspicion of a foreign monarch, the reign of William III witnessed the forging of a sense of identity between ruler and ruled.[26] This sense of common identity underpinned the emergence of one of the most powerful states in eighteenth-century Europe. One of the reasons why the Jacobite threat was so insignificant by the middle of the eighteenth century is that the Pretender and his supporters were no longer faced merely with the challenge of repeating the achievement of William III in 1689; they were now opposed by a much larger and more professional army, supported in turn by a much bigger and more confident state apparatus.

What, then, changed between the seventeenth and eighteenth centuries? First, the population of England was better able to bear the burden imposed by the state. Second, institutions and mechanisms were established whereby the wealth of the country could effectively be tapped in order to finance the war effort. Third, a significant shift took place in perceptions of what was a proper level of taxation. Fourth, the nation's *élite* demonstrated its willingness to trust the post-revolutionary monarchs with the money needed to raise and maintain an army and navy large enough to play a major role in a European war.

The first point is structural and can be explained by the co-incidence of a series of climactic, demographic and economic developments. Geoffrey Parker has recently shown that the middle years of the century experienced a global climatic 'catastrophe', with a series of harsh winters, cool summers, droughts and floods leading to widespread scarcity of food.[27] By the end of the century, however, climatic conditions had become more benign, coinciding with a relaxation of the pressures that the population growth of

[25] James Scott Wheeler, *The Making of a World Power: War and the Military Revolution in the Seventeenth-Century England* (Stroud, 1999), esp. chs 3–4; Braddick, *State Formation in Early Modern England, c.1550–1700* (Cambridge, 2000), pp. 213–21, 253–65.

[26] Colley, *In Defiance of Oligarchy*, pp. 12–13 and n. 28; Tony Claydon, *William III and the Godly Reformation* (Cambridge, 1996), esp. chs 4–6. Cf. Craig Rose, *England in the 1690s: Revolution, Religion and War* (Oxford, 1999), esp. chs 2–4.

[27] G. Parker, 'Crisis and Catastrophe: The Global Crisis of the Seventeenth Century Reconsidered', *American Historical Review*, 113 (2008), 1053–79.

the Tudor and early Stuart period had imposed on the English economy. In the second half of the century population stagnated and probably even declined slightly. At the same time there is clear evidence that agricultural improvement was contributing to the reduction in food prices and also to improvement in diet.[28] The *English* experience was distinctive in degree, if not in general character – at no time after 1680 did the country experience genuine famine, such as occurred in Scotland in the 1690s or in France in 1693 and 1709.[29] Moreover, the boom in trade that took place in the last years of Charles II's reign was not merely cyclical; it was the manifestation of a secular development that was to transform the British economy over the next century and that can be attributed partly to the beginnings of the 'imperial dividend', as the American colonies in particular began to make a significant contribution to the British economy.[30] Certainly, there is clear evidence of a general improvement in living standards, as colonial products such as sugar and tobacco ceased to be luxuries and as a vibrant consumer market developed for household goods and clothing.[31]

Second, the state developed the mechanisms to tap the country's wealth more effectively. This, too, was a long-term process, beginning perhaps with the destruction of the fiscal apparatus of the early Stuart monarchy under the pressure of civil war. As a result the restored regime inherited a taxation system, now overwhelmingly dependent on parliamentary approval, which had the potential to raise much greater revenues than before 1640. During the Restoration significant improvements were effected in the administration of government finance through the strengthening of the authority of the Treasury and the establishment of permanent offices to administer the customs, the excise (itself an innovation of the 1640s) and the hearth tax.[32] The crucial developments, however, took place after 1688 in the 'financial revolution', most notably the creation of the Bank of England and a system for the funding of long-term debt.[33] The revolution was important here, not

28 E.A. Wrigley and R.S. Schofield, *The Population History of England 1541–1871: A Reconstruction* (1981), pp. 207–15; Mark Overton, *Agricultural Revolution in England: The Transformation of the Agrarian Economy, 1500–1850* (Cambridge, 1996).

29 G. Holmes, 'The Achievement of Stability: The Social Context of Politics from the 1680s to the Age of Walpole', in *The Whig Ascendancy: Colloquies on Hanoverian England*, ed. J. Cannon (1981), pp. 1–22.

30 Nuala Zahedieh, *The Capital and the Colonies: London and the Atlantic Economy 1660–1700* (Cambridge, 2010); David Ormrod, *The Rise of Commercial Empires. England and the Netherlands in the Age of Mercantilism, 1650–1770* (Cambridge, 2003), chs 2–3.

31 Jan De Vries, *The Industrious Revolution: Consumer Behavior and the Household Economy 1650 to the Present* (Cambridge, 2008), ch. 4.

32 Braddick, *State Formation*, esp. ch. 6; H. Tomlinson, 'Financial and Administrative Developments in England, 1660–88', in *The Restored Monarchy 1660–1688*, ed. J.R. Jones (1979), pp. 94–117; Wheeler, *Making of a Great Power*, chs 5–7.

33 Dickson, *Financial Revolution*, chs 1, 3; Brewer, *Sinews of Power*, ch. 4; Murphy, *Origins*, ch. 2.

only in plunging Britain into a European war that demanded unprecedented sums of money, but also in bringing to power a group of predominantly whig politicians who were ideologically committed to a national bank and a political economy that supported it.[34] The result was the transformation of the royal debt into the national debt and royal finance into state finance. No longer could M.P.s claim that government revenues were only for the private benefit of the king.[35]

All of this was accompanied by a change in attitudes towards taxation and, more precisely, to the level of taxation which it was thought that the country could bear. Part of the problem for early Stuart monarchs was that their subjects objected to contributing to the royal coffers because they believed that they were already subjected to an unfair tax burden. A century later British perceptions of the share of national income taken by the state had changed dramatically. This is not to say that taxation had ceased to be controversial or that people did not object to paying specific taxes or to the level of taxation. But, relatively, Englishmen believed that they were taxed less heavily than other people in Europe, and particularly the French. Hogarth helped to disseminate the popular image of the prosperous Englishman settling down to his meal of roast beef, while his French counterpart, oppressed by the exactions of an arbitrary monarchy and an over-privileged church, was forced to endure wooden clogs and a bare table.[36] Ironically, as Peter Mathias and Patrick O'Brien have demonstrated, the opposite was true; throughout the eighteenth century the French state consistently took a significantly lower proportion of national income than the British.[37] The perception, however, was deeply engrained. Part of the explanation for it was surely growing economic prosperity: most Englishmen felt richer, and were richer. But part of the explanation lies in structural differences between the English and French economies and tax systems. The importance of overseas trade in the British economy meant that it was possible to raise large sums of money through the imposition of customs revenues on a wide range of goods at the point of entry into the country. At the same time the concentrated nature of much manufacturing facilitated the levying of internal excise duties at the point of production – English beer, for example, tended to be manufactured in breweries, whereas

34 Pincus, *1688*, ch. 12, though his argument that 'political economic issues' were 'central … to the causes' of the revolution is more tendentious. On the argument for a Dutch contribution to these developments, see M. 't Hart, '"The Devil or the Dutch": Holland's Impact on the Financial Revolution in England 1643–94', *Parliaments, Estates and Representation*, 11 (1991), 39–52.

35 Russell, *James and his Parliaments*, p. 77.

36 Michael Duffy, *The Englishman and the Foreigner* (Cambridge, 1986), pp. 35, 156–7.

37 Peter Mathias and Patrick O'Brien, 'Taxation in Britain and France?: A Comparison of the Social and Economic Incidence of Taxes Collected for the Central Governments', *Journal of European Economic History*, V (1976), 601–50.

French wine and cider tended to be produced domestically. As a result, most English indirect taxation was invisible at the point of consumption and most Englishmen had little to do with revenue officials. The French government, by contrast, relied heavily on the taxation of a relatively small number of items, many of which were essential for subsistence, and the country was famously criss-crossed with internal customs barriers. Frenchmen were much more aware of the taxes that they were paying and they regularly came face-to-face with tax collectors.[38]

The fourth change to take place at the end of the seventeenth century was the willingness of the English political *élite* to trust William and Anne with the money needed to wage two lengthy wars against the might of Louis XIV's France. The sums involved were vast: the Nine Years' War cost some £35m and the War of the Spanish Succession around £65m. Taxation covered much of this, averaging over £3.5m per annum during the 1690s and £5.25m between 1701 and 1713;[39] the substantial shortfall was covered by loans, which also had to be approved in parliament. It is the willingness of the English *élite* to vote these enormous sums and to keep on voting them, it is the sudden emergence of a sense of common identity uniting the English *élite* and its rulers, that is so remarkable when viewed against the background of seventeenth-century politics. It is my contention that the revolution of 1688 played a key role in bringing about this change of attitudes. To understand why this is the case, it is necessary to look a little more closely at the causes of political instability in the seventeenth century.

In recent years, despite the vigorous debates that are still continuing about the nature and causes of the puritan revolution and about the destabilizing characteristics of Restoration politics, some kind of consensus appears to have emerged. While debates continue about chronology and about the relative weight of different factors, two issues have come to dominate all others in analyses of the causes of the conflicts of the mid-seventeenth century and the nature of Restoration politics: religion and the constitution. In religion two distinct, though related, issues can be identified. The first is anti-popery, which manifested itself in the commitment to make England a protestant state and nation, and in the fear that the achievement of that goal was constantly threatened, both at home and abroad, by those who wished to return the country to communion with Rome.[40] The second was the debate, itself a product of the Reformation, about the character of the Church of England. It was given focus by the demands of the hotter

38 Brewer, *Sinews of Power*, pp. 100–1; J.C. Riley, *The Seven Years War and the Old Regime in France* (Princeton, NJ, 1986), ch. 2, esp. pp. 53–4.

39 Brewer, *Sinews of Power*, pp. 30, 40.

40 Scott, *England's Troubles*, chs 4–8; Peter Lake, 'Antipopery: The Structure of a Prejudice', in *Conflict in Early Stuart England: Studies in Religion and Politics 1603–42*, ed. Richard Cust and Ann Hughes (1989), pp. 72–106; John Miller, *Popery and Politics in England 1660–1688* (Cambridge, 1973).

sort of protestants, the puritans and later the dissenters, for a church that was more thoroughly reformed, one that was more effectively purged of the remnants of popery.[41] If religion provided one source of controversy through the century, another was to be found in the constitution or, more precisely, in debates about the powers and prerogatives of the monarchy. Time and again, constitutional issues revealed a fault line between those, on the one hand, who supported a strong monarchy, who were advocates of the royal prerogative, and who did not bridle at descriptions of the English king as 'absolute', and those, on the other hand, who insisted that England was a mixed or limited monarchy, who emphasized the subjection of the king to the law, and who perhaps even talked of the co-ordinate power of king and parliament.[42]

Demands for the further reformation of the Church of England need not detain us long in the context of this discussion. The problem of 'dissent' remained a controversial and divisive political issue well into the early eighteenth century, contributing significantly to the ideology of both whiggery and toryism.[43] However, the experience of defeat in 1660 and the Restoration settlement of religion in 1662, which, by excluding the presbyterians, removed from the church those who were most committed to working for its reform, did much to undermine the zeal of the puritans and the call for further reformation lost much of its potential for generating political instability. The failure to comprehend the presbyterians in 1662 removed from the church those who were most committed to working for its reform, and, quite rapidly, the focus of debate shifted away from demands for the radical reform of the national church to discussion of the relationship of dissenters with church and state. This process was accelerated by the growing denominalization of dissent, with the result that, by 1689, desire for comprehension within a 'purified' Church of England had limited appeal even within presbyterianism.[44]

The Restoration settlement, however, did little to remove the other major sources of instability in English politics. If parliament had gone to war with Charles I to impose limitations on his powers, the return of Charles II marked the failure of its efforts, as he was restored without conditions, his

41 Patrick Collinson, *The Birthpangs of Protestant England: Religious and Cultural Change in the Sixteenth and Seventeenth Centuries* (1988); *The Culture of English Puritanism, 1560–1700*, ed. Christopher Durston and Jacqueline Eales (1996), esp. chs 2, 3, 5.

42 Scott, *England's Troubles*, esp. chs 4–8; Alan Cromartie, *The Constitutionalist Revolution: An Essay on the History of England, 1450–1642* (Cambridge, 2006); J.P. Sommerville, *Politics and Ideology in England, 1603–40* (1986).

43 Harris, *Politics under the Later Stuarts*, pp. 152–7; Geoffrey Holmes, 'Religion and Party in Late Stuart England', in *Politics, Religion and Society in England 1679–1742* (1986), pp. 181–216.

44 *The Entring Book of Roger Morrice*, ed. M. Goldie *et al.* (7 vols, Woodbridge, 2007–9), I, 148–246; John Spurr, 'From Puritanism to Dissent, 1660–1700', in *Culture of English Puritanism*, ed. Durston and Eales, pp. 234–65.

powers largely intact. The restored king's marriage to Catherine of Braganza in 1662 also offered a reminder of Charles I's reign, as the practice of the mass at court was once more guaranteed by international treaty and a catholic coterie formed at the heart of English politics based on the household of the queen consort and, from the 1670s, at the court of the duke and duchess of York.[45] Nor were Englishmen reassured by events on the continent, as it was the catholic powers in Europe, and especially in Germany, which had emerged strengthened from the Thirty Years' War.[46]

Throughout the Restoration popery and the constitution were the open sores of English politics, generating instability time and again.[47] There were widespread fears that Charles II was seeking to exploit his prerogative in order to increase the power of the monarchy, at the expense of both the individual and parliament. His 1672 Declaration of Indulgence was denounced by the House of Commons as an illegal extension of the prerogative, since 'no such Power was ever claimed or exercised by any of Your Majesty's Predecessors'.[48] His efforts to build up the army, particularly in the 1670s, were portrayed as a preparation for an attack on the liberties of the subject, an impression that was all the more easily cultivated when troops were used to suppress dissenting conventicles.[49] The attempt, particularly by Danby, to create a loyal court party in parliament was seen as part of a conspiracy to turn that institution into a mere rubber-stamp for royal edicts.[50] These fears were only heightened by the events of James II's reign, as the king launched what many came to see as a fundamental assault on the rights and liberties of Englishmen. The issuing of the declarations of indulgence, suspending the operation of all penal laws in matters of religion; the deprivation of the president and fellows of Magdalen College, Oxford; the attempts to secure the return of a packed parliament, committed in advance to the repeal of the Test and Corporation Acts; the establishment of the ecclesiastical commission; the imprisonment and trial of the seven bishops – all these

45 Miller, *Popery and Politics*, pp. 21–2, 129–30. Moreover, Charles II's most influential mistresses were catholics. Tim Harris, *Restoration: Charles II and his Kingdoms 1660–1685* (2005), pp. 72–3. A vivid sense of the catholic atmosphere at court is provided by the newsletters of Edward Coleman, the secretary to the duchess of York, between 1675 and 1678. Harry Ransom Humanities Research Center, Austin, TX, Pforzheimer MS 103C, Boxes 6–8. Cf. Caroline Hibbard, *Charles I and the Popish Plot* (Chapel Hill, NC, 1983).

46 J.F. Bosher, 'The Franco-Catholic Danger, 1660–1715', *History*, LXXIX (1994), 5–30; W.R. Ward, *Christianity under the Ancien Régime 1648–1789* (Cambridge, 1999).

47 The classic contemporary account, linking the two themes, was Andrew Marvell, *An Account of the Growth of Popery and Arbitrary Government* (1677).

48 *C.J.*, IX, 257.

49 Gerald R. Cragg, *Puritanism in the Period of the Great Persecution 1660–1688* (Cambridge, 1957), p. 38; John Childs, *The Army of Charles II* (1976), p. 70; Anthony Fletcher, 'The Enforcement of the Conventicle Acts 1664–79', in *Persecution and Toleration*, ed. W.J. Sheils (Studies in Church History, 21, 1984), pp. 235–46.

50 Spurr, *England in the 1670s*, p. 67.

events suggested a king who had no regard for the law and was bent on destroying the constitution in pursuit of his 'catholicizing' policies.[51]

The potential for anti-popery to generate instability in the political world of the Restoration was revealed most vividly during the crisis of 1678–81.[52] In the aftermath of the revelation of the popish plot, attention quickly focused on the fact that the heir to the throne, James, duke of York, was a catholic, leading to a vigorous campaign to secure his exclusion from the succession. For many Englishmen, however, the politics of exclusion could only be seen in the wider context of the struggle between protestantism and popery.[53] The Reformation was being threatened abroad, by the advance of the Counter-Reformation on the continent and especially in France, and at home, by a catholic conspiracy at the very heart of the political system. The attitude of many ministers was positively apocalyptic. In dozens of sermons and tracts, they portrayed the popish plot as yet another episode in the long history of the efforts by the emissaries of anti-Christ to overcome the true gospel. In the past, as William Lloyd told the congregation at the funeral of Edmund Godfrey, 'the good Providence of God' had saved the nation. But the message was not entirely reassuring: there was always the possibility that, on this occasion, God would allow it to be destroyed for its sins.[54]

If such attitudes were largely silenced during the years of the tory reaction, they found new expression following James II's accession. Gilbert Burnet was not alone in seeing 1685, the year both of James II's accession and the revocation of the edict of Nantes, as a critical moment in the history of European protestantism, which he described as 'the fifth great crisis of the protestant religion'.[55] The policies of the new king – his abandonment of his alliance with the tories soon after his accession to the throne and his increasingly zealous pursuit of policies designed to secure full religious equality for his co-religionists – soon convinced even the intolerant, persecuting high churchmen of the early 1680s, who had rallied to his support as duke of York, to embrace the idea of protestant union in the face of the catholic threat. It is tempting to see the overtures made by Sancroft and his colleagues to the dissenters are mere tactical posturing, designed to

[51] The best account is now Harris, *Revolution*, ch. 5.

[52] Jonathan Scott, *Algernon Sidney and the Restoration Crisis, 1677–1683* (Cambridge, 1991); Mark Knights, *Politics and Opinion in Crisis, 1678–81* (Cambridge, 1994).

[53] The title of the whig propagandist, Henry Care's newspaper, *Weekly Pacquet of Advice from Rome* (1678–83) makes the connection clear. See also Harris, *Restoration*, pp. 152–3.

[54] W. Lloyd, *A sermon at the funeral of Edmund-Berry Godfrey* (1678), p. 40; W. Johnston, *Revelation Restored. The Apocalypse in Later Seventeenth-century England* (Woodbridge, 2011), ch. 5; D. Wykes, 'Dissenters and the Writing of History: Ralph Thoresby's "Lives and Characters"', in *Fear, Exclusion and Revolution. Roger Morrice and Britain in the 1680s*, ed. J. McElligott (Aldershot, 2006), pp. 180–1.

[55] *Bishop Burnet's History of His Own Time*, ed. M.J. Routh (6 vols, 2nd edn, Oxford, 1833), III, 75. Cf. *Morrice Entring Book*, ed. Goldie et al., IV, 212–13.

persuade James II to return to his old friends. And that, surely, is precisely what they were, at least in part, as was revealed by the retreat of many high churchmen from their more conciliatory attitude towards dissent in the aftermath of James's flight.[56] But that is not the whole story, as many high churchmen also embraced an apocalyptic worldview and prepared themselves for martyrdom in the event that God did, indeed, demonstrate his displeasure towards his chosen people.[57]

II

Viewed in this context, the full significance of the 1688 revolution – and especially of the revolution settlement – becomes apparent. Recent work on the settlement has tended to reassert the view that it was revolutionary, changing the nature of the English monarchy and redefining its powers.[58] How, then, did the constitutional settlement of 1689 contribute to the longer-term shift in political culture that I have been discussing? To answer this question, a brief reconsideration of two key elements of the settlement is necessary.

First, the Declaration of Rights, the document read to William and Mary before they were formally offered the crown and then embodied in statute as part of the Bill of Rights later in 1689, provides a statement about the lawful extent of many of the royal prerogative powers that had been the cause of most debate and controversy earlier in the seventeenth century.[59] While the document was the subject of some debate, particularly in the Commons at the beginning of February 1689, its framing did not generate the kind of set-piece confrontations that characterized disputes about the wording of the offer of the crown.[60] This suggests that the Declaration was able to win support from tories as well as whigs, and that it was drafted very much as a response to what both tories and whigs agreed were abuses of royal power by James II, his ministers and judges, with the intention of 'vindicating and asserting their ancient rights and liberties'.[61] As Tim Harris has recently

56 John Spurr, 'The Church of England, Comprehension and the Toleration Act of 1689', *E.H.R.*, CIV (1989), 927–46.

57 M. Goldie, 'The Political Thought of the Anglican Revolution', in *The Revolutions of 1688*, ed. R. Beddard (Oxford, 1991), pp. 122–4.

58 Harris, *Revolution*, and Pincus, *1688*, may disagree about the nature of the revolution, but both are in no doubt that there *was* a revolution in 1688–9.

59 Cf. the discussions in Schwoerer, *Declaration of Rights, 1689*, which helpfully prints the text of the declaration at pp. 295–8, and Harris, *Revolution*, pp. 329–48.

60 Contrast Anchitell Grey, *Debates in the House of Commons from the year 1667 to the year 1694* (10 vols, 1773), IX, 42–4, 79–83, with pp. 46–52, 53–65, and *The Debate at Large, between the Lords and Commons … Relating to the Word Abdicated, and the Vacancy of the Throne…* (1695).

61 Schwoerer, *Declaration*, p. 296.

shown, there is a compelling case for regarding the Declaration of Rights as a bi-partisan achievement, but that does not mean that it should be seen as a limited, conservative document.[62]

The argument may be illustrated through an examination of four of the main clauses of the Declaration: those relating to the ecclesiastical commission, the suspending and dispensing powers and the standing army. On the first of these, there is no doubt that, contrary to the opinion of some recent historians, the ecclesiastical commission was a court.[63] The commissioners regarded themselves as a court and their proceedings were based on the procedures of ecclesiastical law. There is a strong argument for accepting the arguments of contemporaries, like Bishop Compton, who refused to recognize its authority on the ground that its establishment was 'directly contrary' to the statute of the Long Parliament in 1641 that had abolished the court of high commission.[64] But a few voices could be found, admittedly of figures closely associated with James's policies, such as Lord Chancellor Jeffreys and the propagandist Henry Care, who were prepared to argue that James's ecclesiastical commission was not the same as Charles I's court, that it used only ecclesiastical censures (rather than fines and imprisonment), and that the right to appoint commissioners to act on his behalf was an intrinsic part of the royal supremacy.[65]

The case of the suspending power raised related issues about the nature and extent of the royal supremacy. A powerful body of legal opinion, represented very visibly by the defence counsel at the trial of the seven bishops, argued that the power of the king to suspend penal laws in matters of religion was illegal. In support of their argument they relied very heavily on a resolution of the House of Commons to this effect in 1673 and, while the counsel for the prosecution responded, quite correctly, that a resolution of the Commons did not make law, a case could be made that Charles II, by withdrawing his Declaration of Indulgence, had accepted the arguments of the Commons that English monarchs had never possessed such a power.[66] Significantly, even the bench of judges presiding over the case of the seven bishops was divided over the legality of the suspending power, with Justice Powell stating that he could not find 'in any a case in all our laws. . . that there is any such power in the king'.[67] But, in 1688 there were lawyers who were prepared to defend it, arguing, as the earl of Shaftesbury had done in

62 Harris, *Revolution*, p. 334.

63 J.P. Kenyon, 'The Commission of Ecclesiastical Causes, 1687–8: A Reconsideration', *H.J.*, 34 (1991), 727–36.

64 *The Life of Dr Henry Compton, Lord Bishop of London* (1715?), p. 27.

65 J. Rose, *Godly Kingship in Restoration England: the Politics of the Royal Supremacy* (Cambridge, 2011), pp. 251–67.

66 *A Complete Collection of State Trials*, compiled by T. B. Howell (London, 1809–26), XII, 368.

67 *Ibid.*, p. 427.

1672, that as supreme head of the church the king possessed an intrinsic right, declared and guaranteed by the 1559 Act of Supremacy, to suspend *ecclesiastical* laws.[68]

The dispensing power raised a different set of issues. Whereas a significant body of legal opinion argued that the suspending power was an illegal abuse of the royal prerogative in all cases, as laws could only be suspended by the same authority that had made them, all were agreed both that a power to dispense individuals from the provisions of the law was an intrinsic part of the prerogative and that the king could not dispense with something that was *malum in se*, such as the laws of God. The key issue, therefore, was when it was lawful to dispense. When the framers of the Declaration condemned the dispensing power 'as it hath been assumed and exercised of late', they had in mind above all the mass dispensations from the Test Act and penal laws that had followed the case of *Godden v. Hales* in 1686. There is no doubt that this was a collusive action; there is no doubt that James II went to considerable lengths to remodel the bench to obtain a favourable verdict, dismissing six judges before the case was heard; there is no doubt that the verdict was controversial, with both Burnet and Morrice noting that many were unconvinced by the judges' reasoning.[69] Moreover, the king's actions after the trial, issuing dispensations to hundreds of people so that they were not obliged to qualify themselves for office by taking anglican communion, were commonly seen as an abuse of the prerogative, even by some who supported his right in principle. But the judgment itself had been a ringing endorsement, backed by a substantial body of legal opinion, not only of the king's right to dispense from the penal laws, but also of tory, neo-absolutist thought, asserting clearly and unequivocally, in the words of Lord Chief Justice Herbert, that 'the laws of England are the king's laws'.[70]

The final clause to be considered in this brief overview is one which might appear to offer some of the strongest support to W.A. Speck's claim that 'the Declaration of Right made new law in the guise of declaring the old': that 'the raising or keeping of a standing army within the kingdom in time of peace, unless it be with the consent of parliament, is against the law'.[71] This had certainly been an issue which had agitated Restoration parliaments and, in 1679, the Commons had finally passed a resolution that the maintenance of 'standing forces' within the kingdom was 'illegal'.[72]

68 'A Letter from a Person of Quality', in John Locke, *An Essay Concerning Toleration and Other Writings on Law and Politics 1667–1683*, ed. J. R. Milton and Philip Milton (Oxford, 2006), p. 341; Paul Seaward, 'Shaftesbury and the Royal Supremacy', in *Anthony Ashley Cooper, First Earl of Shaftesbury, 1621–1683* (Farnham, 2011), pp. 51–76.

69 Burnet, *History*, III, 97–100; *Morrice Entring Book*, ed. Goldie et al., III, 146–9.

70 *State Trials*, XI, 1303.

71 W.A. Speck, *Reluctant Revolutionaries. Englishmen and the Revolution of 1688* (Oxford, 1988), p. 162.

72 *C.J.*, IX, 581.

But, as has already been noted, parliamentary resolutions do not make law. There is no doubt that one of the most offensive features of the army under both Charles II and James II was the billeting of soldiers in private houses, an action which contravened both the Petition of Right of 1628 and the Disbanding Act of 1679. But the Declaration of Rights went well beyond billeting and claimed as law something that could not be justified on the basis of any statute before 1689. Even so, it should be remembered that the claim in the Declaration was not entirely spurious; through the Restoration there was a substantial body of opinion which believed that the keeping of a standing army without parliamentary consent was illegal.[73]

The point is not that the Declaration of Rights was a conservative or a radical document, not that its framers believed that they were reasserting the known law or that they were making new law under the guise of declaring the old. These comments have, instead, been intended to highlight the fact that before 1688 the nature and extent of the prerogative powers of the king were contested, particularly on a series of issues which had considerable significance for the rights and liberties of the subject. On some of these issues legal opinion was deeply divided; on others a consensus probably existed that the way in which the king was exercising his powers was against the law, which is one reason why the independence of the judiciary became such an important issue.[74] But on all of the issues James was able to find judges who were prepared to justify his exercise of his prerogative as lawful. In this context it is hardly surprising that many people feared the growth of arbitrary power, nor that they were determined that the revolution settlement would restrict monarchical power.[75] It is clear that the Declaration of Rights was intended to, and did, act as a limitation on the royal prerogative. What triumphed in 1689 was not 'the law' over the illegalities of James II; rather, it was the triumph of a particular interpretation of the law, one which limited the prerogative in ways that Charles II, James II and many of their supporters would have found unacceptable. Moreover, looking to the future, it embedded in English law an interpretation of the prerogative which did much to reassure Englishmen that their rights and liberties could no longer be invaded by the exercise of arbitrary power.

The way in which the revolution settlement contributed to the transformation of English political culture can be further illuminated by a considera-

73 Lois G. Schwoerer, *'No Standing Armies!' The Antiarmy Ideology in Seventeenth-Century England* (Baltimore, MD, 1974), pp. 107–10, 120–1.

74 It was finally resolved in the Act of Settlement in 1701 which provided that, for the future, judges' commissions should be issued *quam diu se bene gesserint*.

75 The importance of the law courts in the construction of Stuart absolutism is vividly highlighted by Roger Morrice's comment, on walking through Westminster Hall on 4 February 1689, that it was the first occasion on which he had been there 'without feare' and 'with true liberty and freedome' since 1662. *Morrice Entring Book*, ed. Goldie et al., IV, 520.

tion of the resolution passed by the House of Commons on 29 January 1689, agreed to by the House of Lords later the same day, and subsequently given legislative force in the Bill of Rights, 'that it hath been found, by Experience, to be inconsistent with the Safety and Welfare of this Protestant Kingdom, to be governed by a Popish Prince'.[76] Arguably this resolution was of even more significance than the Declaration of Rights, though it has been largely ignored by historians, with the exception of Henry Horwitz, perhaps because it seemed a natural and obvious conclusion to draw after the events of James II's reign and the revolution itself.[77] Almost certainly, the neglect of historians is also a consequence of the absence of debate at the time: the surviving sources indicate that the resolution passed through both houses with little discussion and even less opposition.[78] Yet in some ways this was the most remarkable act of the revolution. Essentially the convention was now doing precisely what the exclusionists had been arguing for in 1679–81, precisely what had then caused such deep divisions within the nation, namely excluding catholics from the succession to the English crown. And the implications were exactly the same as in 1679–81. Parliament was asserting its right, this time successfully, to deliberate on and change the law relating to the succession. Then, the cavalier and tory position had been that the succession could not be changed, that even a parliamentary statute could not take away the duke of York's rights as heir. As Lord Chief Justice Finch had said during the trial of John Hampden in 1638, acts of parliament might 'take away flowers and ornaments of the crown, but not the crown itself', and specifically that they could not 'bar a succession'.[79] As one of its first acts, just a week after assembling, the convention asserted parliament's right to a co-ordinate power with the crown, precisely the point condemned by the University of Oxford in its comprehensive statement of tory anglican ideology in the wake of the Rye House Plot.[80] The resolution of 29 January and, subsequently, the Bill of Rights placed a final nail in the pretensions of any future English monarch to an 'absolute power'.

But the significance of this resolution was not merely constitutional. William's invasion had provided a solution to the threat posed by James II to both protestantism and English liberties; the resolution provided guarantees for the future. One of the most destabilizing features of English politics

76 *C.J.*, X, 15; *L.J.*, XIV, 110. As reported to, and agreed by, the Lords, the resolution read 'the Protestant Religion'.

77 Henry Horwitz, '1689 (and All That)', *Parliamentary History*, VI (1987), 23–32; Howard Nenner, 'Sovereignty and the Succession in 1688–9', in *The World of William and Mary: Anglo-Dutch Perspectives on the Revolution of 1688–89*, ed. Dale Hoak and Mordechai Feingold (Stanford, CA, 1996), p. 115.

78 *Grey's Debates*, IX, 26–9.

79 *State Trials*, III, 1235.

80 *A Collection of Scarce and Valuable Tracts*, ed. Sir W. Scott (13 vols, London, 1809–15), VIII, 301–3.

throughout the seventeenth century had been the presence of a catholic faction at court. One of the biggest problem for all Stuart monarchs was that they were not trusted, and, above all, they were not trusted to defend and support the protestant interest. This point was made very clearly by John Birch, one of the few members of the convention to have served in the parliamentary armies of the 1640s:

> These forty years we have been scrambling for our Religion, and have saved but little of it. We have been striving against *Anti-Christ*, Popery, and Tyranny.... King *James* I was so fond of the *Spanish* match ... that he lost the *Palatinate* by it.... When once King *Charles* I married a Papist, all things, from that time forward, went in a contrary way; all things tended to Popery, and a Civil War ... I remember what was said in this House, when the late King *James* [i.e. James II] was married to this Queen: 'Men will follow their interest; and it was his interest to destroy the Protestant Religion, our Laws and Liberties.'[81]

Ultimately, the threat to the Reformation – to protestantism – was an internal one far more than an external one. The real danger was not from Louis XIV, and still less from the pope, but rather from those at court who wished to imitate and emulate him. European history over the previous century taught Englishmen all too clearly the lesson that the greatest threat to the protestantism of a state was to be ruled by a catholic.

Thus, the revolution played a crucial role in bringing political stability to England, both by safeguarding English liberties and by guaranteeing the protestantism of the English state. The dynastic revolution of 1688–9 brought to the throne not merely a protestant, but arguably *the* leader of the protestant interest in Europe.[82] The dynastic settlement guaranteed that England would continue to be governed by a line of protestants for the future. The English *élite* knew that their catholic neighbours were a small minority, who could present no real threat by themselves. After 1689, therefore, the threat of popery and arbitrary power came from England's external enemies, from the exiled Jacobites and above all the French. Instead of causing divisions within English political society, as it had done before 1688, the catholic threat now united Englishmen and helped to provide at least rhetorical justification for a century of warfare.[83]

Educated Englishmen in the late seventeenth century were all too aware of events in Europe.[84] Though separate from Europe, they were part of it,

[81] *Grey's Debates*, IX, 26–7.

[82] Tony Claydon, *William III* (2002), ch. 1; Wout Troost, *William III, the Stadholder King: A Political Biography* (Aldershot, 2005), pp. 95–9.

[83] Linda Colley, *Britons: Forging the Nation 1707–1837* (New Haven, CT, 1992), ch. 1, esp. pp. 18–43.

[84] Tony Claydon, *Europe and the Making of England, 1660–1760* (Cambridge, 2007), esp. ch. 1.

and the patterns of European history were not encouraging. Over much of the continent absolutist monarchies were in the ascendant and the role of representative institutions was in decline; they were abolished, turned into rubber-stamps, or simply ignored.[85] There were very real fears that England might go the same way. Similarly, protestantism was in crisis, as it was pushed back geographically by an assertive Counter-Reformation. Again, there were genuine fears that England might follow Bohemia, Poland and, most recently, France. In the eyes of many, indeed, these two processes were linked – popery and absolutism supported each other and flourished together. In the Netherlands William of Orange was very conscious of being in the front-line of this struggle. Geography meant that England was not quite so exposed, but the presence of a catholic interest at court almost continuously through the seventeenth century raised fears. Throughout the century, there were group of politicians who were suspicious of the court, who distrusted its intentions and who feared that it was about to betray the Reformation. Put together, these two fears of popery and absolutism were hugely destabilizing. They contributed, in large measure, to the crisis of the late 1630s and 1640s and that of the 1670s and 1680s.[86] But the constitutional settlement of 1689, especially the combination of the dynastic aspects of that settlement with the limitations on the prerogative, effected a decisive break with the past. The position of parliament within the constitution was guaranteed and strengthened; the protestant character of the nation was secured. England was set firmly on a path that, in the eighteenth century, was to give her both an identity and constitutional and political structures that were distinctive in Europe. The change in political culture was, of course, a process and developments earlier in the century undoubtedly contributed. But, within months of the revolution, England had become one of the leaders of the protestant interest in Europe, fighting a war against Louis XIV's France, funded by parliament through unprecedented loans, subscribed with some alacrity by the London merchant community and others, and new taxes.

III

Another theme that has received little attention in this volume is the causes of the breakdown of the regime in 1688. It is one thing to claim that 1688–9 witnessed a dynastic and constitutional revolution that had far-reaching effects on English politics; it is quite another thing to argue that that outcome was aimed at or planned by any of the participants. From

85 H.G. Koenigsberger, '*Dominium Regale* or *Dominium Politicum et Regale*', in *Politicians and Virtuosi: Essays in Early Modern History* (1986), pp. 1–25; A.R. Myers, *Parliaments and Estates in Europe to 1789* (1975).

86 For an account that emphasizes the European context, see Scott, *England's Troubles*, Part 1.

different perspectives and with different emphases many historians writing since the tercentenary have portrayed the revolution as unintended. Robert Beddard has called it 'unexpected', while Speck describes 'reluctant revolutionaries', forced into action by William's intervention and James's flight.[87] Mark Goldie has anatomized those high church tories whose opposition to James was intended to force him back into alliance with them, but who, by revealing the weakness of the regime, helped to pave the way for William's invasion.[88] Views such as these have recently been radically challenged by Steve Pincus, who sees the revolution as the outcome of a struggle between two competing visions for the modernization of the English state.[89] What, then, were the aims of the participants in the revolution?

A reappraisal of James II and his policies is long overdue. The view of the king as a 'fool', bent on a course of action that was 'suicidal', remains deeply engrained in the literature.[90] Even those sympathetic to him tend to portray him as an old man in a hurry, blinded by the zeal of a convert to the depth of English anti-popery and rashly determined to push through his policies even at the expense of alienating many of his most loyal supporters.[91] Much attention has focused on whether he was committed to the policy of toleration to which he publicly committed himself in 1687 or whether it was merely a tactical manoeuvre to strengthen the position of his catholic co-religionists. The evidence on this subject, as on so many aspects of James's policies, is deeply contradictory, and not only because he appears to have held different positions at different points in his life. James was much more open than his brother and many reports survive of audiences in which he discussed matters of state at length, but he clearly adapted his comments to his audience.[92] The French ambassador, Paul Barillon, appeared to enjoy a relaxed, even intimate relationship, with the king, but did James's praise of Louis XIV's revocation of the edict of Nantes, for example, reflect his true distaste for protestantism, or was it merely part of his attempt to cultivate good relations with his cousin?[93] But James's personal views on toleration,

[87] R.A. Beddard, 'The Unexpected Whig Revolution of 1688', in *Revolutions of 1688*, ed. Beddard, pp. 11–101; Speck, *Reluctant Revolutionaries*.

[88] Goldie, 'Anglican Revolution'.

[89] Pincus, *1688*, pp. 6–10.

[90] The quotations are taken from D. Ogg, *England in the Age of James II and William III* (Oxford, 1955), pp. 193–4.

[91] John Miller, *James II: A Study in Kingship* (Hove, 1977).

[92] Best known are the reports of his conversations with Barillon (T.N.A., P.R.O. 31/3), some of which are reprinted in Sir John Dalrymple, *Memoirs of Great Britain and Ireland* (2 vols, 1771–3), II, App. Pt 1. Even more revealing, however, is 'A Letter from a Jesuit of Liege', in *Three Letters* [1689?], p. 1. For the authenticity of this document, see Thomas M. McCoog, 'A Letter from a Jesuit of Liège (1687)?', *Recusant History*, XXX (2010), 88–106.

[93] Dalrymple, *Memoirs*, II, Pt 1, 177; B.L., Add. MS 34502: despatch of Pedro Ronquillo, 5 Apr. 1686.

however interesting biographically, reveal little about the course of events during his reign.

What was James II trying to achieve? In broad outline, from the meeting of the second session of his only parliament in November 1685, the king, buoyed by the defeat of the rebellions of Argyle and Monmouth, made it clear that he would not be satisfied with the mere allowance to catholics of freedom to practice their religion; he was determined to be able to employ them in military and civil offices. As the earl of Halifax observed, James had 'discovered what he would be at', though the full scope of the king's ambitions only emerged gradually.[94] He was aiming for far more than toleration for catholics; his policy of 'catholicization' was intended to establish them on a footing of equality with his anglican subjects. Repeal of the Test Acts, allowing them to sit in parliament and serve in state offices, was the central plank of this policy, the implications of which were clear with the appointment from the summer of 1686 of catholic J.P.s, judges and privy councillors, as well as military officers. But James's concerns were much broader, as was revealed by the encouragement of catholic schools across the country, by establishing a catholic college at Oxford through the appointment of the Jesuit Bonaventure Gifford as president of Magdalen College, and by the recognition of catholic bishops. It was also essential, from James's point of view, that the position of catholicism be secured for the future. He was reported to have said, 'I growing old, must make great steps, otherwise ... I shall leave you worse than I found you.'[95] He was conscious that his heir presumptive was a protestant and, even after the birth of the prince of Wales on 10 June 1688, he must have feared that a regent would lack the authority to defend his achievements. So key measures, such as the repeal of the Test Acts, could not rest on prerogative power alone; if he was going to secure lasting changes in the position of catholicism within England, then he needed to secure repeal by parliament. James's long-term aims, however, remain obscure. He clearly expected that the ending of the privileges enjoyed by anglicans, combined with missionary activity, would remove the prejudices of many protestants and lead to widespread conversion. But we simply lack the evidence to know whether he believed that the rights of protestants, as well as catholics, would be guaranteed by a legal toleration, or whether in due course he expected that the success of the catholic revival would render toleration irrelevant.

Once James had become convinced that the anglican tories could not be persuaded to support the repeal of the Test Acts, he issued his Declaration of Indulgence in April 1687, suspending all penal laws in matters of religion and offering a general toleration, in an attempt to construct an alliance

94 *The Parliamentary History of England from the Earliest Period to the Year 1803* (36 vols, 1806–20), IV, 1371.

95 *Three Letters*, p. 1.

of dissenters and catholics. Steve Pincus has suggestively pointed to the influence on James and his court of a Gallican catholic absolutism, but the specifically English context of the king's policies also needs to be appreciated.[96] James's embrace of toleration *may* have been tactical, but it was also a reversion to earlier Stuart policies. After the fall of the earl of Clarendon in 1667, Charles II had constructed a ministry that combined catholics like Clifford with dissenters like Ashley, and in 1672 he issued a Declaration of Indulgence, very similar to James II's, in an attempt to construct a broad base of support for the war against the Dutch Republic.[97] It is important to recognize, however, that James II was not merely trying to construct an alliance of two minorities excluded from the Restoration anglican church-state. As Archbishop Sheldon had succeeded in demonstrating in 1676 with the so-called Compton census, the two groups provided too narrow a foundation on which to build a successful policy.[98] In this sense Halifax's well-known scepticism about James's 'scheme' in 1687–8, reassuring the prince of Orange that it was 'impractical', was well founded.[99] The key to James's policy, however, was not numbers. He was, rather, trying to re-orientate public debate of his policies away from the division between protestant and catholic to focus instead on support for, and opposition to, toleration. The former, the dangers of popery, was the favoured ground of the anglican clergy, who, as Burnet reminds us, engaged in a highly co-ordinated programme of publication between 1686 and 1688.[100] James certainly encouraged the publication and dissemination of treatises, from the royal printer, Henry Hills, and Abraham Woodhead's press at Oxford in particular, intended to demonstrate the truth and merits of the catholic faith. But more important, in this context, are the controversial pamphlets and news-sheets, published in 1687 and 1688 by figures like Henry Care and William Penn, which presented a case for the repeal of the Test Acts and, more generally, mounted a defence of toleration against anglican intolerance.[101] This was not an unrealistic strategy. As Mark Goldie has pointed out, '"Presbyterian" politics' in the 1670s and 1680s extended far beyond those who attended dissenting meeting houses, and on issues such as comprehension the 'Church' and 'dissenting' parties were more or less equal in number.[102]

96 Pincus, *1688*, ch. 5.

97 This period lacks a modern study, but see Maurice Lee, *The Cabal 1667–74* (Urbana, IL, 1965).

98 *The Compton Census of 1676: A Critical Edition*, ed. Anne Whiteman (1986).

99 Dalrymple, *Memoirs*, II, Pt 1, 196.

100 Burnet, *History*, III, 104–5.

101 Scott Sowerby, *Making Toleration: The Repealers and the Glorious Revolution* (Cambridge, MA, forthcoming 2013).

102 *Morrice Entring Book*, ed. Goldie et al., I, 153–4. See also Richard Davis, 'The "Presbyterian" Opposition and the Emergence of Party in the House of Lords in the Reign of Charles II', in *Party and Management in Parliament, 1660–1784*, ed. C. Jones (Leicester, 1984), pp. 1–35.

What about the alleged 'absolutism' of James II? There is no doubt that he was committed to strengthening the power of the crown. Some of the ways in which James sought to stretch – or, in the eyes of his opponents, abuse – his prerogative powers have already been discussed, and it is difficult to sustain the argument that this was only done in pursuit of his policy of 'catholicization'. In Ireland, when new charters were issued to corporations, James was determined, against the advice of his catholic lord deputy, Tyrconnell, to reserve for the crown the right to appoint and remove corporation officers, thus making it possible for a future protestant monarch to reverse the gains made by catholics. The 'imperial pretensions of the English crown' trumped the interests of Irish catholics.[103] More generally, before the birth of a male heir in the summer of 1688 there is no evidence at all that James contemplated attempting to change the succession, although that option was certainly canvassed. The king remained committed to the notion that the law relating to the succession was unalterable, as had been argued by his supporters during the exclusion crisis.[104] It is not necessary, however, to look to France to find the model for James II's absolutism. A strong English tradition of absolutist thought, stretching back at least to the reign – and the writings – of James I and distinct in some respects from French ideas, was available to James II, as it had been to his brother.[105] There was, in fact, no single definition of absolute monarchy, and by the Restoration there was a rich variety of absolutist writing, represented better, perhaps, by the sermons and tracts of high anglican clergy than by the posthumous publication of Filmer's *Patriarcha* (1680).[106] England possessed a stronger tradition than France of criticism of absolutist theory, conflating absolute monarchy with tyranny and arbitrary rule in a manner which exercised a profound influence over later historical studies.[107] But we now need no reminder that absolutism meant rule within the law; absolute rulers were constrained not only by divine and natural law, but also by the laws of the kingdom. James II recognized that statute law could not be unmade by him alone, just as he recognized that he could not tax his subjects without their consent in parliament. He spent most of his reign attempting to secure the *parliamen-*

103 Harris, *Revolution*, p. 136.

104 The very argument that had been used to defend the rights of James himself in 1679–81. Archives des Affaires Etrangères, CPA 164, fo. 28, quoted in Miller, *James II*, p. 126.

105 *King James VI and I: Political Writings*, ed. J.P. Sommerville (Cambridge, 1994); *idem*, 'Absolutism and Royalism', in *The Cambridge History of Political Thought 1450–1700*, ed. J.H. Burns and M. Goldie (Cambridge, 1991), pp. 347–73.

106 James Daly, 'The Idea of Absolute Monarchy in Seventeenth-Century England', *H.J.*, XXI (1978), 227–50; M. Goldie, 'John Locke and Anglican Royalism', *Political Studies*, XXXI (1983), 69–71.

107 E.g. Algernon Sidney, *Discourses Concerning Government*, ed. Thomas G. West (Indianapolis, IN, 1990), pp. 267–70, 398–9, 452–4; J. Locke, *Two Treatises of Government* (1689), bk 1, § 80.

tary repeal of the Test Acts, and he appears to have recognized that the acts could not be repealed by a parliament packed with dispensed catholics.

Should the revolution, then, be viewed as a verdict on James II's government or on Restoration government more generally? This has been one of the questions at the heart of debate about the revolution ever since 1689. To some extent the answer is both. As has already been noted, the revolution provided a resolution to a series of profoundly debstabilizing issues in seventeenth-century politics. It secured the English polity from the threat of popery and it determined that the English monarchy was not absolute. What is more, it is clear that these outcomes were intended by some of the participants in the events of October to December 1688 and that they were the objective of the framers of the revolution settlement in January and February 1689. But to say that the revolution provided an answer is not the same as saying that these problems 'caused' the revolution. Indeed, at the end of 1684 it is very difficult to imagine circumstances in which there could have been a similar reaction to Charles II's government, despite the fears of popery and arbitrary government, which had provoked the crisis of 1678–81 and which continued to infect English politics. The exclusion crisis had demonstrated precisely why Charles II's government was unlikely to disintegrate: a substantial part of the English nation saw a strong monarchy as a bulwark against a recurrence of the disorder of the 1640s and 1650s.[108]

Any explanation of the revolution of 1688–9, therefore, needs to give due weight to contingent factors. Three points stand out in particular. First, James's policy was profoundly destabilizing. His pursuit of 'catholicization' alienated a key group of the strongest supporters of the monarchy, those who had rallied to the defence of James's own right to the succession in 1679–81, who had provided the foot-soldiers throughout the country during Charles II's campaign against the exculsionists during the last four years of his reign, and who had, in the parliament of 1685, enthusiastically voted James II the largest revenue of any Stuart monarch.[109] But the tories were not only important numerically. They were also more significant than any other group in providing and disseminating a powerful monarchical ideology in the aftermath of the civil wars, the 'generation of men ... sprung up among us, who', according to Locke, 'would flatter princes with an Opinion, that they have a Divine Right to absolute Power'.[110] As hinted in Locke's description, however, tory absolutism was an expression of tory anglicanism.

108 Harris, *Restoration*, ch. 4.

109 Despite rumours, no attempt was made in the parliament of 1685 to limit royal power by imposing conditions on the granting of supply. *Memoirs of Sir John Reresby*, ed. Andrew Browning (Glasgow, 1936), p. 362. The contrast with the situation in 1689–90 is illuminating. Clayton Roberts, 'The Constitutional Significance of the Financial Settlement of 1690', *H.J.*, XX (1977), 59–76.

110 Locke, *Two Treatises*, bk 1, § 3.

James II's actions presented them with an awful dilemma. The doctrine of non-resistance did not require that they give the king active support; nor did they take recourse in inaction, at least not until their attempts to force James to change his policies and return to his 'old friends' were overtaken by events in November and December 1688. But, for many, the king's assault on true religion and promotion of a false one demanded that they oppose his policies by all lawful methods – by preaching; by publishing; by petitioning, as the seven bishops did in May 1688 in protest against the declaration of indulgence; and even by refusing to sign an abhorrence of William's invasion.[111]

Second, James failed in his efforts to set the agenda for discussion in the public sphere. Despite attracting significant support from former whig opponents, James's propagandists were unable to re-orientate the debate about his policies into one about toleration and intolerance.[112] Anglican writers worked hard to keep popery at the forefront of people's minds, and the stream of controversial and polemical anti-catholic pamphlets by figures like Sherlock, Stillingfleet, Tenison, Claggett and Wake was supplemented by the re-printing of earlier works.[113] Moreover, sympathy for persecuted dissenting ministers and support for comprehension were not, of course, the same as a commitment to toleration; many presbyterians themselves remained ambivalent about toleration and retained a residual attachment to the concept of a national church.[114] Anglican tories waged a vigorous and effective campaign to woo the dissenters, culminating in Sancroft himself making a commitment to some form of comprehension.[115] But James's bigger problem was that he simply was not trusted. This was not only because a key component of the English tradition of anti-popery was that catholics could not be trusted, but also because there were daily reminders, in reports from France and even Ireland, that, once catholics were in a position of power, persecution would follow, whatever legal guarantees had been offered earlier.[116] James's own earlier apparently enthusiastic support for persecution

111 Goldie, 'Anglican Revolution'; *Morrice Entring Book*, ed. Goldie et al., IV, 322.

112 Mark Goldie, 'John Locke's Circle and James II', *H.J.*, 35 (1992), 557–86.

113 A clear sense of the scale and co-ordination of this campaign can be gleaned from *A Preservative against Popery* (3 vols, 1738), a re-publication of many of the texts from the revolutionary period in the context of a later scare about the spread of popery.

114 See e.g. Morrice's description of non-presbyterian dissenters as 'fanaticks'. *Morrice Entring Book*, ed. Goldie et al., IV, 83, 261, 264, 274.

115 Robert Beddard, 'Observations of a London Clergyman on the Revolution of 1688–9: Being an Excerpt from the Autobiography of Dr William Wake', *The Guildhall Miscellany*, II, 9 (1967), 406–17.

116 Claydon, *Europe and the Making of England*, pp. 162–5; Alasdair Raffe, *The Culture of Controversy: Religious Arguments in Scotland, 1660–1714* (Woodbridge, 2012), pp. 109–10. Roger Morrice's *Entring Book* is full of reports of events in France: see vols 3–4 *passim*.

in England and, especially, Scotland merely confirmed such prejudices.[117] Halifax's famous warning that 'You are therefore to be hugged now, onely that you may be the better squeezed at another time', seemed all too plausible.[118] Perhaps James's biggest failing, given the course to which he was committed, was to recognize that he desperately needed to build trust, even among many of those who had most to gain from his policies.

The third and the most unexpected contingent factor in 1688 was the invasion of William of Orange. That William wished to intervene is not in itself surprising, and it had little to do with English domestic politics. He believed that both the protestant cause in Europe and, above all, the security of the Dutch republic were threatened by the aggression and ambitions of Louis XIV, and England offered perhaps the best way of redressing the balance of power.[119] He had been disappointed that his marriage to Princess Mary in 1677 had not led to a closer alliance, and through most of the 1680s his relations with his uncle had been strained. By the winter of 1687–8 the clouds of war were gathering and the close relations between James II and Louis XIV suggested that the best that William could hope for was English neutrality. But a renewal of the Anglo-French alliance which had almost destroyed the Republic in 1672 appeared a real threat. William probably made the decision to invade in May 1688. Certainly by June plans were being made and the invasion armada began to be assembled. William's own dynastic ambitions seem of little relevance: what he wanted was effective control of English foreign policy, though he surely realized that the most effective way of securing this was by seizing the crown.[120] What is remarkable is not that William wanted to launch an invasion, but that he could. As Jonathan Israel has pointed out, the invasion was impossible without the support of the States of Holland and the States General. Given the attitude of both bodies through the 1680s, their readiness to declare war against England and France, to launch a pre-emptive strike against England and to entrust their armed forces to the stadholder all represent dramatic shifts of policy, which are all the more remarkable as the resources of the Dutch state – an army of at least 21,000 men, including the best of their regiments, and a fleet of some 500 vessels – were being committed to what can only be described as a highly risky strategy.[121] The Dutch were braving the autumn gales to launch a combined operation, of a scale unparalleled

[117] See e.g. his well publicized speech to the Scottish parliament in 1681 demanding action to suppress 'Seditious and Rebellious Conventicles'. *His Majesties Gracious Letter to his Parliament of Scotland: With the Speech of His Royal Highness the Duke…* (1681), p. 5.

[118] *The Works of George Savile, Marquis of Halifax*, ed. M. Brown (3 vols, Oxford, 1989), I, 252.

[119] Claydon, *William III*, pp. 28–35.

[120] How secure could William have felt at the head of an Anglo-Dutch army in Europe with James II, either in England or in exile, still as king *de iure*?

[121] Jonathan I. Israel, 'The Dutch Role in the Glorious Revolution', in *The Anglo-Dutch*

in European history, against a state with a large army and a powerful navy. Failure, even getting bogged down in a military campaign in England, would have left them dangerously exposed to the armies of Louis XIV. And it very nearly did not happen. The support of Amsterdam was essential, for both finance and materials, but only at the end of September did the city council, provoked by Louis XIV's intensification of the *guerre de commerce*, finally give its backing to William.[122]

IV

The essays in this volume are linked by two agendas. First, all agree that the events of 1688–9 were revolutionary. Second, they share the belief that our understanding of the revolution can be enhanced by the British, Atlantic and European perspectives that have played such a large part in defining recent scholarship on the early modern period as a whole. All of these approaches have their critics, and all have sometimes been subject to exaggerated claims for their novelty. But there is no doubt that they have forced us to address new questions about the revolution and to approach old questions in fresh ways. By bringing together some of this work in a volume that is, quite deliberately, not anglocentric in focus, we hope that we have illuminated both the interactions between the different parts of the Atlantic archipelago, its colonial possessions and Europe during the second great crisis of the Stuart monarchy, and some of the peculiarities of the experiences of the various territories subject to Stuart rule. This afterword has been more anglocentric, partly in order to address some of the major historical debates that it was not possible to cover in earlier chapters. It seemed important to make that point that 1688–9 marks a decisive moment in the transformation of *English* political culture and of the *English* state. But it must be emphasized that, while some of the revolutionaries were keen to implement changes that contributed to that transformation, the key event of the revolution, the removal of James, was dependent on a series of contingencies. There is no doubt that, by the spring of 1688 and arguably much earlier, James's regime was in crisis; the outcome of that crisis and the role of James in any re-structured English/British polity was far from certain. I want to conclude by suggesting some ways in which the transformation of the English state links to the concerns of British, Atlantic and European histories.

One of the main arguments of this chapter has been that the revolution removed two of the most destabilizing features of English politics in

Moment: Essays on the Glorious Revolution and its World Impact, ed. J.I. Israel (Cambridge, 1991), pp. 105–11.

122 *Ibid.*, pp. 112–19.

the seventeenth century: the beliefs that English liberties were being undermined by the crown and that popery at court was threatening the cause of true religion. The removal of these fears helped to unleash the power of the English state. Despite some residual, and not unjustified, concerns about the absolutist ambitions of William III, the English *élite* were prepared to trust their monarch with unprecedented sums of money, to commit themselves to involvement in war on an unparalleled scale, and to collaborate in the rapid development of what became arguably the most powerful fiscal-military state in eighteenth-century Europe.[123] But what were the implications of these developments for the other parts of the Stuart realms?

First, to an extent that has rarely been adequately recognized by eighteenth-century historians, the revolution turned England (and then Britain) into a European state. Only the accident of William's early death meant that the 'union' between England and the Dutch Republic was relatively short-lived – and, in 1689, it was by no means certain that William and Mary would have no children. By the time of William's death the implications of the revolutionary settlement of the crown had been made explicit, with the vesting of succession after the death of Anne in the electors of Hanover; from 1714 the dynastic union with Hanover put Britain at the heart of the European state-system throughout the rest of the eighteenth century. One of the most significant implications of this, as has been revealed by Andrew Thompson, was that England/Britain became the leader of the protestant interest in Europe, not only in resisting the catholic absolutism of Louis XIV, but also, particularly under George I and George II, in playing an active role in the religious politics of the Holy Roman Empire and providing a natural destination for successive waves of protestant refugees from Europe.[124]

Second, the development of English power transformed its relationship with its colonies, both in the Americas and in the East. The revolution in England facilitated the reaction in the colonies against those moves towards greater metropolitan control, represented most strikingly by the Dominion of New England.[125] In some ways the revolution created highly localized and diverse governmental and constitutional structures, which, in the coming years, were relatively easily adapted and extended to incorporate within the empire very different territories, including the overwhelmingly catholic Minorca and Quebec. But in important ways the revolution tied the colonies more closely into the imperial economic system. Commerce, above all

[123] Mark Goldie and Clare Jackson, 'Williamite Tyranny and the Whig Jacobites', in *Redefining William III: The Impact of the King-Stadholder in International Context*, ed. Esther Mijers and David Onnekink (Aldershot, 2007), pp. 177–99. See Miller, *James II*, p. 176 and n. for James's awareness of William's absolutist inclinations.

[124] Andrew C. Thompson, *Britain, Hanover and the Protestant Interest, 1688–1756* (Woodbridge, 2006).

[125] See Chapter 8 of this book and Owen Stanwood, *The Empire Reformed. English America in the Age of the Glorious Revolution* (Philadelphia, PA, 2011).

trade with the Americas, was essential in providing the revenues on which the fiscal-military state depended, quite apart from the colonies' growing importance in supplying the materials necessary to keep the navy afloat. The defence and expansion of the North Atlantic and, increasingly, the Indian trade became ever more important aspects of state policy.[126] Even more directly, the emergence of the English/British fiscal-military state put the colonies in the front line of its defence. Jamaica and Barbados, Pennsylvania and New York, and Bengal all had far more direct experience of warfare in the eighteenth century than the inhabitants of England.

Third, the revolution triggered a significant shift in the balance of power within the British Isles. The immediate effect of events in England during the winter of 1688–9 was to provoke and facilitate a catholic revolution in Ireland under the leadership of Earl Tyrconnel, James II's lord deputy, aimed at creating an Irish state independent of English control. In Scotland the collapse of James's power provided the opportunity for a presbyterian revolution that installed William as king, but which was more radical than in England and which partly dismantled the mechanisms through which Stuart kings had controlled the country. But the rapid development and expansion of the *English* state, a process in which the revolution of 1688 was of central importance, changed the balance of power in the three kingdoms fundamentally. The English revolution was exported to Ireland by force in 1690–1; the protestant minority was then bluntly reminded of its dependence on the power of the English state by the passage of the Declaratory Act, asserting the constitutional supremacy of the British parliament, in 1720. When the Scottish parliament played its trump card in 1704 by threatening to settle the crown away from the house of Hanover, it, too, was subjected to a brutal lesson in realpolitik, as the passage of the Aliens Act by the English parliament reminded the Scots of the economic and political advantages of union. The Act of Union agreed by the two kingdoms in 1707 guaranteed the security essential to the English state if it was to continue to pursue its international ambitions. The Scots and, to a lesser extent, the Irish certainly came to enjoy the benefits of empire in the later eighteenth century,[127] but the British state, as created at the beginning of the century, was dominated by England and the apparatus of the fiscal-military state was overwhelmingly English.

The kind of dynastic agglomeration that the British state became in the eighteenth century was not unusual in Europe. One only has to look at the Habsburg monarchy to see another example of what H.G. Koenigsberger

126 Philip J. Stern, *The Company-State: Corporate Sovereignty and the Early Modern Foundations of the British Empire in India* (New York, 2011) both highlights the importance of India within the eighteenth-century empire and emphasizes the variety of 'constitutional' forms in the empire's governance.

127 Colley, *Britons*, esp. chs 3–4.

described as a 'composite' monarchy.[128] With the acquisition of Silesia in 1740, Frederick II found himself the ruler of a territory with a majority catholic population, as the English were in Ireland. The Dutch Republic was another major power with strong representative institutions. The French possessed a rival commercial empire in India and the Americas. But it can be argued that, by the end of the eighteenth century, the British empire was even more complex – geographically, ethnically, religiously and constitutionally – than the Habsburg empire or any of its other rivals. The peculiarities of the British state – above all, the interaction between its English, British, European and colonial dimensions – deserve greater attention. Among the great European powers the British state of the eighteenth century was distinctive, in polity, in economy and in composition. This state was, in significant measure, the creation of the revolution of 1688.

128 Koenigsberger, '*Dominium Regale* or *Dominium Politicum et Regale*'; J.H. Elliott, 'A Europe of Composite Monarchies', *Past and Present*, 137 (1992), 48–71. The tendency towards the creation of unitary states in the eighteenth century, while plausible when viewed from within Britain, looks very different, however, from the vantage points of Hanover, Boston, Quebec or Calcutta.

Index

STUDIES IN EARLY MODERN CULTURAL, POLITICAL AND SOCIAL HISTORY

I

Women of Quality
Accepting and Contesting Ideals of Femininity in England, 1690–1760
Ingrid H. Tague

II

Restoration Scotland, 1660–1690
Royalist Politics, Religion and Ideas
Clare Jackson

III

Britain, Hanover and the Protestant Interest, 1688–1756
Andrew C. Thompson

IV

Hanover and the British Empire, 1700–1837
Nick Harding

V

The Personal Rule of Charles II, 1681–85
Grant Tapsell

VI

Royalism, Print and Censorship in Revolutionary England
Jason McElligott

VII

The English Catholic Community, 1688–1745
Politics, Culture and Ideology
Gabriel Glickman

VIII

England and the 1641 Irish Rebellion
Joseph Cope

IX

Culture and Politics at the Court of Charles II, 1660–1685
Matthew Jenkinson

X

Commune, Country and Commonwealth:
The People of Cirencester, 1117–1643
David Rollison

XI

An Enlightenment Statesman in Whig Britain
Lord Shelburne in Context, 1737–1805
Edited by Nigel Aston and Clarissa Campbell Orr

XII
London's News Press and the Thirty Years War
Jayne E. E. Boys

XIII
God, Duty and Community in English Economic Life, 1660–1720
Brodie Waddell

XIV
Remaking English Society: Social Relations and Social Change in Early Modern England
Edited by Steve Hindle, Alexandra Shepard and John Walter

XV
Common Law and Enlightenment in England, 1689–1750
Julia Rudolph

XVI
The Final Crisis of the Stuart Monarchy: The Revolutions of 1688–91 in their British, Atlantic and European Contexts
Edited by Stephen Taylor and Tim Harris

XVII
The Civil Wars after 1660: Public Remembering in Late Stuart England
Matthew Neufeld

XVIII
The Nature of the English Revolution Revisited
Edited by Stephen Taylor and Grant Tapsell

XIX
The King's Irishmen: The Irish in the Exiled Court of Charles II, 1649–1660
Mark R. F. Williams

XX
Scotland in the Age of Two Revolutions
Edited by Sharon Adams and Julian Goodare

XXI
Alehouses and Good Fellowship in Early Modern England
Mark Hailwood

XXII
Social Relations and Urban Space: Norwich, 1600–1700
Fiona Williamson